R.C. SPROUL

CLASSIC TEACHINGS
ON THE NATURE OF GOD

R. C. SPROUL

The Holiness of God
Chosen by God
Pleasing God

THREE VOLUMES IN ONE

CLASSIC TEACHINGS
ON THE NATURE OF GOD

HENDRICKSON PUBLISHERS

CLASSIC TEACHINGS ON THE NATURE OF GOD

Hendrickson Publishers Marketing, LLC
P. O. Box 3473
Peabody, Massachusetts 01961-3473

ISBN 978-1-59856-468-6
Reprinted by permission of Tyndale Publishing House, Inc.

The Holiness of God

Chosen by God

Pleasing God

Printed in the United States of America
Fourth Hendrickson Edition Printing -- February 2018

Library of Congress Cataloging-in-Publication Data

Sproul, R. C. (Robert Charles), 1939-
  Classic teachings on the nature of God / R.C. Sproul.
    p. cm.
  ISBN 978-1-59856-468-6 (alk. paper)
1. God (Christianity—Holiness. 2. Predestination. 3. Christian
life--Reformed authors. I. Sproul, R. C. (Robert Charles), 1939-
Holiness of God. II. Sproul, R. C. (Robert Charles), 1939- Chosen by
God. III. Sproul, R. C. (Robert Charles), 1939- Pleasing God. IV. Title.

BT147.S66 2010
231'.4--dc22

                    2009048961

Contents

THE HOLINESS OF GOD

R. C. SPROUL

*To Kaki and Ryan
and to their generation,
that they may live during
a new reformation*

Contents

Acknowledgments

My special thanks go to Wendell Hawley for his warm and kind encouragement in this project. If the book has any clarity, the credit must go to my wife, Vesta, who is my most ruthless and loving editor.

ONE

❦

The Holy Grail

Gaily bedight, a gallant knight
In sunshine and in shadow;
Riding along, singing a song,
In search of El Dorado.

EDGAR ALLAN POE

I was compelled to leave the room. A deep, undeniable summons disturbed my sleep; something holy called me. The only sound was the rhythmic ticking of the clock on my desk. It seemed vague and unreal, as if it were in a chamber, submerged under fathoms of water. I had reached the beginning edge of slumber, where the line between consciousness and unconsciousness is blurred. I was suspended in that moment when one hangs precariously on the edge, a moment when sounds from the outside world still intrude on the quietness of one's brain, that moment just before surrender to the night occurs. Asleep, but not yet asleep. Awake, but not alert. Still vulnerable to the inner summons that said, "Get up. Get out of this room."

The summons became stronger, more urgent, impossible to ignore. A burst of wakefulness made me jerk upright and swing my legs over the side of the bed and onto the floor. Sleep vanished in an instant, and my body sprang into resolute action. Within seconds I was dressed and on the way out of my college dormitory. A quick glance at the clock registered the time in my mind. Ten minutes before midnight.

The night air was cold, turning the snow of the morning to a hard-crusted blanket. I felt the crunch under my feet as I walked toward the center of campus. The moon cast a ghostly pall on the college buildings, whose gutters were adorned with giant icicles—dripping water arrested in space, solid daggers of ice that resembled frozen fangs. No human architect could design these gargoyles of nature.

The gears of the clock atop Old Main Tower began to grind, and the arms met and embraced vertically. I heard the dull groan of the machinery a split second before the chimes began to ring. Four musical tones signaled the full hour. They were followed by the steady, sonorous striking of twelve. I counted them in my mind, as I always did, checking for a possible error in their number. But they never missed. Exactly twelve strokes pealed from the tower like an angry judge's gavel banging on metal.

The chapel was in the shadow of Old Main Tower. The door was made of heavy oak with a Gothic arch. I swung it open and entered the narthex. The door fell shut behind me with a clanging sound that reverberated from the stone walls of the nave.

The echo startled me. It was a strange contrast to the sounds of daily chapel services, where the opening and closing of the doors were muffled by the sounds of students shuffling to their assigned places. Now the sound of the door was amplified into the void of midnight.

I waited for a moment in the narthex, allowing my eyes a few seconds to adjust to the darkness. The faint glow of the moon seeped through the muted stained-glass windows. I could make out the outline of the pews and the center aisle that led to the chancel steps. I felt a majestic sense of space, accented by the vaulted arches of the ceiling. They seemed to draw my soul upward, a sense of height that evoked a feeling of a giant hand reaching down to pick me up.

I moved slowly and deliberately toward the chancel steps. The sound of my shoes against the stone floor evoked terror-filled images of German soldiers marching in hobnailed boots along cobblestone streets. Each step resounded down the center aisle as I reached the carpet-covered chancel.

There I sank to my knees. I had reached my destination. I was ready to meet the source of the summons that had disturbed my rest.

I was in a posture of prayer, but I had nothing to say. I knelt there quietly, allowing the sense of the presence of a holy God to fill me. The beat of my heart was telltale, a *thump-thump* against my chest. An icy chill started at the base of my spine and crept up my neck. Fear swept over me. I fought the impulse to run from the foreboding presence that gripped me.

The terror passed, but soon it was followed by another wave. This wave was different. It flooded my soul with unspeakable peace, a peace that brought instant rest and repose to my troubled spirit. At once I was comfortable. I wanted to linger there. To say nothing. To do nothing. Simply to bask in the presence of God.

That moment was life transforming. Something deep in my spirit was being settled once for all. From this moment there could be no turning back; there could be no erasure of the indelible imprint of its power. I was alone with God. A holy God. An awesome God. A God who could fill me with terror in one second and with peace in the next. I knew in that hour that I had tasted of the Holy Grail. Within me was born a new thirst that could never be fully satisfied in this world. I resolved to learn more, to pursue this God who lived in dark Gothic cathedrals and who invaded my dormitory room to rouse me from complacent slumber.

What makes a college student seek the presence of God in the late hours? Something happened in a classroom that afternoon that drove me to the chapel. I was a new Christian. My conversion had been sudden and dramatic, a replica for me of the Damascus Road. My life had been turned upside down, and I was filled with zeal for the sweetness of Christ. I was consumed with a new passion. To study Scripture. To learn how to pray. To conquer the vices that assaulted my character. To grow in grace. I wanted desperately to make my life count for Christ. My soul was singing, "Lord, I want to be a Christian."

But something was missing in my early Christian life. I had abundant zeal, but it was marked by a shallowness, a kind of simplicity that was making me a one-dimensional person. I was a Unitarian of sorts, a Unitarian of the second person of the Trinity. I knew who Jesus was, but God the Father was shrouded in mystery. He was hidden, an enigma to my mind and a stranger to my soul. A dark veil covered His face.

My philosophy class changed that.

It was a course that had held little interest for me. I could hardly wait to get the tedious requirement behind me. I had chosen to major in Bible and thought the abstract speculations that went on in philosophy class were a waste of time. Listening to philosophers quarrel about reason and doubt seemed empty. I found no food for my soul, nothing to inflame my imagination, just dull and difficult intellectual puzzles that left me cold. Until that winter afternoon.

The lecture that day was about a Christian philosopher whose name was Aurelius Augustine. In the course of history, he had been canonized by the Roman Catholic church. Everyone spoke of him as Saint Augustine. The professor lectured on Augustine's views of the creation of the world.

I was familiar with the biblical account of creation. I knew that the Old Testament opens with the words, "In the beginning God created the heavens and the earth." But I had never thought deeply about the original act of creation. Augustine probed into this glorious mystery and raised the question, "How was it done?"

"In the beginning . . ."

It sounds like the start of a fairy tale: "Once upon a time." The trouble is that in the beginning there was no time as we understand it to be "once upon."

We think of beginnings as starting points somewhere in the middle of a period of history. Cinderella had a mother and a grandmother. Her story that began "once upon a time" did not begin at the absolute beginning. Before Cinderella there were kings and queens, rocks and trees, horses, jackrabbits, daffodils.

What was there before the beginning of Genesis 1? The people God created had no parents or grandparents. They had no history books to read because there was no history. Before the creation there were no kings or queens or rocks or trees. There was nothing; nothing, of course, except God.

Here is where I got an Excedrin headache in my philosophy class. Before the world began, there was nothing. But what in the world is "nothing"? Have you ever tried to think about nothing? Where can we find it? Obviously nowhere. Why? Because it is nothing, and nothing doesn't exist. It can't exist, because if it did, then it would be something and not nothing. Are you starting to get a headache like mine? Think about it for a second. I can't tell you to think about "it" because nothing isn't an "it." I can only say "nothing isn't."

So how can we think about nothing? We can't. It is simply impossible. If we try to think of nothing, we always wind up thinking of something. As soon as I try to think about nothing, I start imagining a lot of "empty" air. But air is something. It has weight and substance. I know that because of what happens if a nail goes through the tire of my car.

Jonathan Edwards once said that nothing is what sleeping rocks dream about. That doesn't help much. My son offered me a better definition of *nothing*. When he was in junior high, I asked him when he came home from school, "What did you do today, Son?" The reply was the same every day: "Nuthin'." So the best explanation I can give of "nothing" is "that which my son used to do every day in junior high."

Our understanding of creativity involves the shaping and forming of paint, clay, notes on paper, or some other substance. In our experience we have not been able to find a painter who paints without paint or a writer who writes without words or a composer who composes without notes. Artists must start with *something*. What artists do is shape, form, or rearrange other materials. But they never work with nothing.

Saint Augustine taught that God created the world out of nothing. Creation was something like the magician pulling a rabbit out of a hat. Except God didn't have a rabbit, and He didn't even have a hat.

My next-door neighbor is a skilled cabinetmaker. One of his specialties is constructing cabinets for professional magicians. He has given me a tour of his workshop and has shown me how the magician's boxes and cabinets are made. The trick is the clever use of mirrors. When the magician walks onstage and displays an empty box or an empty hat, what you see is only half the box or half the hat. Take the "empty" hat, for example. A mirror is fixed in the exact middle of the hat. The mirror reflects the empty side of the hat, giving an exact mirror image. The illusion creates the visual effect of seeing both sides of an empty hat. In fact you see only half the hat. The other half has plenty of room to conceal snow-white doves or a plump rabbit. Not much magic to it, is there?

God did not create the world with mirrors. To do that He would have required half a world to start with and a giant mirror to conceal the other half. Creation involved the bringing into existence of everything that is, including mirrors. God created the world from nothing. Once there was nothing, then suddenly, by the command of God, there was a universe.

Again we ask, How did He do it? The only hint the Bible gives is that God called the universe into being. Augustine called that act the "divine imperative" or the "divine fiat." We all know that an imperative is a command. So is a fiat. When Augustine spoke of a fiat, he was not thinking of a little Italian car. The dictionary defines *fiat* as a command or an act of the will that creates something.

At the present moment I am writing this book on a computer manufactured by IBM. It is an amazing piece of machinery, quite complicated in all its parts. The machine is designed to respond to certain commands. If I make a mistake while I am typing on the keyboard, I do not have to reach for an eraser. To correct my errors, I merely punch in a command, and the computer corrects it. The computer works by fiat. But the power of my fiat is limited. The only fiats that work are the ones that are already programmed into the computer. I would love simply to be able to say to the computer, "Write this whole book for me, please, while I go out and play golf." My machine can't do that. I can yell at the screen with the strongest imperative I know: "Write that book!" but the thing is too obstinate to comply.

God's fiats are not so limited. He can create by the sheer force of His divine command. He can bring something out of nothing, life out of death. He can do these things by the sound of His voice.

The first sound uttered in the universe was the voice of God commanding, "Let there be!" It is improper to say that this was the first sound "in" the universe because until the sound was made there was no universe for it to be in. God shouted into a void. Perhaps it was a kind of primal scream directed at the empty darkness.

The command created its own molecules to carry the sound waves of God's voice farther and farther into space. Yet sound waves would take too long. The speed of this imperative exceeded the speed of light. As soon as the words left the Creator's mouth, things began to happen. Where His voice reverberated, stars appeared, glowing in unspeakable brilliance in tempo with the songs of angels. The force of divine energy splattered against the sky like a kaleidoscope of color hurled from the palette of a powerful artist. Comets crisscrossed the sky with flashing tails like Fourth of July skyrockets.

The act of creation was the first event in history. It was also the most dazzling. The supreme Architect gazed at His complex blueprint and shouted commands for the boundaries of the world to be set. He spoke, and the seas were shut behind doors, and the clouds were filled with dew. He bound the Pleiades and buckled the belt of Orion. He spoke again, and the earth began to fill with orchards in full bloom. Blossoms burst forth like springtime in Mississippi. The lavender hues of plum trees danced with the brilliance of azaleas and forsythia.

God spoke once more, and the waters teemed with living things. The snail sneaked beneath the shadowy form of the stingray, while the great marlin broke the surface of the water to promenade on the waves with his tail. Again He spoke, and the roar of the lion and the bleating of sheep were heard. Four-footed animals, eight-legged spiders, and winged insects appeared.

And God said, "That's good."

Then God stooped to earth and carefully fashioned a piece of clay. He lifted it gently to His lips and breathed into it. The clay began to move. It began to think. It began to feel. It began to worship. It was alive and stamped with the image of its Creator.

Consider the raising of Lazarus from the dead. How did Jesus do it? He did not enter the tomb where the rotting corpse of Lazarus was laid out; He did not have to administer mouth-to-mouth resuscitation. He stood outside the tomb, at a distance, and cried with a loud voice, "Lazarus, come forth!" Blood began to flow through the veins of Lazarus, and brain waves started to pulsate. In a burst of life Lazarus quit his grave and walked out. That is fiat creation, the power of the divine imperative.

Some modern theorists believe that the world was created by nothing. Note the difference between saying that the world was created *from* nothing and saying that the universe was created *by* nothing. In this modern view the rabbit comes out of the hat without a rabbit, a hat, or even a magician. The modern view is far more miraculous than the biblical view. It suggests that nothing created something. More than that, it holds that nothing created everything—quite a feat indeed!

Now surely there aren't serious people running around in this scientific age claiming that the universe was created by nothing, are there? Yes. Scores of them. To be sure, they usually don't say it quite the way I have said it, and they'd probably be annoyed with me for stating their views in such a manner. They'd undoubtedly protest that I have given a distorted caricature of their sophisticated position. Okay. True—they don't say that the universe was created by nothing; they say that the universe was created by chance.

But chance is no thing. It has no weight, no measurements, no power. It is merely a word we use to describe mathematical possibilities. It can do nothing. It can do nothing because it is nothing. To say that the universe was created by chance is to say that it came from nothing.

That is intellectual madness. What are the chances that the universe was created by chance?

Saint Augustine understood that the world could not be created by chance. He knew that it required something or someone with power—the very power of creation—to get the job done. He knew that something cannot come from nothing. He understood that somewhere, somehow, something or someone had to have the power of being. If not, then nothing would now exist.

The Bible says, "In the beginning God." The God we worship is the God who has always been. He alone can create beings, because He alone has the *power of being.* He is not nothing. He is not chance. He is pure Being, the One who has the power to be *all by Himself.* He alone is eternal. He alone has power over death. He alone can call worlds into being by fiat, by the power of His command. Such power is staggering, awesome. It is deserving of respect, of humble adoration.

It was the words of Augustine—that God created the world out of nothing by the sheer power of His voice—that drove me to the chapel at midnight.

I know what it means to be converted. I know what it means to be born again. I also understand that a person can be born again only once. When the Holy Spirit quickens our souls to new life in Christ, He does not stop His work. He continues to work on us. He continues to change us.

My experience in the classroom, thinking about the creation of the world, was like being born again a second time. It was like being converted, not merely to God the Son, but to God the Father. Suddenly I had a passion to know God the Father. I wanted to know Him in His majesty, to know Him in His power, to know Him in His august holiness.

My "conversion" to God the Father was not without its attending difficulties. Though I was deeply impressed by the notion of a God who created a whole universe from nothing, I was troubled by the fact that the world we live in is a place filled with sorrows. It is a world riddled with evil. My next question was, How could a good and holy God create a world that is in such a mess? As I studied the Old Testament, I was also bothered by the stories about God's ordering the slaughter of women and children, of God's killing Uzzah instantly for touching the ark of the covenant, and by other narratives that seemed to reveal a brutal side to the character of God. How could I ever come to love such a God?

The one concept, the central idea I kept meeting in Scripture, was the idea that God is *holy*. The word was foreign to me. I wasn't sure what it meant. I made the question a matter of diligent and persistent search. Today I am still absorbed with the question of the holiness of God. I am convinced that it is one of the most important ideas that a Christian can ever grapple with. It is basic to our whole understanding of God and of Christianity.

The idea of holiness is so central to biblical teaching that it is said of God, "Holy is his name" (Luke 1:49). His name is holy because He is holy. He is not always treated with holy reverence. His name is tramped through the dirt of this world. It functions as a curse word, a platform for the obscene. That the world has little respect for God is vividly seen by the way the world regards His name. No honor. No reverence. No awe before Him.

If I were to ask a group of Christians what the top priority of the church is, I am sure I would get a wide variety of answers. Some would say evangelism, others social action, and still others spiritual nurture. But I have yet to hear anyone talk about what Jesus' priorities were.

What is the first petition of the Lord's Prayer? Jesus said, "This, then, is how you should pray: 'Our Father in heaven . . .' " (Matt. 6:9). The first line of the prayer is not a petition. It is a form of personal address. The prayer continues: "hallowed be your name, your kingdom come" (Matt. 6:9–10). We often confuse the words "hallowed be your name" with part of the address, as if the words were "hallowed *is* your name." In that case the words would merely be an ascription of praise to God. But that is not how Jesus said it. He uttered it as a petition, as the first petition. We should be praying that God's name be hallowed, that God be regarded as holy.

There is a kind of sequence within the prayer. God's kingdom will never come where His name is not considered holy. His will is not done on earth as it is in heaven if His name is desecrated here. In heaven the name of God is holy. It is breathed by angels in a sacred hush. Heaven is a place where reverence for God is total. It is foolish to look for the kingdom anywhere God is not revered.

How we understand the person and character of God the Father affects every aspect of our lives. It affects far more than what we normally call the "religious" aspects of our lives. If God is the Creator of the entire universe, then it must follow that He is the Lord of the whole universe. No part of the world is outside of His lordship. That means that no part of my life must be outside of His lordship. His holy character has something to say about economics, politics, athletics, romance— everything with which we are involved.

God is inescapable. There is no place we can hide from Him. Not only does He penetrate every aspect of our lives, but He penetrates it in His majestic holiness. Therefore we must seek to understand what the holy is. We dare not seek to avoid it. There can be no worship, no spiritual growth, no true obedience without it. It defines our goal as Christians. God has declared, "Be holy, because I am holy" (Lev. 11:44).

To reach that goal, we must understand what holiness is.

Allowing God's Holiness to Touch Our Lives

As you reflect about what you have learned and rediscovered about God's holiness, answer these questions. Use a journal to record your responses to God's holiness, or discuss your responses with a friend.

1. When you think of God as holy, what comes to your mind?
2. Describe a time when you were overcome by God's holiness.
3. Are you attracted to God's holiness?
4. What does it mean for you to be holy in the coming week?

~⊙~

TWO

Holy, Holy, Holy

Weave a circle round him thrice,
And close your eyes with holy dread.
For he on honey-dew hath fed,
And drunk the milk of Paradise.

SAMUEL TAYLOR COLERIDGE

The prophet in Old Testament Israel was a lonely man. He was a rugged individualist singled out by God for a painful task. He served as a prosecuting attorney of sorts, the appointed spokesman of the Supreme Judge of heaven and earth to bring suit against those who had sinned against the bench.

The prophet was not an earthly philosopher who wrote his opinions for scholars to discuss; he was not a playwright who composed dramas for public entertainment. He was a messenger, a herald of a cosmic king. His announcements were prefaced by the words "Thus says the Lord" (NASB).

The record of the lives of the prophets reads like a history of martyrs. Their history sounds like a casualty report from the Third Division in World War II. The life expectancy of a prophet was that of a marine lieutenant in combat.

When it is said of Jesus that "He was despised and rejected by men, a man of sorrows, and familiar with suffering" (Isa. 53:3), it is clear that He stood in a long line of men whom God had appointed to such suffering. The prophet's curse was solitude; his home was often a cave. The desert was his traditional meeting place with God. Nakedness was sometimes his wardrobe, a wooden stock his necktie. His songs were composed with tears.

Such a man was Isaiah ben Amoz.

In the panoply of Old Testament heroes, Isaiah stands out in stellar relief. He was a prophet of prophets, a leader of leaders. He is called a "major prophet" because of the vast size of the written material that bears his name.

As a prophet, Isaiah was unusual. Most prophets were of humble origins: peasants, shepherds, farmers. Isaiah was of the nobility. He was a recognized statesman, having access to the royal court of his day. He consorted with princes and kings. God used him to speak to several monarchs of Judah, including Uzziah, Jotham, Ahaz, and Hezekiah.

What set a prophet of Israel apart from all other men was the sacred auspices of his call. His call was not from men. He could not apply for the job. He had to be selected—chosen directly and immediately by God. And the call was sovereign; it could not be refused. (Jeremiah tried to refuse his call but was abruptly reminded by God that He had consecrated Jeremiah from his mother's womb. When, after a term in this office, Jeremiah sought to resign, God refused to accept his resignation.) The job of prophet was for life. There was no quitting or retiring with pension.

The record of the call of Isaiah is perhaps the most dramatic of all such calls recorded for us in the Old Testament. We are told that it came to pass in the year that King Uzziah died.

King Uzziah died in the eighth century B.C. His reign was important in Jewish history. He was one of the better kings who ruled over Judah. He was not a David, but neither was he noted for the corruption that characterized the kings of the north, such as Ahab. Uzziah ascended to the throne when he was sixteen years old. He reigned in Jerusalem for fifty-two years. Think of it, fifty-two years! In the past fifty-two years, the United States has witnessed the administrations of Truman, Eisenhower, Kennedy, Johnson, Nixon, Ford, Carter, Reagan, Bush, Clinton, and Bush. But many people in Jerusalem lived their entire lives under the reign of King Uzziah.

The Bible tells us that Uzziah began his reign in godliness, doing "what was right in the eyes of the LORD" (2 Chron. 26:4). He sought after God, and God blessed him. He was victorious in battle over the Philistines and other nations. He built towers in Jerusalem and strengthened the city walls. He dug massive cisterns in the desert and stimulated great expansion in the nation's agriculture. He restored the military power of Judah to a standard almost as high as it had been under David. For most of his career Uzziah was noted as a great and beloved king.

The story of Uzziah ends with a sad note, however. The last years of his life were like those of a Shakespearean tragic hero. His career was marred by the sin of pride committed after he acquired great wealth and power. He tried to play God. He boldly entered the temple and arrogantly claimed for himself the rights that God had given only to the priests. When the priests of the temple tried to stop his act of sacrilege, Uzziah became enraged. While he was screaming at them in fury, leprosy broke out on his forehead. The Bible says of him: "He lived in a separate house, being a leper, . . . cut off from the house of the LORD" (2 Chron. 26:21, NASB). When Uzziah died, in spite of the shame of his later years,

it was a time of national mourning. Isaiah went to the temple, presumably looking for consolation in a time of national and personal grief. He got more than
he bargained for: "In the year that King Uzziah died, I saw the Lord seated on a
throne, high and exalted, and the train of his robe filled the temple" (Isa. 6:1).

The king was dead. But when Isaiah entered the temple, he saw another
king, the Ultimate King, the One who sat forever on the throne of Judah. He
saw the Lord.

Notice how in Isaiah 6:1 the word *Lord* is printed. It begins with a capital letter
and then is finished with lowercase letters. This stands in contrast with the word
Lord that occurs later in the text and frequently in Scripture. Sometimes the
word *Lord* appears in all capital letters—Lord. This is not an error in printing or
a mere inconsistency on the part of the translator. Most English translations of
the Bible follow this device of rendering the word *Lord* sometimes in lowercase
letters and other times in uppercase letters. The reason for this difference is that
two different Hebrew words are used in the original text, but both are rendered
in English by the word *Lord.*

When the word *Lord* occurs in lowercase letters, the translator is indicating to us that the word *adonai* is found in the Hebrew Bible. Adonai means
"sovereign one." It is not the name of God. It is a title for God, indeed the
supreme title given to God in the Old Testament. When Lord appears in all
capital letters it indicates that the word *Jahweh* is used in the Old Testament.
Jahweh is the sacred name of God, the name by which God revealed Himself to
Moses in the burning bush. This is the unspeakable name, the ineffable name,
the holy name that is guarded from profanity in the life of Israel. Normally it
occurs only with the use of its four consonants—*yhwh*. It is therefore referred
to as the sacred tetragrammaton, the unspeakable four letters.

We see, for example, this contrast in words found in the Psalms. Psalm 8
reads, "O Lord, our Lord, how majestic is your name in all the earth!" (Ps. 8:1).
What the Jew was saying was, "O Jahweh, our Adonai, how excellent is your
name in all the earth." Or we could render it, "O God, our sovereign one, how
excellent. . . ." Again we read in Psalm 110: "The Lord says to my Lord: 'Sit at
my right hand' " (Ps. 110:1). Here the psalmist is saying, "God said to my sovereign, sit at my right hand."

Lord is the name of God; *Lord* is His title. We speak of President George W.
Bush. *George* is his name; *president* is his title. If the highest office in our land is
the office of president, so the highest office and title in Israel was the office of
Sovereign. The title *adonai* was reserved for God. It was the title that was given
to Jesus in the New Testament. When Christ is called "Lord," He is invested with

the New Testament equivalent of the Old Testament *adonai*. Jesus is called the King of kings and Lord of lords, gaining a title that beforehand was reserved only for God the Father, the supreme Sovereign of heaven and earth.

These different uses of the words LORD and *Lord* indicate the care with which people communicated God's holy nature. In some ways that is similar to my choosing to use capital letters when I use a pronoun to refer to God. Because God is unspeakably holy, I cannot bring myself to refer to Him as "him," even though my younger readers may be bothered by what they perceive to be an outdated use of capital letters. To me it is a gesture of respect and awe for a holy God.

When Isaiah came to the temple, there was a crisis of sovereignty in the land. Uzziah was dead. The eyes of Isaiah were opened to see the real king of the nation. He saw God seated on the throne, the sovereign one.

Humans are not allowed to see the face of God. The Scriptures warn that no person can see God and live. We remember Moses' request when he ascended the holy mountain of God. Moses had been an eyewitness of astonishing miracles. He had heard the voice of God speaking to him out of the burning bush. He had witnessed the river Nile turn into blood. He had tasted manna from heaven and had gazed upon the pillar of cloud and the pillar of fire. He had seen the chariots of Pharaoh inundated by the waves of the Red Sea. Still he was not satisfied. He wanted more. He craved the ultimate spiritual experience. He inquired of the Lord on the mountain, "Let me see your face. Show me your glory." The request was denied:

> And the LORD said, "I will cause all my goodness to pass in front
> of you, and I will proclaim my name, the LORD, in your presence.
> I will have mercy on whom I will have mercy, and I will have
> compassion on whom I will have compassion. But," he said, "you
> cannot see my face, for no one may see me and live."
>
> Then the LORD said, "There is a place near me where you may
> stand on a rock. When my glory passes by, I will put you in a
> cleft in the rock and cover you with my hand until I have passed
> by. Then I will remove my hand and you will see my back; but
> my face must not be seen." (Exod. 33:19–23)

When God told Moses that he could see His back, the literal reading of the text can be translated "hindquarters." God allowed Moses to see His hindquarters but never His face. When Moses returned from the mount, his face

was shining. The people were terrified, and they shrank away from him in horror. Moses' face was too dazzling for them to look upon. So Moses put a veil
over his face so that the people could approach him. This experience of terror
was directed at the face of a man who had come so close to God that he was
reflecting God's glory. This was a reflection of the glory from the back of God,
not the refulgent glory of His face. If people are terrified by the sight of the
reflected glory of the back parts of God, how can anyone stand to gaze directly
into His holy face?

Yet the final goal of every Christian is to be allowed to see what was denied
to Moses. We want to see Him face-to-face. We want to bask in the radiant glory
of His divine countenance. It was the hope of every Jew, a hope instilled in the
most famous and beloved benediction of Israel:

> The LORD bless you
>   and keep you;
> the LORD make his face shine upon you
>   and be gracious to you;
> the LORD turn his face toward you
>   and give you peace. (Num. 6:24–26)

This hope, crystallized in the benediction of Israel, becomes more than
a hope for the Christian—it becomes a promise. John tells in his first letter:
"We are children of God, and what we will be has not yet been made known.
But we know that when he appears, we shall be like him, for we shall see him
as he is" (1 John 3:2). Here is the promise of God: We shall see Him as He is.
Theologians call this future expectation the beatific vision. We will see God *as*
He is. This means that someday we will see God face-to-face. We will not see
the reflected glory of a burning bush or a pillar of cloud. We will see Him as
He is, as He is in His pure, divine essence.

Right now it is impossible for us to see God in His pure essence. Before
that can ever happen, we must be purified. When Jesus taught the Beatitudes,
He promised only a distinct group the vision of God: "Blessed are the pure
in heart, for they will see God" (Matt. 5:8). None of us in this world is pure
in heart. It is our impurity that prevents us from seeing God. The problem is
not with our eyes; it is with our hearts. Only after we are purified and totally
sanctified in heaven will we have the capacity to gaze upon Him face-to-face.
"Above him were seraphs, each with six wings: With two wings they covered
their faces, with two they covered their feet, and with two they were flying"
(Isa. 6:2).

The seraphim are not sinful humans burdened with impure hearts. Yet as angelic beings, they are still creatures, and even in their lofty status as consorts of the heavenly host it is necessary for them to shield their eyes from a direct gaze on the face of God. They are fearfully and wonderfully made, equipped by their Creator with a special pair of wings to cover their faces in His majestic presence.

The seraphim have a second pair of wings. The second pair is used to cover their feet. This equipment is not intended as a sort of angelic shoe to protect the soles of their feet or to facilitate walking in the heavenly temple. The covering of the feet is for a different reason, a reason reminiscent of Moses' experience with the burning bush:

> There the angel of the LORD appeared to him in flames of fire from within a bush. Moses saw that though the bush was on fire it did not burn up. So Moses thought, "I will go over and see this strange sight—why the bush does not burn up."
>
> When the LORD saw that he had gone over to look, God called to him from within the bush, "Moses, Moses!"
>
> And Moses said, "Here I am."
>
> "Do not come any closer," God said. "Take off your sandals, for the place where you are standing is holy ground." (Exod. 3:2–5)

God commanded Moses to take off his shoes. Moses was standing on holy ground. The ground was made holy by the presence of God. The act of removing the shoes was a symbol of Moses' recognition that he was of the earth—earthy. Human feet, sometimes called "feet of clay," symbolize our creatureliness. It is our feet that link us to the earth.

The seraphim are not of the earth. Their feet are not made of clay. As angels, they are spirit beings. Nevertheless they remain creatures, and the imagery of Isaiah's vision suggests that they too must cover their feet, acknowledging their creatureliness in the exalted presence of God.

Here we encounter the crux of Isaiah's vision. It is the song of the seraphim that reveals the awesome message of this text. "And they were calling to one another: 'Holy, holy, holy is the LORD Almighty; the whole earth is full of his glory' " (Isa. 6:3). The song is the repetition of a single word—*holy*. Three times the word is sung in succession, giving the church its most august anthem. The song is called the *Trisagion*, which means simply the "three times holy."

The significance of the repetition of the word *holy* can be easily missed. It represents a peculiar literary device that is found in Hebrew forms of literature, especially in poetry. The repetition is a form of emphasis. When we want to emphasize the importance of something in English, we have several devices from which to choose. We may underline the important words or print them in italics or boldface type. We may attach an exclamation point following the words or set them off in quotation marks. These are all devices to call the reader's attention to something that is especially important.

The Old Testament Jew also had different techniques to indicate emphasis. One such device was the method of repetition. We see Jesus' use of repetition with the words "Truly, truly, I say to you" (NASB). Here the double use of *truly* was a sign that what He was about to say was of crucial importance. The word translated "truly" is the ancient word *amen*. We normally think of the word *amen* as something people say at the end of a sermon or of a prayer. It means simply, "It is true." Jesus used it as a preface instead of a response.

A humorous use of the repetition device may be seen in Genesis 14. The story of the battle of the kings in the Valley of Siddim mentions men who fell in the great tar pits of the region. Some translators call them asphalt pits, or bitumen pits, or simply great pits. Why the confusion in translation? Exactly what kind of pits were they? The Hebrew is unclear. The original text gives the Hebrew word for pit and then simply repeats it. The story speaks literally of pit pits. The Jew was saying that there are pits and there are pits. Some pits are pittier than other pits. These pits—the pit pits—were the pittiest pits of all. It is one thing to fall into a pit. But if you fall into a pit pit, you are in deep trouble.

On a handful of occasions the Bible repeats something to the third degree. To mention something three times in succession is to elevate it to the superlative degree, to attach to it emphasis of superimportance. For example, the dreadful judgment of God is declared in the book of Revelation by the eagle who cried in midair with a loud voice: "Woe! Woe! Woe to the inhabitants of the earth" (Rev. 8:13). Or we hear it in the mocking sarcasm of Jeremiah's temple speech when he chided the people for calling out in hypocrisy, "This is the temple of the LORD, the temple of the LORD, the temple of the LORD!" (Jer. 7:4).

Only once in sacred Scripture is an attribute of God elevated to the third degree. Only once is a characteristic of God mentioned three times in succession. The Bible says that God is holy, holy, holy. Not that He is merely holy, or even holy, holy. He is holy, holy, holy. The Bible never says that God is love, love, love; or mercy, mercy, mercy; or wrath, wrath, wrath; or justice, justice, justice. It does say that He is holy, holy, holy, that the whole earth is full of His glory.

"At the sound of their voices the doorposts and thresholds shook and the temple was filled with smoke" (Isa. 6:4).

A recent survey of people who used to be church members revealed that the main reason they stopped going to church was that they found it boring. It is difficult for many people to find worship a thrilling and moving experience. We note here, when God appeared in the temple, the doors and the thresholds were moved. The inert matter of doorposts, the inanimate thresholds, the wood and metal that could neither hear nor speak had the good sense to be moved by the presence of God. The literal meaning of the text is that they were shaken. They began to quake where they stood.

"Woe to me!" I cried. "I am ruined! For I am a man of unclean lips, and I live among a people of unclean lips, and my eyes have seen the King, the LORD Almighty" (Isa. 6:5).

The doors of the temple were not the only things that were shaking. The thing that quaked the most in the building was the body of Isaiah. When he saw the living God, the reigning monarch of the universe displayed before his eyes in all of His holiness, Isaiah cried out, "Woe is me!"

The cry of Isaiah sounds strange to the modern ear. It is rare that we hear people today use the word *woe*. Since this word is old-fashioned and archaic, some modern translators have preferred to substitute another word in its place. That is a serious mistake. The word *woe* is a crucial biblical word that we cannot afford to ignore. It has a special meaning.

When we think of woes, we think of the troubles encountered in melodramas set in the old-time nickelodeons. *The Perils of Pauline* showed the heroine wringing her hands in anguish as the heartless landlord came to foreclose on her mortgage. Or we think of Mighty Mouse flying from his cloud to streak to the rescue of his girlfriend, who is being tied to the railroad tracks by Oilcan Harry. She cries, "Woe is me!"

The term *woe* has gone the way of other worn-out exclamations like *alas* or *alack* or *forsooth*. The only language that has kept the expression in current usage is Yiddish. Modern Jews still declare their frustrations by exclaiming "Oy vay!" which is a shortened version of the full expression *oy vay ist mer.* Oy vay is Yiddish for "Oh woe," an abbreviation for the full expression, "Oh woe is me!"

The full force of Isaiah's exclamation must be seen against the background of a special form of speech found in the Bible. When prophets announced their messages, the most frequent form the divine utterances took was the *oracle.* The oracles were announcements from God; they could be good news or bad news. The positive oracles were prefaced by the word *blessed.* When Jesus preached the Sermon on the Mount, He used the form of the oracle, saying, "Blessed are the poor in spirit," "Blessed are those who mourn," "Blessed are those who hunger and thirst." His audience understood that He was using the formula of the prophet, the oracle that brought good tidings.

Jesus also used the negative form of the oracle. When He spoke out in angry denunciation of the Pharisees, He pronounced the judgment of God upon their heads by saying to them, "Woe to you, scribes and Pharisees, hypocrites!" (Matt. 23:13–29, NASB). He said this so often that it began to sound like a litany. On the lips of a prophet the word *woe* is an announcement of doom. In the Bible, cities are doomed, nations are doomed, individuals are doomed—all by uttering the oracle of woe.

Isaiah's use of *woe* was extraordinary. When he saw the Lord, he pronounced the judgment of God upon himself. "Woe to me!" he cried, calling down the curse of God, the utter anathema of judgment and doom upon his own head. It was one thing for a prophet to curse another person in the name of God; it was quite another for a prophet to put that curse upon himself.

Immediately following the curse of doom, Isaiah cried, "I am ruined." I prefer the older translation that read, "For I am undone." We can readily see why more modern translations have made the change from *undone* to *ruined*. Nobody speaks today about being undone. But the word is more vivid in what it conveys than the word *ruined*.

To be undone means to come apart at the seams, to be unraveled. What Isaiah was expressing is what modern psychologists describe as the experience of personal disintegration. To disintegrate means exactly what the word suggests, *dis integrate*. To integrate something is to put pieces together into a unified whole. When schools are integrated, children from two different races are placed together to form one student body. The word *integrity* comes from this root, suggesting a person whose life is whole or wholesome. In modern slang we say, "That person has got it all together."

If ever there was a man of integrity, it was Isaiah ben Amoz. He was a whole man, a together type of a fellow. He was considered by his contemporaries as the most righteous man in the nation. He was respected as a paragon of virtue. Then he caught one sudden glimpse of a holy God. In that single moment, all of his self-esteem was shattered. In a brief second he was exposed, made naked beneath the gaze of the absolute standard of holiness. As long as Isaiah could compare himself to other mortals, he was able to sustain a lofty opinion of his own character. The instant he measured himself by the ultimate standard, he was destroyed—morally and spiritually annihilated. He was undone. He came apart. His sense of integrity collapsed.

The sudden realization of ruin was linked to Isaiah's mouth. He cried, "I am a man of unclean lips." Strange. We might have expected him to say, "I am a man of unclean habits," or, "I am a man of unclean thoughts." Instead he called attention immediately to his mouth. In effect he said, "I have a dirty mouth." Why this focus on his mouth?

Perhaps a clue to Isaiah's utterance may be found in the words of Jesus when He said that it's not what goes into people's mouths that defiles them; it's what comes out of their mouths that defiles them. Or we could look to the discourse on the tongue written by James, the Lord's brother:

> The tongue also is a fire, a world of evil among the parts of the body. It corrupts the whole person, sets the whole course of his life on fire, and is itself set on fire by hell.
>
> All kinds of animals, birds, reptiles and creatures of the sea are being tamed and have been tamed by man, but no man can tame the tongue. It is a restless evil, full of deadly poison.
>
> With the tongue we praise our Lord and Father, and with it we curse men, who have been made in God's likeness. Out of the same mouth come praise and cursing. My brothers, this should not be. Can both fresh water and salt water flow from the same spring? My brothers, can a fig tree bear olives, or a grapevine bear figs? Neither can a salt spring produce fresh water. (James 3:6–12)

The tongue is a restless evil, full of deadly poison. This was the realization of Isaiah. He recognized that he was not alone in his dilemma. He understood that the whole nation was infected with dirty mouths: "I live among a people of unclean lips." In the flash of the moment Isaiah had a new and radical understanding of sin. He saw that it was pervasive, in himself and in everyone else.

We are fortunate in one respect: God does not appear to us in the way He appeared to Isaiah. Who could stand it? God normally reveals our sinfulness to us a bit at a time. We experience a gradual recognition of our own corruption. God showed Isaiah his corruption all at once. No wonder he was ruined.

Isaiah explained it this way: "My eyes have seen the King, the Lord Almighty" (Isa. 6:5). He saw the holiness of God. For the first time in his life Isaiah really understood who God was. At the same instant, for the first time Isaiah really understood who Isaiah was.

"Then one of the seraphs flew to me with a live coal in his hand, which he had taken with tongs from the altar. With it he touched my mouth and said, 'See, this has touched your lips; your guilt is taken away and your sin atoned for' " (Isa. 6:6–7).

Isaiah was groveling on the floor. Every nerve fiber in his body was trembling. He was looking for a place to hide, praying that somehow the earth would cover him or the roof of the temple would fall upon him—anything to get him out from under the holy gaze of God. But there was nowhere to hide. He was naked and alone before God. Unlike Adam, Isaiah had no Eve to comfort him, no fig leaves to conceal him. His was pure moral anguish, the kind that rips out the heart of a man and tears his soul to pieces. Guilt, guilt, guilt. Relentless guilt screamed from his every pore.

The holy God is also a God of grace. He refused to allow His servant to continue on his belly without comfort. He took immediate steps to cleanse the man and restore his soul. He commanded one of the seraphim to jump into action. The angelic creature moved swiftly, flying to the altar with tongs. From the burning fire, the seraph took a glowing coal, too hot to touch even for an angel, and flew to Isaiah.

The seraph pressed the white-hot coal to the lips of the prophet and seared them. The lips are one of the most sensitive parts of human flesh, the meeting point of the kiss. Here Isaiah felt the holy flame burning his mouth. The acrid smell of burning flesh filled his nostrils, but that sensation was dulled by the excruciating pain of the heat. This was a severe mercy, a painful act of cleansing. Isaiah's wound was being cauterized, the dirt in his mouth was being burned away. He was refined by holy fire.

In this divine act of cleansing, Isaiah experienced a forgiveness that went beyond the purification of his lips. He was cleansed throughout, forgiven to the core, but not without the awful pain of repentance. He went beyond cheap grace and the easy utterance "I'm sorry." He was in mourning for his sin, overcome with moral grief, and God sent an angel to heal him. His sin was taken away. His dignity remained intact. His guilt was removed, but his humanity was not insulted. The conviction that he felt was constructive. His was no cruel and unusual punishment. A second of burning flesh on the lips brought a healing that would extend to eternity. In a moment, the disintegrated prophet was whole again. His mouth was purged. He was clean.

"Then I heard the voice of the Lord saying, 'Whom shall I send? And who will go for us?'

And I said, 'Here am I. Send me!' " (Isa. 6:8)

Isaiah's vision took on a new dimension. Until this point he had seen the glory of God; he had heard the song of the seraphim; he had felt the burning coal upon his lips. Now for the first time he heard the voice of God. Suddenly the angels were silent, and the voice boomed throughout the temple, the voice that Scripture elsewhere describes as the sound of many waters. That voice echoed with the piercing questions: "Whom shall I send? And who will go for us?"

There is a pattern here, a pattern repeated in history. God appears, people quake in terror, God forgives and heals, God sends. From brokenness to mission is the human pattern. When God asked, "Whom shall I *send?*" Isaiah understood the force of the word. To be "sent" meant to function as an emissary for God, to be a spokesman for the deity. In the New Testament the word *apostle* meant "one who is sent." The Old Testament counterpart to the New Testament apostle was the prophet. God was looking for a volunteer to enter the lonely, grueling office of prophet. "Whom shall I send?"

Notice Isaiah's answer: "Here am I, send me." There is a crucial difference between saying, "Here am I" and saying, "Here I am." Had he said, "Here I am," that would have merely indicated his location. But he was interested in more than giving God his location. He said, "Here am I." With these words Isaiah was stepping forward to volunteer. His answer was simply, "I will go. Look no further. Send me."

Two important things must be noted in Isaiah's reply. The first is that he was not Humpty-Dumpty. In the nursery rhyme the fall of Mr. Dumpty is tragic because no one in the entire kingdom had the power to put him together again. Yet he was no more fragile than Isaiah. Isaiah was shattered into as many pieces as any fallen egg. But God put him together again. God was able to take a shattered man and send him into the ministry. He took a sinful man and made him a prophet. He took a man with a dirty mouth and made him God's spokesman.

The second important thing we learn from this event is that God's work of grace on Isaiah's soul did not annihilate his personal identity. Isaiah said, "Here am I." Isaiah could still speak in terms of "I." He still had an identity. He still had a personality. Far from God seeking to destroy the "self," as many distortions of Christianity would claim, God redeems the self. He heals the self so that it may be useful and fulfilled in the mission to which the person is called. Isaiah's personality was overhauled but not annihilated. He was still Isaiah ben Amoz when he left the temple. He was the same person, but his mouth was clean.

Ministers are noteworthy of their calling. All preachers are vulnerable to the charge of hypocrisy. In fact, the more faithful preachers are to the Word of God in their preaching, the more liable they are to the charge of hypocrisy. Why? Because the more faithful people are to the Word of God, the higher the message is that they will preach. The higher the message, the further they will be from obeying it themselves.

I cringe inside when I speak in churches about the holiness of God. I can anticipate the responses of the people. They leave the sanctuary convinced that they have just been in the presence of a holy man. Because they hear me preach about holiness, they assume I must be as holy as the message I preach. That's when I want to cry, "Woe is me."

It's dangerous to assume that because a person is drawn to holiness in his study that he is thereby a holy man. There is irony here. I am sure that the reason I have a deep hunger to learn of the holiness of God is precisely because I am not holy. I am a profane man—a man who spends more time out of the temple than in it. But I have had just enough of a taste of the majesty of God to want more. I know what it means to be a forgiven man and what it means to be sent on a mission. My soul cries for more. My soul needs more.

Allowing God's Holiness to Touch Our Lives

As you reflect about what you have learned and rediscovered about God's holiness, answer these questions. Use a journal to record your responses to God's holiness, or discuss your responses with a friend.

1. Have you ever had an experience in which you were overcome by God's presence, in which you were "undone" by God's presence?
2. Isaiah's response to God's revelation of His holiness was "Woe is me." What is your response?
3. In what ways do you need to be refined by the fire of God's holiness?
4. What aspect of God's holiness, as described in this chapter, causes you to worship Him more fully?
5. Use the hymn at the end of this book [The Holiness of God] to express your worship to God.

THREE

The Fearful Mystery

What is that which gleams through me
and smites my heart without wounding it?
I am both a-shudder and aglow.
A-shudder, in so far as I am unlike it,
aglow in so far as I am like it.

SAINT AUGUSTINE

Here we are, already in the third chapter of this book, and I still have not defined what it means to be holy.

I wish I could postpone the task even further. The difficulties involved in defining holiness are vast. There is so much to holiness, and it is so foreign to us that the task seems almost impossible. In a very real sense, the word *holy* is a foreign word. But even when we run up against foreign words, we hope that a foreign language dictionary can rescue us by providing a clear translation. The problem we face, however, is that the word *holy* is foreign to all languages. No dictionary is adequate to the task.

Our problem with definition is made more difficult by the fact that in the Bible the word *holy* is used in more than one way. In a sense the Bible uses *holy* in a way that is very closely related to God's goodness. It has been customary to define *holy* as "purity, free from every stain, wholly perfect and immaculate in every detail."

Purity is the first word most of us think of when we hear the word *holy*. To be sure, the Bible does use the word this way. But the idea of purity or of moral perfection is at best the secondary meaning of the term in the Bible. When the seraphim sang their song, they were saying far more than that God was "purity, purity, purity."

The primary meaning of *holy* is "separate." It comes from an ancient word that means "to cut," or "to separate." To translate this basic meaning into contemporary language would be to use the phrase "a cut apart." Perhaps even more accurate would be the phrase "a cut above something." When we find a garment or another piece of merchandise that is outstanding, that has a superior excellence, we use the expression that it is "a cut above the rest."

God's holiness is more than just separateness. His holiness is also transcendent. The word *transcendence* means literally "to climb across." It is defined as "exceeding usual limits." To transcend is to rise above something, to go above and beyond a certain limit. When we speak of the transcendence of God, we are talking about that sense in which God is above and beyond us. Transcendence describes His supreme and absolute greatness. The word is used to describe God's relationship to the world. He is higher than the world. He has absolute power over the world. The world has no power over Him. Transcendence describes God in His consuming majesty, His exalted loftiness. It points to the infinite distance that separates Him from every creature. He is an infinite cut above everything else.

When the Bible calls God holy, it means primarily that God is transcendentally separate. He is so far above and beyond us that He seems almost totally foreign to us. To be holy is to be "other," to be different in a special way. The same basic meaning is used when the word *holy* is applied to earthly things. Look carefully at the following list of things the Bible speaks of as holy:

holy ground	holy nation
holy Sabbath	holy anointing oil
Holy Place	holy jubilee
holy linen coat	holy field
holy house	holy water
holy tithe	holy ark
holy censers	Holy City
holy bread	holy word
holy seed	holy ones
holy covenant	Holy of Holies
holy convocation	

This list is by no means exhaustive. It serves to show us that the word *holy* is applied to all sorts of things besides God. In every case the word *holy* is used to express something other than a moral or ethical quality. The things that are holy are things that are set apart, separated from the rest. They have been separated from the commonplace, consecrated to the Lord and to His service.

The things in the list are not holy in themselves. To become holy they first must be consecrated or sanctified by God. God alone is holy in Himself. Only God can sanctify something else. Only God can give the touch that changes it from the commonplace to something special, different, and apart.

Notice how the Old Testament regards things that have been made holy. Whatever is holy carries a peculiar character. It has been separated from a common use. It may not be touched; it may not be eaten; it may not be used for common matters. It is special.

Where does purity come in? We are so accustomed to equating holiness with purity or ethical perfection that we look for the idea when the word *holy* appears. When things are made holy, when they are consecrated, they are set apart unto purity. They are to be used in a pure way. They are to reflect purity as well as simple apartness. Purity is not excluded from the idea of the holy; it is contained within it. But the point we must remember is that the idea of the holy is never exhausted by the idea of purity. It includes purity but is much more than that. It is purity and transcendence. It is a transcendent purity.

When we use the word *holy* to describe God, we face another problem. We often describe God by compiling a list of qualities or characteristics that we call attributes. We say that God is a spirit, that He knows everything, that He is loving, just, merciful, gracious, and so on. The tendency is to add the idea of the holy to this long list of attributes as one attribute among many. But when the word *holy* is applied to God, it does not signify one single attribute. On the contrary, God is called holy in a general sense. The word is used as a synonym for His deity. That is, the word *holy* calls attention to all that God is. It reminds us that His love is holy love, His justice is holy justice, His mercy is holy mercy, His knowledge is holy knowledge, His spirit is holy spirit.

We have seen that the term *holy* calls attention to the transcendence of God, the sense in which He is above and beyond the world. We have also seen that God can reach down and consecrate special things in this world and make them holy. His touch on the common makes the common suddenly uncommon. Again we say that nothing in this world is holy in itself. Only God can make something holy. Only God can consecrate.

When we call things holy when they are not holy, we commit the sin of idolatry. We give to common things the respect, awe, worship, and adoration that belong only to God. To worship the creature instead of the Creator is the essence of idolatry.

In antiquity, idol makers were involved in a lucrative business. Some idols were made from wood, others from stone, and some from precious metals. The idol maker went to the marketplace and purchased the best materials and then went to his workshop to ply his craft. He worked long hours shaping images from the material, using his best tools and instruments. When he was finished, he swept up the floor of his workshop and carefully put his tools away in a cupboard. He then got down on his knees and started to talk to the idol he had just fashioned. Imagine talking to a dumb piece of wood or stone. The thing couldn't possibly hear what was being said. It could offer no reply. It could render no assistance. It was deaf, dumb, mute, and impotent. Yet people would ascribe holy power and worship to these objects.

Some idolaters were a bit more sophisticated. They didn't worship images of stone or totem poles. They began to worship the sun or the moon or even an abstract idea. But the sun is also a creature. There is nothing transcendent and holy about the moon. These things are all part of nature. They are all created. They may be impressive, but they do not go above and beyond the creaturely. They are not holy.

To worship an idol involves calling something holy when it is not holy. Remember, only God can consecrate. (When a minister "consecrates" a marriage or a communion wafer, it is understood that he is merely proclaiming a reality that God has already consecrated. This is an authorized use of human consecration.) When a human being tries to consecrate what God has never consecrated, it is not a genuine act of consecration. It is an act of desecration. It is an act of idolatry.

Early in the twentieth century a German scholar made an unusual and interesting study of the holy. The man's name was Rudolf Otto. Otto attempted to study the holy in a scientific way. He examined how people from different cultures and nations behave when they encounter something they regard as holy. He explored the human feelings people have when they meet the holy.

The first important discovery Otto made was that people have a difficult time describing the holy. Otto noticed that although certain things could be said about the holy, there always remained an element that defied explanation. It was not that this element was irrational. No, it was more super-rational, above the limits of our minds. There was something extra about human experience with the holy, something that could not be put into words. This is what Otto called a kind of *plus*. The plus is that part of the holy experience that people grope for words to express. It is the spiritual element that defies adequate description.

Otto coined a special term for the holy. He called it the *mysterium tremendum*. A simple translation of this concept is the "awful mystery." Otto described it like this:

> The feeling of it may at times come sweeping like a gentle tide,
> pervading the mind with a tranquil mood of deepest worship.

It may pass over into a more set and lasting attitude of the soul, continuing, as it were, thrillingly vibrant and resonant, until at last it dies away and the soul resumes its "profane," non-religious mood of everyday experience. It may burst in sudden eruption up from the depths of the soul with spasms and convulsions, or lead to the strangest excitements, to intoxicated frenzy, to transport, and to ecstasy. It has its wild and demonic forms and can sink to an almost grisly horror and shuddering. It has its crude barbaric antecedents and early manifestations, and again it may be developed into something beautiful and pure and glorious. It may become the hushed, trembling, and speechless humility of the creature in the presence of—whom or what? In the presence of that which is a *mystery* inexpressible and above all creatures.[1]

Otto spoke of the *tremendum* (awe-fulness) because of the fear the holy provokes in us. The holy fills us with a kind of dread. We use expressions like "My blood ran icy cold" or "My flesh crept."

We think of the Negro spiritual: "Were you there when they crucified my Lord?" The refrain of the song says, "Sometimes it causes me to tremble . . . tremble . . . tremble."

We tend to have mixed feelings about the holy. There is a sense in which we are at the same time attracted to it and repulsed by it. Something draws us toward it, while at the same time we want to run away from it. We can't seem to decide which way we want it. Part of us yearns for the holy, while part of us despises it. We can't live with it, and we can't live without it.

Our attitude toward the holy is close to our attitude toward ghost stories and horror movies. Children beg their parents to tell them ghost stories until they get so frightened they beg them to stop. I hate to take my wife to scary movies. She loves to see them until she sees them—or, I should say, doesn't see them. We go through the same pattern each time. First she clutches my arm and digs her fingernails into my flesh. The only relief I get is when she removes her hands from my arm so she can use both hands to cover her eyes. The next step is when she leaves her seat and goes to the rear of the theater where she can stand with her back against a solid wall. There she can be sure nothing is going to jump out from behind her and grab her. The final step is when she leaves the theater altogether and seeks refuge in the lobby. Yet she tells me that she loves to go to such movies. (There must be a theological illustration in there somewhere.)

Perhaps the clearest example of this strange phenomenon of people's mixed feelings to the holy comes from the world of radio. Before the advent of television, the radio program was the zenith of home entertainment. We were treated to daily operas sponsored by soap companies. Duz gave us *Ma Perkins*. Other soap companies gave us *Our Gal Sunday, One Man's Family, Lorenzo Jones and His Wife, Belle,* and a host of others.

The evening programs were given to action and adventure with *The Lone Ranger, Superman, Tennessee Jed, Hop Harrigan,* and so on. My favorites were the mystery programs like *Gangbusters, The Shadow,* and *Suspense.*

The scary program of all scary programs began with the eerie sound of a creaking door opening. It sounded like fingernails scratching a blackboard. It evoked the image in my head of an ancient, musty vault being opened. With the sound of the creaking door came the sonorous voice of the announcer saying, "INNER SANCTUM!"

What is so scary about the words *inner sanctum?* What do the words mean? *Inner sanctum* simply means "within the holy." Nothing is more dreadful to us, more terrifying to the mind, than to be brought within the holy. Here we begin to tremble as we are brought into the presence of the *mysterium tremendum.*

The mysterious character of a holy God is contained in the Latin word *augustus.* The early Christians had problems giving this title to Caesar. To the Christian, no person was worthy of the title *august.* Only God could properly be called the august one. To be august is to be awe-inspiring, or awe-ful. In the ultimate sense only God is awe-ful.

In Otto's study of the human experience of the holy, he discovered that the clearest sensation that human beings have when they experience the holy is an overpowering and overwhelming sense of creatureliness. That is, when we are aware of the presence of God, we become most aware of ourselves as creatures. When we meet the Absolute, we know immediately that we are not absolute. When we meet the Infinite, we become acutely conscious that we are finite. When we meet the Eternal, we know we are temporal. To meet God is a powerful study in contrasts.

Our contrast with the "Other" is overwhelming. We think of the prophet Jeremiah and of his complaint to God: "O LORD, you deceived me, and I was deceived; you overpowered me and prevailed" (Jer. 20:7).

Here it sounds as if Jeremiah was afflicted by a bad case of stuttering. Normally the Bible is brief in its expressions, having a kind of economy of language. Jeremiah breaks the rule by taking the time to state the utterly obvious. He says,

"You deceived me, and I was deceived." The last phrase is a waste of words. Of course Jeremiah was deceived. If God deceived him, how could he possibly be anything but deceived? If God overpowered him, how could he be anything but overwhelmed?

But maybe Jeremiah just wanted to make sure that God understood him when he registered his complaint. Perhaps he was using the Hebrew method of repetition to indicate emphasis. Jeremiah was deceived and overpowered. He was feeling helpless, impotent before the absolute power of God. In this moment Jeremiah was supremely aware of his own creatureliness.

Being reminded that we are creatures is not always a pleasant thing. The words of Satan's original temptation are hard to erase from our minds. "Ye shall be as gods" (Gen. 3:5, KJV). This ghastly lie of Satan's is one lie we would dearly love to be able to believe. If we could be like gods, we would be immortal, infallible, and irresistible. We would have a host of other powers that we presently do not and cannot possess.

Death often frightens us. When we see another person die, we are reminded that we are also mortal, that someday death will come to us. It is a thought we try to push from our minds. We are uncomfortable when another's death rudely intrudes into our lives and reminds us of what we will face at some unknown future date. Death reminds us that we are creatures. Yet as fearsome as death is, it is nothing compared with meeting a holy God. When we encounter Him, the totality of our creatureliness breaks upon us and shatters the myth that we have believed about ourselves, the myth that we are demigods, junior-grade deities who will try to live forever.

As mortal creatures, we are exposed to all sorts of fears. We are anxious people, given to phobias. Some people are afraid of cats, others of snakes, and still others of crowded places or lofty heights. These phobias gnaw at us and disturb our inner peace.

There is a special kind of phobia from which we all suffer. It is called *xenophobia*. Xenophobia is a fear (and sometimes a hatred) of strangers or foreigners or of anything that is strange or foreign. God is the ultimate object of our xenophobia. He is the ultimate stranger. He is the ultimate foreigner. He is holy, and we are not.

We fear God because He is holy. Our fear is not the healthy fear that the Bible encourages us to have. Our fear is a servile fear, a fear born of dread. God is too great for us; He is too awesome. He makes difficult demands on us. He is the mysterious Stranger who threatens our security. In His presence we quake and tremble. Meeting Him personally may be our greatest trauma.

Allowing God's Holiness to Touch Our Lives

As you reflect about what you have learned and rediscovered about God's holiness, answer these questions. Use a journal to record your responses to God's holiness, or discuss your responses with a friend.

1. In what ways is God an awe-ful mystery to you?
2. Does God's mystery comfort you or frighten you?
3. What do you learn about yourself as you comprehend the mystery of God's holiness?
4. During the coming week, how will you worship God for the mystery of His holiness?

FOUR

The Trauma of Holiness

Hence that dread and amazement with which,
as Scripture uniformly relates, holy men were struck
and overwhelmed whenever they beheld the
presence of God. . . . Men are never duly touched
and impressed with a conviction of their insignificance
until they have contrasted themselves with
the majesty of God.

JOHN CALVIN

I t was a dark and stormy night.

I have waited for a long time to be able to begin a story with this classic expression. This introductory sentence has been so abused that some literary friends have started a club called the Dark and Stormy Night Club. Each year they present awards for the worst opening lines of books and essays.

Perhaps by the time Mark wrote his Gospel, there already was a Dark and Stormy Night Club. Notice how he begins his telling of Jesus calming the storm: "That day when evening came, he said to his disciples, 'Let us go over to the other side' " (Mark 4:35).

Jesus and His disciples were in Galilee. Jesus had been teaching the crowds who gathered on the shore of the large lake that was called the Sea of Galilee. This body of water is one of nature's grand designs. The lake fills a basin that is surrounded by mountains. Its fresh water is an important source of life to the arid countryside of Palestine.

The disciples were professional fishermen, seasoned veterans of the lake. They knew the lake's currents, its moods, and its beauty. The Sea of Galilee is like an enchanting woman whose moods are fiercely changeable. Every sailor in the region is warned of the fickleness of this body of water. Because of its peculiar location in the mountains between the Mediterranean Sea and the desert, the lake is exposed to strange quirks of nature. Violent winds can come across its surface as if they are blowing through a funnel. These winds come without warning and can turn the tranquil lake into a roaring tempest in a matter of seconds. Even with today's modern equipment, some people refuse to sail on the Sea of Galilee for fear of perishing under the wrath of the lake's violent moods.

The disciples had two things in their favor. They were veterans, and they were with the Master. When Jesus suggested that they make an evening crossing, the disciples felt no fear. They prepared their boats and made ready to cross. Then the sea had a temper tantrum; the Lady of the Lake went berserk: "A furious squall came up, and the waves broke over the boat, so that it was nearly swamped" (Mark 4:37).

The thing every Galilean fisherman feared the most happened. The unpredictable tempest hit, its violence threatening to capsize the boat. Even the strongest swimmer could not survive if hurled into the water. The men gripped the gunwales until their knuckles were white. These were crude fishing boats, not schooners or ocean liners. One sudden twist, one high wave hitting broadside could send them all to their deaths. They fought the sea furiously, trying to keep the bow into the waves. Perhaps it was here that the sailor's prayer was first uttered: "O Lord, Your sea is so great, and my boat is so small."

Jesus was sound asleep in the back of the boat. He was taking a nap. I have seen similar behavior. I have been in airplanes during violent storms. I have experienced sudden losses of altitude when the plane drops like a stone for thousands of feet, leaving my stomach on the ceiling. I have heard passengers screaming in terror and seen stewardesses at the edge of panic—all while the man next to me sleeps like a baby. I've wanted to grab the fellow and shake him awake saying, "What's the matter with you? Don't you have the good sense to be scared?"

The Bible says that Jesus was sleeping on a cushion. While everybody else was in panic, Jesus was in peaceful slumber. The disciples were annoyed. Their feelings were a mixture of fear and anger. They moved to awaken Jesus. I don't know what they thought He could do about the situation. The text makes it clear that they certainly didn't expect Him to do what He did. For all intents and purposes, their situation was hopeless. The waves were getting bigger and more violent every second.

The disciples had no idea what Jesus would do. They were like people anywhere. When people are in danger, when they are threatened by peril and don't know what to do, they immediately look to their leader. It is the job of the leader to know what the next step is, even if there is no possible next step. "The disciples woke him and said to him, 'Teacher, don't you care if we drown?' " (Mark 4:38).

Their question was not really a question. It was an accusation. The suggestion was thinly veiled. They were actually saying, "You don't care if we drown." They were charging the Son of God with a lack of compassion. This outrageous attack on Jesus is consistent with mankind's customary attitude toward God. God has to listen to complaints like these from an ungrateful humanity every day. Heaven is bombarded with the repeated charges of angry people. God is called "unloving," "cruel," and "aloof," as if He has not done enough to prove His compassion for us.

There is no indication in the text that Jesus made any reply to the disciples' "question." His answer skipped over words to direct action. He saved His words for the sea and the storm:

> He got up, rebuked the wind and said to the waves, "Quiet! Be still!" Then the wind died down and it was completely calm.
>
> He said to his disciples, "Why are you so afraid? Do you still have no faith?" (Mark 4:39, 40)

The life of Jesus was a blaze of miracles. He performed so many that it is easy for us to become jaded in the hearing of them. We can read this narrative and skip quickly over to the next page without being moved. Yet we have here one of the most astonishing of all Jesus' miracles. We have an event that made a special impression on the disciples. It was a miracle that was mind boggling, even to them.

Jesus controlled the fierce forces of nature by the sound of His voice. He didn't say a prayer. He didn't ask the Father to deliver them from the tempest. He dealt with the situation directly. He uttered a command, a divine imperative. Instantly nature obeyed. The wind heard the voice of its Creator. The sea recognized the command of its Lord. Instantly the wind ceased. Not a zephyr could be felt in the air. The sea became like glass, without the tiniest ripple.

Notice the reaction of the disciples. The sea was now calm, but they were still agitated: "They were terrified and asked each other, 'Who is this? Even the wind and the waves obey him!'" (Mark 4:41).

We see a strange pattern unfolding here. That the storm and raging sea frightened the disciples is not surprising. But once the danger passed and the sea was calm, it would seem that their fear would vanish as suddenly as the storm. It didn't happen that way. Now that the sea was calm, the fear of the disciples *increased*. How do we account for that?

It was the father of modern psychiatry, Sigmund Freud, who once espoused the theory that people invent religion out of a fear of nature. We feel helpless before an earthquake, a flood, or a ravaging disease. So, said Freud, we invent a God who has power over the earthquake, flood, and disease. God is personal. We can talk to Him. We can try to bargain with Him. We can plead with Him to save us from the destructive forces of nature. We are not able to plead with earthquakes, negotiate with floods, or bargain with cancer. So, the theory goes, we invent God to help us deal with these scary things.

What is significant about this scriptural story is that the disciples' fear increased after the threat of the storm was removed. The storm had made them afraid. Jesus' action to still the tempest made them more afraid. In the power of Christ they met something more frightening than they had ever met in nature. They were in the presence of the holy. We wonder what Freud would have said about that. Why would the disciples invent a God whose holiness was more terrifying than the forces of nature that provoked them to invent a god in the first place? We can understand it if people invented an unholy god, a god who brought only comfort. But why a god more scary than the earthquake, flood, or disease? It is one thing to fall victim to the flood or to fall prey to cancer; *it is another thing to fall into the hands of the living God.*

The words that the disciples spoke after Jesus calmed the sea are very revealing. They cried out, "Who is this?" The King James Version expresses the question like this: "What manner of man is this, that even the wind and the sea obey him?" The question was "What *manner* of man is this?" They were asking a question of *kind*. They were looking for a category to put Jesus in, a category with which they were familiar. If we can classify people into certain types, we know immediately how to deal with them. We respond one way to hostile people and another way to friendly people. We react one way to intellectual types and another way to social types. The disciples could find no category adequate to capture the person of Jesus. He was beyond typecasting. He was *sui generis*—in a class by Himself.

The disciples had never met a man like this. He was one of a kind, a complete foreigner. They had met all different kinds of men before—tall men, short men, fat men, skinny men, smart men, and stupid men. They had met Greeks, Romans, Syrians, Egyptians, Samaritans, and fellow Jews. But they had never met a holy man, a man who could speak to wind and waves and have them obey Him.

That Jesus could sleep through the storm at sea was strange enough. But it was not unique. I think again of my fellow airplane passenger who dozed while I was gripped with panic. It may be rare to meet people who can slumber through a crisis, but it is not unprecedented. I was impressed with my friend on the plane. But he did not awaken and yell out the window to the wind and make it stop at his command. If he had done that, I would have looked around for a parachute.

Jesus was different. He possessed an awesome otherness. He was the supreme mysterious stranger. He made people uncomfortable.

The account of Christ calming the storm had a kind of instant replay in Jesus' ministry. Luke gives the setting as the Lake of Gennesaret. It seems that at times the Jews had trouble making up their minds what to call the large body of water nestled in the hills of Galilee. The Lake of Gennesaret was one and the same body of water that is elsewhere called the Sea of Galilee.

> One day as Jesus was standing by the Lake of Gennesaret, with the people crowding around him and listening to the word of God, he saw at the water's edge two boats, left there by the fishermen, who were washing their nets. He got into one of the boats, the one belonging to Simon, and asked him to put out a little from shore. Then he sat down and taught the people from the boat.
>
> When he had finished speaking, he said to Simon, "Put out into deep water, and let down the nets for a catch."
>
> Simon answered, "Master, we've worked hard all night and haven't caught anything. But because you say so, I will let down the nets."
>
> When they had done so, they caught such a large number of fish that their nets began to break. So they signaled their partners in the other boat to come and help them, and they came and filled both boats so full that they began to sink. (Luke 5:1–7)

If ever there was a time when the disciples displayed annoyance and irritation with Jesus, this was the occasion. Simon Peter was tired. He had been up all night and was frustrated by the lack of success in his fishing. The catch had been terrible. Such an experience was enough to put a professional fisherman in a foul mood. Add to his weariness the additional frustration of dealing with the multitudes who were pushing around him all morning as Jesus was teaching. When Jesus' sermon was finished, Simon was ready to go home and go to bed. But Jesus wanted to go fishing. He had a marvelous idea about casting out into the deep water.

It doesn't require a lot of imagination to read between the lines and catch Simon's seething sarcasm. "Master, we've worked hard all night and haven't caught anything. But because you say so, I will let down the nets." Real respect for the wisdom of Jesus in this circumstance would have had Simon saying, simply, "I will let down the nets." Instead, he found it necessary to register his frustration. It is as if he said, "Look, Jesus, you are a marvelous teacher. Your words keep us all spellbound. In matters of religion you confound us all. But, please, give us a little bit of credit. We are professionals. We know the fishing business. We have been out there all night and nothing—zilch. The fish just aren't running. Let's go home, go to bed, and try again later. But if you insist, if we must humor you, then, of course we will let down the nets."

I can see Simon Peter exchanging a knowing glance with Andrew and muttering complaints under his breath as he hoisted the nets that he had just cleaned and threw them overboard. He must have been thinking to himself, *Blasted teachers! They're all alike. They think they know everything.*

We know how it turned out. No sooner had Peter dropped the nets where Jesus told him, than it seemed as if every fish in the Lake of Gennesaret jumped into them. It was as if the fish were having a contest to see who could jump in first. "Last one in is a rotten eel!"

So many fish filled the nets that the strain was too great. The nets began to break. When the other disciples rushed to the scene with their boat, it was still not enough. Both boats were so filled to the brim with fish that the vessels began to sink. This was the most extraordinary catch the fishermen had ever witnessed.

How did Peter react? How would you have reacted? I know what I would have done. I would have pulled out a contract on the spot. I would have asked Jesus to show up at the dock once a month for five minutes. I would have owned the most lucrative fishing business in history.

Business and profits were the things furthest from Peter's mind. When the nets were bursting, Peter couldn't even see the fish. All he could see was Jesus. Hear what he said: "When Simon Peter saw this, he fell at Jesus' knees and said, 'Go away from me, Lord; I am a sinful man!' " (Luke 5:8).

At that moment Peter realized that he was in the presence of the Holy Incarnate. He was desperately uncomfortable. His initial response was one of worship. He fell to his knees before Christ. Instead of saying something like, "Lord, I adore You, I magnify You," he said, "Please go away. Please leave. I can't stand it."

The history of the life of Christ is a history of multitudes of people pushing through crowds just to get close to Him. It is the leper crying, "Have mercy on me." It is the woman who had been bleeding for twelve years reaching out to touch the hem of His garment. It is the thief on the cross straining to hear Jesus' dying words. It is people saying, "Come close to me. Look at me. Touch me."

Not so Peter. His anguished plea was different: He asked Jesus to depart, to give him space, to leave him alone.

Why? We need not speculate here. It is not necessary to read between the lines because the lines themselves state precisely why Peter wanted Jesus gone: "I am a sinful man!" Sinful people are not comfortable in the presence of the holy. The cliché is that misery loves company. Another is that there is fellowship among thieves. But thieves do not seek the consoling presence of the fellowship of police officers. Sinful misery does not love the company of purity.

We notice that Jesus did not lecture Peter about his sins. There was no rebuke, no word of judgment. All Jesus did was to show Peter how to catch fish. But when the holy is manifest, no words are needed to express it. Peter got a message that was impossible to miss. The transcendent standard of all righteousness and all purity blazed before his eyes. Like Isaiah before him, Peter was undone.

One of the strange facts of history is the consistently good reputation Jesus of Nazareth enjoys even with unbelievers. It is rare for an unbeliever to speak unkindly of Jesus. People who are openly hostile to the church and who hold Christians in contempt are often unsparing in their praise for Jesus. Even Friedrich Nietzsche, who announced the death of God and lamented the decadence of the church, spoke of Jesus as a model of the heroic. In the final years of his life, which were spent in a lunatic asylum, Nietzsche expressed his own insanity by signing his letters, "The Crucified One."

The overwhelming testimony of the world is to the incomparable perfection of Jesus. Even George Bernard Shaw, when critical of Jesus, could think of no higher standard than Christ Himself. He said of Jesus, "There were times when he did not behave as a Christian." We cannot miss the irony of Shaw's criticism.

In terms of moral excellence, even those who do not ascribe to the deity or saviorhood of Christ applaud Jesus the man. Like Pontius Pilate they declare, "Ecce homo." "Behold the man!" "I find no fault in Him."

With all the applause Jesus gets, it seems difficult to understand why His contemporaries killed Him. Why did the multitudes scream for His blood? Why did the Pharisees loathe Him? Why was such a nice, upright fellow condemned to death by the highest religious court in the land?

To understand this mystery we might look to modern-day Palestine for an answer. The pilgrim who visits Jerusalem is stunned by the magnificence of the venerable city. At night the ancient walls are bathed by floodlights, giving a magical look to the Holy City. If one approaches the city from the Mount of Olives and passes through the Valley of Kidron along the winding road, he or she will see the standing memorial of the Tomb of the Prophets adorning the roadway along the Eastern Wall near the pinnacle of the temple. The memorial has been standing there for centuries, dating all the way back to the time of Christ. There, in bold relief, are the sculpted figures of the great prophets of the Old Testament, like a Jewish miniature Mount Rushmore.

In Jesus' day the Old Testament prophets were venerated. They were the great folk heroes from the past. Yet when they were alive they were hated, scorned, rejected, despised, persecuted, and killed by their contemporaries.

Stephen was the first Christian martyr. He was killed by a furious mob because he reminded his audience of the blood that was on their hands:

> You stiff-necked people, with uncircumcised hearts and ears! You are just like your fathers: You always resist the Holy Spirit! Was there ever a prophet your fathers did not persecute? They even killed those who predicted the coming of the Righteous One. And now you have betrayed and murdered him—you who have received the law that was put into effect through angels but have not obeyed it. (Acts 7:51–53)

We might expect that these stinging words from Stephen would have pierced the hearts of his hearers and led them to repentance. But such was not the effect: "When they heard this, they were furious and gnashed their teeth at him. . . .

"At this they covered their ears and, yelling at the top of their voices, they all rushed at him, dragged him out of the city and began to stone him" (Acts 7:54, 57, 58).

People have an appreciation for moral excellence, as long as it is removed a safe distance from them. The Jews honored the prophets, from a distance. The world honors Christ, from a distance.

Peter wanted to be with Jesus, until He got too close. Then Peter cried, "Please leave."

In the 1970s, the book *The Peter Principle* by Laurence Peter and Raymond Hull reached the top of the best-seller lists. The fundamental point of its teaching has since become an axiom in the business world: that people tend to rise to their level of incompetence in the corporate structures. The Peter Principle has nothing to do with Simon Peter except that it partially explains why Peter was uncomfortable in the presence of Jesus.

The Peter Principle involves the questions of competence and incompetence. The axiom that people tend to rise to the level of their incompetence is based on a study of promotions in the business world. When people do well, they are promoted. They rise up a notch in the organization. Their upward climb is finally arrested at a certain point. It is the point where they cease to do well. When they stop doing well, they stop getting promoted and are doomed to spend the rest of their days working at a level that is one step above their level of competency. People get locked into their level of incompetency, a tragedy for them and for their companies.

Not everyone gets caught in the trap of the Peter Principle. Authors Peter and Hull mention two categories of people who escape the trap: the super-incompetent and the super-competent. The super-incompetent people have no opportunity to move up to their level of incompetence because they are already incompetent. There is no level at which they are competent. They are incompetent at the lowest level of the organization. These people are weeded out of the organization early.

The real irony is found in the other group that "escapes" the Peter Principle. This group is that of the super-competent. How do super-competent people rise through the corporate structures to get to the top? They don't. The book asserts that the great difficulty super-competent people have in rising up the corporate ladder is that they represent a massive threat to those above them. Their bosses are frightened by them, fearful that they will displace them. Super-competent people represent a clear and present danger that their superiors will lose their seats of honor and power. Super-competent people succeed not by moving up the organizational ladder but also by making jumping moves from one organization to another, moving higher up as they go.

It is easy for us to dismiss Peter and Hull's theory as pure cynicism. We can point to countless examples of people who have had meteoric rises in companies and reached the very top. More than one chief executive officer started in the company as a clerk. Peter and Hull would reply, of course, that these dramatic Horatio Alger stories are the exceptions that prove the rule.

Whatever the true statistics are, the indisputable fact remains that there are numerous occasions where super-competent people are frozen at a low level because they threaten those above them. Not everyone applauds success. I remember a senior student I had in my college teaching days. She was the best female student I had ever had. Her cumulative average was a solid 4.0. Her work was extraordinary.

I was shocked when I graded one of her senior exams, which she flunked miserably. Her performance was such a radical departure from her normal level that I knew something was seriously wrong. I called her into my office for a meeting and asked her what went wrong. She immediately burst into tears and between sobs confessed that she had intentionally failed the exam. When I asked her why, she explained that as she was nearing graduation, she was experiencing a growing fear that she would never find a husband. "None of the guys want to date me," she said. "They all think that I'm too smart, that I'm just a brain." She poured out a heart-wrenching tale of loneliness and a personal feeling of being ostracized from the social life on campus. She was feeling like a pariah.

This student had committed the socially unpardonable sin. She had broken the curve. I know what it means to grade on a curve both from the vantage point of the student and of the teacher. I remember my student days and the dreadful feeling of walking out of a classroom after doing poorly on a test. I remember how it was music to my ears when teachers said that they would grade the test on a curve. That meant if I got only 60 percent on the test, the curve might promote me from a D to a C, or even to a B if enough people did poorly. This put me in a position where I was rooting for the other students to fail.

But there was always one in the crowd. When everyone else was making 20s and 30s on the test, giving incontrovertible evidence that the test was unfair, and the teacher would be morally bound to grade by the curve, there was the inevitable brain who would make 100 percent on the test. I can't ever recall the students rising to their feet to offer the brain a standing ovation. Nobody likes curve breakers. They make us all look bad.

Jesus Christ was a curve breaker. He was the supreme curve buster. He was the ultimate super-competent. The outcasts of society loved Him because He paid attention to them. But those who held the seats of honor and power could not tolerate Christ.

The party of the Jews who declared themselves the mortal enemies of Jesus were the Pharisees.

The Pharisees traced their beginnings to the period of history between the close of the Old Testament period and the beginning of the New Testament period. The sect was started by men who had a great zeal for the Law. The word *Pharisee* literally meant "one who is separated." The Pharisees separated themselves unto holiness. The pursuit of holiness was the chief business of their lives. They majored in holiness. If any group should have thrown their hats in the air when the holy appeared on the scene, it was the Pharisees.

Through their singular devotion to the pursuit of holiness, the Pharisees achieved a level of popular respect for piety and righteousness that was without parallel. They had no peers. They were accorded lofty human praise. They were welcomed to privileged seats in the banquet halls. They were admired as experts in religion. Their uniforms were decorated with the tassels of their exalted ranks. They could be seen practicing their virtue in public places. They fasted where everyone could see them. They bowed their heads in solemn prayer on the street corners and restaurants. No one missed the clang of the coin in the beggar's cup when the Pharisees gave alms. Their "holiness" was plain for everyone to see.

Jesus called them hypocrites.

Jesus pronounced upon them the prophetic oracle of doom: "Woe to you, teachers of the law and Pharisees, you hypocrites! You travel over land and sea to win a single convert, and when he becomes one, you make him twice as much a son of hell as you are" (Matt. 23:15). Jesus' denunciation of the Pharisees was severe. He criticized them for several counts of hypocrisy. Let us examine a few of the charges Jesus brought against them:

> The teachers of the law and the Pharisees sit in Moses' seat. So
> you must obey them and do everything they tell you. But do not
> do what they do, for they do not practice what they preach. They
> tie up heavy loads and put them on men's shoulders, but they
> themselves are not willing to lift a finger to move them.

> Everything they do is done for men to see: They make their
> phylacteries wide and the tassels on their garments long; they
> love the place of honor at banquets and the most important seats
> in the synagogues; they love to be greeted in the marketplaces
> and to have men call them "Rabbi." (Matt. 23:2–7)

There was no understated elegance about the Pharisees. There was no au-thentic beauty to their holiness. They were showy and ostentatious in their outward displays. Their holiness was a sham. The hypocrite was a playactor of righteousness:

> Woe to you, teachers of the law and Pharisees, you hypocrites!
> You clean the outside of the cup and dish, but inside they are full
> of greed and self-indulgence. Blind Pharisee! First clean the inside
> of the cup and dish, and then the outside also will be clean.

> Woe to you, teachers of the law and Pharisees, you hypocrites!
> You are like whitewashed tombs, which look beautiful on the

outside but on the inside are full of dead men's bones and everything unclean. In the same way, on the outside you appear to people as righteous but on the inside you are full of hypocrisy and wickedness. (Matt. 23:25–28)

The images Jesus used are striking. He pictures the Pharisees as being like cups that are clean only on the outside. Imagine going to a restaurant and having the waiter put a cup in front of you that is sparkling clean on the outside but is filled with the residue of yesterday's coffee grounds on the inside of the cup. It would do little to enhance your appetite. So was the service of the Pharisees. As whitewashed tombs conceal the grisly truth of bodily decomposition and putrefying flesh, so the facade of the Pharisees hid from view the rottenness of their souls.

Consider for a moment a few brief epithets that Jesus reserved for the Pharisees: "You snakes!" "You brood of vipers!" "Blind guides!" "Sons of hell!" "Blind fools!" These forms of address can hardly be considered compliments. Jesus spared no invectives in His denunciations of these men. His words were uncharacteristically harsh, though not unjustifiably harsh. They were different from His usual style. The normal form of rebuke He made to sinners was gentle. He spoke tenderly, though firmly, to the woman caught in adultery and to the woman at the well. It seems that Jesus saved His severe comments for the big boys, the theological professionals. With them He asked no quarter and gave none.

We might argue that the Pharisees hated Jesus because He was so critical of them. No one likes to be criticized, especially people who are accustomed to praise. But the venom of the Pharisees went deeper than that. It is safe to assume that had Jesus said nothing to them, they still would have despised Him. His mere presence was enough to cause them to recoil from Him.

It has been said that nothing dispels a lie faster than the truth; nothing exposes the counterfeit faster than the genuine. Clever counterfeit dollars may be unnoticed by the untrained eye. What every counterfeiter fears is that someone will examine his bogus bill while holding a genuine one next to it. The presence of Jesus represented the presence of the genuine in the midst of the bogus. Here authentic holiness appeared; the counterfeiters of holiness were not pleased.

The Sadducees had the same problem with Jesus. They were the exalted priestly class of the day. They took their name from the Old Testament priest Zadok, whose name, in turn, was taken from the Jewish word for "righteous." If the Pharisees considered themselves to be the holy ones, the Sadducees claimed to be the righteous ones. With the appearance of Jesus, their righteousness took on the luster of unrighteousness. Their curve was broken too.

The resentment of the Pharisees and Sadducees toward Jesus began as a petty annoyance, moved to the level of a smoldering rage, and finally exploded in vehement demands for His death. They simply could not tolerate Him. On the Sea of Galilee the disciples were unable to find a category fitting for Christ; they could not answer their own question, "What manner of man is this?" The Pharisees and the Sadducees had a ready answer. They created categories for Jesus: He was a "blasphemer" and a "devil." He had to go. The super-competent had to be destroyed.

The incarnate Christ is no longer walking the earth. He has ascended into heaven. No one sees Him or speaks audibly with Him in the flesh today. Yet the threatening power of His holiness is still felt. Sometimes it is transferred to His people. As the Jews at the foot of Mount Sinai fled in terror from the dazzling face of Moses, so people today get uncomfortable in the mere presence of Christians.

Struggling with the Dutch language was one of the most difficult aspects of my education. When I went to Holland to study, I was bewildered by this language that had such a lilting sound to it. Its vowel sounds were almost impossible for me to pronounce, and the language was rich in strange idioms. Just when I would think that I had the language under control, I would hear an expression that totally mystified me.

Such was the expression I heard at a dinner party at a friend's house in Amsterdam. The conversation was animated until suddenly there was a gap, an unplanned break in the conversation that brought with it a brief awkward silence. To break the silence, one of my Dutch friends said, *"Er gaat een Domine voorbij!"* I replied, "What did you say?" The strange phrase was repeated. I knew what the words meant, but the expression made no sense. To break the awkward silence, he had said, "A minister walked by!"

Again I asked my friends for an explanation. They explained that it was a custom in Holland to use this expression whenever an awkward silence threatened a lively conversation. To say that a minister walked by was to offer an explanation for the sudden silence. The idea was that nothing could ruin the conviviality of a party faster than the presence of a clergyman. When the minister appears, the fun is over. There can be no more laughter, no more lively conversation, only a stilted silence. When such silences came, the only explanation could be that a minister had just walked by.

I experience the same phenomenon frequently on the golf course. If I get paired with strangers, everything goes fine until they ask me what I do. As soon as they find out I am a clergyman, the whole atmosphere changes. They begin to stand farther away from me as we speak, giving me extra space. It is as if they suddenly realize that I have some dreadful disease, and it might be contagious. Profuse apologies usually follow regarding their language. "I'm sorry for swearing. I didn't know that you were a minister." As if the minister never heard such words before or that it was unthinkable that in his whole life such words had ever passed over his lips. The Isaiah-complex of the dirty mouth is still with us.

Scripture says that "the wicked flee when no one pursues" (Prov. 28:1, NKJV). Luther stated it this way, "The pagan trembles at the rustling of a leaf." The uncomfortable feeling that is provoked by the presence of clergymen is fallout from the identification of the church with Christ. It can have strange effects on people.

In the 1970s, one of the leading golfers on the professional tour was invited to play in a foursome with Gerald Ford (then president of the United States), Jack Nicklaus, and Billy Graham. The golfer was especially in awe of playing with Ford and Billy Graham (he had played frequently with Nicklaus before).

After the round of golf was finished, one of the other pros came up to the golfer and asked, "Hey, what was it like playing with the president and with Billy Graham?"

The pro unleashed a torrent of cursing, and in a disgusted manner said, "I don't need Billy Graham stuffing religion down my throat." With that he turned on his heel and stormed off, heading for the practice tee.

His friend followed the angry pro to the practice tee. The pro took out his driver and started to beat out balls in fury. His neck was crimson, and it looked as if steam was coming from his ears. His friend said nothing. He sat on a bench and watched. After a few minutes the anger of the pro was spent. He settled down. His friend said quietly, "Was Billy a little rough on you out there?"

The pro heaved an embarrassed sigh and said, "No, he didn't even mention religion. I just had a bad round."

Astonishing. Billy Graham had said not a word about God, Jesus, or religion, yet the pro had stormed away after the game accusing Billy of trying to ram religion down his throat. How can we explain this? It's really not difficult. Billy Graham didn't have to say a word; he didn't have to give a single sideward glance to make the pro feel uncomfortable. Billy Graham is so identified with religion, so associated with the things of God, that his very presence is enough to smother the wicked person who flees when no one pursues. Luther was right, pagans do tremble at the rustling of a leaf. They feel the hound of heaven breathing down their neck. They feel crowded by holiness, even if it is made present only by an imperfect, partially sanctified human vessel.

The golf pro's reaction to Billy Graham was similar to Peter's reaction to Jesus Christ. "Go away from me, Lord; I am a sinful man!" Both felt the trauma of the presence of the holy. Holiness provokes hatred. The greater the holiness, the greater the human hostility toward it. It seems insane. No man was ever more loving than Jesus Christ. Yet even His love made people angry. His love was a perfect love, a transcendent and holy love, but His very love brought trauma to people. This kind of love is so majestic we can't stand it.

A well-known story in American literature describes a kind of love that destroys. It is a freakish love, a love so intense that it crushes the object of its affection. Students of the writing of John Steinbeck have suggested that his famous character Lennie, in *Of Mice and Men,* was in fact a Christ figure.

Lennie a Christ figure? Many Christians are offended by the suggestion. Lennie is a big, dumb brute. He is a murderer. How could such a person ever serve as a Christ figure?

Of Mice and Men is the story of two migrant workers, Lennie and George, who wander over the countryside from job to job, dreaming of the day when they can own their own farm. Steinbeck describes them:

> Both were dressed in denim trousers and in denim coats with brass buttons. Both wore black, shapeless hats, and both carried tight blanket rolls slung over their shoulders. The first man was small and quick, dark of face, with restless eyes and sharp, strong features. Every part of him was defined: small, strong hands, slender arms, a thin and bony nose. Behind him walked his opposite, a huge man, shapeless of face, with large, pale eyes, with wide sloping shoulders; and he walked heavily, dragging his feet a little, the way a bear drags his paws. His arms did not swing at his sides but hung loosely.

Notice the contrast in the two characters. George's face is clearly defined. Lennie is "shapeless of face." There is something incomprehensible about this hulk of a man. He walks like a bear, but he has the mind of a naïve child. Lennie is mentally retarded. He is virtually helpless without George. George has to take care of him and speak to him in the simplest of terms.

Lennie has a strange quirk. He loves little furry animals—mice, rabbits, and the like. He dreams of the day when George will get their farm and he can keep rabbits and mice of his own. But Lennie has a problem. He doesn't understand his own strength. When he picks up a field mouse or a rabbit, all he wants to do is love it, to shower his affection on it. But the furry creatures don't understand. They are frightened and try to escape Lennie's grasp. Lennie squeezes them so he can hold them still to receive his love. Unintentionally he kills them, squeezing the life out of them with his heavy hands.

Lennie's preoccupation with little furry creatures is a constant source of annoyance to George. He gets upset when he discovers that Lennie is walking around with a dead mouse in his jacket pocket. The thing is rank. But George loves Lennie like a son and patiently abides these foibles. The climax of the book comes when Lennie finds himself alone with the foreman's wife:

> Curley's wife laughed at him. "You're nuts," she said. "But you're a kinda nice fella. Jus' like a big baby. But a person can see kinda what you mean. When I'm doin' my hair sometimes I jus' set an' stroke it 'cause it's so soft." To show how she did it, she ran her fingers over the top of her head. "Some people got kinda coarse hair," she said complacently. "Take Curley. His hair is jus' like wire. But mine is soft and fine. 'Course I brush it a lot. That makes it fine. Here—feel right here." She took Lennie's hand and put it on her head. "Feel right aroun' there an' see how soft it is."
>
> Lennie's big fingers fell to stroking her hair.
>
> "Don't you muss it up," she said.
>
> Lennie said, "Oh! That's nice," and he stroked harder. "Oh, that's nice."
>
> "Look out, now, you'll muss it." And then she cried angrily, "You stop it now, you'll mess it all up." She jerked her head sideways, and Lennie's fingers closed on her hair and hung on. "Let go," she cried. "You let go!"
>
> Lennie was in a panic. His face was contorted. She screamed then, and Lennie's other hand closed over her mouth and nose. "Please don't," he begged. "Oh! Please don't do that. George'll be mad."

She struggled violently under his hands. Her feet battered on the hay and she writhed to be free; and from under Lennie's hand came a muffled scream. Lennie began to cry with fright. "Oh! Please don't do none of that," he begged. "George gonna say I done a bad thing. He ain't gonna let me tend no rabbits." He moved his hand a little and her hoarse cry came out. Then Lennie grew angry. "Now don't," he said, "I don't want you to yell. You gonna get me in trouble jus' like George says you will. Now don't you do that." And she continued to struggle, and her eyes were wild with terror. He shook her then, and he was angry with her. "Don't you go yellin'," he said, and he shook her; and her body flopped like a fish. And then she was still, for Lennie had broken her neck.

It was one thing for Lennie to kill mice, quite another to kill people. This time his strange quirk had gone too far. George led Lennie away, fleeing into the countryside from the pursuing posse. They reached the edge of a deep green pool of the Salinas River. They sat down to rest and began to talk. Lennie waited for George to scold him for doing a bad thing. Then Lennie asked George to tell him again about the farm they would own someday.

Lennie said, "Tell how it's gonna be." George had been listening to the distant sounds. For a moment he was businesslike. "Look acrost the river, Lennie, an' I'll tell you so you can almost see it."

Lennie turned his head and looked off across the pool and up the darkening slopes of the Gabilans. "We gonna get a little place," George began.

While Lennie was locked in reverie, seeing in the distance the longed-for farm, George took a Luger out of his pocket. Lennie's attention was riveted on the imaginary rabbits and chickens that were dancing in front of his eyes. As the posse came closer, George took aim and pulled the trigger.

Slim, the leader of the posse, was the first at the scene.

He went over and looked down at Lennie, and then he looked back at George. "Right in the back of the head," he said softly.

Slim came directly to George and sat down beside him, sat very close to him. "Never you mind," said Slim. "A guy got to sometimes."

"A guy got to sometimes." Sometimes people have to be executed, people who are destructive. People who crush other people cannot be tolerated. Never mind that the force behind Lennie's destructive acts was a force of childlike, innocent love. His love had no ulterior motives, no hint of seduction. His was a pure love; a love so intense that it strangled people who resisted it. George had no alternative. He knew Lennie could not survive in this world. Lennie had to die. Lennie traumatized everyone and everything he touched.

So it was with Christ. The world could tolerate Jesus; they could love Him, but only at a distance. Christ is safe for us if securely bound by space and time. But a present Christ could not survive in a world of hostile men. It was the judgment of Caiaphas that, for the good of the nation, Jesus must die. Sometimes ya just got to.

Allowing God's Holiness to Touch Our Lives

As you reflect about what you have learned and rediscovered about God's holiness, answer these questions. Use a journal to record your responses to God's holiness, or discuss your responses with a friend.

1. Is your view of God's holiness like Peter's? Do you want to run from it?
2. Have you ever experienced the trauma of God's holiness?
3. Describe a time when you were comforted by God's holiness.
4. Of what aspect of God's holiness were you most aware this past week?

〜◆〜

FIVE

The Insanity
of Luther

Let God be God.

MARTIN LUTHER

If we fix our minds on the holiness of God, the result might be disturbing. Martin Luther's spirit was troubled by a deep knowledge of the character of God. Luther's unusual personality was shaped in part by his study of God. Was his personality enhanced or distorted? Was his spirit purified or demented by his encounter with God?

"Love God? Sometimes I hate Him." This is a strange quote to hear from the lips of a man as respected for his religious zeal as Luther. But he said it. He was noted for making outrageous statements. "Sometimes Christ seems to me nothing more than an angry judge who comes to me with a sword in His hand."

Was the man crazy? Before we try to answer that question, let us examine some of the features of Luther's life and behavior that have prompted the judgment that he was, in fact, insane.

The first key to Luther's profile is found in his tempestuous outbursts of anger and his intemperate language. He was fond of calling his critics "dogs." "The dogs are starting to bark," he would say when reactions from his critics reached his ears. His language was at times earthy, salted with scatological references.

Consider an example of Luther's reply to the diatribe of Erasmus:

> It seemed a complete waste of time to reply to your arguments.
> I have already myself refuted them over and over again, and
> Philip Melancthon, in his unsurpassed volume on the doctrines
> of theology, has trampled them in the dust. That book of his,
> to my mind, deserves not merely to live as long as books are
> read, but to take its place in the Church's canon; whereas your

book, by comparison, struck me as so worthless and poor that my heart went out to you for having defiled your lovely, brilliant flow of language with such vile stuff. I thought it outrageous to convey material of so low a quality in the trappings of such rare eloquence; it is like using gold or silver dishes to carry garden rubbish or dung.[1]

Luther's tempestuous behavior came to the surface in an important meeting at Marburg. Leaders of the new Protestant movement came together to iron out disagreements about the Lord's Supper. In the midst of the dialogue Luther began to pound his fist on the table, saying over and over again, *"Hoc est corpus meum, hoc est corpus meum."* ("This is my body.") His antics were similar to the shoe-banging tantrum made famous by Nikita Khrushchev at the United Nations.

Luther was unquestionably intemperate at times. He was given to bombast. His insults, calling people dogs, were often severe. But these issues, though enough to raise questions about his propriety, are hardly matters that bear on his sanity.

But there is more to the matter than Luther's speech patterns. His behavior was at times downright bizarre. He was afflicted by an assortment of phobias. A well-known story recalls that Luther was walking in the midst of a severe thunderstorm when a bolt of lightning crashed so close to him that he was thrown to the ground. The great church historian and biographer of Luther, Roland Bainton, tells the story:

> On a sultry day in July of the year 1505 a lonely traveler was trudging over a parched road on the outskirts of the Saxon village of Stotternheim. He was a young man, short but sturdy, and wore the dress of a university student. As he approached the village, the sky became overcast. Suddenly there was a shower, then a crashing storm. A bolt of lightning rived the gloom and knocked the man to the ground. Struggling to rise, he cried in terror, "St. Anne, help me! I will become a monk."
>
> The man who thus called upon a saint was later to repudiate the cult of saints. He who vowed to become a monk was later to renounce monasticism. A loyal son of the Catholic Church, he was later to shatter the structure of medieval catholicism. A devoted servant of the pope, he was later to identify the popes with Antichrist. For this young man was Martin Luther.[2]

Shortly after this experience, Luther paid his vow. He quit his studies in law and entered the monastery, much to the dismay of his father, Hans.

The fear of violent death as an expression of divine judgment and punishment haunted Luther. He suffered from stomach ailments throughout his life as well as from kidney stones, a most painful malady. On more than one occasion he predicted his death. Numerous times he was sure that he was only days or weeks away from the grave. The lightning bolt seared in his memory a scar that he never forgot.

Not everyone reacts the same way to a close brush with death from lightning. On June 27, 1975, three professional golfers were knocked to the ground by a lightning bolt during the Western Open near Chicago. One of the three, Lee Trevino, suffered a back injury that severely hampered his future career. When interviewed on a television talk show about the incident, the host inquired of Trevino, "What did you learn from the experience?"

In typical "Merry Mex" fashion Trevino replied, "I learned that if the Almighty wants to play through, you better get out of His way." Then he added, "I should have been holding a 1-iron over my head during the storm."

The host was puzzled by this cryptic statement and bit. "Why is that?" he asked.

Trevino's eyes twinkled, and he quipped, "Because not even God can hit a 1-iron."

Trevino gained some jokes for his repertoire from his experience. Luther gained a new career as a monk and a theologian.

Luther's chronic stomach troubles have also been linked to a psychosomatic problem. His neurotic phobias all seemed to go directly to his stomach, destroying his digestion. His problem with flatulence has become legendary, due in part to his own exaggeration of it. His writings are sprinkled with references to his constant belching and breaking of wind. He said, "If I break wind in Wittenburg, they will hear it in Leipzig."

Fortunately Luther was able to find a sanctified use for his flatulence. He advised his students that the breaking of wind was a most effective device to repel the attacks of the devil. Elsewhere Luther spoke of resisting Satan by throwing an inkwell at him. Luther described his battle with Satan in the terms of a man under siege. He was sure that he was a personal target of the prince of hell.

The Satan stories are ripe with fodder for practicing psychologists, who see in these accounts two indications of mental imbalance. On the one hand Luther is thought to have suffered from hallucinations, and on the other from delusions of grandeur that the prince of darkness would single him out as his favorite target.

Yet from the vantage point of church history, it should not surprise us to think that in the sixteenth century, satanic energy might most strongly be focused on Martin Luther.

Another episode that has caused psychiatrists to raise their eyebrows was the celebration of Luther's first mass. Luther had distinguished himself already as a budding theologian and was not shy. His future as a dramatic pulpiteer and master public orator was still unknown to his contemporaries.

The celebration of his first mass following his ordination was Luther's public debut as a cleric. Old Hans Luther had almost made his peace with his son's decision to give up a lucrative career in law in favor of the monastic life. He was feeling some pride—"My son, the priest." The scheduled celebration was seen as a time for family pride, and Luther's relatives joined the public to observe his celebration.

None in attendance expected what happened. Luther began the ceremony with great poise, exuding a priestly bearing of confidence and self-control. When he came to the Prayer of Consecration—that moment in the mass when Luther would exercise his priestly authority for the first time to evoke the power of God to perform the great miracle of transubstantiation (the changing of the elements of bread and wine to the real body and blood of Christ)—Luther faltered.

He froze at the altar. He seemed transfixed. His eyes were glassy, and beads of perspiration formed on his forehead. A nervous hush filled the congregation as they silently urged the young priest on. Hans Luther was growing uncomfortable, feeling a wave of parental embarrassment sweep over him. His son's lower lip began to quiver. He was trying to speak the words of the mass, but no words came forth from his mouth. He went limp and returned to the table where his father and the family guests were seated. He had failed. He had ruined the mass and disgraced himself and his father. Hans was furious. He had just made a generous contribution to the monastery and now felt humiliated in the very place he came to witness his son's honor. He lashed out at Martin and questioned whether his son was fit to be a priest. Martin defended his calling by appealing to the heavenly summons he felt in the lightning-bolt experience. Hans rejoined, "God grant it was not an apparition of the devil."

What happened at the altar? Luther offers his own explanation at the paralysis that struck when he was supposed to say the words, "We offer unto thee, the living, the true, the eternal God." He said:

At these words I was utterly stupefied and terror-stricken. I thought to myself, "With what tongue shall I address such majesty, seeing that all men ought to tremble in the presence of even an earthly prince? Who am I, that I should lift up mine eyes or raise my hands to the divine Majesty? The angels surround him. At his nod the earth trembles. And shall I, a miserable little pygmy, say 'I want this, I ask for that'? For I am dust and ashes and full of sin and I am speaking to the living, eternal and the true God."[3]

But these episodes are minor considerations in the question of Luther's sanity. Our attention must move to one of the most dramatic moments of Luther's life, a dramatic moment for all of Christendom. The supreme trial of Luther's life, the occasion for his utmost test, came at the Imperial Diet of Worms in the year 1521. Before the princes of the church and state, in the presence of the Holy Roman Emperor Charles, a coal miner's son was on trial for heresy.

Events had run out of control since the theological professor had tacked his Ninety-five Theses on the door of All Saints Church at Wittenburg. These were points of issue Luther was announcing for theological debate and dispute. He had no desire to flame them into a national or international fire. Some people, probably students, got hold of the theses and made use of the marvelous new invention of Gutenberg. Within two weeks the theses were the talk of Germany. Bainton borrows an expression from Karl Barth to explain what happened: "Luther was like a man climbing in the darkness a winding staircase in the steeple of an ancient cathedral. In the blackness he reached out to steady himself, and his hand laid hold of a rope. He was startled to hear the clanging of a bell."[4]

A whirlwind of controversy followed. The theses were forwarded to Rome, to Pope Leo. Legend has it that Leo read them and said, "Luther is a drunken German. He will feel different when he is sober." The fight was carried on between monastic orders and theologians. Luther engaged in debates, the most serious in Augsburg and Leipzig. Finally Luther was censured by the publication of a papal bull. Its title, *Exsurge Domine,* came from its opening words: "Arise, O Lord, and judge thy cause. A wild boar has invaded thy vineyard."

After the bull was published, Luther's books were burned in Rome. He appealed for a hearing to the emperor. Finally the Diet met at Worms, where Luther was granted a safe conduct for travel to appear.

What happened at Worms was the stuff that legends are made of. In fact legends have arisen from the events. Hollywood has given its touch of glamour to the scene. The image of Luther that prevails is that of a valiant hero defying a wicked authority structure. Luther is asked, "Will you recant of your writings?"

We imagine Luther standing tall, unintimidated by the officials there, and saying with fist clenched in the air, "Here I stand!" Then we see him turn on his heel and walk boldly from the hall while the people cheer. He mounts his white horse and gallops off into the sunset to begin the Protestant Reformation.

That is not how it happened.

The first session met on April 17. The air was electric with excitement over the showdown. Luther had spoken boldly before his arrival, saying: "This shall be my recantation at Worms: 'Previously I said the pope is the vicar of Christ. I recant. Now I say the pope is the adversary of Christ and the apostle of the Devil.' "[5]

The crowd was expecting more bold statements. They held their breath, waiting for the wild boar to go on the rampage.

When the Imperial Diet opened, Luther stood in the center of the great hall. By his side was a table that contained his controversial books. An official asked Luther if the books were his. He replied in a voice that was barely a whisper: "The books are all mine, and I have written more." Then came the decisive question of Luther's readiness to recant. The assembly waited for his response. There was no raised fist, no defiant challenge. Again Luther answered almost inaudibly, "I beg you, give me time to think it over." As he had done at his first mass, Luther faltered. His confidence deserted him; the wild boar was suddenly like a whimpering pup. The emperor was shocked by the request and wondered if it might simply be a stalling tactic, a theological filibuster. Yet he granted clemency until the morrow, giving Luther twenty-four hours to think it over.

That night, in the solitude of his room, Luther wrote what I believe to be one of the most moving prayers ever written. His prayer reveals the soul of a humble man prostrate before his God, desperately seeking the courage to stand alone before hostile men. For Luther it was a private Gethsemane:

> O God, Almighty God everlasting! how dreadful is the world! behold how its mouth opens to swallow me up, and how small is my faith in thee! . . . Oh! the weakness of the flesh, and the power of Satan! If I am to depend upon any strength of this world—all is over. . . . The knell is struck. . . . Sentence is gone forth. . . . O God! O God! O thou, my God! help me against all the wisdom of this world. Do this, I beseech thee; thou shouldst do this . . . by thy own mighty power. . . . The work is not mine, but thine. I have no business here. . . . I have nothing

to contend for with these great men of the world! I would
gladly pass my days in happiness and peace. But the cause is
thine. . . . And it is righteous and everlasting! O Lord! help me!
O faithful and unchangeable God! I lean not upon man. It were
vain! Whatever is of man is tottering, whatever proceeds from
him must fail. My God! my God! does thou not hear? My God!
art thou no longer living? Nay, thou canst not die. Thou dost
but hide thyself. Thou hast chosen me for this work. I know
it! . . . Therefore, O God, accomplish thine own will! Forsake
me not, for the sake of thy well-beloved Son, Jesus Christ, my
defense, my buckler, and my stronghold. Lord—where art
thou? . . . My God, where art thou? . . . Come! I pray thee, I
am ready. . . . Behold me prepared to lay down my life for thy
truth . . . suffering like a lamb. For the cause is holy. It is thine
own! . . . I will not let thee go! no, nor yet for all eternity! And
though the world should be thronged with devils—and this
body, which is the work of thine hands, should be cast forth,
trodden under foot, cut in pieces, . . . consumed to ashes,
my soul is thine. Yes, I have thine own word to assure me of
it. My soul belongs to thee, and will abide with thee forever!
Amen! O God send help! . . . Amen![6]

Late the next afternoon Luther returned to the hall. This time his voice did
not quake or quiver. He tried to answer the question by giving a speech. His
inquisitor finally demanded an answer: "I ask you, Martin—answer candidly
and without horns—do you or do you not repudiate your books and the errors
which they contain?"[7]

Luther replied:

Since then Your Majesty and your lordships desire a simple
reply, I will answer without horns and without teeth. Unless I
am convicted by Scripture and plain reason—I do not accept the
authority of popes and councils, for they have contradicted each
other—my conscience is captive to the Word of God. I cannot
and I will not recant anything, for to go against conscience is
neither right nor safe. Here I stand, I cannot do otherwise. God
help me. Amen.[8]

The words of a crazy man? Perhaps. The question is raised how one man
dare stand against pope and emperor, councils and creeds, against the entire

organized authority of Christendom. What arrogance there must be to contradict the finest scholars and the highest officials of the church, to set his own powers of mind and biblical interpretation against that of the whole world. Is this egomania? Is it megalomania? Are these the musings of a biblical genius, a courageous saint, or the ravings of a maniac? Whatever the verdict, this lonely stand, for good or for evil, divided Christendom asunder.

As important as this event was to the church and to the personal history of Martin Luther, it was not the chief reason future scholars would judge Luther insane. There was something even more extraordinary, more morbid, indeed macabre about the man. It had to do with Luther's behavioral patterns while he was a monk in the monastery.

As a monk, Luther devoted himself to a rigorous kind of austerity. He set out to be the perfect monk. He fasted for days and indulged in severe forms of self-flagellation. He went beyond the rules of the monastery in matters of self-denial. His prayer vigils were longer than anyone else's. He refused the normal allotment of blankets and almost froze to death. He punished his body so severely that he later commented it was in the monk's cell that he did permanent damage to his digestive system. He wrote about his experience: "I was a good monk, and I kept the rule of my order so strictly that I may say that if ever a monk got to heaven by his monkery, it was I. All my brothers in the monastery who knew me will bear me out. If I had kept on any longer, I should have killed myself with vigils, prayers, reading, and other work."[9]

The most bizarre of Luther's practices involved his habit of daily confession. The requirement was that all one's sins be confessed. Luther could not go a day without sinning, so he felt it necessary to go to the confessional every day, seeking absolution.

Confession was a regular part of the monastic life. The other brothers came regularly to their confessors and said, "Father, I have sinned. Last night I stayed up after 'lights out' and read my Bible with a candle." Or, "Yesterday at lunchtime I coveted Brother Philip's potato salad." (How much trouble can a monk get into in a monastery?) The Father Confessor would hear the confession, grant priestly absolution, and assign a small penance to be performed. That was it. The whole transaction took only a few minutes.

Not so with Brother Martin. He was driving his Father Confessor to distraction. Luther was not satisfied with a brief recitation of his sins. He wanted to make sure that no sin in his life was left unconfessed. He entered the confessional and stayed for hours every day. On one occasion Luther spent six hours confessing the sins he had committed in the previous day!

The superiors of the monastery began to wonder about Luther. They considered the possibility that he was a "goldbricker," preferring to spend his waking hours in the confessional rather than to study and perform his other tasks. Concern arose that perhaps he was mentally unbalanced, rapidly moving to serious psychosis. His mentor, Staupitz, finally grew angry and scolded Luther: " 'Look here,' he said, 'if you expect Christ to forgive you, come in with something to forgive—parricide, blasphemy, adultery—instead of all these peccadilloes. . . . Man, God is not angry with you. You are angry with God. Don't you know that God commands you to hope?' "[10]

Here it is! Here is the aspect of Luther that has most brought the verdict of insanity. The man was radically abnormal. His guilt complex was unlike anyone's before him. He was so morbid in his guilt, so disturbed in his emotions, that he could no longer function as a normal human being. He could not even function as a normal monk. He was still running from the lightning bolt. Bainton sums up his condition:

> In consequence the most frightful insecurity beset him. Panic
> invaded his spirit. The conscience became so disquieted as to
> start and tremble at the stirring of a wind-blown leaf. The horror
> of nightmare gripped the soul, the dread of one waking in the
> dusk to look into the eyes of him who has come to take his life.
> The heavenly champions all withdrew; the fiend beckoned with
> leering summons to the impotent soul. These were the torments
> which Luther repeatedly testified were far worse than any
> physical ailment that he had ever endured.
>
> His description tallies so well with a recognized type of
> mental malady that again one is tempted to wonder whether
> his disturbance should be regarded as arising from authentic
> religious difficulties or from gastric or glandular deficiencies.[11]

What accounts for Luther's behavior? One thing is certain: Whatever defense mechanisms normal people have to mute the accusing voice of conscience, Luther was lacking.

Some theorists argue that people may have a more accurate view of reality when they are insane than when they are sane. We think of the anxiety-stricken man who goes to the psychiatrist and complains that he is so paralyzed by fear that he cannot attend a church picnic. When the psychiatrist probes, the man explains that he could be involved in a car crash on the way to the picnic, be struck by a poisonous snake while at the picnic, be hit by lightning if a storm comes up, or choke to death on a hot dog.

All of these fears represent sober possibilities. Life is dangerous business. Nowhere are we safe from a multitude of life-threatening dangers. Howard Hughes, with all his millions, could not find an environment where he was totally safe from the attack of hostile germs. The psychiatrist cannot prove that all picnics are safe. The man's perception of all the things that could go wrong is accurate, but he is still abnormal because he has lost the defenses that enable us to ignore the clear and present dangers that surround us every day.

One aspect of Luther's background and personality is often overlooked by the psychological analysts. They miss the point that before Luther went to the monastery, he had already distinguished himself as one of the brightest young minds in Europe in the field of jurisprudence. Luther was brilliant. There was nothing wrong with his brain. His grasp of subtle and difficult points of the law made him a standout. Some heralded him as a legal genius.

It has been said many times that there is a fine line between genius and insanity and that some people move back and forth across it. Perhaps that was the problem Luther had.

He was not crazy. He was a genius. He had a superior understanding of law. Once he applied his astute legal mind to the law of God, he saw things that many people miss.

Luther examined the Great Commandment, " 'Love the Lord your God with all your heart and with all your soul and with all your strength and with all your mind'; and, 'Love your neighbor as yourself' " (Luke 10:27). Then he asked himself, "What is the Great Transgression?" Some answer this question by saying that the great sin is murder, adultery, blasphemy, or unbelief. Luther disagreed. He concluded that if the Great Commandment was to love God with all the heart, then the Great Transgression was to fail to love God with all the heart. He saw a balance between great obligations and great sins.

Most people do not think that way. None of us keeps the Great Commandment for five minutes. We may think that we do in a surface way, but on a moment's reflection it is clear that we don't love God with our whole heart or our whole mind or our whole strength. We don't love our neighbor as we love ourselves. We may do everything in our power to avoid thinking about this at a deep level, but there is always that nagging sense in the back of our minds to accuse us of the certain knowledge that, in fact, we violate the Great Commandment every day. Like Isaiah, we also know that no one else keeps the Great Commandment either. Herein is our comfort: Nobody is perfect. We all fall short of perfect love for God, so why worry about it? It doesn't drive sane people to the confessional for six hours a day. If God punished everyone who failed to keep the Great Commandment, He would have to punish everyone in the world. The test is too great, too demanding; it is not fair. God will have to judge us all on a curve.

Luther didn't see it that way. He realized that if God graded on a curve, He would have to compromise His own holiness. To count on God doing so is supreme arrogance and supreme foolishness as well. God does not lower His own standards to accommodate us. He remains altogether holy, altogether righteous, and altogether just. But we are unjust, and therein lies our dilemma. Luther's legal mind was haunted by the question, How can an unjust person survive in the presence of a just God? Where everyone else was at ease in the matter, Luther was in agony: "Do you not know that God dwells in light inaccessible? We weak and ignorant creatures want to probe and understand the incomprehensible majesty of the unfathomable light of the wonder of God. We approach; we prepare ourselves to approach. What wonder then that his majesty overpowers us and shatters!"[12]

Luther was the polar opposite to the biblical character of the rich young ruler who came to Jesus inquiring about his salvation: "A certain ruler asked him, 'Good teacher, what must I do to inherit eternal life?' 'Why do you call me good?' Jesus answered. 'No one is good—except God alone. You know the commandments: "Do not commit adultery, do not murder, do not steal, do not give false testimony, honor your father and mother" ' " (Luke 18:18–20).

People often miss something in this well-known meeting between Jesus and the rich ruler. It is the significance of the man's greeting to Jesus. He called Him "Good teacher."

Jesus did not miss the significance of it. Jesus knew at once that He was talking to a man who had a superficial understanding of the meaning of the word *good*. The man wanted to talk to Jesus about salvation. Instead, Jesus subtly turned the conversation around to a discussion about what goodness was. He took the opportunity to give the man an unforgettable lesson on the meaning of "good."

Jesus focused on the man's greeting: "Why do you call me good?" He accented the question with a further qualification: "No one is good—except God alone." Let a red alert sound here. Some people, even learned theologians, have stumbled over Jesus' comments. Some hear Jesus saying in effect, "Why are you calling me good? I am not good. Only God is good. I am not God. I am not good."

By no means was Jesus denying His own deity here. And He was not denying His own goodness. Given the right understanding, it would have been perfectly fitting for the rich ruler to call Jesus good. Jesus was good. He was the incarnation of the good. The point is, however, that the rich man was not aware of that. He was honoring Jesus as a great teacher, but that is all he saw in Him. He had no idea he was speaking to God Incarnate.

The rich young ruler obviously did not know his Bible. He had failed to understand the meaning of Psalm 14:

> The fool says in his heart,
> "There is no God."
> They are corrupt, their deeds are vile;
> there is no one who does good.
>
> The LORD looks down from heaven
> on the sons of men
> to see if there are any who understand,
> any who seek God.
> All have turned aside,
> they have together become corrupt;
> there is no one who does good,
> not even one. (Ps. 14:1–3)

This psalm is quoted and amplified in the New Testament by the apostle Paul. The message is unmistakable. No one does good, not even one. The "not even one" erases all possibility for misunderstanding. The indictment allows for no exceptions save for the Son of God, who alone achieves goodness.

The human spirit recoils from such a universal indictment. Surely the Scriptures exaggerate. We know several people who do good. We see people perform good deeds frequently. We grant that no one is perfect. We all slip up from time to time. But we do perform a few good deeds now and then, don't we? No! This is precisely the way the rich young ruler was thinking. He was measuring goodness by the wrong standard. He was evaluating good deeds from an outward vantage point.

God commands that we do certain good things. He commands us to give to the poor. We give to the poor. That is a good deed, isn't it? Yes and no. It is good in the sense that our outward act conforms to what God commands. In that sense we do good often. But God also looks at the heart. He is concerned about our deepest motivations. For a good deed to pass the standard of God's goodness, it must flow out of a heart that loves God perfectly and loves our neighbor perfectly as well. Since none of us achieves that perfect love for God and our neighbor, all of our outwardly good deeds are tarnished. They carry the blemish of the imperfections of our inner motivations. The logic of the Bible is this: Since no one has a perfect heart, no one does a perfect deed.

The law of God is the mirror of true righteousness. When we set our works before this mirror, the reflection in it tells us of our imperfections. Jesus held this mirror up before the eyes of the rich young ruler: "You know the commandments: 'Do not commit adultery, do not murder, do not steal. . . .' " (Luke 18:20). It is important to note here that the commandments Jesus listed for the young ruler were those included in the so-called second table of the law, the commandments that deal with our responsibilities toward fellow human beings. These are the commandments that concern adultery, murder, stealing, and so on. Noticeably absent in Jesus' summary were the first few commandments that deal explicitly with our direct obligations to God.

How did the rich man answer? He was not bothered. He looked calmly in the mirror and saw no imperfections. He replied: "All these I have kept since I was a boy" (Luke 18:21).

Imagine the arrogance or the ignorance of the man. I find it difficult to understand Jesus' patience. I could not have contained myself. I would have instantly expressed my indignation by saying something like, "What! You have kept the Ten Commandments since you were a boy! You haven't kept any of the Ten Commandments for the last five minutes. Didn't you hear the Sermon on the Mount? Don't you realize that if you are unjustly angry with someone, you have violated the deeper meaning of the law against murder? Don't you know that if you lust after a woman, you break the deeper law of adultery? Don't you ever covet? Do you always honor your parents? You are mad or blind. Your obedience has been superficial at best. You obey only on the surface."

That is how I would have handled it. But it is not the way Jesus handled it. Jesus was more subtle, and more effective: "When Jesus heard this, he said to him, 'You still lack one thing. Sell everything you have and give to the poor, and you will have treasure in heaven. Then come, follow me' " (Luke 18:22).

If ever Jesus spoke with tongue in cheek, it was here. If we take Jesus' words literally, we would be forced to conclude that the conversation took place between the two most righteous men in history, that it was a dialogue between the Lamb without blemish and a lamb with only one blemish. I would be delighted to hear from Jesus that my moral perfection lacked only one thing.

We know better. If we speculate and try to get into the secret recesses of Jesus' mind, we can imagine a thought process that went something like this: *Oh, you have kept all the commandments since you were a child. Well, let's see. What is the first commandment? Oh, yes, "You shall have no other gods before me." Let's see how you do with that one.*

Jesus put him to the test. If anything in the rich man's life came before God, it was his money. Jesus set the challenge precisely at this point, at the point of the man's obedience to commandment number one: "Go, sell all that you have. . . ."

What did the man do? How did he handle his only blemish? He walked away sorrowfully, for he had great possessions. The man was put to the test of the Ten Commandments, and he flunked out after the first question.

The point of this narrative is not to lay down a law that a Christian must get rid of all private property. The point is for us to understand what obedience is and what goodness actually requires. Jesus called the man's bluff, and the man folded.

When Jesus met another young man centuries later, He did not have to go through an elaborate object lesson to help the man understand his sin. He never said to Luther, *"One* thing you lack." Luther already knew that he lacked a multitude of things. He was a lawyer; he had studied the Old Testament Law; he knew the demands of a pure and holy God, and it was driving him crazy.

The genius of Luther ran up against a legal dilemma that he could not solve. There seemed to be no solution possible. The question that nagged him day and night was how a just God could accept an unjust man. He knew that his eternal destiny rode on the answer. But he could not find the answer. Lesser minds went merrily along their way, enjoying the bliss of ignorance. They were satisfied to think that God would compromise His own excellence and let them into heaven. After all, heaven would not be the marvelous place it was cracked up to be if they were excluded from it. God must grade on a curve. Boys will be boys, and God is big enough not to get all excited about a few moral blemishes.

Two things separated Luther from the rest of men: First, he knew who God was. Second, he understood the demands of God's law. He had mastered the law. Unless he came to understand the gospel, he would die in torment.

Then it happened: Luther's ultimate religious experience. There were no lightning bolts, no flying inkwells. It took place in quietness, in the solitude of his study. Luther's so-called "tower experience" changed the course of world history. It was an experience that involved a new understanding of God, a new understanding of His divine justice. It was an understanding of how God can be merciful without compromising His justice. It was a new understanding of how a holy God expresses a holy love:

> I greatly longed to understand Paul's Epistle to the Romans and nothing stood in the way but that one expression, "the justice of God," because I took it to mean that justice whereby God is just and deals justly in punishing the unjust. My situation was that, although an impeccable monk, I stood before God as a sinner troubled in conscience, and I had no confidence that my merit would assuage him. Therefore I did not love a just and angry God, but rather hated and murmured against him. Yet I clung to the dear Paul and had a great yearning to know what he meant.
>
> Night and day I pondered until I saw the connection between the justice of God and the statement that "the just shall live by faith." Then I grasped that the justice of God is that righteousness by which through grace and sheer mercy God justifies us through faith. Thereupon I felt myself to be reborn and to have gone through open doors into paradise. The whole of Scripture took on a new meaning, and whereas before the "justice of God" had filled me with hate, now it became to me inexpressibly sweet in greater love. This passage of Paul became to me a gate of heaven. . . .
>
> If you have a true faith that Christ is your Saviour, then at once you have a gracious God, for faith leads you in and opens up God's heart and will, that you should see pure grace and overflowing love. This it is to behold God in faith that you should look upon his fatherly, friendly heart, in which there is no anger nor ungraciousness. He who sees God as angry does not see him rightly but looks only on a curtain as if a dark cloud had been drawn across his face.[13]

Like Isaiah before him, Luther felt the burning coal on his lips. He knew what it meant to be undone. He was shattered by the mirror of a holy God. He said later that before he could get a taste of heaven, God had to dangle him first over the pit of hell. God did not drop His servant into the pit; He saved his life from the pit. He proved that He was a God who was both just and the justifier. When Luther understood the gospel for the first time, the doors of paradise swung open, and he walked through.

"The just shall live by faith." This was the battle cry of the Protestant Reformation. The idea that justification is by faith alone, by the merits of Christ alone, was so central to the gospel that Luther called it "the article upon which the church stands or falls." Luther knew that it was the article by which he would stand or fall.

Once Luther grasped Paul's teaching in Romans, he was reborn. The burden of his guilt was lifted. The crazed torment was ended. This meant so much to the man that he was able to stand against pope and council, prince and emperor, and, if necessary, the whole world. He had walked through the gates of paradise, and no one was going to drag him back. Luther was a Protestant who knew what he was protesting.

Was Luther crazy? Perhaps. But if he was, our prayer is that God would send to this earth an epidemic of such insanity that we too may taste of the righteousness that is by faith alone.

Allowing God's Holiness to Touch Our Lives

As you reflect about what you have learned and rediscovered about God's holiness, answer these questions. Use a journal to record your responses to God's holiness, or discuss your responses with a friend.

1. When you look into the mirror of God's holiness, what do you see? What do you learn about yourself and about God?
2. What do you do with your guilt about your sin?
3. What does "the just shall live by faith" mean to you personally?
4. How can you worship God for justifying you?

SIX

✦◆✦

Holy Justice

*Justice is regarded as the highest
of all virtues, more admirable than
morning star and evening star.*

ARISTOTLE

Martin Luther understood how serious the problem is for unjust people to live in the presence of a just and holy God. Just as Luther was a monk of monks, so Paul was a Pharisee of Pharisees. Both were brilliant men, highly educated. It was said of Paul that he was the most educated man in Palestine at the time of his conversion. He had the equivalent of two Ph.D.s by the time he was twenty-one years old. He also struggled deeply with the law and the question of the justice of God. Luther the monk and Paul the Pharisee both were consumed by the problem of holy justice. They were both students of the Old Testament Law before they became advocates of the gospel.

Whoever reads the Old Testament must struggle with the apparent brutality of God's judgment found there. For many people this is as far as they read. They stumble over the violent passages we call the "hard sayings." Some people see these sayings as sufficient reason to reject Christianity out of hand. These hard sayings seem ample reason to hold the Old Testament God in contempt. Others try to soften the blow by turning the Old Testament into a religious parable or by applying a method of cut and paste, assigning the more brutal passages to the level of primitive myth. Some even go so far as to argue that the Old Testament God is a different God from the New Testament God—a shadowy God with a bad temper, a kind of demonic deity whose blazing wrath is beneath the dignity of the New Testament God of love.

In this chapter I want to stare the Old Testament God right in the eye. I want to look at the most difficult, most offensive passages we can find in the Old Testament and see if we can make any sense of them. We will look at the swift and sudden judgment that falls on Nadab and Abihu, the sons of Aaron; we will look at God's striking Uzzah dead for touching the ark of the covenant;

we will look at the lengthy list of crimes for which God commanded capital punishment; we will look at the slaughter of women and children allegedly done under the orders of God. Be warned. This chapter is not for the weak of stomach or of heart. We will stare into the abyss of the Most Terrible, if you are willing to read along.

Let's look first at Nadab and Abihu. These two men were priests, sons of Aaron, the high priest. God had personally selected Aaron to be the first high priest. Together with Moses, Aaron had led the people of Israel through the wilderness. "Aaron's sons Nadab and Abihu took their censers, put fire in them and added incense; and they offered unauthorized fire before the LORD, contrary to his command. So fire came out from the presence of the LORD and consumed them, and they died before the LORD" (Lev. 10:1, 2). If any people in Israel had a close relationship with God, it was Moses and Aaron. One might expect a little leeway from God in dealing with Aaron's sons. But there was none. For one transgression at the altar, God reacted swiftly and violently, wiping them out on the spot. It was not as if they profaned the altar with prostitutes or offered human sacrifices as did the Molech cult. All Nadab and Abihu did was offer some "strange fire" there. We are not sure exactly what the strange fire was. It sounds as if the situation was merely a question of young priests doing some creative experimenting with the liturgy. A censurable offense, perhaps. But the death penalty? Without the benefit of a trial? Immediate, summary execution?

Throughout the years people have tried to offer a natural explanation for what happened to Nadab and Abihu. Immanuel Velikovsky, scientist friend of Albert Einstein's, was one of those people.

Velikovsky shocked the geological world with his theories that changes in the earth's surface were made suddenly by a catastrophic upheaval caused by a planet or giant comet that came so close to the earth that it reversed the magnetic poles and forced the earth to start spinning in the opposite direction. Imagine a top spinning as fast as it can. Then, instantly, it is made to spin in the opposite direction. If there were water inside the top, what would happen to it? It would become a tidal wave in the opposite direction. Part of Velikovsky's theory suggests that a meteoric shower bombarded the earth that included within its content great volumes of petroleum, filling the fissures on the earth's surface and causing great deposits of oil to form under the earth. (Consider the oil-rich region of the Middle East.)

This theory suggests that Nadab and Abihu found some oil lying around, and they wondered what it was. They decided to see how it worked if it was mixed with the burning substances at the altar. When they put it in the fire, *whoosh*, it ignited and exploded, killing the priests instantly. In a primitive society this would be viewed as a sudden act of judgment by the gods. In Velikovsky's view, the deaths of Nadab and Abihu were accidents, a tragic case of children playing with unknown fire.

The Bible views the story differently. The Bible records the event as a supernatural judgment of God. It may have been enacted through natural means, but it is clear that the death of Nadab and Abihu was no accident. It must be ascribed to the wrath and judgment of God.

How did Aaron view the event? I suppose he was angry and hurt. It was a calamity for Aaron and his remaining family. He had dedicated his entire life to the service of God. His sons were following in his footsteps. He could remember the day of their consecration and the pride he felt when they were set apart for the priesthood. It was a family matter. What thanks did he get from the God he served? God summarily executed his sons for what appeared to be a minor infraction of the rules of the altar.

Aaron rushed to see Moses and tell him about it. It was as if Aaron were saying, "Okay, God, I'm going to tell on you. I'm going straight to Moses. You're going to have to deal with us both on this one." So Aaron went to Moses and pled his case: "Moses then said to Aaron, 'This is what the LORD spoke of when he said: "Among those who approach me I will show myself holy; in the sight of all the people I will be honored"'" (Lev. 10:3).

Moses gave Aaron the answer of the Lord. He reminded him of the original consecration of the priests. They had been set apart for a sacred task and solemnly charged with the precise requirements of their office. They had the privilege of ministering before a holy God. Each vessel in the tabernacle was made to precise specifications, and each item was sanctified by elaborate measures commanded by God. There was no ambiguity to be found in these commands. With respect to the altar of incense, Aaron and his sons were specifically instructed in the proper procedures. God had spoken:

> Do not offer on this altar any other incense or any burnt offering
> or grain offering, and do not pour a drink offering on it. Once
> a year Aaron shall make atonement on its horns. This annual
> atonement must be made with the blood of the atoning sin
> offering for the generations to come. It is most holy to the LORD.
> (Exod. 30:9, 10)

The instructions had been clear. The altar of incense was declared by God to be "most holy." When Nadab and Abihu offered strange or unauthorized fire on it, they were acting in clear defiance of God. Theirs was an act of blatant rebellion, an inexcusable profaning of the Holy Place. They committed a sin of arrogance, an act of treason against God: They profaned a most holy place.

God's judgment was swift. His explanation to Moses was clear: "I will show myself holy; in the sight of all the people I will be honored." These were not words of future prophecy or prediction. When God said, "I will," He meant it as a divine command, a command no one dare countermand.

The capstone of this episode is found in the last sentence of Leviticus 10:3: "Aaron remained silent."

What else could Aaron do? The debate was over. The evidence was in, and God had rendered His verdict. The sons of Aaron had been explicitly forbidden from offering such fire. They committed an act of disobedience, and God had lowered the gavel of His justice on them. So Aaron was silent. He held his peace. He could think of no excuse to offer, no protest to make. Like sinners at the Last Judgment, his mouth was stopped.

Here is an example of God's punitive justice, the justice by which He punishes the guilty. Is this punishment cruel and unusual? Does it in fact go beyond the limits of justice and cross the border into injustice?

Built into our concept of justice is the idea that the punishment must fit the crime. If the punishment is more severe than the crime, then an injustice has been committed. The Bible makes it clear that Nadab and Abihu could not plead ignorance as an excuse for their sin. God had made His instructions clear to them. They knew that they were not allowed to offer unauthorized fire on the altar. That they sinned is easy for us to see. But they never dreamed their sin was so serious that it would prompt God to execute them on the spot. Here we meet an example that screams of harshness from the hand of God, of a punishment that is far too cruel and unusual for the crime. Such a measure of punishment not only puzzles us, it staggers us.

How do we square this narrative with what Genesis teaches earlier about the character of God's justice? Genesis asserts that the judge of all the earth *will do right* (Gen. 18:25). The basic assumption of Israel is that God's judgments are always according to righteousness. His justice is never unfair, never whimsical, never tyrannical. It is impossible for God to be unjust, because His justice is holy.

If we struggle with the story of Nadab and Abihu, we meet even greater difficulty with the story of Uzzah. When David ascended to the kingship of Israel, he moved quickly to consolidate his kingdom. He conferred with his officers and military commanders and decided to bring the ark of the covenant, Israel's most sacred vessel, out of "retirement" and back to a central place. The ark had been captured by the Philistines; and it was said that in that fateful day, the glory had departed from Israel. When the sacred ark was captured, Israel's greatest treasure was stolen and carried off to the pagan temple of Dagon. When the ark was returned, it was placed in safekeeping awaiting the appropriate time for its public restoration to a position of prominence in the midst of the nation. Finally, the hour came, and David wanted the glory back. He said: " 'Let us bring the ark of our God back to us, for we did not inquire of it during the reign of Saul.' The whole assembly agreed to do this, because it seemed right to all the people" (1 Chron. 13:3 4).

The ark was the rallying point for the nation. It was the throne of God, the sacred seat of the Most High. It had been constructed and ornamented by the strict design of God Himself. It was to be housed in the *Sanctus Sanctorum,* the Holy of Holies. The ark was a chest made of acacia wood, overlaid with gold on the inside and outside. It had a gold molding around it. Four gold rings were fastened to its feet so that poles could be inserted through the rings to carry the chest. The poles were also made of acacia wood and overlaid with gold.

The lid of the chest was called an "atonement cover." It was also made of pure gold. Two cherubim made of hammered gold were mounted on each end of the chest, facing each other with their wings spread upward. This was the sacred object that David ordered returned to Jerusalem.

> They moved the ark of God from Abinadab's house on a new cart, with Uzzah and Ahio guiding it. David and all the Israelites were celebrating with all their might before God, with songs and with harps, lyres, tambourines, cymbals and trumpets.
>
> When they came to the threshing floor of Kidon, Uzzah reached out his hand to steady the ark, because the oxen stumbled. The LORD's anger burned against Uzzah, and he struck him down because he had put his hand on the ark. So he died there before God.
>
> Then David was angry because the LORD's wrath had broken out against Uzzah. (1 Chron. 13:7–11)

If God made David angry with this violent outburst of wrath, how much more unsettled does it make a reader who is unskilled in theology? David was a man after God's own heart. Not only was he a masterful king, an accomplished musician, and a champion warrior, but he was also a premier theologian.

Even more than the case of Nadab and Abihu, the execution of Uzzah stirs protests from readers who have been taught that God is a God of love and kindness. The Bible says of God that He is long-suffering and slow to anger. It sure didn't take His anger long to reach the boiling point with Uzzah. Uzzah touched the ark, and *wham!* God exploded in fury.

Again, efforts have been made to soften the harshness of this account by seeking a natural explanation for Uzzah's death. It has been suggested that Uzzah had so much respect for the sacred ark that when he touched it, he was so overcome with fright that he had a heart attack and died on the spot. He was plain scared to death. This explanation absolves God of any responsibility in the matter. The biblical writer's interpretation is merely an example of primitive superstition sprinkled throughout the Old Testament.

People reach for such explanations not only because our culture has an incurable allergy to all things supernatural but also because the story so offends our sense of justice. Look again at what happened. The ark was being transported by oxcart toward Jerusalem. It was a joyous day of national celebration. The glory was returning to the Holy City. The roads were crowded with people. The gala parade was punctuated by the sounds of the harps, lyres, tambourines, cymbals, and trumpets. Imagine the spectacle: It was like a parade with seventy-six trombones. People danced in the streets.

The oxen suddenly stumbled, and the cart tottered precariously. The chest slid from its mooring and was in danger of falling into the dirt and being sullied by the mud. It was unthinkable that this precious object be desecrated by falling in the dirt.

Surely Uzzah's reaction was instinctive. He did what any pious Jew would do to keep the ark from falling into the mud. He reached out his hand to steady the ark, to protect the holy object from falling. It was not a premeditated act of defiance toward God. It was a reflex action. From our vantage point it seems like an act of heroism. We think that Uzzah should have heard the voice of God shouting down from heaven, crying, "Thank you, Uzzah!"

God didn't do that.

Instead, He killed Uzzah. He slaughtered him on the spot. Another summary execution.

What was Uzzah's sin? To answer that, we must look back in Jewish history to the formation of the priesthood and the special commands that God had given them. To be a priest in Israel, one had to be from the tribe of Levi. All priests were Levites, but not all Levites were priests. A special family branch of the Levites were the clan of Kohathites. As the name indicates, these were the descendants of Kohath. The Kohathites were consecrated by God to a highly specialized task. They were trained for one basic job—to take care of the sacred articles of the tabernacle: "This is the work of the Kohathites in the Tent of Meeting: the care of the most holy things" (Num. 4:4).

It is important to remember that the tabernacle was a tent. It was portable. When the tribes of Israel moved, they carried the tabernacle with them so that God would be in their midst. When the tabernacle was transported, it was necessary first to cover and shield the holy vessels. We read, "After Aaron and his sons have finished covering the holy furnishings and all the holy articles, and when the camp is ready to move, the Kohathites are to come to do the carrying. *But they must not touch the holy things or they will die.* The Kohathites are to carry those things that are in the Tent of Meeting" (Num. 4:15, italics added).

To reinforce this command, God adds further provisions and stipulations:

> The LORD said to Moses and Aaron, "See that the Kohathite
> tribal clans are not cut off from the Levites. So that they may
> live and not die when they come near the most holy things, do
> this for them: Aaron and his sons are to go into the sanctuary
> and assign to each man his work and what he is to carry. But the
> Kohathites must not go in to look at the holy things, even for a
> moment, or they will die." (Num. 4:17–20)

Uzzah was probably a Kohathite. He knew exactly what his duties were. He had been trained thoroughly in the discipline of his calling. He understood that God had declared that the touching of the ark of the covenant was a capital offense. No Kohathite, under any circumstance, was ever permitted to touch the ark. No emergency was grounds for breaking that inviolate command. The elaborate construction of the ark, complete with golden rings through which long poles were inserted, was so fashioned as to make it clear that the ark itself was not to be touched. The men commissioned to transport the ark could touch only the poles and the rings. Then it was the task of the Kohathites to carry the ark by these long poles. No provision was made for hurrying the procedure by transporting the ark via an oxcart.

We must ask the question, What was the ark doing on an oxcart in the first place? God was so strict about the holy things of the tabernacle that the Kohathites were not allowed even to gaze upon the ark. This, too, was a capital crime. God had decreed that if a Kohathite merely glanced at the ark in the Holy of Holies for an instant, he would die. Not only was Uzzah forbidden to touch the ark, he was forbidden even to look at it.

He touched it anyway. He stretched out his hand and placed it squarely on the ark, steadying it in place lest it fall to the ground. An act of holy heroism? No! It was an act of arrogance, a sin of presumption. Uzzah assumed that his hand was less polluted than the earth. But it wasn't the ground or the mud that would desecrate the ark; it was the touch of man. The earth is an obedient creature. It does what God tells it to do. It brings forth its yield in its season. It obeys the laws of nature that God has established. When the temperature falls to a certain point, the ground freezes. When water is added to the dust, it becomes mud, just as God designed it. The ground doesn't commit cosmic treason. There is nothing polluted about the ground.

God did not want His holy throne touched by that which was contaminated by evil, that which was in rebellion to Him, that which by its ungodly revolt had brought the whole creation to ruin and caused the ground and the sky and the waters of the sea to groan together in travail, waiting for the day of redemption. Man. It was man's touch that was forbidden.

Uzzah was not an innocent man. He was not punished without a warning. He was not punished without violating a law. There was no caprice in this act of divine judgment. There was nothing arbitrary or whimsical about what God did in that moment. But there was something unusual about it. The execution's suddenness and finality take us by surprise and at once shock and offend us.

There is a reason why we are offended, indeed angered, by the story of Uzzah and the story of Nadab and Abihu. We find these things difficult to stomach because we do not understand four vitally important biblical concepts: *holiness, justice, sin,* and *grace.* We do not understand what it means to be holy. We do not understand what justice is. We do not understand what sin is. We do not understand what grace is.

The story of Uzzah is an example of divine justice. It is not an example of divine mercy. But we cannot begin to understand divine mercy until we first have some understanding of divine justice.

When the Bible speaks of God's justice, it usually links it to divine righteousness. God's justice is *according to righteousness.* There is no such thing as justice according to unrighteousness. There is no such thing as evil justice in God. The justice of God is always and ever an expression of His holy character.

The word *justice* in the Bible refers to a conformity to a rule or a norm. God plays by the rules. The ultimate norm of justice is His own holy character. His righteousness is of two sorts. We distinguish God's internal righteousness from His external righteousness. What God *does* is always consistent with who God *is.* He always acts according to His holy character. God's internal righteousness is the moral excellence of His character. It is rooted in His absolute purity. There is no "shadow of turning" in Him. As a holy God, He is utterly incapable of an unholy act. Only unholy beings commit unjust and unrighteous acts.

There is a consistency in God, a "straightness" about Him. Human unrighteousness is often described in terms of our being not straight. We are crooked. It is not by accident that we often refer to criminals as "crooks." Crooks are so called because they are crooked; they are not straight. God is straight. His straightness is seen in His outward behavior, His external righteousness. In all eternity God has never done a crooked thing. He killed Nadab and Abihu. He killed Uzzah. He did the same thing to Ananias and Sapphira in the New Testament. These were righteous acts of judgment.

The Bible clearly teaches that God is the Supreme Judge of the universe. The question we ask after reading about Uzzah is this: Is God qualified for the job? To function as the Supreme Judge of heaven and earth, He ought to be just. If the Supreme Judge is unjust, we have no hope of justice ever prevailing. We know that earthly judges can be corrupt. They take bribes; they show partiality; at times they act from ignorance. They make mistakes.

Not so with God. There is no corruption in Him. No one can bribe Him. He refuses to show partiality. He shows no favoritism (Acts 10:34). He never acts out of ignorance. He does not make mistakes. Bumper stickers in this world may demand, "Impeach Nixon," but only a fool asks for the impeachment of God.

The patriarch Abraham wrestled with the question of the justice of God. God announced that He was going to destroy Sodom and Gomorrah. He planned to annihilate the cities totally—men, women, and children. Abraham was disturbed by this, concerned that in the visitation of divine wrath on the cities, the innocent would perish along with the guilty. If God wiped out the cities in an act of judgment, Abraham feared that the judgment would be indiscriminate, like a teacher punishing a whole class for the sins of one student:

> Then Abraham approached him and said: "Will you sweep
> away the righteous with the wicked? What if there are fifty
> righteous people in the city? Will you really sweep it away and
> not spare the place for the sake of the fifty righteous people in
> it? Far be it from you to do such a thing—to kill the righteous
> with the wicked, treating the righteous and the wicked alike.
> Far be it from you! Will not the Judge of all the earth do right?"
> (Gen. 18:23–25)

"Will not the Judge of all the earth do right?" A more rhetorical question has never been asked. Abraham assumed that to kill the righteous along with the wicked was far removed from any possibility with God. "Far be it from you!" Abraham had no idea how far such an act would be from God. There was never a remote possibility that God would kill innocent people along with the guilty. For God to do that, He would have to cease being holy. He would have to stop being God.

God was willing to bend over backward for Abraham. He said He would spare the whole city if Abraham could find forty-five righteous people in it. He would spare it for the sake of thirty, for the sake of ten. Abraham's task was made more simple by 80 percent. All he had to do was to find ten righteous people, and God would spare the whole city. The implication of the text is that God would have spared it for *one* person if Abraham could find one. What happened to Sodom and Gomorrah? "Early the next morning Abraham got up and returned to the place where he had stood before the LORD. He looked down toward Sodom and Gomorrah, toward all the land of the plain, and he saw dense smoke rising from the land, like smoke from a furnace" (Gen. 19:27, 28).

The Judge of heaven and earth did right. No innocent people were punished. God's justice is never divorced from His righteousness. He never condemns the innocent. He never clears the guilty. He never punishes with undue severity. He never fails to reward righteousness. His justice is perfect justice.

God does not always act with justice. Sometimes He acts with mercy. Mercy is not justice, but it also is not injustice. Injustice violates righteousness. Mercy manifests kindness and grace and does no violence to righteousness. We may see *nonjustice* in God, which is *mercy,* but we never see *injustice* in God.

Again we ask, What about the obvious difference between the tone of the New Testament and that of the Old Testament? The Old Testament seems to show God as being more harsh than the New Testament does. Consider the matter of capital punishment in the Old Testament. The Old Testament lists numerous crimes that are punishable by death, including the following:

striking or cursing parents	homosexual practices
desecrating sacrificial offerings	incest
murder	bestiality
kidnapping	prostitution of virgins
idolatry	rape
child sacrifice	practicing false
blasphemy	prophecy
Sabbath violations	refusing to obey the
the practice of magic	verdict of a priest-
consulting mediums	judge
and wizards	bearing false witness in
unlawful divorce	a capital case

This is a partial list of Old Testament crimes that called for the death penalty. Against the tone of the New Testament the list seems harsh.

A few years ago *Time* magazine reported an incident that took place in the state of Maryland. A truck driver was arrested for drunk and disorderly conduct. When the police officers arrived on the scene to arrest the man, he became abusive. He used filthy language in a boisterous manner, calling the officers every name he could think of. The police were infuriated by his verbal abuse. When the man was brought before the magistrate, he was still being abusive. The maximum penalty the magistrate could impose for drunk and disorderly conduct was a one-hundred-dollar fine and thirty days in jail.

The magistrate became so angry that he wanted to "throw the book" at him. He found an antiquated law still on the books in Maryland; it was in disuse but had never been repealed. The statute prohibited public blasphemy.

Since the man had publicly profaned and blasphemed the name of God as part of the verbal abuse he hurled at the police, the magistrate tacked on another one-hundred-dollar fine and an additional thirty days in jail.

The *Time* news editor reported this incident in a spirit of moral outrage. His complaint was not that penalties for blasphemy involved a violation of the separation of church and state. His outrage was based on his charge that to put a man in jail for sixty days and to fine him two hundred dollars was a gross miscarriage of justice. Such a penalty was too severe. It was cruel and unusual.

Evidently the news editor was not upset about the penalties imposed for drunk and disorderly conduct. It was the punishment for blasphemy that he could not handle. This is in strong contrast to the law code God established in Israel. The truck driver could rejoice that he wasn't arrested by Aaron. In the Old Testament the best lawyer in Israel could not get his client a one-hundred-dollar fine for public blasphemy. The question we face is, What is worse, creating a public disturbance by getting drunk, or publicly insulting the dignity of a holy God? The news editor gave his answer. God gave a different one. If the Old Testament laws were in effect today, every television network executive would have long ago been executed.

We cannot deny that the New Testament seems to reduce the number of capital offenses. By comparison the Old Testament seems radically severe. What we fail to remember, however, is that the Old Testament list represents a massive reduction in capital crimes from the original list. The Old Testament code represents a bending over backward of divine patience and forbearance. The Old Testament Law is one of astonishing grace.

Astonishing grace? I will say it again. The Old Testament list of capital crimes represents a massive reduction of the original list. It is an astonishing measure of grace. The Old Testament record is chiefly a record of the grace of God.

How so? To make sense out of my strange words, we must go back to the beginning, to the original rules of the universe. What was the penalty for sin in the original created order? "The soul who sins is the one who will die" (Ezek. 18:4). In creation all sin is deemed worthy of death. Every sin is a capital offense.

In creation God is not obliged to give us the gift of life. He is not in debt to us. The gift of life comes by His grace and stands under His divine authority. The task that is given to mankind in creation is to bear witness to the holiness of God, to be His image bearer. We are made to mirror and reflect the holiness of God. We are made to be His ambassadors.

God put Adam and Eve on probation and said, "If you sin, you will die." Sin brings the loss of the gift of life. The right to life is forfeited by sin. Once people sin, they forfeit any claim on God to human existence. Now the big question: When was the penalty for sin to be meted out in creation? Was the penalty stated like this: "If you sin, then someday you will die"? No! The penalty for sin was clearly stated by God: "When you eat of it you will surely die" (Gen. 2:17).

In creation the penalty for sin was not only death, but instant death. Death that very day: death as swiftly as it fell on Nadab and Abihu; death as sudden as it wiped out Uzzah; death as quick as it befell Ananias and Sapphira. "The day that you sin you will surely die."

Numerous commentators have tried to soften the divine warning by interpreting the "death" of Genesis 2 as a kind of spiritual death. That is not what the text says. The death penalty of which God warned was real death, death in the full sense of the word. To be sure, Adam and Eve did suffer spiritual death that very day, but God granted mercy in terms of the full measure of the penalty. We have a saying that "justice delayed is justice denied." Not always. In the case of creation and mankind's fall, the full measure of justice was delayed so grace would have time to work. Here the delay of justice was not the denial of justice but the establishing of mercy and grace.

Yet the death penalty was imposed and is still imposed. All people die. We may live out our three score and ten and then die. But die we shall, because we are all under the death penalty for sin. We are all sitting on death row awaiting execution. The greatest mass killer of all time was not Adolf Hitler or Joseph Stalin. The greatest mass killer of all is nature. Everyone falls victim to nature, which does not operate independently from God. Nature is merely the avenger of a holy God.

Was it unjust for God to say to Adam and Eve that they would die when they sinned? Think about it. Was it evil for God to impose the death penalty for all sin? If you say yes, be careful. If you say yes, you are saying it as an expression of the very fallen, sinful nature that exposes you to the death penalty in the first place. If you say yes, you slander the character of God. If you say yes, you do violence to His holiness. If you say yes, you assail the righteous Judge of all the earth. If you say yes, you have never come to grips with what sin is. We must not say yes. We must say no and say it with conviction.

Is the death penalty for sin unjust? By no means. Remember that God voluntarily created us. He gave us the highest privilege of being His image bearers. He made us but a little lower than the angels. He freely gave us dominion over all the earth. We are not turtles. We are not fireflies. We are not caterpillars or coyotes. We are people. We are the image bearers of the holy and majestic King of the cosmos.

We have not used the gift of life for the purpose God intended. Life on this planet has become the arena in which we daily carry out the work of cosmic treason. Our crime is far more serious, far more destructive than that of Benedict Arnold. No traitor to any king or nation has even approached the wickedness of our treason before God.

Sin is cosmic treason. Sin is treason against a perfectly pure Sovereign. It is an act of supreme ingratitude toward the One to whom we owe everything, to the One who has given us life itself. Have you ever considered the deeper implications of the slightest sin, of the most minute peccadillo? What are we saying to our Creator when we disobey Him at the slightest point? We are saying no to the righteousness of God. We are saying, "God, Your law is not good. My judgment is better than Yours. Your authority does not apply to me. I am above and beyond Your jurisdiction. I have the right to do what I want to do, not what You command me to do."

The slightest sin is an act of defiance against cosmic authority. It is a revolutionary act, a rebellious act in which we are setting ourselves in opposition to the One to whom we owe everything. It is an insult to His holiness. We become false witnesses to God. When we sin as the image bearers of God, we are saying to the whole creation, to all of nature under our dominion, to the birds of the air and the beasts of the field: "This is how God is. This is how your Creator behaves. Look in this mirror; look at us, and you will see the character of the Almighty." We say to the world, "God is covetous; God is ruthless; God is bitter; God is a murderer, a thief, a slanderer, an adulterer. God is all of these things that we are doing."

When people join together in sin, they "speak of kings and things." It is the ultimate conspiracy. We reach for the crown and plot for the throne, saying in effect to God, "We will not have You rule over us." The psalmist put it this way:

> Why do the nations conspire
>   and the peoples plot in vain?
> The kings of the earth take their stand
>   and the rulers gather together
> against the LORD
>   and against his Anointed One.
> "Let us break their chains," they say,
>   "and throw off their fetters." (Ps. 2:1–3)

When we sin, we not only commit treason against God, but we also do violence to each other. Sin violates people. There is nothing abstract about it. By my sin I hurt human beings. I injure their person; I despoil their goods; I impair their reputation; I rob from them a precious quality of life; I crush their dreams and aspirations for happiness. When I dishonor God, I dishonor all people who bear His image. Is it any wonder, then, that God takes sin so seriously?

Hans Küng, the controversial Roman Catholic theologian, writing about the seemingly harsh judgments of sin God makes in the Old Testament, says that the most mysterious aspect of the mystery of sin is not that the sinner deserves to die, but rather that the sinner in the average situation continues to exist.

Küng asks the right question. The issue is not why does God punish sin but why does He permit the ongoing human rebellion? What prince, what king, what ruler would display so much patience with a continually rebellious populace?

The key to Küng's observation is that he speaks of sinners' continuing to live in the average situation. That is, it is customary or usual for God to be forbearing. He is indeed long-suffering, patient, and slow to anger. In fact He is so slow to anger that when His anger does erupt, we are shocked and offended by it. We forget rather quickly that God's patience is designed to lead us to repentance, to give us time to be redeemed. Instead of taking advantage of this patience by coming humbly to Him for forgiveness, we use this grace as an opportunity to become more bold in our sin. We delude ourselves into thinking that either God doesn't care about it, or that He is powerless to punish us.

The supreme folly is that we think we will get away with our revolt.

Far from being a history of a harsh God, the Old Testament is the record of a God who is patient in the extreme. The Old Testament is the history of a persistently stiff-necked people who rebel time after time against God. The people became slaves in a foreign land. They cried out to God. God heard their groans and moved to redeem them. He parted the Red Sea to let them out of bondage. They responded by worshiping a golden calf.

We must still face the difficult question of the conquest of Canaan. There God explicitly commanded the slaughter of men, women, and children. The Promised Land was given to Israel by a bloody sword, a sword dripping with the blood of infants and women. God directly issued the order for the bloodbath:

> When the LORD your God brings you into the land you are entering to possess and drives out before you many nations— the Hittites, Girgashites, Amorites, Canaanites, Perizzites, Hivites and Jebusites, seven nations larger and stronger than you—and when the LORD your God has delivered them over to you and you have defeated them, then you must destroy them totally. Make no treaty with them, and show them no mercy. (Deut. 7:1, 2)

Why did God issue such a command? How could He have ordered the slaughter of women and children? Again we find modern attempts to soften the event. A curriculum for high school students prepared by a major church denomination in the United States explained that in light of the New Testament revelation of God's love, we know that God did not ever issue such a belligerent command. The Old Testament is merely the record of a primitive warlike group of Hebrews who tried to justify ruthless policies by attributing them to a divine sanction.

The writers of the curriculum did not believe that God ever issued such a command. It was to be a case of intrusion of mythology into the biblical record. Such interpretations overlook some vital aspects of the matter. First, there is a historical precedent that is far more severe than the conquest of Canaan—the Flood. In the Flood God destroyed the entire population of the world except for Noah and his family. The Flood was a "conquest of Canaan" on a grand scale. More important is the failure to understand the nature of sin. The assumption of the commentators is that God wiped out innocent people in Canaan. Of the multitudes of women and children living in Canaan, none was innocent. The conquest of Canaan was an explicit expression of God's righteous judgment on a wicked nation. He made that point clear to Israel. He also made it clear to the people of Israel that they also were not innocent. It was not as if God destroyed a wicked people for the sake of a righteous people. To the Canaanites God poured out justice. To the Jews God poured out mercy. He was quick to remind the Jews of that:

> After the LORD your God has driven them out before you, do
> not say to yourself, "The LORD has brought me here to take
> possession of this land because of my righteousness." No, it is
> on account of the wickedness of these nations that the LORD
> is going to drive them out before you. It is not because of your
> righteousness or your integrity that you are going in to take
> possession of their land; but on account of the wickedness of
> these nations, the LORD your God will drive them out before
> you, to accomplish what he swore to your fathers, to Abraham,
> Isaac and Jacob. Understand, then, that it is not because of your
> righteousness that the LORD your God is giving you this good
> land to possess, for you are a stiff-necked people. (Deut. 9:4–6)

Three times in this passage God reminded the people of Israel that it was not because of their righteousness that He would defeat the Canaanites. He wanted to make that point clear. Israel might have been tempted to jump to the conclusion that God was "on their side" because they were better than pagan nations. God's announcement made that inference impossible.

The holiness of God is at the heart of the issue of the conquest of Canaan. It was because of His holiness that the act was ordained. On the one hand He moved to punish the insult to His holiness that was daily perpetrated by the Canaanites. On the other hand He was preparing a land and a nation for a holy purpose. God commanded that no mercy be shown toward the inhabitants of the land. He explained why:

> Do not intermarry with them. Do not give your daughters to
> their sons or take their daughters for your sons, for they will
> turn your sons away from following me to serve other gods, and
> the LORD's anger will burn against you and will quickly destroy
> you. This is what you are to do to them: Break down their altars,
> smash their sacred stones, cut down their Asherah poles and
> burn their idols in the fire. For you are a people holy to the LORD
> your God. The LORD your God has chosen you out of all the
> peoples on the face of the earth to be his people, his treasured
> possession. (Deut. 7:3–6)

God did not choose Israel because Israel was already holy. He chose them to *make* them holy. Israel was called to be holy in two senses of the word. They were called to be different, to be set apart as a vehicle of God's plan of redemption.

They were also called to be holy in the sense of being purified. Pagan practices were to be absent from Israel's midst. They were to be sanctified by drawing near to God. Salvation for the nations was to come out of Israel. The Promised Land was to be the breeding ground for the coming Messiah. There was no room for pagan shrines and pagan rites. God ordained a scorched-earth policy to purge the land for future salvation.

We have labored the problems of the acts of divine justice found in the Old Testament. We have tried to show that God's justice was neither whimsical nor unwarranted. We must add that there is no real conflict between the God of the Old Testament and the God of the New Testament. It was the Old Testament God whom Christ called "Father." It was the God of Abraham, Isaac, and Jacob who so loved the world that He sent His one and only Son to redeem it. It was Jesus' meat and drink to do the will of this God. It was zeal for the God who slew Nadab, Abihu, and Uzzah that consumed Christ. It was the God who destroyed the world by a flood who pours the waters of His grace out to us.

The false conflict between the two testaments may be seen in the most brutal act of divine vengeance ever recorded in Scripture. It is not found in the Old Testament but in the New Testament. The most violent expression of God's wrath and justice is seen in the Cross. If ever a person had room to complain of injustice, it was Jesus. He was the only innocent man ever to be punished by God. If we stagger at the wrath of God, let us stagger at the Cross. Here is where our astonishment should be focused. If we have cause for moral outrage, let it be directed at Golgotha.

The Cross was at once the most horrible and the most beautiful example of God's wrath. It was the most just and the most gracious act in history. God would have been more than unjust, He would have been diabolical to punish Jesus if Jesus had not first willingly taken on Himself the sins of the world. Once Christ had done that, once He volunteered to be the Lamb of God, laden with our sin, then He became the most grotesque and vile thing on this planet. With the concentrated load of sin He carried, He became utterly repugnant to the Father. God poured out His wrath on this obscene thing. God made Christ accursed for the sin He bore. Herein was God's holy justice perfectly manifest. Yet it was done for us. He took what justice demanded from us. This "for us" aspect of the Cross is what displays the majesty of its grace. At the same time justice and grace, wrath and mercy. It is too astonishing to fathom.

We cringe at God's justice because its expression is so unusual. As Küng observed, God's usual course of action is one of grace. Grace no longer amazes us. We have grown used to it; we take it for granted.

Perhaps the best illustration of this may be found in the teaching of Jesus:

> Now there were some present at that time who told Jesus about the Galileans whose blood Pilate had mixed with their sacrifices. Jesus answered, "Do you think that these Galileans were worse sinners than all the other Galileans because they suffered this way? I tell you, no! But unless you repent, you too will all perish. Or those eighteen who died when the tower in Siloam fell on them—do you think they were more guilty than all the others living in Jerusalem? I tell you, no! But unless you repent, you too will all perish." (Luke 13:1–5)

This is one of the most difficult of the "hard sayings" of Jesus. The question is raised, What about the people Pilate slaughtered, or the innocent people killed by the falling of the tower? Where was God in these events? The question under discussion was, How could God allow these things to happen? The question is actually a thinly veiled accusation. The issue was, as always, How can God allow innocent people to suffer?

We can hear the implied protest in the question. The eighteen innocent people were walking down the street minding their own business. They were not engaged in playing "sidewalk superintendent." They were not heckling the construction workers. They were not running away after robbing a bank. They just were "there," at the wrong time and in the wrong place. They suffered the consequences of a fatal accident.

Note Jesus' response. He did not say, "I am very sorry to hear about this tragedy. These things happen, and there is not much we can do about it. It was fate. An accident. As good Christians you have to learn to accept the bad with the good. Keep a stiff upper lip. Be good Stoics! I know I taught you that the One who keeps Israel neither slumbers nor sleeps. But that was a poetic statement, a bit of hyperbole. Do you realize what a difficult task it is for My Father to run the universe? It gets tiring. Every now and then He must take a nap. On the afternoon in question He was very weary and grabbed forty winks. While He was nodding, the tower fell. I am sorry about that, and I will report your grievance to Him. I will ask Him to be a bit more careful in the future."

Jesus did not say, "I know I told you that My Father notices the landing of every sparrow and that He numbers the hairs on your head. Do you realize how many sparrows there are flying around? And the hairs on your head! The afternoon the tower fell, my Father was busy counting the hairs on the head of a particularly bushy-haired fellow. He was concentrating so hard on the fellow's head that He overlooked the falling tower. I will suggest that He get His priorities in order and not spend so much time with sparrows and hair."

No. Instead, Jesus rebuked the people for putting their amazement in the wrong place. He said, "Unless you repent, you too will all perish." In effect what Jesus was saying was this: "You people are asking the wrong question. You should be asking Me, 'Why didn't that tower fall on my head?' "

In two decades of teaching theology, I have had countless students ask me why God doesn't save everybody. Only once did a student come to me and say, "There is something I just can't figure out. Why did God redeem *me*?"

We are not really surprised that God has redeemed us. Somewhere deep inside, in the secret chambers of our hearts, we harbor the notion that God owes us His mercy. Heaven would not be quite the same if we were excluded from it. We know that we are sinners, but we are surely not as bad as we could be. There are enough redeeming features to our personalities that if God is really just, He will include us in salvation. What amazes us is justice, not grace.

Our tendency to take grace for granted was powerfully demonstrated while I was teaching college students. I had the assignment of teaching a freshman Old Testament course to 250 students at a Christian college. On the first day of class I went over the course assignments carefully. My experience taught me that the assignment of term papers required a special degree of explanation. This course required three short papers. I explained to the students that the first paper was due on my desk by noon the last day of September. No extensions were to be given except for students who were physically confined to the infirmary or who had deaths in the immediate family. If the paper was not turned in on time, the student would receive an F for the assignment. The students acknowledged that they understood the requirements.

On the last day of September, 225 students dutifully handed in their term papers. Twenty-five students stood, quaking in terror, full of remorse. They cried out, "Oh, Professor Sproul. We are so sorry. We didn't budget our time properly. We didn't make the proper adjustment from high school to college. Please don't give us an F. Please, oh, please give us an extension."

I bowed to their pleas for mercy. "All right," I said. "I'll give you a break this time. But, remember, the next assignment is due the last day of October."

The students were profuse in their gratitude and filled the air with solemn promises of being on time for the next assignment. Then came the last day of October. Two hundred students came with their papers. Fifty students came empty-handed. They were nervous but not in panic. When I asked for their papers, again they were contrite. "Oh, Professor. It was Homecoming Week. Besides it is midterm, and all of our assignments are due in other classes. Please give us one more chance. We promise it will never happen again."

Once more I relented. I said, "Okay, but this is the last time. If you are late for the next paper, it will be an F. No excuses, no whining. F. Is that clear?"

"Oh, yes, Professor. You are terrific." Spontaneously the class began to sing, "We love you, Prof Sproul. Oh, yes we do." I was Mr. Popularity.

Can you guess what happened on the last day of November? Right. One hundred and fifty students came with their term papers. The other hundred strolled into the lecture hall utterly unconcerned. "Where are your term papers?" I asked.

One student replied, "Oh, don't worry, Prof, we're working on them. We'll have them for you in a couple of days, no sweat."

I picked up my lethal black grade book and began taking down names. "Johnson! Do you have your paper?"

"No sir" came the reply.

"F," I said as I wrote the grade in the book. "Muldaney! Do you have your paper?"

Again, "No sir" was the reply. I marked another F in the book.

The students reacted with unmitigated fury. They howled in protest, screaming, "That's not fair!"

I looked at one of the howling students. "Lavery! You think it's not fair?"

"Yes," he growled in response.

"I see. It's justice you want? I seem to recall that you were late with your paper the last time. If you insist on justice, you will certainly get it. I'll not only give you an F for this assignment, but I'll change your last grade to the F you so richly deserved."

The student was stunned. He had no more arguments to make. He apologized for being so hasty and was suddenly happy to settle for one F instead of two.

The students had quickly taken my mercy for granted. They assumed it. When justice suddenly fell, they were unprepared for it. It came as a shock, and they were outraged. This, after only two doses of mercy in the space of two months.

The normal activity of God involves far more mercy than I showed those students with their term papers. Old Testament history covers hundreds of years. In that time God was repeatedly merciful. When His divine judgment fell on Nadab or Uzzah, the response was shock and outrage. We have come to expect

God to be merciful. From there the next step is easy: We demand it. When it is not forthcoming, our first response is anger against God, coupled with the protest: "It isn't fair." We soon forget that with our first sin we have forfeited all rights to the gift of life. That I am drawing breath this morning is an act of divine mercy. God owes me nothing. I owe Him everything. If He allows a tower to fall on my head this afternoon, I cannot claim injustice.

One of our basic problems is the confusion of justice and mercy. We live in a world where injustices happen. They happen among people. Every one of us at some time has been a victim of injustice at the hands of another person. Every one of us at some time has committed an injustice against another person. People treat each other unfairly. One thing is certain: No matter how much injustice I have suffered from the hands of other people, I have never suffered the slightest injustice from the hand of God.

Suppose a person falsely accuses me of stealing money. Charges are brought against me, and I am arrested and sent to prison. On the human level, I have been a victim of gross injustice. I have every right to cry out to God and plead for vindication in this world. I can complain about being falsely persecuted. God is angry with people for unjustly putting me in prison. God promises to vindicate me from this injustice someday. Injustice is real, and it happens every day in this world.

The injustices we suffer are all of a *horizontal* sort. They happen between actors in this world. Yet standing over and above this world is the Great Judge of all. My relationship to Him is vertical. In terms of that vertical relationship I never suffer an injustice. Though people may mistreat me, God never does. That God allows a human being to treat me unjustly is just of God. While I may complain to God about the human, horizontal injustice I have suffered, I cannot rise up and accuse God of committing a vertical injustice by allowing the human injustice to befall me. God would be perfectly just to allow me to be thrown in prison for life for a crime I didn't commit. I may be innocent before other people, but I am guilty before God.

We often blame God for the injustices done to us and harbor in our souls the bitter feeling that God has not been fair toward us. Even if we recognize that He is gracious, we think that He has not been gracious enough. We think we deserve more grace.

Please read that last sentence again: *We think we deserve more grace.* What is wrong with that sentence? Grammatically it is fine. But there is something seriously wrong with the content, with the meaning of the sentence.

It is impossible for anyone, anywhere, anytime to *deserve* grace. Grace by definition is undeserved. As soon as we talk about deserving something, we are no longer talking about grace; we are talking about justice. Only justice can be deserved. God is never obligated to be merciful. Mercy and grace must be voluntary or they are no longer mercy and grace. God never "owes" grace. He reminds us more than once: "I will have mercy on whom I will have mercy" (Exod. 33:19). This is the divine prerogative. God reserves for Himself the supreme right of executive clemency.

Suppose ten people sin and sin equally. Suppose God punishes five of them and is merciful to the other five. Is this injustice? No! In this situation five people get justice and five get mercy. No one gets injustice. What we tend to assume is this: If God is merciful to five, He must be equally merciful to the other five. Why? He is never obligated to be merciful. If He is merciful to nine of the ten, the tenth cannot claim to be a victim of injustice. God never owes mercy. God is not obliged to treat all people equally. Maybe I'd better say that again. *God is never obliged to treat all people equally.* If He were ever unjust to us, we would have reason to complain. But simply because He grants mercy to my neighbor, it gives me no claim on His mercy. Again we must remember that mercy is always voluntary. "I will have mercy on whom I will have mercy."

I will receive only justice or mercy from God. I never receive injustice from His hand. We may request that God help us get justice at the hands of other people, but we would be utterly foolish ever to ask Him for justice from Himself. I warn my students: "Don't ever ask God for justice—you might get it."

It is the confusion between justice and mercy that makes us shrink in horror when we read the stories of Nadab, Abihu, and Uzzah. When God's justice falls, we are offended because we think God owes perpetual mercy. We must not take His grace for granted. We must never lose our capacity to be amazed by grace. We sing the song "Amazing Justice." Our lyrics tend to go like this:

> Amazing Justice, cruel and sharp
>   That wounds a saint like me:
> I'm so darn good it makes no sense—
>   The tower fell on me!

I remember preaching a "practice sermon" in preaching class in seminary. In my sermon I was extolling the marvels of God's grace. As the hymn says, I spoke of "God's grace, infinite grace."

At the end of my sermon the professor had a question for me. "Mr. Sproul," he said, "where did you ever get the idea that God's grace is infinite? Is there absolutely no limit to His grace?" As soon as he asked that question, I knew I was in trouble. I could quote him chapter and verse of the hymn that taught me that, but somehow I couldn't come up with a single Scripture verse that taught God's grace is infinite.

The reason I couldn't find any Scripture passage to support my statement is because there is none. God's grace is not infinite. God is infinite, and God is gracious. We experience the grace of an infinite God, but grace is not infinite. God sets limits to His patience and forbearance. He warns us over and over again that someday the ax will fall and His judgment will be poured out.

Since it is our tendency to take grace for granted, my guess is that God found it necessary from time to time to remind Israel that grace must never be assumed. On rare but dramatic occasions He showed the dreadful power of His justice. He killed Nadab and Abihu. He killed Uzzah. He commanded the slaughter of the Canaanites. It is as if He were saying, "Be careful. While you enjoy the benefits of My grace, don't forget My justice. Don't forget the gravity of sin. Remember that I am holy."

Allowing God's Holiness to Touch Our Lives

As you reflect about what you have learned and rediscovered about God's holiness, answer these questions. Use a journal to record your responses to God's holiness, or discuss your responses with a friend.

1. In what ways does God's justice frighten you? In what ways does it comfort you?
2. What is your response when you realize that you deserve to die because of your sin?
3. What is your response when you realize that God's justice demanded Christ's death for you?
4. In what ways has God demonstrated His mercy to you?

~⚬~

SEVEN

War and Peace
with a Holy God

If man is not made for God,
why is he only happy in God?
If man is made for God,
why is he so opposed to God?

BLAISE PASCAL

The biblical record contains the stories of men and women who have wrestled with God. The very name *Israel* means "one who struggles with God." God is holy. He is high above us, transcendent. Yet He is a God with whom we can wrestle. In our wrestling match the goal is not final war but final peace. Some have found it. In this chapter we will look at examples of people who have gone to the mat with God and come away at peace. We will look at Jacob, Job, Habakkuk, and Saul of Tarsus. Then we will examine what it means to make peace with God.

Jacob was a rascal. His name means "supplanter." He was the fellow who deceived his father, conned his brother, and entered into an ungodly conspiracy with his mother. It is hard to imagine that the son of Isaac and the grandson of Abraham could be so corrupt. But in the course of Jacob's life, he underwent a radical transformation. It started at Bethel: "Jacob left Beersheba and set out for Haran. When he reached a certain place, he stopped for the night because the sun had set. Taking one of the stones there, he put it under his head and lay down to sleep" (Gen. 28:10, 11).

Travel in ancient Palestine was often an ordeal. Night brought danger from marauding thieves and wild beasts. On Jacob's journey there was no way station for him to seek lodging. He traveled as far as he could until the sun went down. At that point he made camp under the stars. His pillow for the night was a stone. When he settled into sleep, he had a dream that was destined to change his life:

> He had a dream in which he saw a stairway resting on the earth, with its top reaching to heaven, and the angels of God were ascending and descending on it. There above it stood the LORD, and he said: "I am the LORD, the God of your father Abraham and the God of Isaac. I will give you and your descendants the land on which you are lying. Your descendants will be like the dust of the earth, and you will spread out to the west and to the east, to the north and to the south. All peoples on earth will be blessed through you and your offspring. I am with you and will watch over you wherever you go, and I will bring you back to this land. I will not leave you until I have done what I have promised you."
> (Gen. 28:12–15)

The stairway Jacob saw in his dream is commonly referred to as "Jacob's ladder." It served as a bridge between heaven and earth. Up to this point in his life Jacob was not in touch with heavenly things. He had a profound sense of the *absence of God*. It seems strange that a son of Isaac and grandson of Abraham would be so "secular." Abraham had spoken with God. Surely young Jacob had sat around campfires and heard stories from his father and grandfather. He must have known about God's order to Abraham to sacrifice Isaac on an altar at Mount Moriah.

Jacob's life had been lived out on the plane of this world. Talk about heavenly matters had made little impression on him. His mind was fixed on the earth. As far as he was concerned, there was an unbridgeable chasm between heaven and earth. If there was a God, He was so remote, so utterly transcendent that He had no relevance to Jacob's life. This God of whom his parents spoke was too high for Jacob to reach—until he had a dream.

The dream featured a stairway. The stairway was a contact point, a connection between the realm of the holy and the realm of the profane. On the stairway Jacob saw angels ascending and descending. They were moving in both directions, from earth to heaven and from heaven to earth. The traffic was continuous. They moved from his presence to God's presence. At the top of the staircase Jacob saw the figure of God. God spoke to him, confirming the promise that He had made earlier to Abraham and Isaac. The promise of God would continue to future generations. It was going to pass through Jacob. He would be the carrier of the covenant oath that God had sworn. God promised to be with Jacob wherever he went and to stay with him until all the promises had been accomplished.

Whatever happened to Jacob's ladder? The image virtually disappears in Old Testament history. Centuries pass with no mention of it. Then suddenly, it appears again in the New Testament:

> Philip found Nathanael and told him, "We have found the one Moses wrote about in the Law, and about whom the prophets also wrote—Jesus of Nazareth, the son of Joseph."
>
> "Nazareth! Can anything good come from there?" Nathanael asked.
>
> "Come and see," said Philip.
>
> When Jesus saw Nathanael approaching, he said of him, "Here is a true Israelite, in whom there is nothing false."
>
> "How do you know me?" Nathanael asked.
>
> Jesus answered, "I saw you while you were still under the fig tree before Philip called you."
>
> Then Nathanael declared, "Rabbi, you are the Son of God; you are the King of Israel."
>
> Jesus said, "You believe because I told you I saw you under the fig tree. You shall see greater things than that." He then added, "I tell you the truth, you shall see heaven open, and the angels of God ascending and descending on the Son of Man." (John 1:45–51)

Jesus' words to Nathanael were radical. In this conversation He declared that He is the ladder of Jacob; He is the bridge between heaven and earth; He is the one who spans the chasm between the Transcendent One and mere humans. The angels of God ascend and descend on Him. He makes the absent God present among us. Was this what Jacob saw in a dim, shadowy way?

When Jacob awoke from his dream, he was stunned. He was overcome by the power of his nighttime vision. "When Jacob awoke from his sleep, he thought, 'Surely the LORD is in this place, and I was not aware of it.' He was afraid and said, 'How awesome is this place! This is none other than the house of God; this is the gate of heaven'" (Gen. 28:16, 17).

The name of the place where Jacob had his dream became known as Bethel. In Hebrew, the word *Bethel* means "house of God." There was no tabernacle there, no temple, no church. Jacob called it the house of God because there the Holy One made Himself known. Jacob's words are typical of the plight contemporary culture feels. Ours is a day when people feel a sense of the absence of God. We see no burning bushes, no pillars of fire, no incarnate Christ walking in our midst. We feel abandoned, thrown to the waters of a hostile or, even worse, indifferent universe. We seem locked into a world from which there is no exit, no stairway to the stars.

Jacob felt the same way until he had his dream. His words are relevant to our modern situation. "Surely the LORD is in this place, and I was not aware of it." God was there all the time. He was not remote from Jacob, but Jacob had missed Him all of his life. Jacob was unaware of the presence of God. This tragic ignorance of God's presence is played out in our culture every day in the lives of millions of people. God is here, but we are unaware. The moment awareness of His divine presence begins, the deepest personal struggle a person can experience begins as well. The dream did not end Jacob's struggle. It was the beginning of a struggle that was for keeps. From that moment on, he was fighting for his own soul.

"How awesome is this place!" This was Jacob's response to being in the house of God. People do not normally feel that way in church. There is no sense of awe, no sense of being in the presence of One who makes us tremble. People in awe never complain that church is boring.

Scholars do not agree on the precise time of Jacob's conversion. Some locate it here at Bethel, when he had the overwhelming sense of God's presence. Others pinpoint it years later in Jacob's life when he had his fateful wrestling match with God:

> That night Jacob got up and took his two wives, his two maidservants and his eleven sons and crossed the ford of the Jabbok. After he had sent them across the stream, he sent over all his possessions. So Jacob was left alone, and a man wrestled with him till daybreak. When the man saw that he could not overpower him, he touched the socket of Jacob's hip so that his hip was wrenched as he wrestled with the man. Then the man said, "Let me go, for it is daybreak."
>
> But Jacob replied, "I will not let you go unless you bless me."
>
> The man asked him, "What is your name?"
>
> "Jacob," he answered.

Then the man said, "Your name will no longer be Jacob, but Israel, because you have struggled with God and with men and have overcome."

Jacob said, "Please tell me your name."

But he replied, "Why do you ask my name?" Then he blessed him there.

So Jacob called the place Peniel, saying, "It is because I saw God face to face, and yet my life was spared." (Gen. 32:22–30)

Obviously the "man" Jacob wrestled was more than a man—he was the angel of God. The battle was fierce, raging through the night with neither combatant gaining the upper hand. Finally the angel used the overpowering might of God to touch the socket of Jacob's hip. Jacob's "victory" was not one of conquest but of survival. He walked away from the duel, but he walked with a limp for the rest of his life.

The discussion with the angel about names is significant. The angel demanded the name of Jacob. The demand for the name was similar to the custom we have today of indicating surrender by saying "uncle." For the combatant to yield his name meant that he was acknowledging the superiority of the other party. The yielding of the name was an act of submission. When Jacob surrendered his name, he surrendered his soul. He relinquished authority over his own life. With the surrender came a new name, a new identity. *Israel.*

In defeat Jacob was still hoping for a draw, a tie that would leave his pride intact. Even a split decision would help. He said to the angel, "Please tell me your name." Note the difference in the name-exchange issue. The angel demanded Jacob's name, and Jacob surrendered it. Jacob politely requested the angel's name and did not get it. This was the final act of divine conquest. There are no draws with God, no split decisions. When we wrestle with the Almighty, we lose. He is the undefeated champion of the universe.

The Holy One cannot be defeated in personal combat. But there is some consolation here. Jacob wrestled with God and lived. He was beaten. He was left crippled, but he survived that battle. At least we can learn from this that God will engage us in our honest struggles. We may wrestle with the Holy One. Indeed, for the transforming power of God to change our lives, we must wrestle with Him. We must know what it means to fight with God all night if we are also to know what it means to experience the sweetness of the soul's surrender.

No one ever carried on a livelier, more strident debate with God than did Job. If ever a man seemed to have a right to challenge God, it was Job. Job had been declared righteous by God Himself, and still he was afflicted with immeasurable misery. The drama of Job makes it seem as if the poor man was nothing more than a pawn in a cosmic struggle between God and Satan. God allowed Job to be put to a test. His possessions were stolen; his family was destroyed; and finally he was afflicted with a tormenting scourge of boils. He found no relief from his pain. His bodily anguish soon affected his soul.

I once talked to an elderly woman who was battling cancer with chemotherapy. She suffered the side effects of nausea from the treatments. I asked her how her spirits were holding up, and she offered a most candid reply: "It is hard to be a Christian when your head is in the toilet." The woman understood the close connection between body and soul. It is extremely difficult to be spiritual when the body is afflicted with unremitting pain.

Yet Job did not blaspheme. He cried out, "Though he slay me, yet will I hope in him" (Job 13:15). Even his wife tried to get him to find ultimate relief. Her advice was simple and to the point: "Curse God and die!" (Job 2:9).

Job refused to take the easy way out. He suffered the counsel of fools by listening to the advice of his friends. Finally he rose up to challenge God on the matter. He faced God alone, wrestling and struggling for answers to his misery. God's reply was hardly comforting:

Then the LORD answered Job out of the storm. He said:

"Who is this that darkens my counsel
    with words without knowledge?
Brace yourself like a man;
    I will question you,
and you shall answer me.

Where were you when I laid the earth's foundation?
    Tell me, if you understand.
Who marked off its dimensions? Surely you know!
    Who stretched a measuring line across it?
On what were its footings set,
    or who laid its cornerstone—
while the morning stars sang together
    and all the angels shouted for joy?

Who shut up the sea behind doors
    when it burst forth from the womb,

> when I made the clouds its garment
>> and wrapped it in thick darkness,
> when I fixed limits for it
>> and set its doors and bars in place,
> when I said, 'This far you may come and no farther;
>> here is where your proud waves halt'?" (Job 38:1–11)

This was a very difficult oral examination. Job demanded answers from God. Instead of answers he received a bundle of questions in return. God rebuked Job for casting a dark shadow over divine wisdom by his own ignorance. It was as if God said, "Okay, Job, you want to interrogate me? Fine, I'll answer your questions, but first I have a few for you." Like bullets from a rapid-fire machine gun, God shot out questions, each one more intimidating than the last. Finally Job spoke:

Then Job answered the LORD:

> "I am unworthy—how can I reply to you?
>> I put my hand over my mouth.
> I spoke once, but I have no answer—
>> twice, but I will say no more." (Job 40:3–5)

Consider the image Job used. He said that he would place his hand over his mouth. He gagged himself. He covered his lips with his hand lest any more foolish words escape his mouth. He was sorry that he ever challenged God. He recognized that his words had been presumptuous. He had said all he wanted to say.

But the interrogation continued. God was not yet finished with the examination. He asked a series of questions that overwhelmed Job: "Would you discredit my justice? Would you condemn me to justify yourself?" (Job 40:8).

Here the issue is plain. Job's challenge flies into the teeth of divine justice. His charges are an insult to a holy God. God's question rings in Job's ears: "Will you condemn me to justify yourself?" There is no doubt that Job longed to be justified. He was sick of the accusations of his friends. He did not understand why he was so miserable. He prayed for vindication. But his desire had gone out of control. He was on the verge of trading God's justification for his own. He had crossed a line in the debate, suggesting that perhaps God had done evil. God asked him straight out, "Do you want to condemn me so that you can be exonerated?"

The full weight of God's questions fell hard on Job. He was almost crushed by them. Finally he took his hand away from his mouth and spoke again. This time there were no accusations in his words. He broke his vow of silence only to voice his contrition:

> I know that you can do all things;
>> no plan of yours can be thwarted.
> You asked, "Who is this that obscures my counsel without knowledge?"
>> Surely I spoke of things I did not understand,
>> things too wonderful for me to know.
> You said, "Listen now, and I will speak;
>> I will question you, and you shall answer me."
> My ears had heard of you
>> but now my eyes have seen you.
> Therefore I despise myself and
>> repent in dust and ashes. (Job 42:2–6)

When we read this section of the book of Job, we may get the idea that God was bullying Job. He cried out for answers, and God said that He would answer Job's questions. But the answers never came forth. To be sure, there was a condition attached to the promise of answers: Job was required to answer first. But Job flunked his exam. God then gave no answers.

Yet Job was satisfied. Even though God gave no answers, Job's questions were put to rest. He received a higher answer than any direct reply could have provided. God answered Job's questions not with words but with Himself. As soon as Job saw who God is, Job was satisfied. Seeing the manifestation of God was all that he needed. He was able to leave the details in God's hands. Once God Himself was no longer shrouded in mystery, Job was able to live comfortably with a few unanswered questions. When God appeared, Job was so busy repenting that he did not have time for further challenges. His rage was redirected to himself: "I despise myself and repent in dust and ashes."

We point now to one more Old Testament man who challenged God. The prophet Habakkuk took God to task for doing things that offended his sense of justice. The prophet was appalled that God's people should suffer at the hands of a nation that was more wicked than they were themselves. On the surface it looked as if God had abandoned His promises to the Jews and had become a turncoat, giving His divine allegiance to the wicked Babylonians. For Habakkuk this was comparable to a modern-day Jew wondering if God was on Hitler's side during the Holocaust. Habakkuk's complaint was registered with a loud protest:

> How long, O LORD, must I call for help,
>   but you do not listen?
> Or cry out to you, "Violence!"
>   but you do not save?
> Why do you make me look at injustice?
>   Why do you tolerate wrong?
> Destruction and violence are before me;
>   there is strife, and conflict abounds.
> Therefore the law is paralyzed,
>   and justice never prevails.
> The wicked hem in the righteous,
>   so that justice is perverted. (Hab. 1:2–4)

Habakkuk was flaming angry. His complaint was so heated that he overdid it a bit. He said, "Justice never prevails." Surely in this world there is injustice that awaits final rectification, but to say that justice *never* prevails is going overboard. Like Job, Habakkuk demanded some answers. He went to the mat with God and was prepared to wrestle it out. He stood in his watchtower, waiting for a reply from the Almighty. When God finally spoke, Habakkuk's reaction was like Job's:

> I heard and my heart pounded,
>   my lips quivered at the sound;
> decay crept into my bones,
>   and my legs trembled." (Hab. 3:16)

The response of the prophet was like that of a small child who is scolded by a parent. His heart palpitated, and his lips began to quiver. We have all seen small children on the verge of tears. They try to hold back the flood, but the tremor in the lower lip gives them away. Here was a grown man whose lips quivered in the presence of God. He felt a kind of internal rottenness, a decay entering his very bones. The skeletal structure of the man felt as if it were collapsing. The trembling of the *mysterium tremendum* attacked his legs; his knees began to knock. He walked away from his wrestling match with God, but he walked on wobbly legs.

With the appearance of God, all of Habakkuk's angry protests ceased. Suddenly the tone of his speech changed from one of bitter despair to one of unwavering confidence and hope:

Though the fig tree does not bud
and there are no grapes on the vines,
though the olive crop fails
and the fields produce no food,
though there are no sheep in the pen
and no cattle in the stalls,
yet I will rejoice in the LORD,
I will be joyful in God my Savior." (Hab. 3:17, 18)

Habakkuk was now as fierce in his joy as he had been in his despair. He was able to rest absolutely in God's sovereignty. His words, translated into modern jargon, might sound like this: "Even if the budget is never balanced, even if the stock market crashes, even if food prices skyrocket, even if my child never recovers from her illness, even if I lose my job, and even if we lose our home—yet will I rejoice in the God of my salvation."

Jacob, Job, and Habakkuk all declared war on God. They all stormed the battlements of heaven. They were all defeated, yet they all came away from the struggle with uplifted souls. They paid a price in pain. God allowed the debate, but the battle was fierce before peace was established.

Saul of Tarsus felt the same overpowering conquest by God. He was a zealot for the Pharisees, totally repulsed by the advent of a new sect called Christianity. He was determined to wipe Christians from the face of the earth. Commissioned by the authorities, he went from house to house rounding up early Christian believers and casting them into prison. He stood on the sidelines during the stoning of Stephen and applauded the act. He was gleeful when he gained a new assignment to go to Damascus to continue his massacre of Christians. It was on the Damascus Road that he met the Holy One. He recounted the scene during his trial before King Agrippa:

> About noon, O king, as I was on the road, I saw a light from heaven, brighter than the sun, blazing around me and my companions. We all fell to the ground, and I heard a voice saying to me in Aramaic, "Saul, Saul, why do you persecute me? It is hard for you to kick against the goads."
>
> Then I asked, "Who are you, Lord?"
>
> "I am Jesus, whom you are persecuting," the Lord replied. "Now get up and stand on your feet. I have appeared to you to appoint

you as a servant and as a witness of what you have seen of me and what I will show you. I will rescue you from your own people and from the Gentiles. I am sending you to them to open their eyes and turn them from darkness to light, and from the power of Satan to God, so that they may receive forgiveness of sins and a place among those who are sanctified by faith in me."

So then, King Agrippa, I was not disobedient to the vision from heaven. (Acts 26:13–19)

Saul was zealous in his pursuit of righteousness. He was a Pharisee of Pharisees, a man committed to legal perfection. The irony of his zeal is seen in that the more zealous he was for his goals, the more opposed he actually became to the work of God. Not that God is opposed to the pursuit of righteousness. God is for the pursuit of righteousness, but He stands against the proud and the arrogant. He stands against those who are swelled up with self-righteousness. While Saul was convinced he was fighting for God, he was actually fighting against God. In this ironic battle he was doomed to an ultimate confrontation with the very Christ he opposed.

One of the names by which God is revealed in the Old Testament is the name *El Shaddai*. The name means "the thunderer" or "the overpowerer." It was by the name El Shaddai that God appeared to Job. What Job experienced was the awesome power of a sovereign God who overpowers all people and is Himself overpowered by no one. Saul met the Overpowerer on the road to Damascus.

Saul described his experience on the desert road as starting with the appearance of a dazzling light. The desert road at noonday was a place where the brilliance of the sun was particularly strong, piercing the day through a very thin atmosphere. Under normal conditions the sunshine there is intense. For any other light to be noticed against the backdrop of the desert sun, it must have been extraordinary. Saul spoke of a light more brilliant, more dazzling than the sun. He described it as a "light from heaven."

The expression "light from heaven" does not mean a light from the sky. The sun shines from the sky. Saul was in the presence of the heavenly glory of God. God's glory is the outward manifestation of His holiness. The effulgence of His glory is so scintillating, so brilliant that it eclipses the noonday sun. In the book of Revelation we read of the appearance of the new Jerusalem, the city that comes down from heaven: "I did not see a temple in the city, because the Lord God Almighty and the Lamb are its temple. The city does not need the sun or the moon to shine on it, for the glory of God gives it light, and the Lamb is its lamp" (Rev. 21:22, 23).

The new Jerusalem has no sun simply because it has no need for the sun. The glory of God and of His Christ is so bright that the sun itself is overpowered by it. Saul was blinded by its rays. Consider what happens to people if they gaze directly into the sun. In times of solar eclipse people are attracted by the strange sight of a shadow passing over the sun. There is a strong temptation to fix our gaze directly at it. Yet, even in eclipse we find it is painful and dangerous to look directly at the sun. We are warned by the news media at such times not to make attempts to look directly at it, lest we do serious damage to our eyes. If we cannot gaze directly at the sun during an eclipse, how much more severe would be the brilliance that literally outshines the sun? The glory of God reaches a magnitude of brightness far beyond that of the sun shining at full strength.

No angel appeared to wrestle with Saul. Yet some supernatural force threw him to the ground. In an instant Saul was blinded. There was no warning, no whisper of wind to alert him. Sovereignly and powerfully he was knocked flat to the desert floor.

With the light from heaven came also a voice. The voice is elsewhere described as the sound of many waters, a voice that roars like a booming waterfall that is cascading over rocks. Saul identified the voice as speaking in the Aramaic tongue, the native language of Jesus. The voice addressed Saul personally, in the form of the repetition of his name: "Saul, Saul." This double form of address indicated a greeting of personal intimacy. It was the way God addressed Moses at the burning bush and Abraham at his altar on Mount Moriah. It was the form by which Jesus cried over Jerusalem and addressed His Father in His darkest hour on the cross.

"Saul, Saul, why do you persecute me?" Notice that the voice did not inquire why Saul was persecuting Christ's church. It was rather, "Why do you persecute *me?*" To attack the church of Christ is to attack Him. Then the question: "Why do you kick against the goads?" The ox goads were sharp spikes implanted in a wooden frame that were fastened to oxcarts behind the oxen. If an ox became stubborn and refused to move forward, it sometimes registered its stubbornness by kicking its feet backward into the goad. Imagine how dumb an ox would be if after once kicking the goad, it became so furious that it kicked it again and again. The more it kicks the goads, the more pain it inflicts on itself. It is like a man banging his head against the wall and finding solace in how good it feels when he stops.

The voice was saying to Saul, "You dumb ox! How stupid it is to keep kicking the goads. You cannot win. Your battle is futile. It is time to surrender." Saul's response was a simple question, but the question was loaded: "Who are you, Lord?" Saul did not know the identity of the One who had just overpowered him, but of one thing he was certain—whoever it was, He was Lord.

In this experience Saul became Paul just as Jacob had become Israel. The battle was over. Saul struggled with God and lost. Here, like Isaiah, Saul received his call, his commission to apostleship. His life was changed, and the course of world history was changed with it. In defeat Paul found peace.

After telling this story to King Agrippa, Paul added these words: "So then, King Agrippa, I was not disobedient to the vision from heaven." As zealous as Saul had been in his fight *against* Christ, he became even more zealous in his fight *for* Christ. He had a vision of God's holiness that was so intense, he never forgot it. He contemplated it and expounded its meaning throughout his epistles. He became a man who understood what it meant to be justified. For him the holy war was over, and he entered into a holy peace. He became the apostle whose writings awakened Luther in the monastery and gave to the Christian church the recipe for an abiding peace with God.

The struggle we have with a holy God is rooted in the conflict between God's righteousness and our unrighteousness. He is just, and we are unjust. This tension creates fear, hostility, and anger within us toward God. The unjust person does not desire the company of a just judge. We become fugitives, fleeing from the presence of One whose glory can blind us and whose justice can condemn us. We are at war with Him unless or until we are justified. Only the justified person can be comfortable in the presence of a holy God.

The apostle Paul sets forth immediate benefits—fruits of justification. In his Epistle to the Romans he explains what happens to us when we are justified, when we are covered by Christ's righteousness, which is by faith: "Therefore, since we have been justified through faith, we have peace with God through our Lord Jesus Christ, through whom we have gained access by faith into this grace in which we now stand. And we rejoice in the hope of the glory of God" (Rom. 5:1, 2).

The first fruit of our justification is *peace with God.* To the ancient Jew peace was a precious but elusive commodity. The present-day turmoil in the Middle East seems like a replay of ancient history. From the days of the conquest of Canaan to the period of Roman occupation in New Testament times, there were only a few years when Israel was not at war. The location of Palestine as a pivotal land bridge between Africa and Asia made it a corridor not only for trade but also for warfare. Tiny Israel often found itself caught between competing world powers and was used like a military Ping-Pong ball.

The Jews longed for peace. They yearned for the day when swords would be beaten into plowshares. They waited for the era when the Prince of Peace would come to end the incessant hostilities. So important to the Jews was their quest for peace, that the very word *peace* became a daily greeting. Where we say hello or good-bye, Jews simply said shalom. To this day the greeting *shalom* remains an integral part of Jewish vocabulary.

The word *peace* had its primary reference to the cessation of military conflict. But a deeper meaning was attached to it as well. The Jews were also deeply concerned for inner peace, for the tranquil rest of the soul that meant an end to a troubled spirit. We have a similar concept in view when we speak of "peace of mind."

I remember the sultry summer day in 1945 when I was busy playing stickball in the streets of Chicago. At that time my world consisted of the piece of real estate that extended from one manhole cover to the next. All that was important to me was that my turn at bat had finally come. I was most annoyed when the first pitch was interrupted by an outbreak of chaos and noise all around me. People started running out of apartment doors, screaming and beating dishpans with wooden spoons. I thought for a moment it might be the end of the world. It was certainly the end of my stickball game. In the riotous confusion I saw my mother rushing toward me with tears streaming down her face. She scooped me up in her arms and squeezed me, sobbing over and over again, "It's over. It's over. It's over!"

It was VJ Day, 1945. I wasn't sure what it all meant, but one thing was clear. It meant that the war had ended and that my father was coming home. No more airmail to faraway countries. No more listening to the daily news reports about battle casualties. No more silk banners adorned with stars hanging in the window. No more crushing of tin soup cans. No more ration coupons. The war was over, and peace had come to us at last.

That moment of jubilation left a lasting impression on my childhood brain. I learned that peace is an important thing, a cause for unbridled celebration when it was established and for bitter remorse when it was lost.

The impression I got that day in the streets of Chicago was that peace had arrived forever. I had no idea how fragile it was. It seemed like a very short time before news reporters like Gabriel Heater were giving ominous warnings about troop buildups in China, the nuclear threat of Russia, and the blockade of Berlin. The peace of America was short lived, yielding once more to warfare in Korea and then again in Vietnam.

Fragile. Unstable. Tenuous. These are the normal conditions of earthly peace. Peace treaties, like rules, seem to be made to be broken. A million Neville Chamberlains leaning over balconies with hands outstretched, declaring, "We have achieved peace for our time" would not ensure that human history is ever anything but one continuous Munich.

We soon learn not to trust too heavily in peace. War intrudes too quickly, too easily. Yet we long for a lasting peace that we can depend on. This is precisely the kind of peace the apostle Paul declared in his Epistle to the Romans.

When our holy war with God ceases; when we, like Luther, walk through the doors of paradise, when we are justified by faith, the war ends forever. With the cleansing from sin and the declaration of divine forgiveness we enter into an eternal peace treaty with God. The firstfruit of our justification is peace with God. This peace is a holy peace, a peace unblemished and transcendent. It is a peace that cannot be destroyed.

When God signs a peace treaty, it is signed for perpetuity. The war is over, forever and ever. Of course we still sin; we still rebel; we still commit acts of hostility toward God. But God is not a cobelligerent. He will not be drawn into warfare with us. We have an advocate with the Father. We have a mediator who keeps the peace. He rules over the peace because He is both the Prince of Peace and He is *our* peace.

We are now called the children of God, a title granted in blessing to those who are peacemakers. Our sins are now dealt with by a Father, not a military commander. We have peace. It is our possession, sealed and guaranteed for us by Christ.

Our peace with God is not fragile; it is stable. When we sin, God is displeased, and He will move to correct us and convict us of our sin. But He does not go to war against us. His bow is no longer bent, and the arrows of His wrath are no longer aimed at our hearts. He does not rattle His sword every time we break the treaty.

The peace of justification is not only external. The deepest longings for inward peace are also met in Christ. It was St. Augustine who once prayed, "Thou hast made us for Thyself, and our heart is restless, until it finds its rest in Thee." We all know what it means to be stricken with inner restlessness. We know the gnawing feelings of emptiness and guilt that come from estrangement from God. Once our peace is established, that awful emptiness is filled, and our hearts may be still.

The New Testament calls this peace the peace that passes understanding. It is a holy peace, a peace that is "other" than routine earthly peace. It is the kind of peace that only Christ can bestow. It is the kind of peace that Christ Himself possessed.

We know from the Gospel records that Jesus had few possessions in this world. He owned no home; He had no place to lay His head. He had no business or corporate stocks. His one possession was His robe. That valuable robe was stolen from Him by those appointed to execute Him. It would seem, then, that He died penniless, with no inheritance to bequeath to His heirs.

We are the heirs of Christ. At first glance it would seem that we are heirs without an inheritance. Yet the Bible makes it clear that God has been pleased to give His kingdom to His beloved Son. Jesus had an inheritance from His Father, and that inheritance He has passed on to us. He promised that someday we will hear the words, "Come, you who are blessed by my Father; take your inheritance, the kingdom prepared for you since the creation of the world" (Matt. 25:34).

The kingdom of God is not our only inheritance. In His last will and testament, Jesus left His heirs something else, something very special: "Peace I leave with you; my peace I give you. I do not give to you as the world gives. Do not let your hearts be troubled and do not be afraid" (John 14:27).

This is the legacy of Christ: *peace.* It is His peace that is our inheritance. He gives the gift in a way that is different from gifts that are given in this world. There are no ulterior motives and no sinister strings attached. He gives us His peace not for His benefit but for ours. It is an otherworldly gift given in an other worldly manner. It is ours to keep forever.

Peace is only one immediate fruit of justification. Added to this holy peace is something else: *access.* The word *access* is crucial to anyone who has ever wrestled with a holy God. We see signs all around us about access. One sign may read, "No Access," and another reads, "Limited Access." At one time in history a "No Access" sign was posted at the gates of Paradise. Even the Old Testament temple allowed ordinary people no access to the throne of God. Even the high priest's access was "limited" to once a year under very guarded circumstances. A thick veil separated the Holy of Holies from the rest of the temple. It was off-limits. Restricted. No admission was permitted to the rank-and-file believer.

The moment Jesus was slain, the instant the Just One died for the unjust, the veil in the temple was torn. The presence of God became accessible to us. For the Christian the "No Access" sign was removed from the gates of paradise. We may now walk freely on holy ground. We have access to His grace, but even more, we have access to Him. Justified people need no longer say to the Holy One, "Depart from me, for I am a sinful man." Now we can feel welcome in the presence of a holy God. We can take our questions to Him. He is not too remote to hear our cries. We come as those covered by the righteousness of Christ. I repeat: *We can feel welcome in the presence of God.* To be sure we still come in awe, in a spirit of reverence and adoration, but the tremendous news is that we can come:

> Therefore, since we have a great high priest who has gone
> through the heavens, Jesus the Son of God, let us hold firmly
> to the faith we profess. For we do not have a high priest who is
> unable to sympathize with our weaknesses, but we have one who
> has been tempted in every way, just as we are—yet was without
> sin. Let us then approach the throne of grace with confidence, so
> that we may receive mercy and find grace to help us in our time
> of need. (Heb. 4:14–16)

The Bible invites us to approach the throne of grace with confidence. Other translators use the word *boldness.* As justified people we may be bold in approaching God. To be bold or confident must not be confused with being arrogant or flip. Uzzah was more than bold; he was arrogant. Nadab and Abihu went beyond confidence to insulting the majesty of God. We are to come into His presence boldly and in confidence. There is no need to retreat from Him or to hesitate to enter. But when we come, we must remember two things: (1) who He is; and (2) who we are.

For the Christian the holy war is over; the peace has been established. Access to the Father is ours. But we still must tremble before our God. He is still holy. Our trembling is the tremor of awe and veneration, not the trembling of the coward or the pagan frightened by the rustling of a leaf. Luther explained it this way: We are to fear God not with a servile fear like that of a prisoner before his tormentor but as children who do not wish to displease their beloved Father. We come to Him in confidence; we come to Him in boldness; we have access. We have a holy peace.

Allowing God's Holiness to Touch Our Lives

As you reflect about what you have learned and rediscovered about God's holiness, answer these questions. Use a journal to record your responses to God's holiness, or discuss your responses with a friend.

1. Has God ever engaged you in an honest struggle, as He did Jacob? What was the outcome?
2. Have you ever challenged God, as Job did? What was God's response?

3. Habakkuk's battle with God ended in a bold statement of faith: "Even if _____ happens, yet I will rejoice in the Lord." What are the "even if's" in your life? Are you willing to surrender them to the Lord?

4. What does it mean to you personally that Christ's death offers us unending peace with God?

5. How will you worship God for giving us unlimited access to Himself?

✦

EIGHT

Be Holy Because
I Am Holy

Apollyon, beware what you do;
for I am in the king's highway,
the way of holiness;
Therefore take heed to yourself.

JOHN BUNYAN

Christians in the early church were called saints. Since that time the word *saint* has undergone strong changes in our vocabulary. Now the word *saint* conjures up images of a super-righteous person, a person of extraordinary piety and spiritual power. The Roman Catholic Church has made it a title for those who have been canonized into a special list of spiritual heroes and heroines.

The Bible uses the word *saint* for the rank-and-file believer. In the New Testament all of the people of God enjoy the title *saint*. The word means simply "holy one." The New Testament saints were the holy ones. It seems odd that the term is used for believers who were struggling with all sorts of sin. When we read the epistles of Paul, we are struck by the fact that he addresses the people as saints and then goes on to rebuke them for their foolish and sinful behavior.

The saints of Scripture were called saints not because they were already pure but because they were people who were set apart and called to purity. The word *holy* has the same two meanings when applied to people as it has when it is applied to God. We recall that when the word *holy* is used to describe God, it not only calls attention to that sense in which He is different or apart from us, but it also calls attention to His absolute purity. But we are not God; we are not transcendent; we are certainly not pure. How then can the Bible possibly call us "holy ones"?

To answer that question, we must look back to the Old Testament. When God led Israel out of bondage in Egypt and made them a special nation, He set them apart. He called them His chosen people and gave them a special commission. He said to them, "Be holy, because I am holy" (Lev. 11:44).

This special call to Israel was really not new. It did not begin with Moses or even with Abraham. The call to holiness was first given to Adam and Eve. This was the original assignment of the human race. We were created in the image of God. To be God's image meant, among other things, that we were made to mirror and reflect God's character. We were created to shine forth to the world the holiness of God. This was the chief end of man, the very reason for our existence.

Presbyterian churches have made use of the Westminster Catechism in the instruction of children. The first question of the catechism reads: "What is the chief end of man?" The question asks about the primary responsibility carried by every human being. The answer to the question reads: "Man's chief end is to glorify God and to enjoy Him forever."

I had a hard time with that question when I was a boy. I couldn't quite put the two parts of the answer together. I was unable to see how enjoyment fit with glorifying God. I realized that to glorify God involved some kind of obedience to His holy law. That did not sound like much fun. Already I knew the conflict between my own enjoyment and obeying the laws of God. I dutifully recited the required answer even though I had no real understanding of it. I saw God as a barrier to joy. To live to His glory as my chief goal was not what I had in mind. I guess Adam and Eve had a little trouble with it too.

A big problem I had in my youth was that I did not quite understand the difference between happiness and pleasure. I would like to report to you that since I have become a man, I have put away all childish things. Unhappily, that is not the case. There are still childish things that cling to my adult life. I still struggle with the difference between happiness and pleasure. I know the difference in my head, but it has not yet reached my bloodstream.

I have committed many sins in my life. Not one of my sins has ever made me happy. None has ever added a single ounce of happiness to my life. Quite the contrary. Sin has added an abundance of unhappiness to my life. I stand amazed at those famous personalities who, in the course of television or magazine interviews, declare that if they had their lives to live over, they would do nothing differently. Such foolishness staggers my imagination. There are multitudes of things I would love to have the chance to do over. Now it is quite possible that with a second chance, I would make the same foolish mistakes, but I'd still like the chance to try.

My sins have not brought me happiness. But my sins have brought me pleasure. I like pleasure. I am still very much attracted to pleasure. Pleasure can be great fun. And not all pleasures are sins. There is much pleasure to be found in righteousness. But the difference is still there. Sin can be pleasurable, but it never brings happiness.

Now if I understand all this, why would I ever be tempted to sin? It seems silly that anyone who knows the difference between happiness and pleasure would continue to trade happiness for pleasure. It seems utterly stupid for a person to do something that he knows will rob him of his happiness. Yet we do it. The mystery of sin is not only that it is wicked and destructive but also that it is so downright stupid.

I smoked cigarettes for years. I never really kept count, but my guess is that during those years, hundreds of people called my attention to the fact that smoking was not a good thing for me to be doing. They were merely pointing out to me the obvious, telling me what every smoker in America already knows. Before I was ever converted to Christianity, I knew full well that smoking was harmful to me. I knew it before the surgeon general ever put a warning label on cigarette packages. I knew it from the first cigarette I ever smoked. Yet I continued to do it. Sheer madness. That is what sin is.

Have you ever done anything that you felt like doing even though your head told you it was wrong? If you answer no to that question, you are either lying or deluded. We all fall into this trap. We do what we feel like doing rather than what we know we ought to do. No wonder we cry like Paul, "What a wretched man I am! Who will rescue me from this body of death?" (Rom. 7:24).

Our problem is that we have been called to be holy, and we are not holy. Yet again the question arises, If we are not holy, why does the Bible call us saints?

The Bible calls us "holy ones." We are holy because we have been consecrated to God. We have been set apart. We have been called to a life that is different. The Christian life is a life of nonconformity. The idea of nonconformity is expressed in Romans:

> Therefore, I urge you, brothers, in view of God's mercy, to offer your bodies as living sacrifices, holy and pleasing to God—this is your spiritual act of worship. Do not conform any longer to the pattern of this world, but be transformed by the renewing of your mind. Then you will be able to test and approve what God's will is—his good, pleasing and perfect will. (Rom. 12:1, 2)

In the Old Testament, worship centered on the altar with the presentations of sacrifices offered to God. For the most part, these sacrifices of animals and various grains were made as sin offerings. In themselves the animal sacrifices had no power to atone for sins. They were symbols that pointed forward to the one great sacrifice that would be made on the cross. After the perfect Lamb was slain, the altar sacrifices ceased. The Christian church has no provision for animal sacrifices anymore because it has no need for such sacrifices. To offer them now would be to insult the perfection of Christ's sacrifice.

Because the days of animal sacrifices are over, many people assume that all sacrifices offered to God are abhorrent to Him. That is simply not true. Here the apostle Paul calls for a new kind of sacrifice, a *living sacrifice* of our bodies. We are to give to God not our grains or our animals, but ourselves. This new sacrifice is not an act of atonement; it is not a sin offering. The sacrifice of our bodies to God is a thank offering. It follows upon Paul's word *therefore.*

When we see the word *therefore* in the text of Scripture, we are immediately alerted that a conclusion is coming. The word *therefore* links what has been previously said to what is about to be concluded. In Romans 12 the "therefore" refers to all the apostle has stated in the previous chapters regarding Christ's saving work on our behalf. The word drives us forward to the only proper conclusion we can draw from His work. In light of the gracious justification that Christ has achieved for us, the only reasonable conclusion we can reach is that we ought to present ourselves totally to God as walking, breathing, living sacrifices.

What does the living sacrifice look like? Paul first describes it in terms of nonconformity. "Do not conform any longer to the pattern of this world." Here is the point at which many Christians have gone astray. It is clear that we are to be nonconformists. But it is difficult to understand precisely what kind of nonconformity is called for. Nonconformity is a tricky matter and can easily be reduced to superficiality.

It is a tragedy that the matter of nonconformity has been treated by Christians at a shallow level. The simplistic way of not conforming is to see what is in style in our culture and then do the opposite. If short hair is in vogue, the nonconformist wears long hair. If going to movies is popular, then Christians avoid movies as "worldly." The extreme case of this may be seen in groups that refuse to wear buttons or use electricity because such things, too, are worldly.

A superficial style of nonconformity is the classical pharisaical trap. The kingdom of God is not about buttons, movies, or dancing. The concern of God is not focused on what we eat or what we drink. The call of nonconformity is a call to a deeper level of righteousness that goes beyond externals. When piety is defined exclusively in terms of externals, the whole point of the apostle's teaching has been lost. Somehow we have failed to hear Jesus' words that it is not what goes into a person's mouth that defiles a person, but what comes out of that mouth. We still want to make the kingdom a matter of eating and drinking.

Why are such distortions rampant in Christian circles? The only answer I can give is sin. Our marks of piety can actually be evidences of impiety. When we major in minors and blow insignificant trifles out of proportion, we imitate the Pharisees. When we make dancing and movies the test of spirituality, we are guilty of substituting a cheap morality for a genuine one. We do these things to obscure the deeper issues of righteousness. Anyone can avoid dancing or going to movies. These require no great effort of moral courage. What is difficult is to control the tongue, to act with integrity, to reveal the fruit of the Spirit.

I have never heard a sermon on coveting. I have heard plenty of sermons about the evils of whiskey, but none on the evils of covetousness. Strange. To be sure, the Bible declares that drunkenness is sin, but drunkenness never made the top-ten list. True nonconformists stop coveting; they stop gossiping; they stop slandering; they stop hating and feeling bitter; they start to practice the fruit of the Spirit.

Jesus rebuked the Pharisees for their preoccupation with external matters:

> Woe to you, teachers of the law and Pharisees, you hypocrites!
> You give a tenth of your spices—mint, dill and cummin. But you
> have neglected the more important matters of the law—justice,
> mercy and faithfulness. You should have practiced the latter,
> without neglecting the former. You blind guides! You strain out a
> gnat but swallow a camel. (Matt. 23:23, 24)

Jesus rebuked the scribes and the Pharisees for neglecting weighty matters and overemphasizing minor matters. He saw this issue not as an *either-or* matter but a *both-and* matter. Tithes were to be paid, but not as a substitute for paying great care to issues of justice, mercy, and fidelity. The Pharisees took care of outward, external, visible matters of piety but ignored the higher spiritual issues.

Anyone can be a nonconformist for nonconformity's sake. Again I want to emphasize that this is a cheap piety. What we are ultimately called to is more than nonconformity; we are called to *transformation*. We notice that the words *conform* and *transform* both contain the same root word *form*. The only difference between the two words is found in the prefixes. The prefix *con* means "with." To conform, then, is to be "with the structures or forms." In our culture a conformist is someone who is "with it." A nonconformist may be regarded as someone who is "out of it." If the goal of the Christian is to be "out of it," then I am afraid we have been all too successful.

The prefix *trans* means "across" or "beyond." When we are called to be transformed, it means that we are to rise above the forms and the structures of this world. We are not to follow the world's lead but to cut across it and rise above it to a higher calling and style. This is a call to transcendent excellence, not a call to sloppy "out-of-it-ness." Christians who give themselves as living sacrifices and offer their worship in this way are people with a high standard of discipline. They are not satisfied with superficial forms of righteousness. The "saints" are called to a rigorous pursuit of the kingdom of God. They are called to depth in their spiritual understanding.

The key method Paul underscores as the means to the transformed life is by the "renewal of the mind." This means nothing more and nothing less than education. Serious education. In-depth education. Disciplined education in the things of God. It calls for a mastery of the Word of God. We need to be people whose lives have changed because our minds have changed.

True transformation comes by gaining a new understanding of God, ourselves, and the world. What we are after ultimately is to be conformed to the image of Christ. We are to be like Jesus, though not in the sense that we can ever gain deity. We are not god-men. But our humanity is to mirror and reflect the perfect humanity of Jesus. A tall order!

To be conformed to Jesus, we must first begin to think as Jesus did. We need the "mind of Christ." We need to value the things He values and despise the things He despises. We need to have the same priorities He has. We need to consider weighty the things that He considers weighty.

That cannot happen without a mastery of His Word. The key to spiritual growth is in-depth Christian education that requires a serious level of sacrifice.

That is the call to excellence we have received. We are not to be like the rest of the world, content to live our lives with a superficial understanding of God. We are to grow dissatisfied with spiritual milk and hunger after spiritual meat.

To be a saint means to be separated. But it means more than that. The saint also is to be involved in a vital process of sanctification. We are to be purified daily in the growing pursuit of holiness. If we are justified, we must also be sanctified.

Luther used a wonderful Latin phrase to describe the status of the justified sinner: *simul justus et peccator.* Let's look at the phrase a word at a time to discern its meaning for us. *Simul* is the Latin word from which our English word *simultaneous* is derived; it means "at one and the same time." *Justus* is the Latin from which our word *just* comes, and *et* is the Latin word for "and." The word *peccator* is probably least familiar to us. We derive the English words *impeccable* and *peccadillo* from it. It is the Latin word for "sinner." Putting the words together, we get *simul justus et peccator*: "at the same time just and sinner." That is what saints are, people who are at one and the same time just, yet sinful.

That saints are still sinners is obvious. How then can they be just? Saints are just because they have been justified. In and of themselves they are not just. They are made just in God's sight by the righteousness of Christ. This is what justification by faith is about. When we put our personal trust for our salvation in Christ and in Him alone, then God transfers to our account all of the righteousness of Jesus. His justness becomes ours when we believe in Him. It is a legal transaction. The transfer of righteousness is like an accounting transaction where no real property is exchanged. That is, God puts Jesus' righteousness in my account while I am still a sinner.

This all sounds something like a fraud, as if God is playing legal games. He counts us righteous even when in and of ourselves we are not righteous. But this is the gospel! This is the Good News, that we can carry an account of perfect righteousness before the judgment throne of a just and holy God. It is the righteousness of Christ that becomes ours by faith. It is no fraud and much less a game. The transaction is real. God's declaration is serious. Christ's righteousness is really put in our account. God sees us as righteous because we have been covered and clothed by the righteousness of Jesus. It is not simply that Jesus pays our debts for us by dying. His life is as important to us as His death. Not only does Christ take our sins, our debts, and our demerits, but He also gives us His obedience, His assets, and His merits. That is the only way an unjust person can ever stand in the presence of a just and holy God.

This concept of a transfer of righteousness is fraught with peril. It is easily confused and seriously abused. Some people assume that if we believe in Christ, we never have to worry about changing our lives. Justification by faith may be viewed as a license to sin. If we have the righteousness of Christ, why should we worry about changing our sinful ways? Since our good works can't get us into heaven, why should we be concerned about them at all? Such questions never ought to pass over the lips of a truly justified person.

When Luther boldly declared the biblical doctrine of justification by faith alone, he said, "Justification is by faith alone, but not by a faith that is alone." James had said it earlier in a different way. He said that "faith without deeds is dead" (James 2:26). True faith, or saving faith, is what Luther called a *fides viva*, a "living faith." It is a faith that immediately brings forth the fruits of repentance and righteousness. If we say we have faith, but no works follow, that is clear evidence that our faith is not genuine. True faith always produces real conformity to Christ. If justification happens to us, then sanctification will surely follow. If there is no sanctification, it means that there never was any justification.

The instant we believe, we are immediately justified. God does not wait for our good works before He declares us just. We are still sinners when the declaration comes.

How much time elapses before the sinner begins to become pure? The answer is *none*. There is no time lapse between our justification and the *beginning* of our sanctification. But there is a great time lapse between our justification and the *completion* of our sanctification.

Luther used a simple analogy to explain it. He described the condition of a patient who was mortally ill. The doctor proclaimed that he had medicine that would surely cure the man. The instant the medicine was administered, the doctor declared that the patient was well. At that instant the patient was still sick, but as soon as the medicine passed his lips and entered his body, the patient began to get well. So it is with our justification. As soon as we truly believe, at that very instant we start to get better; the process of becoming pure and holy is underway, and its future completion is certain.

The goal of Christian growth is the achievement of righteousness. In the Christian world today such a statement may sound radical. Christians hardly ever talk about righteousness. The word has almost become a swear word. Nearly any other term is preferred to the word *righteousness*. I have never had a student, a parishioner, or any other person come to me and ask, "How can I become righteous?"

Many people have spoken to me about being ethical, moral, spiritual, or even pious. But nobody seems to want to talk about being righteous. Perhaps it is because we know it is a sin to be self-righteous. The word *righteous* sounds a bit pharisaical. It sounds more spiritual to talk about being spiritual than it does to talk about being righteous.

To be spiritual has only one real purpose. It is a means to an end, not the end itself. The goal of all spiritual exercise must be the goal of righteousness. God calls us to be holy. Christ sets the priority of the Christian life: "But seek first his kingdom and his righteousness, and all these things will be given to you as well" (Matt. 6:33). The goal is righteousness.

How can we know if we are moving ahead in our pursuit of righteousness? How can we know if we are making real progress in our call to be holy? The Bible sheds light on these questions. Righteous people are known by their fruit. They become holy by the sanctifying power of the Holy Spirit working in them and on them. The Holy Spirit knows what holiness is. He is called the Holy Spirit not only because He is holy Himself but also because He is working to produce holiness in us.

The fruit of righteousness is that fruit that is exercised in us by the Holy Spirit. If we want to be holy, if we have a real hunger for righteousness, then we must focus our attention on the fruit of the Holy Spirit.

The fruit of the Holy Spirit is set forth for us in stark contrast to the fruit of our sinful nature:

> The acts of the sinful nature are obvious: sexual immorality, impurity and debauchery; idolatry and witchcraft; hatred, discord, jealousy, fits of rage, selfish ambition, dissensions, factions and envy; drunkenness, orgies, and the like. I warn you, as I did before, that those who live like this will not inherit the kingdom of God. (Gal. 5:19–21)

In this passage Paul echoes Jesus' warning about the loss of the kingdom of God. People whose lives are characterized by the styles mentioned above will not inherit the kingdom of God. This is not to say that any sin we commit will mean the forfeiture of heaven. Paul is talking about a lifestyle that is habitually and consistently characterized by the vices mentioned. The list includes both external and internal sins, sins of the body and sins of the heart.

The sins listed may be described as gross and heinous sins. The New Testament recognizes degrees of sins. Some sins are worse than others. This important point is often overlooked by Christians. Protestants particularly struggle with the concept of gradations or degrees of sin. This is partly due to a reaction to the Roman Catholic idea of two kinds of sins: mortal and venial. Rome calls certain sins "mortal" because they are so serious that they kill the grace in our soul. Lesser sins are called "venial"; they fall short of destroying saving grace.

We tend to think that sin is sin and that no sin is greater than any other. We think of Jesus' teaching in the Sermon on the Mount that to lust after a woman is to be guilty of adultery. We are aware that the Bible teaches if we sin against one point of the law, we sin against the whole law. These two biblical teachings can easily confuse us about the degrees of sin.

When Jesus said that to lust is to violate the law against adultery, He did not say or imply that lust is *as bad as* the full act of adultery. His point was that the full measure of the law prohibited more than the actual act of adultery. The law has a broader application. The Pharisees thought that because they never committed the actual act of adultery, they were free of sin against the law. They assumed that if they actually refrained from killing people, they were keeping the law against killing. They failed to see that unjust anger and hatred were also included in the wider meaning of the law against killing.

Jesus taught that hate is a sin against another person's life. Hatred violates people. It is not as severe as actual murder, but it is nevertheless a sin. The smallest sin involves a sin against the whole law. The law is the standard of holiness for us. In our slightest transgression we sin against that standard; we violate the call to holiness. Again, that does not imply that every sin is as wicked as every other sin. Jesus repeatedly spoke of degrees of punishment in hell as well as of those whose guilt was greater than others.

The idea of gradations of sin is important for us to keep in mind so we understand the difference between *sin* and *gross sin*. Again, all of our sins require forgiveness. All of our sins are acts of treason against God. We need a Savior for our "little" sins as well as for the "major" ones. But some sins are more significant than others, and we need to identify which these are, lest we fall into the pharisaical trap of majoring in the minors.

Consider the attention that is given to the problem of being overweight in our society. Each year people in the United States spend billions of dollars on dieting. There are some excellent reasons for us to keep our body weight under control. We know that obesity is a major health problem. We also know that gluttony is a sin. We are prone to stuffing and stretching the temple of the Holy Spirit. But the accent on our national concern for slimness is not so much a focus on health or gluttony as it is a view based on cosmetics. We want to be slim so that we will look nice. There is nothing wrong with that. But slimness is not the highest measure we can find for holiness. No one has ever hurt me because they were overweight. They have hurt me because they slandered me. We spend little money controlling the slander problem. Maybe it is because some things are more difficult to control than weight. Some people have mastered the art of appetite control. No one has mastered the art of tongue control.

Think of the people whom you consider to be the most godly people you've met. How much does their weight enter into the godliness you've admired? How many of these godly people have vicious tongues? It's a contradiction in terms, isn't it? Godliness and an uncontrolled tongue are incompatible.

The fruit of the Spirit stands in vivid contrast to the sins of the flesh. The fruit of the Spirit yields the virtues we recognize in godly people. Consider the fruit Paul mentions: "But the fruit of the Spirit is love, joy, peace, patience, kindness, goodness, faithfulness, gentleness and self-control" (Gal. 5:22, 23).

These are the marks of a person who is growing in holiness. These are the virtues we are called to cultivate. To yield the fruit of the Spirit, we must practice the fruit of the Spirit. The Spirit is at work within us to assist us in the practice of the fruit, but we are called to strive with all our might to produce this fruit.

In this list of the fruit of the Spirit, the apostle gives us a recipe for our sanctification. We all like to learn things in ten easy lessons. There is nothing easy about becoming holy. Yet, the Bible does make it easy for us to know what holiness is supposed to look like. The fruit of the Spirit—that is where our focus must be. Paul simplifies it for us. He adds the following words to his list of virtues that comprise the fruit of the Spirit: "Against such things there is no law. Those who belong to Christ Jesus have crucified the sinful nature with its passions and desires. Since we live by the Spirit, let us keep in step with the Spirit. Let us not become conceited, provoking and envying each other" (Gal. 5:23–26).

Allowing God's Holiness to Touch Our Lives

As you reflect about what you have learned and rediscovered about God's holiness, answer these questions. Use a journal to record your responses to God's holiness, or discuss your responses with a friend.

1. What does it mean to you to be holy, to live a holy life?
2. How are you trying to renew your mind?
3. How do you respond when you realize that God has justified you by transferring to your account all of Christ's righteousness?
4. What fruit has the Holy Spirit been developing in your life?
5. In what ways do you want to grow in holiness?

NINE

God in the Hands of Angry Sinners

*Almost every natural man
that hears of hell, flatters himself
that he shall escape it.*

JONATHAN EDWARDS

Perhaps the most famous sermon ever preached in America was Jonathan Edwards's sermon "Sinners in the Hands of an Angry God." Not only has the sermon been reproduced in countless catalogs of preaching, but it is also included in most anthologies of early American literature. So scandalous is this vivid portrayal of unconverted people's precarious state under the threat of hell that some modern analysts have called it utterly sadistic.

Edwards's sermon is filled with graphic images of the fury of divine wrath and the horror of the relentless punishment of the wicked in hell. Such sermons are out of vogue in our age and generally considered in poor taste and based on a pre-enlightened theology. Sermons stressing the fierce wrath of a holy God aimed at impenitent human hearts do not fit with the civic meeting hall atmosphere of the local church. Gone are the Gothic arches; gone are the stained-glass windows; gone are the sermons that stir the soul to moral anguish. Ours is an upbeat generation with the accent on self-improvement and a broad-minded view of sin.

Our thinking goes like this: If there is a God at all, He is certainly not holy. If He is perchance holy, He is not just. Even if He is both holy and just, we need not fear because His love and mercy override His holy justice. If we can stomach His holy and just character, we can rest in one thing: He cannot possess wrath.

If we think soberly for five seconds, we must see our error. If God is holy at all, if God has an ounce of justice in His character, indeed if God exists as God, how could He possibly be anything else but angry with us? We violate

His holiness; we insult His justice; we make light of His grace. These things can hardly please Him.

Edwards understood the nature of God's holiness. He perceived that unholy people have much to fear from such a God. Edwards had little need to justify a scare theology. His consuming need was to preach about God's holiness; to preach it vividly, emphatically, convincingly, and powerfully. He did this not out of a sadistic delight in frightening people but out of compassion. He loved his congregation enough to warn them of the dreadful consequences of facing the wrath of God. He was not concerned with laying a guilt trip on his people but with awakening them to the peril they faced if they remained unconverted.

Let's examine a section of the sermon to get but a taste of its flavor:

> The God that holds you over the pit of hell, much as one holds a spider, or some loathsome insect, over the fire, abhors you, and is dreadfully provoked: his wrath towards you burns like fire; he looks upon you as worthy of nothing else, but to be cast into the fire; he is of purer eyes than to bear to have you in his sight; you are ten thousand times more abominable in his eyes, than the most hateful venomous serpent is in ours. You have offended him infinitely more than ever a stubborn rebel did his prince; and yet, it is nothing but his hand that holds you from falling into the fire every moment. It is to be ascribed to nothing else, that you did not go to hell the last night; that you were suffered to awake again in this world, after you closed your eyes to sleep. And there is no other reason to be given, why you have not dropped into hell since you arose in the morning, but that God's hand has held you up. There is no other reason to be given why you have not gone to hell, since you have sat here in the house of God, provoking his pure eyes by your sinful wicked manner of attending his solemn worship. Yea, there is nothing else that is to be given as a reason why you do not this very moment drop down into hell.
>
> O sinner! consider the fearful danger you are in: it is a great furnace of wrath, a wide and bottomless pit, full of the fire of wrath, that you are held over in the hand of that God, whose wrath is provoked and incensed as much against you, as against many of the damned in hell. You hang by a slender thread, with the flames of divine wrath flashing about it, and ready every moment to singe it, and burn it asunder; and you have no interest in any Mediator, and nothing to lay hold of to save

yourself, nothing to keep off the flames of wrath, nothing of
your own, nothing that you ever have done, nothing that you can
do, to induce God to spare you one moment.[1]

The pace of the sermon is relentless. Edwards strikes blow after blow to the
conscience-stricken hearts of his congregation. He draws graphic images from
the Bible, all designed to warn sinners of their peril. He tells them that they are
walking on slippery places with the danger of falling from their own weight. He
says that they are walking across the pit of hell on a wooden bridge supported
by rotten planks that may break at any second. He speaks of invisible arrows
that, like a pestilence, fly at noonday. He warns that God's bow is bent and that
the arrows of His wrath are aimed at their hearts. He describes God's wrath as
great waters rushing against the floodgates of a dam. If the dam should break,
the sinners would be inundated by a deluge. He reminds his hearers that there is
nothing between them and hell but air:

> Your wickedness makes you as if it were heavy as lead, and to
> tend downwards with great weight and pressure towards hell;
> and if God should let you go, you would immediately sink and
> swiftly descend and plunge into the bottomless gulf; and your
> healthy constitution, and your own care and prudence, and best
> contrivance, and all your righteousness, would have no more
> influence to uphold you and keep you out of hell, than a spider's
> web would have to stop a falling rock.[2]

In the application section of the sermon, Edwards places great stress on the
nature and severity of God's wrath. Central to his thinking is the clear notion
that a holy God must also be a wrathful God. He lists several key points about
God's wrath that we dare not overlook.

1. *God's wrath is divine.* The wrath of which Edwards preached was the
wrath of an infinite God. He contrasts God's wrath with human anger or the
wrath of a king for his subject. Human wrath terminates. It has an ending point.
It is limited. God's wrath can go on forever.

2. *God's wrath is fierce.* The Bible repeatedly likens God's wrath to a wine-
press of fierceness. In hell there is no moderation or mercy given. God's anger
is not mere annoyance or a mild displeasure. It is a consuming rage against the
unrepentant.

3. *God's wrath is everlasting.* There is no end to the anger of God directed
against those in hell. If we had any compassion for other people, we would wail
at the thought of a single one of them falling into the pit of hell. We could not

stand to hear the cries of the damned for five seconds. To be exposed to God's fury for a moment would be more than we could bear. To contemplate it for eternity is too awful to consider. With sermons like this we do not want to be awakened. We long for blissful slumber, for the repose of tranquil sleep.

The tragedy for us is that in spite of the clear warnings of Scripture and of Jesus' sober teaching on this subject, we continue to be at ease about the future punishment of the wicked. If God is to be believed at all, we must face the awful truth that someday His furious wrath will be poured out. Edwards observed:

> Almost every natural man that hears of hell, flatters himself that he shall escape it; he depends upon himself for his own security; he flatters himself in what he has done, in what he is now doing, or what he intends to do. Every one lays out matters in his own mind how he shall avoid damnation, and flatters himself that he contrives well for himself, and that his schemes will not fail.[3]

How do we react to Edwards's sermon? Does it provoke a sense of fear? Does it make us angry? Are we feeling like a multitude of people who have nothing but scorn for any ideas about hell and everlasting punishment? Do we consider the wrath of God as a primitive or obscene concept? Is the very notion of hell an insult to us? If so, it is clear that the God we worship is not a holy God: Indeed He is not God at all. If we despise the justice of God, we are not Christians. We stand in a position that is every bit as precarious as the one that Edwards so graphically described. If we hate the wrath of God, it is because we hate God Himself. We may protest vehemently against these charges, but our vehemence only confirms our hostility toward God. We may say emphatically, "No, it is not God I hate; it is Edwards that I hate. God is altogether sweet to me. My God is a God of love." But a loving God who has no wrath is no God. He is an idol of our own making as much as if we carved Him out of stone.

Jonathan Edwards preached another famous sermon that can be viewed as a sequel of sorts to "Sinners in the Hands of an Angry God." He titled the sermon "Men Naturally God's Enemies." If I can presume to improve Edwards's title, I would suggest instead "God in the Hands of Angry Sinners."

If we are unconverted, one thing is absolutely certain: *We hate God.* The Bible is unambiguous about this point. We are God's enemies. We are inwardly sworn to His ultimate destruction. It is as natural for us to hate God as it is for rain to moisten the earth when it falls. Now our annoyance may turn to outrage. We heartily disavow what I have just written. We are quite willing to acknowledge that we are sinners. We are quick to admit that we do not love God as much as we ought. But who among us will admit to hating God?

Romans 5 teaches clearly: "When we were God's enemies, we were reconciled to him through the death of his Son" (Rom. 5:10). The central motif of the New Testament is the theme of reconciliation. Reconciliation is not necessary for those who love each other. God's love for us is not in doubt. The shadow of doubt hangs over us. It is our love for God that is in question. The natural human mind, what the Bible calls the "carnal mind," is at enmity with God.

We reveal our natural hostility for God by the low esteem we have for Him. We consider Him unworthy of our total devotion. We take no delight in contemplating Him. Even for the Christian, worship is often difficult and prayer a burdensome duty. Our natural tendency is to flee as far as possible from His presence. His Word rebounds from our minds like a basketball from a backboard.

By nature, our attitude toward God is not one of mere indifference. It is a posture of malice. We oppose His government and refuse His rule over us. Our natural hearts are devoid of affection for Him; they are cold, frozen to His holiness. By nature, the love of God is not in us.

As Edwards noted, it is not enough to say that the natural human mind views God as an enemy. We must be more precise. God is our *mortal* enemy. He represents the highest possible threat to our sinful desires. His repugnance to us is absolute, knowing no lesser degrees. No amount of persuasion from philosophers or theologians can induce us to love God. We despise His very existence and would do anything in our power to rid the universe of His holy presence.

If God were to expose His life to our hands, He would not be safe for a second. We would not ignore Him; we would destroy Him. This charge may seem extravagant and irresponsible until we examine once more the record of what happened when God did appear in Christ. Christ was not simply killed. He was murdered by malicious people. The crowds howled for His blood. It was not enough merely to do away with Him, but it had to be done with the accompaniment of scorn and humiliation. We know that His divine nature did not perish on the cross. It was His humanity that was put to death. Had God exposed the divine nature to execution, had He made His divine essence vulnerable to the executioner's nails, then Christ would still be dead and God would be absent from heaven. Had the sword pierced the soul of God, the ultimate revolution would have been successful, and mankind would now be king.

But, we protest, we are Christians. We are lovers of God. We have experienced reconciliation. We have been born of the Spirit and have had the love of God shed abroad in our hearts. We are no longer enemies but friends. All of these things are true for the Christian. But we must be careful, remembering that with our conversion our natural human natures were not annihilated. There remains a vestige of our fallen nature with which we must struggle every day. There still resides a corner of the soul that takes no delight in God. We see its ragged edge in our continued sin, and we can observe it in our lethargic worship. It manifests itself even in our theology.

It has been said that historically three generic types of theology compete for acceptance within the Christian church: Pelagianism, Semi-Pelagianism, and Augustinianism.

Pelagianism is not Christian. It is not merely sub-Christian but strongly anti-Christian. It is basically a theology of unbelief. That it has a stranglehold on many churches is testimony to the power of people's natural enmity toward God. To the Pelagian or liberal there is no supernatural activity. They do not believe in miracles, in Christ's deity, the Atonement, the Resurrection, the Ascension, or the Second Coming. In a word, there is no biblical Christianity to it. It is sheer paganism masquerading as piety.

What of Semi-Pelagianism? It is clearly Christian with its passionate confession of the deity of Christ and its confidence in the Atonement, the Resurrection, and the rest. Semi-Pelagianism is the majority report among evangelical Christians and probably represents the theology of the vast majority of people who read this book. But I am convinced that with all of its virtues, Semi-Pelagianism still represents a theology of compromise with our natural inclinations. It has a glaring defect in its understanding of God. Though it salutes the holiness of God and protests loudly that it believes in God's sovereignty, it still entertains delusions about our ability to incline ourselves to God, to make "decisions" to be born again. It declares that fallen people, who are at enmity with God, can be persuaded to be reconciled even before their sinful hearts are changed. It has people who are not born again seeing a kingdom Christ declared could not be seen and entering a kingdom that cannot be entered without rebirth. Evangelicals today have unconverted sinners who are dead in trespasses and sin bringing themselves to life by *choosing to be born again*. Christ made it clear that dead people cannot choose anything, that the flesh counts for nothing, and that we must be born of the Spirit before we can even see the kingdom of God, let alone enter it. The failure of modern evangelicalism is the failure to understand the holiness of God. If that one point were grasped, there would be no more talk of mortal enemies of Christ coming to Jesus by their own power.

Only Augustinianism sees grace as central to its theology. When we understand the character of God, when we grasp something of His holiness, then we begin to understand the radical character of our sin and helplessness. Helpless sinners can survive only by grace. Our strength is futile in itself; we are spiritually impotent without the assistance of a merciful God. We may dislike giving our attention to God's wrath and justice, but until we incline ourselves to these aspects of God's nature, we will never appreciate what has been wrought for us by grace. Even Edwards's sermon on sinners in God's hands was not designed to stress the flames of hell. The resounding accent falls not on the fiery pit but on the hands of the God who holds us and rescues us from it. The hands of God are gracious hands. They alone have the power to rescue us from certain destruction.

How can we love a holy God? The simplest answer I can give to this vital question is that we can't. Loving a holy God is beyond our moral power. The only kind of God we can love by our sinful nature is an unholy god, an idol made by our own hands. Unless we are born of the Spirit of God, unless God sheds His holy love in our hearts, unless He stoops in His grace to change our hearts, we will not love Him. He is the One who takes the initiative to restore our souls. Without Him we can do nothing of righteousness. Without Him we would be doomed to everlasting alienation from His holiness. We can love Him only because He first loved us. To love a holy God requires grace, grace strong enough to pierce our hardened hearts and awaken our moribund souls.

If we are in Christ, we have been awakened already. We have been raised from spiritual death unto spiritual life. But we still have "sleepers" in our eyes, and at times we walk about like zombies. We retain a certain fear of drawing near to God. We still tremble at the foot of His holy mountain.

Yet as we grow in our knowledge of Him, we gain a deeper love for His purity and sense a deeper dependence on His grace. We learn that He is altogether worthy of our adoration. The fruit of our growing love for Him is the increase of reverence for His name. We love Him now because we see His loveliness. We adore Him now because we see His majesty. We obey Him now because His Holy Spirit dwells within us.

Allowing God's Holiness to Touch Our Lives

As you reflect about what you have learned and rediscovered about God's holiness, answer these questions. Use a journal to record your responses to God's holiness, or discuss your responses with a friend.

1. How do you respond to Jonathan Edwards's sermon? Is it compassionate?
2. How does understanding God's wrath help you honor Him as a holy God?
3. In what ways do you need God to help you love Him?

TEN

❧

Looking beyond Shadows

Truth is always about something,
but reality is that about which truth is.

C. S. LEWIS

T he psalmist was stirred to feelings of awe and reverence as he contemplated the arena in which he lived. As he turned his gaze toward the sky, the realm of the heavens, he was provoked to express his deepest thoughts:

> When I consider your heavens,
>> the work of your fingers,
> the moon and the stars,
>> which you have set in place,
> what is man that you are mindful of him,
>> the son of man that you care for him?
> You made him a little lower than the heavenly beings
>> and crowned him with glory and honor. (Ps. 8:3–5)

These were not the sentiments of a professional astronomer or a primitive astrologer. They were the reflections of an ordinary person who was contemplating his small place in a vast universe. The psalmist had no concept of an expanding universe that contained billions of stars and innumerable galaxies. He had no thoughts of exploding novae or of spiral nebulae. He had never heard of Big-Bang cosmology. From his vantage point in space and time, the sky appeared to be a domed canopy whose luminaries were perhaps only a few miles high in the sky.

I wonder what David would have thought if someone suggested to him that the light from the nearest star (apart from our own sun) took four and a half years to reach planet Earth while traveling at the speed of 186,000 miles per second? It is almost impossible for us to contemplate such distances and spatial enormity, even though we live on this side of the Copernican Revolution. When we consider that our planet is twenty-five thousand miles in circumference and that light can go around the world seven and a half times in a single second, we are reduced to sheer astonishment. That astonishment is compounded almost infinitely when we think of the number of seconds in a day, not to mention the number of seconds in four and a half years. But that measurement is only to the nearest star. We have no meaningful analogies to use to contemplate the distance to the furthest star. Indeed we don't even know what star is the furthest star, because in all likelihood it has not been discovered yet.

With the meager resources the psalmist had when he gazed into the night sky of Palestine, he was overwhelmed by the weighty sense of contrast between the magnificence of the heavens and the relative obscurity and insignificance of his own life. By considering the stars, he was forced to ask the ultimate question about his own existence: "What is man that you are mindful of him?" (Ps. 8:4).

We might expect that his conclusion would have been that he was virtually nothing, an insignificant blip on the radar screen of history or a meaningless speck in a cosmic desert. But such was not his conclusion. He expressed a high view of the significance of life on this planet and of the value and dignity of humanity. He spoke of the crown of glory and honor with which the Creator touched this tiny part of creation.

How was the psalmist able to rise to such optimistic heights? Was it merely a case of delusions of grandeur? Was the psalmist armed with a knowledge that was able to bridge the enormous gap between heaven and earth? Perhaps it was because the psalmist was able to perceive something to which we have become almost completely blind. Perhaps it was because the psalmist could see past the stars and the moon to the One who set them in the heavens in the first place.

In his letter to the Romans, the apostle Paul wrote of the revelation that God makes of Himself in and through nature. He says, "For since the creation of the world God's invisible qualities—his eternal power and divine nature—have been clearly seen, being understood from what has been made, so that men are without excuse" (Rom. 1:20).

What Paul says here is startling. He acknowledges the invisibility of God. Yet he speaks of the invisible things of God as being seen. If something is seen, it is not invisible; if it is invisible, it cannot be seen. Why then does the apostle speak of seeing the invisible? Paul was not speaking nonsense or uttering riddles. What he means is this: What cannot be seen *directly* can be seen *indirectly*. In the realm of theology, what Paul is describing is called *mediate revelation*.

Mediate revelation involves a communication or unveiling that takes place through some medium. We use the term *medium* to refer to a source of communication such as newspapers, radio, and television. We receive the information we call news not by being direct eyewitnesses of the events but by reading about them in the print media, by hearing them on the radio, or by watching them on television. Television is such a powerful medium that we may *think* that we are actual eyewitnesses of the events we see on the screen. As we watch a football game in live time, we may feel that we are actually there at the scene. But, of course, we are not. We are watching transmitted images, or pictures, of the event. The game is "visible" to us only via "tele-vision," a medium of communication.

When we turn our attention to the stars, we are engaged in the use of another medium. To look at a star or the moon is not to look at the face of God. It is to look at the handiwork of God. When we gaze at "The Nightwatch" in the Rijksmuseum in Amsterdam, we are not looking at Rembrandt. We are looking at a painting that came from his hand. That painting tells us something about the man who painted it, but it certainly does not tell us everything about him.

Of course, nature in its fullness is a far greater masterpiece than anything Rembrandt ever created. Nature provides us with a much bigger picture than "The Nightwatch." And it reveals far more of its Creator than a painting ever can of its artist. Paul declares that the medium of nature makes visible the invisible power and deity of God Himself.

Paul makes it clear that everybody sees this manifestation of God's majesty. This revelation gets through to all people so that all people see it clearly. The force of Paul's assertion is that every person who has ever lived knows that there is a God and is aware of His transcendent majesty and holiness. The medium God has selected to reveal Himself universally is so clear and so potent that it leaves no one with an excuse. It is a medium far more powerful and effective for its task than a television broadcast. A Barbara Walters interview with God could not show us as much of God as nature does.

Though all people receive this knowledge of God, they will not all readily acknowledge it. After the apostle wrests all excuses from the people's hands, he declares:

> For although they knew God, they neither glorified him as
> God nor gave thanks to him, but their thinking became futile
> and their foolish hearts were darkened. Although they claimed
> to be wise, they became fools and exchanged the glory of the
> immortal God for images made to look like mortal man and
> birds and animals and reptiles. (Rom. 1:21–23)

Have you ever met Michael Jordan? How would I answer that question if it were asked of me? I could answer it in two different ways. I could say, "Yes, I've met Michael. I've seen him and talked to him." Or I could say, "No, I've never met the man." Both of these answers are true as far as they go. I have seen Michael Jordan. I've seen him on television. I have spoken to him. I have shouted at him while watching the Bulls play on television. Yet, it is also true that I have never met the man. Usually when we talk like this, we add the qualifier "in person." We understand the difference between the real person and the image of the person.

Paul is saying that the real person of God is really known through the real revelation that takes place in the real realm of nature. But the problem is that in the case of God, we distort our knowledge of Him by replacing Him with an image that we create ourselves. This is the essence of idolatry: replacing the reality with a counterfeit. We distort the truth of God and reshape our understanding of Him according to our own preferences, leaving us with a God who is anything but holy.

Again, it is important to note that Paul does not bring a universal indictment against humanity for the failure to know God. That is not our problem. It is not that we fail to know that God is and who God is; it is that we refuse to *believe* what we know to be true. Here we face a problem that is not an intellectual problem. It is a moral problem. It is the problem of dishonesty.

All idolatry is rooted in this fundamental dishonesty. Paul describes this in terms of an exchange, which is a dishonest exchange: "They exchanged the truth of God for a lie, and worshiped and served created things rather than the Creator—who is forever praised. Amen" (Rom. 1:25).

The dishonest exchange that is in view here is the substitution of the creature for the Creator, an exchange that is dishonest precisely because we know better. The late Carl Sagan spoke of the sense of awe and reverence that he felt when he contemplated the intricacies of the cosmos. But Sagan made it clear that this reverence was not for the Author of the cosmos but for the cosmos itself. Sagan's response to the stars was diametrically opposed to the psalmist's response. The psalmist was moved to worship the God who created nature and reveals Himself through nature, not to worship nature itself. This reflects the essential differences between godliness and paganism. Pagans confuse the creature and the Creator. They attribute the glory that properly belongs to God to the creature.

We remember that Paul sees human sin in people's refusal to honor God as God. This refusal is done even though people know the eternal power and deity of the Creator. This refusal to honor God as God is what I think Paul has in mind when he asserts that people refuse to believe what they know is true about God.

The striking conclusion we reach from the apostle's teaching is that God's holiness is not an obscure or arcane secret that may be discovered only by some spiritually elite group of people. Rather God's holiness is on display daily for everyone to see. Again it is not merely that it is available to be seen for those who earnestly search for it. Rather Paul's point is that God's holiness *is seen*, and it is seen clearly.

Elsewhere the apostle indicates that the knowledge of God that is given through creation is not a knowledge we warmly receive and embrace. Instead it is our nature to abhor this knowledge of God's holiness. It is characteristic of the reprobate mind not to want to retain God in our knowledge. We prefer to change the holy into something less than holy. It is this rejection of God's majesty that leaves us with minds that are darkened. It results in a massive foolishness that has disastrous consequences for our lives. Once we refuse to honor God as God, our whole view of life and the world becomes distorted.

Let's return to Psalm 8. Before the psalmist speaks of his contemplation of the stars and the moon and the heavens, he utters a poignant doxology:

> O LORD, our Lord,
>> how majestic is your name in all the earth!
> You have set your glory above the heavens. (Ps. 8:1)

The crucial point that is affirmed by the psalmist is that God's glory is *above the heavens.* The glory of God transcends all creaturely glory. Indeed what glory may be found in this world is borrowed or derived from the Creator's hand. The psalmist is obviously a regenerate man. The psalmist is pleased to honor God as God and to acknowledge the truth of the revelation given in nature. He lifts his eyes above and beyond the splendor of the heavens and rejoices in the glory that is revealed through them.

In his work *The Republic*, Plato uses an illustration that has become famous. Plato tells of men who are chained in the dark interior of a cave. They receive warmth and light from a small fire. All that the men can observe are the flickering shadows cast on the wall of the cave by the fire. This is the extent of their vision. All the reality that they know is that of the shadows. It is not until they are liberated from the confines of the darkness and emerge into the light of day that they can perceive reality as it is. In the meantime, they confuse the shadows on the wall with the real truth.

Plato's analogy was designed to illustrate the difference between what he called *knowledge* and *opinion*. Opinion rests on assumptions drawn from shadows. It fails to penetrate truth. For Plato all knowledge that rests solely on observations of this external world is not true knowledge, but a mere shadow of the truth. To get to the truth, one must get beyond the immediate realm of sense perception to the eternal realm of ultimate reality. He sought to go beyond the phenomena to the ultimate truth and reality.

Though Plato's analogy was written centuries ago, it may be a fitting commentary of the spirit of our own age. We pride ourselves in modern science's explosion of knowledge of the external world. The expansion of the scope of our knowledge has moved well beyond the limits imposed by our naked powers of perception. We probe the realm of the infinitesimal by means of the microscope and the realm of the distant by means of the telescope. Our vision of the near and of the distant now far exceeds what was reached by previous explorations.

Our view of the world around us and the world above us has been so greatly enhanced that it would seem that we have been catapulted into a majestic theater that gives daily displays of remarkable glory. Yet our view of the world is perhaps more earthbound and nearsighted than ever before. Ours is the age of myopia, an age in which we declare that the sum total of reality is the here and now. This is an unprecedented kind of secularism. In our quest for liberation from the sacred and creaturely independence, we have succeeded only in cutting ourselves off from the sacred. We live in a smaller cave than Plato envisioned, and the shadows we behold are cast not by a roaring fire but by rapidly cooling, smoldering embers.

In his *Institutes of the Christian Religion,* sixteenth-century theologian John Calvin offered another analogy, that of the blindfold. He argued that nature is a massive theater, indeed a glorious theater of divine revelation. But we walk through this theater as if we were wearing blindfolds. Calvin's point was not to deny that we actually receive knowledge from natural revelation. Rather he was speaking of the state of people who willfully refuse to turn their gaze to the obvious. We put the blindfolds on ourselves, and then we stumble along, cursing the darkness. The analogy is one designed to underscore human folly, which prefers darkness to light and creatures to the Creator.

Calvin remarks:

> But as the greater part of mankind, enslaved by error, walk
> blindfold in this glorious theater, he exclaims that it is a rare
> and singular wisdom to meditate carefully on these works of

God, which many, who seem sharp-sighted in other respects, behold without profit. It is indeed true that the brightest manifestation of divine glory finds not one genuine spectator among a hundred. Still neither his power nor his wisdom is shrouded in darkness.[1]

We are creatures who prefer life in the cave to the full light of the blazing sun. The glory of God is all around us. We cannot miss it. However, we not only fail to stop and smell the flowers, but we also fail to notice the glory of the flowers' Maker.

Indeed the featured presentation in the theater of divine majesty in which we walk daily is God's glory. The psalmist declares that the sky and all of nature sing out God's glory and majesty.

We see the inseparable link between God's holiness and His glory. His glory is the outward manifestation of His most perfect being. It is His heaviness or weightiness that is displayed. The Scripture frequently speaks of the cloud of God's glory that at times is made outwardly visible. It is the *shekinah*. This glory cloud overshadowed the disciples on the Mount of Transfiguration. It served as the escort for Jesus in His ascension into heaven and will bear Him when He returns. This glory cloud is so dazzling that it can effect blindness in those who look at it directly, as the apostle Paul did on the road to Damascus.

When God's glory erupted in its full measure in biblical times, the result was terror in all who beheld it. But this cloud of glory is not the only manifestation of God's presence in the Bible. He appeared also in various theophanies such as the burning bush, the pillar of fire, and the tongues of fire that fell at Pentecost. To a lesser degree His glory is manifest everywhere at all times. It can no more be extinguished than can the light of the sun. The sun may be obscured by cloud cover or even undergo periodic eclipses, but such phenomena do not utterly quench its light.

Calvin used the metaphor of "spectacles" or "eyeglasses" to describe our perception of God's glory. He spoke of the spectacles of faith by which believers look beyond the surface of things to feast their eyes on the glory that is plainly there.

The Bible speaks of those who have eyes to see and ears to hear. This reference is not to the ordinary power of the senses but of the ability to cut through the darkness and cacophony of sin to see and hear the truth. With regeneration, the scales fall from our eyes so that we can truly perceive what we see and truly understand what we hear (Mark 4:12). This capacity grows as we mature in our faith.

A few years ago I took up sketching and oil painting as a pastime. My amateur work will never adorn the walls of serious art galleries. I stumble along with this hobby, learning through trial and error. In my earliest instruction, I was told to look at the world around me in a different way. I was taught to pay attention to nuances of shade and shadow, to observe color and texture. Before this exercise, when I passed trees along the road, I saw only trees. Now when I look at trees, I notice the peculiar texture of the bark and the colors highlighted in the leaves. These nuances were always there. I just never noticed them before. Each of these nuances has its own medium to announce the presence of God's glory.

When we are engaged with painting and other art forms, we are interested in beauty. The very concept of beauty is profoundly difficult to define. It is elusive and controversial. The discipline of philosophy has its own subcategory of aesthetics, which seeks to determine norms for beauty. Historically there have been many competing schools of aesthetic thought. Many people have concluded that there are no rules for beauty, that it is purely a subjective matter. Others, dating back to Aristotle and beyond, have argued for objective criteria for beauty. The subjectivists find refuge in the slogan that "beauty is in the eye of the beholder." This tends to reduce beauty to personal taste or preference, such as found in the various flavors of ice cream. Here one person's beauty is another person's ugliness.

On the other hand some schools of thought have tried to find objective norms by which to judge beauty. Thinkers like Aristotle, Aquinas, and Edwards, for example, have seen beauty based in matters of proportionality, symmetry, complexity, harmony, and the like. The intricate symmetry of complex parts points to elements of beauty. Though it is admitted that the simple may be beautiful, it is more often the harmonic composition of complex parts that points to beauty. We understand the difference between the presentation of stick figures and the structure of the human figure depicted in Michelangelo's work. Likewise, we note the difference between a child playing "Twinkle, Twinkle, Little Star" with one finger and a concert pianist playing Beethoven's *Piano Concerto no. 4.*

What emerges in great art and great music is a depth of dimension that does not quickly become stale or trite. Think, for example, of the difference between Bach's "Jesu, Joy of Man's Desiring" and a current popular song or movie theme. Some popular songs endure for years, but most are short-lived. If, for example, you sat and listened to a popular song for six hours straight, chances are you would become bored with it. Yet if you were to listen intently and continuously to a Bach masterpiece, the piece tends to become more and more fascinating as you discover more intricate nuances to it.

Sometimes people think I am strange when I mention the beauty of professional football games. How could something so primal and violent be said to contain any beauty in it? What I enjoy is watching superbly conditioned athletes who have reached the apex of their sport working together to execute a single movement. Eleven men on one side of the ball each have a specific function to perform in a single play designed to advance the ball only a few feet, while another eleven men on the other side of the ball work together as a unit to prevent that progress. The execution of a play involves a kind of orchestration that requires harmony rather than dissonance. When the harmony is lost, the ball is fumbled or the play is otherwise thwarted.

In all of this, be it art or sport, is revealed a kind of beauty that has profound theological implications. The Old Testament frequently refers to the beauty of God's holiness. Even the garments God designed for Aaron and the priests were designed "for glory and for beauty" (Exod. 28:2, NASB). These references indicate a significant relationship between the holy and the beautiful. We are accustomed to thinking in terms of an inherent relationship between goodness and holiness and between truth and holiness. But truth and goodness are merely two legs of a three-legged stool. The third leg is the element of beauty.

In biblical categories, there is a triad of virtues, all of which point beyond themselves to the holiness of God. This triad is composed of the *good*, the *true*, and the *beautiful*. Let's explore each one.

The ancient philosophers such as Plato and Aristotle sought for what they called the *summum bonum*, or the "highest good." It was this quest that drove them to postulate the existence of God. In their own way, they were attesting what is basic to biblical faith, that the highest good is found in God Himself. He is the norm of norms, and He is without norm. All good finds its root in Him and in His character. He is the fountain of all that is good, and all that is good, in turn, points back to Him. It is only when God is banished from human thought that an ethic of relativism is embraced. But relativism is not so much an ethic as it is an antiethic, which forms the basis of godlessness. It was Dostoyevsky who declared that "If there is no God, then all things are permissible." He understood that without the highest good, there can be no good at all. All "goods" are measured against the ultimate standard of God's goodness.

Just as all goodness finds its definition in the ground of God's goodness, so all truth is judged according to the standard of the truth of God. He is the supreme Author of truth. All that is true not only flows from Him, but it also reflects His character. The ancient theologians understood that all truth is God's truth and that all truth "meets at the top." What is meant by this expression is that no truth is independent of God or contradicts what He declares to be true. Philosophers have offered various theories of truth. One of the most persistent is the so-called *correspondence theory of truth*. This concept defines truth as that which corresponds to reality. The problem with this naked definition is that people have different perceptions of what is true. So the argument ensues: "Truth as perceived by whom?" To transcend this difficulty, we must add to the basic definition the words "as perceived by God." With this addition, the full definition becomes "Truth is that which corresponds to reality as perceived by God." God's perception of truth is perfect. He sees all things from the perspective of eternity. He knows the structure of all reality, both big and small. What He reveals in the Bible is always consistent with His self-revelation in nature. What we learn from the study of nature must square with what we learn from the study of grace. Both spheres belong to God. God is not the author of confusion. He is incapable of speaking lies or contradictions. This is what is meant by the idea that all truth meets at the top. It is not that somehow God can reconcile real contradictions but that no real contradictions infect the clarity of His truth. God's truth is holy truth. That is, His truth expresses His own character. Insofar as He is the fountainhead of all truth, all truth points back to Him. Since all truth points to Him, all truth is sacred. The sacredness of truth is what makes the lie so diabolical in that it distorts our perception of the very character of God.

Just as truth and goodness are rooted in God's character, so is beauty. God Himself is the ground of all unity and diversity, of simplicity and complexity. His very being is internally consistent and harmonious and proportionate. In Him there are no distortions, no disorder, no ugliness. His voice admits to no noise or cacophony. The works of His hands are cosmos, not chaos. Chaos is marked by disorder and confusion; it is manifest irrationally. The beauty of God is a sane and rational beauty in that His being is one of perfect sanity and order. Insofar as the beautiful bears witness to these qualities, they bear witness to Him. Edgar Allan Poe understood that in beauty one encounters the dimension of the sublime, a dimension that is not irrational but may be transrational. That is, beauty, though it involves the mind, goes beyond the limits of mere cognition. When we are "moved" by great works of art, we are gripped by an affective sense that stirs the soul as well as the mind. To cultivate an appreciation for beauty is to set our course to follow after the sublime Author of all beauty.

Medieval theologians used the Latin phrase *ens perfectissimus* to refer to God. The phrase may be translated by the words "the most perfect being." Here the theologians used an expression that is a bit misleading. To say that something or someone is the most perfect being involves a redundancy. Real perfection does not admit to degrees. Something that is truly perfect in every

respect cannot become more perfect or most perfect. We speak like this because we are accustomed to dealing with things that are imperfect. Imperfect
things can be improved, but the perfect cannot. It should suffice us to say of
God simply that He is perfect. Why then did the theologians use the superlative degree to speak of God's perfection? The answer must be found in their
desire to underscore the reality of God's perfection so clearly that they would
eliminate any possibility of suggesting the slightest lack of perfection in God's
character. It was a legitimate use of hyperbole to speak of most perfect.

God's perfection applies to all of His attributes. His power is perfect; it has
no weaknesses or any possibility of weakness. His knowledge is not only omniscient but reflects perfect omniscience. There is nothing that God does not
know or that He could possibly learn. Some modern theologians have tried to
declare that God is omniscient but that His omniscience is a limited omniscience.
They assert that God knows everything He can possibly know, but He does not
and cannot know certain things, especially the future decisions of free agents.
But a limited omniscience is simply not omniscience. And it is not perfect.
This view of limited omniscience robs God of His holy omniscience, which
is a perfect omniscience. God's love, His wrath, His mercy—all that He is—is
perfect. Not only is He perfect, but He is eternally and immutably so. There
never was a time when God was less than perfect, and there is no possibility that
in the future He may slip into any kind of imperfection. What has been with
God will be so forever. His perfection is immutable. It cannot change.

Shadows in a cave are given to change. They dance and flicker with ever-
changing shape and brightness. To contemplate the truly holy and to go beyond
the surface of creaturely things, we need to get out of our self-made cave and
walk in the glorious light of God's holiness.

Allowing God's Holiness to Touch Our Lives

As you reflect about what you have learned and rediscovered about God's
holiness, answer these questions. Use a journal to record your responses to
God's holiness, or discuss your responses with a friend.

1. Describe a recent experience in which God revealed Himself to you
   through nature.
2. In what ways do we worship creation rather than the Creator?
3. How do things that are good, true, and beautiful reflect God's
   holiness? How does this truth help shape your priorities?
4. How will you worship God for His holiness?

Holy Space and Holy Time

Where, except in the present,
can the Eternal be met?

C. S. LEWIS

No Exit. This famous play written by the French existentialist philosopher Jean Paul Sartre depicts his view that hell is other people, a realm from which there is no exit. The same title may be used to describe our contemporary culture's view of our world. We are a generation of people who feel trapped in the here and now. We sense no access to the heavenly or to the realm of the transcendent. There seems to be an unbridgeable chasm that cuts us off from the arena of the holy. We are doomed, it seems, to live out our days chained to the profane.

As I write these words, a spacecraft is hurtling toward outer space. The astronauts on board are traveling to make repairs and enhancements for the Hubble telescope, which is transmitting to earth unprecedented views of the outer reaches of the universe. As a result, astronomers scramble for new adjustments in their paradigms of cosmology. A myriad of new data impose their presence on us, screaming for explanation. Few scientists still hold to the antiquated view of a steady-state universe, a theory that is being pushed aside by evidence that our universe is ever expanding.

The eighteenth century saw the appearance of a new religion called Deism, which represented a compromise between classical Christian theism and atheistic naturalism. The favorite metaphor of Deism was that of the Divine Clockmaker. God was viewed as the First Cause, who created the world just as a clockmaker designs and constructs a clock. Deists envisioned that just as the clockmaker fits together the springs and gears and then winds up the clock so that it can run on its own inherent power, so God, the great Designer and Maker of the universe, created the world and then stepped back to let the world run by its own mechanical laws. They believe that God made the world a closed system and that He remains eternally aloof from its operation.

The Deists see no daily providence, no sacred intrusions from above, and no real possibility of meaningful communication from below.

Deism did not last long as a viable religion. It was not satisfying to either the classical theist or the hard-boiled naturalist. So it quickly passed from the scene. Its abiding significance, however, may be seen in at least two important ways. The first is that, though Deism represented a tiny blip on the radar scope of history, the blip occurred at precisely the time when the United States of America was in its formative stages. Deism was in vogue during the drafting of the Declaration of Independence and the Constitution, and to some degree even traditional Christians at that time accepted Deism's view of natural law.

The second point of Deism's impact was that it favored a view of a closed mechanistic universe that left no room for divine intrusion. Although the religion of Deism is long since past, its view of the world remains current. Many people in our culture think of the world as one that operates by fixed natural laws that function in a manner similar to a winding clock. All causes for all events are rooted strictly in nature, and God is left with nothing to do but to abide as a remote and distant spectator of human events. In our society, religion is limited to a kind of personal therapy for people who have difficulty dealing with the difficulties of life. Ours is a profane existence, with no sense of the presence of the holy.

But people have always looked for a window or door to the transcendent. We seek a threshold that will lead us over the border from the profane to the sacred. It is a quest for sacred space, for ground that is holy ground. Mircea Eliade, one of the leading historians of religion of the twentieth century, has written of this human quest in his book *The Sacred and the Profane*. Eliade insists that we have never been able to create an existence of pure and utter profanity. He says, "To whatever degree he may have desacralized the world, the man who has made his choice in favor of a profane life never succeeds in completely doing away with religious behavior."[1] Humanity seems to be incurably *homo religiosis*. Even within the confines of a closed universe, people seek some place that will serve as a point of access to the transcendent. We feel an aching void that screams to be filled by the holy. We long for holy space.

In Moses' encounter with God in the wilderness, he experienced a threshold to holy space:

> Now Moses was tending the flock of Jethro his father-in-law, the
> priest of Midian, and he led the flock to the far side of the desert
> and came to Horeb, the mountain of God. There the angel of
> the LORD appeared to him in flames of fire from within a bush.
> Moses saw that though the bush was on fire it did not burn up.

So Moses thought, "I will go over and see this strange sight—why the bush does not burn up."

When the LORD saw that he had gone over to look, God called to him from within the bush, "Moses! Moses!"

And Moses said, "Here I am."

"Do not come any closer," God said. "Take off your sandals, for the place where you are standing is holy ground." Then he said, "I am the God of your father, the God of Abraham, the God of Isaac and the God of Jacob." At this, Moses hid his face, because he was afraid to look at God. (Exod. 3:1–6)

In this experience of theophany, God commanded Moses to keep himself a safe distance from God's immediate presence. Moses was forbidden to come too close. Then God commanded him to remove his sandals. We have seen in our discussion of the prophet Isaiah's vision that there is a link between the covering of the seraphim's feet and the uncovering of Moses' feet in this event. In both cases the feet point to the condition of creatureliness. In any case Moses was told to remove his sandals because he was standing on holy ground. Moses had entered into holy space. At some point in his walk toward the burning bush, he had crossed a border marking the line between the sacred and the profane. Being a fallen creature of this world, Moses himself was profane. Yet here he dared to walk on earth that was now holy.

The holy space Moses occupied was made holy by God's presence. The composition of the earth at this spot was no different from the earth on the rest of the desert floor. The sacred character of this spot was not intrinsic but extrinsic. That is, it was *made* sacred by a super-added presence. The event that occurred there loaned an extraordinary dimension to the ordinary. The common space had become uncommon by virtue of God's appearance at that spot.

What Moses experienced at the burning bush was not only a theophany but also a hierophany. Just as the word *theophany* refers to a visible manifestation of God, the term *hierophany* refers to an outward manifestation of the holy. Eliade comments, "Every sacred space implies a hierophany, an irruption of the sacred that results in detaching a territory from the surrounding cosmic milieu and making it qualitatively different."[2]

We see a second biblical example of holy space in the account of Jacob's experience at Bethel. In commenting on this Old Testament story, the historian Eliade notes:

When Jacob in his dream at Haran saw a ladder reaching to heaven, with angels ascending and descending on it, and heard the LORD speaking from above it, saying: "I am the Lord God of Abraham," he awoke and was afraid and cried out: "How dreadful is this place: this is none other but the house of God, and this is the gate of heaven." And he took the stone that had been his pillow, and set it up as a monument, and poured oil on the top of it. He called the place Beth-el, that is, house of God (Genesis 28:12–19). The symbolism implicit in the expression "gate of heaven" is rich and complex; the theophany that occurs in a place consecrates it by the very fact that it makes it open above—that is, in communication with heaven, the paradoxical point of passage from one mode of being to another.[3]

Several significant images are connected in the interplay of this event. The first is the image of the ladder with the ascending and descending angels. Again we see that the ladder serves as a connecting link between heaven and earth, the sacred and the profane. The ladder describes a way out of the seemingly closed universe. Second, this holy space receives a new name, *Beth-el*, precisely because it is deemed not only the "house of God" but also, perhaps even more important, a virtual gateway. The house does not merely have a portal, it *is* a portal, a door that provides access to heaven.

The third significant dimension of imagery (and I choose the word *significant* for its literal value of that which is "sign bearing") is the image of the stone. Originally the stone was a common piece of rock used for a common purpose in antiquity, namely to serve as a pillow for Jacob's head as he slept during the night. After the hierophany, the stone is assigned a different purpose. It is transformed from its common purpose to an uncommon purpose. It is anointed with oil in a simple rite of consecration so that it may become a sacred mark for sacred space. It marks what Eliade calls a place of passage between heaven and earth.

Sacred space in biblical times is frequently marked as a place of passage. We see this in the account of Noah and his family as they survive the Deluge:

By the twenty-seventh day of the second month the earth was completely dry.

Then God said to Noah, "Come out of the ark, you and your wife and your sons and their wives. Bring out every kind of

living creature that is with you—the birds, the animals, and
all the creatures that move along the ground—so they can
multiply on the earth and be fruitful and increase in number
upon it."

So Noah came out, together with his sons and his wife and his
sons' wives. All the animals and all the creatures that move along
the ground and all the birds—everything that moves on the
earth—came out of the ark, one kind after another.

Then Noah built an altar to the LORD and, taking some of all the
clean animals and clean birds, he sacrificed burnt offerings on it.
(Gen. 8:14–20)

As soon as the waters receded and Noah and his family were able to leave
the ark, they built an altar. The immediate purpose for the altar was to provide
a platform for making an offering to God. But that was not the only function
of the altar. The altar also served to mark the spot of a new beginning, to
delineate the place where the passage from destruction to redemption had
taken place.

We see similar episodes sprinkled throughout the Old Testament:

The LORD appeared to Abram and said, "To your offspring I will
give this land." So he built an altar there to the LORD, who had
appeared to him.

From there he went on toward the hills east of Bethel and
pitched his tent, with Bethel on the west and Ai on the east.
There he built an altar to the LORD and called on the name of the
LORD. (Gen. 12:7, 8)

From there he went up to Beersheba. That night the LORD
appeared to him and said, "I am the God of your father
Abraham. Do not be afraid, for I am with you; I will bless you
and will increase the number of your descendants for the sake of
my servant Abraham."

Isaac built an altar there and called on the name of the LORD.
There he pitched his tent, and there his servants dug a well.
(Gen. 26:23–25)

When Moses went and told the people all the LORD's words and
laws, they responded with one voice, "Everything the LORD has

said we will do." Moses then wrote down everything the LORD had said.

He got up early the next morning and built an altar at the foot of the mountain and set up twelve stone pillars representing the twelve tribes of Israel. (Exod. 24:3, 4)

These passages illustrate instances in which an altar marks sacred space, a crucial passage. Each passage demonstrates a bridge from the merely profane to the holy, either through God's appearance to people or through significant decisions that set the people apart as holy.

Our contact with the holy is not merely an encounter with a different dimension of reality; it is the meeting with Absolute Reality. Christianity is not about involvement with religious experience as a tangent. It involves a meeting with a holy God, who forms the center, or core, of human existence. The Christian faith is theocentric. God is not at the edge of Christians' lives but at the very center. God defines our entire life and worldview.

In our contemporary experience, we experience holy space in church sanctuaries. The biblical word *church* refers to people, not buildings. Yet when people gather for worship, they need a physical place of meeting. Because the church building is the place designed for worship, we have come to abbreviate the term *church building* as simply *church*. In this sense, churches are designed and built to serve as a kind of sacred space reserved for a place of encounter with the holy.

Church architecture varies. Every church building communicates some kind of nonverbal message. In the past, the Gothic cathedral was designed to focus attention on God's transcendence. The use of high ceilings, vaulted space, towers, and spires all served to communicate that in this building, people met with the holy. While some contemporary church buildings still use spires and vaulted ceilings to suggest God's awesome holiness, other church buildings have been designed to create a fellowship facility. These churches can look more like town meeting halls or even theaters. In some of these churches, the sanctuary becomes a stage, and the congregation becomes an audience. The trend may be seen as a profanation of sacred space to remove any discomfort suggested by the presence and the terror of our holy God. In these settings people are comfortable with other people as they enjoy fellowship with one another.

What is often lost in these functional church designs is the profound sense of *threshold*. A threshold is a place of transition. It signals a change from one realm to another. A friend recently told me of a threshold experience she and her family had. While staying with a relative in St. Louis, my friend, her husband, and two children visited the St. Louis cathedral. As the family walked from the parking lot to the front of the cathedral, they joked and chatted about the warm weather, the emerging daffodils, and other ordinary things. Once they stepped out of the sunlight into the cathedral, the talking abruptly stopped. They were stunned into silence by the magnificent mosaic work that arched high above them in the cathedral's foyer. My friend was especially intrigued by the behavior of her daughter, who had never before been in a cathedral. The teenager started to tiptoe around, as if the sound of her footsteps or the mere touch of her shoes on the floor would disturb something. As the mother and daughter walked into the sanctuary, where 43 million mosaic tiles in over eight thousand shades of color depicted stories from the Bible and from the life of St. Louis, the daughter emitted groans of awe as she stood for ten minutes looking up at the arched ceiling. She then sat in one of the pews, slowly pivoting her head to take in the walls around her. All the while, this normally talkative teenager said nothing. She was overcome by the beauty, the stillness, the holy space. Wanting to explore the transepts and chapels that lined the front of the cathedral, the daughter left the pew and set out to get a closer look. But after having gone only a few steps, she returned to the pew to ask her mother, "Is it all right for me to walk over there?" The mother explained where it was acceptable for her to walk and what places were off-limits.

As my friend watched her daughter explore the rest of the cathedral, the mother realized that without having been told, this teenager had sensed that she was in a holy space. She had crossed a threshold. Also, without having discussed it, this teenager sensed that she, in her humanity, was profane. The sound of her voice, the sound of her footsteps, the touch of her shoes on the floor was somehow offensive to the holiness revealed in this place. She was on holy ground.

It can be argued that such threshold thinking obscures the biblical truth that God is omnipresent and that all of creation is sacred as the theater of God's operations. But the Bible is much more positive about the idea of space. The consecration of sacred space does not end with the close of the Old Testament. It is rooted and grounded in the act of creation itself, and something profoundly important to the human spirit is lost when it is neglected.

Each of our lives is marked by sacred sites that we cherish in our memories. I have an uncanny sense of respect for the room in which I was converted to Christ. I am well aware that the room holds no special power and that it was not the room that converted me. Yet it was *the place* where I first met Christ. This sacred space will always remain as a special place in my life.

In 1996, I led a tour of the sites that were significant to the life of Martin Luther. I visited the Wittenburg church on whose door Luther had tacked his Ninety-five Theses. I was in Erfurt, where he was ordained, and in the Wartburg Castle, where he translated the Bible. Christian history was made in these places. They have a certain sacred significance for me. I had similar feelings when I visited Calvin's church in Geneva and Knox's church in Scotland. Yet these all pale in significance when compared with a journey to the Holy Land. There I felt the place was almost haunted as we stood on the Mount of Olives or walked on the Via Dolorosa. Pilgrims from all over the world have a common sense of the extraordinary when they enter places made sacred by the visitation of God Incarnate. These sites are holy because they were touched by His presence.

God's holiness touches not only space but also time. The Greek language of the New Testament has two different words that can be translated *time*. The first is *chronos*, which usually refers to the ordinary moment-by-moment passing of time. Words like *chronicle, chronology,* and *chronometer* all are derived from this Greek word. The second Greek word for time is *kairos*. Kairos refers to special moments that have particular significance. We lack a precise word to translate it into English. The closest we come is the word *historic*. We recognize that all historic events are also historical events, but not all historical events are historic ones. Any event that takes place in history is *historical*. Yet we reserve the term *historic* for events of peculiar importance. Historic events are pivotal moments that shape history from that point on.

In biblical history, kairotic events take place within the context of chronos. Christianity is not a religion that is based simply on vertical events that are wrested out of the context of history. The biblical faith is rooted and grounded within the plane of real history. Though the Bible reveals a special kind of history the scholars call *redemptive* history, it is nevertheless committed to the idea that the redemption that is revealed is revealed in redemptive *history*.

Kairotic events include such crucial moments as the Creation, the Fall, the Exodus, the Captivity, the Incarnation, the Cross, the Resurrection, the Ascension, and Pentecost. These events are watershed moments in God's work in history. They are filled with redemptive significance.

Such kairotic events are often marked in the Bible with the elements of sacred time. These times indicate extraordinary moments of interruptions or intrusions into this world by the holy. In our culture we have the custom of marking certain days with the designation *holiday*, which is an abbreviation for the phrase "holy day." Not every holiday celebrated in our country carries religious connotations with it. Most holidays signify little interest in the holiness of God. Yet because they are deemed particularly important as focal points of remembrance, they are "set apart" from the common or ordinary days of the calendar year.

We are familiar with cultural "rites of passage" that mark off transitional moments in our own lives. These rites are not always linked to religious occasions. In fact, some of the rites may be profane or linked to mythology. But the rites are deemed important precisely because they mark a threshold or moment of transition from one stage or status to another. The popular ballad "Graduation Day" glorified experiences of New Year's Eve, football victories, and the like as being "moments to remember." We mark such times of passage with celebrations, feasts, greeting cards, and other cultural symbols.

The Christian faith includes a significant dimension of sacred time. Sacred time, however, is rooted in real history, not mythology. The first account of sacred time is accomplished by God Himself in His work of creation:

> Thus the heavens and the earth were completed in all their vast array.
>
> By the seventh day God had finished the work he had been doing; so on the seventh day he rested from all his work. And God blessed the seventh day and made it holy, because on it he rested from all the work of creating that he had done. (Gen. 2:1–3)

God set apart the seventh day as sacred time. When God handed down the Ten Commandments at Mount Sinai, He again announced this seventh day, the Sabbath, as holy, a sacred time that would be integral to the life and faith of Israel. In Christian history the sacred time of the Sabbath has three distinct orientations. The first is the commemoration of God's work of creation. The second is the celebration of God's work of redemption. The third is the celebration of the future promise of the consummation of redemption when we enter our Sabbath rest in heaven. Thus the whole scope of redemptive history, from start to finish, is made sacred in the observance of the Sabbath.

Even profane people try to break out of the monotony of the daily rhythm of time. They seek respite from the weariness of labor. They may even say, "Thank God, it's Friday." The weekend is "set apart" for breaks in the rhythm of labor. People seek the special time of the party or the happy hour. They celebrate their own special days such as birthdays or wedding anniversaries. They seek relief from the here and now. But these celebrations are markedly different from the sacred time Christians celebrate. Eliade remarks at length about this:

For religious man, on the contrary, profane temporal duration can be periodically arrested; for certain rituals have the power to interrupt it by periods of a sacred time that is nonhistorical (in the sense that it does not belong to the historical present). Just as a church constitutes a break in plane in the profane space of a modern city, the service celebrated inside it marks a break in profane temporal duration. It is no longer today's historical time that is present—but the time in which the historical existence of Jesus Christ occurred, the time sanctified by his preaching, by his passion, death, and resurrection.[4]

Each Sabbath day, believers observe sacred time in the context of worship. It is the keeping holy of the Sabbath day that marks the regular sacred time for the Christian. The worship service is a marking of a special liturgical time. Because of the reality of the Incarnation, history itself becomes sacred for the Christian. We mark our calendars with reference to time that is B.C. or A.D. We have a theology of history because we realize that there is a holy purpose to history, even our salvation.

In the Old Testament the chief moment of sacred time is that which marked the remembrance of the Exodus from Egypt and the Passover. God instituted an annual feast to celebrate this act of redemption:

> This is a day you are to commemorate; for the generations to come you shall celebrate it as a festival to the LORD—a lasting ordinance. For seven days you are to eat bread made without yeast. On the first day remove the yeast from your houses, for whoever eats anything with yeast in it from the first day through the seventh must be cut off from Israel. On the first day hold a sacred assembly, and another one on the seventh day. Do no work at all on these days, except to prepare food for everyone to eat—that is all you may do.
>
> Celebrate the Feast of Unleavened Bread, because it was on this very day that I brought your divisions out of Egypt. Celebrate this day as a lasting ordinance for the generations to come. (Exod. 12:14–17)

Similarly, the New Testament sees the replacing of the Passover celebration by the commemoration of the Lord's Supper. The sacrament of the Lord's Supper was first instituted by Christ in the context of the celebration of the Passover. During the Passover meal, Jesus changed the significance of the liturgy as part of the institution of the New Covenant, wherein the elements that were formerly used to recall the Exodus now are used to express the supreme Exodus that would be accomplished by His death on the cross:

> While they were eating, Jesus took bread, gave thanks and broke it, and gave it to his disciples, saying, "Take and eat; this is my body."

> Then he took the cup, gave thanks and offered it to them, saying, "Drink from it, all of you. This is my blood of the covenant, which is poured out for many for the forgiveness of sins. I tell you, I will not drink of this fruit of the vine from now on until that day when I drink it anew with you in my Father's kingdom." (Matt. 26:26–29)

The celebration of the Lord's Supper involves sacred time in three distinct ways. First, it looks to the past, instructing believers to remember and to show forth Christ's death by this observance. Second, it focuses on the present moment of celebration, in which Christ meets with His people to nurture them and strengthen them in their sanctification. Third, it looks to the future, to the certain hope of their reunion with Christ in heaven, where they will participate in the banquet feast of the Lamb and His bride.

In sacred space and sacred time Christians find the presence of the holy. The bars that seek to shut out the transcendent are shattered, and the present time becomes defined by the intrusion of the holy. When we erect barriers to these intrusions, dikes to keep them from flooding our souls, we exchange the holy for the profane and rob both God of His glory and ourselves of His grace.

Soli Deo gloria.

Allowing God's Holiness to Touch Our Lives

As you reflect about what you have learned and rediscovered about God's holiness, answer these questions. Use a journal to record your responses to God's holiness, or discuss your responses with a friend.

1. Where have you experienced a sense of threshold, of sacred space?
2. In what ways have you looked for a doorway to holy space? Do you go to a specific place—in your home, in your church, in nature—to feel closer to God?
3. What holy times can you pinpoint in your life?
4. How can you cultivate the sense of God's presence and holiness in your life?

Glory to the Holy One

R. C. Sproul

Stuart Sacks
1991

* if only 2 Timps tune to A & D; play notes in parenthesis

Ho - ly, ho - ly, ho - ly, cried the ser - aph throng;

Glo - ry to the Ho - ly One, Is the an - gel's song.

Interlude

song. 3. With song.

(Bb, Eb, F)**

allargando   5. Come,   an - gel quick and

meno mosso

mf — *ff*

** if only 2 timps, tune to Bb, Eb; play notes in parenthesis

Notes

CHAPTER 3—THE FEARFUL MYSTERY

1. Rudolf Otto, *The Idea of the Holy* (Oxford: Oxford University Press, 1950), 12–13.

CHAPTER 5—THE INSANITY OF LUTHER

1. Martin Luther, *The Bondage of the Will*, trans. J. I. Packer and O. R. Johnson (Old Tappan, N.J.: Revell, 1970), 63.
2. Roland Bainton, *Here I Stand* (Nashville: Abingdon, 1950), 15.
3. Ibid., 30.
4. Ibid., 64.
5. Ibid., 139.
6. Ewald M. Plass, ed., *What Luther Says* (St. Louis: Concordia, 1959), 1107–8.
7. Bainton, *Here I Stand*, 144.
8. Ibid.
9. Ibid., 34.
10. Ibid., 41.
11. Ibid., 42.
12. Ibid., 43.
13. Ibid., 50.

CHAPTER 9—GOD IN THE HANDS OF ANGRY SINNERS

1. *The Works of Jonathan Edwards, vol. II* (Carlisle, Penn.: Banner of Truth, 1974), 10.
2. Ibid., 9.
3. Ibid., 8.

CHAPTER 10—LOOKING BEYOND SHADOWS

1. John Calvin, *The Institutes of the Christian Religion, vol. I*, trans. Henry Beveridge (Grand Rapids: Eerdmans, 1964), 57.

CHAPTER 11—HOLY SPACE AND HOLY TIME

1. Mircea Eliade, *The Sacred and the Profane* (New York: Harper & Row, 1961), 23.
2. Ibid., 26.
3. Ibid.
4. Ibid., 72

CHOSEN BY GOD

R. C. SPROUL

Contents

One

The Struggle

Baseball. Hot dogs. Apple pie. Chevrolet. These are all things American. To complete the mix we must add the great American motto: "We will not discuss religion or politics."

Mottoes are made to be broken. Perhaps no American rule is broken more frequently than the one about not discussing religion or politics. We embark on such discussions repeatedly. And when the topic turns to religion, it often gravitates to the issue of predestination. Sadly, that often means the end of discussion and the beginning of argument, yielding more heat than light.

Arguing about predestination is virtually irresistible. (Pardon the pun.) The topic is so juicy. It provides an opportunity to spar about all things philosophical. When the issue flares up, we suddenly become super-patriotic, guarding the tree of human liberty with more zeal and tenacity than Patrick Henry ever dreamed of. The specter of an all-powerful God making choices for us, and perhaps even against us, makes us scream, "Give me free will or give me death!"

The very word *predestination* has an ominous ring to it. It is linked to the despairing notion of fatalism and somehow suggests that within its pale we are reduced to meaningless puppets. The word conjures up visions of a diabolical deity who plays capricious games with our lives. We seem to be subjected to the whims of horrible decrees that were fixed in concrete long before we were born. Better that our lives were fixed by the stars, for then at least we could find clues to our destiny in the daily horoscopes.

Add to the horror of the word *predestination* the public image of its most famous teacher, John Calvin, and we shudder all the more. We see Calvin portrayed as a stern and grim-faced tyrant, a sixteenth-century Ichabod Crane who found fiendish delight in the burning of recalcitrant heretics. It is enough to cause us to retreat from the discussion altogether and reaffirm our commitment never to discuss religion and politics.

With a topic people find so unpleasant, it is a wonder that we ever discuss it at all. Why do we speak of it? Because we enjoy unpleasantness? Not at all.

We discuss it because we cannot avoid it. It is a doctrine plainly set forth in the Bible. We talk about predestination because the Bible talks about predestination. If we desire to build our theology on the Bible, we run head on into this concept. We soon discover that John Calvin did not invent it.

Virtually all Christian churches have some formal doctrine of predestination. To be sure, the doctrine of predestination found in the Roman Catholic Church is different from that in the Presbyterian Church. The Lutherans have a different view of the matter from the Episcopalians.

The fact that such variant views of predestination abound only underscores the fact that if we are biblical in our thinking we must have some doctrine of predestination. We cannot ignore such well-known passages as:

> Just as He chose us in Him before the foundation of the world,
> that we should be holy and without blame before Him in love,
> having *predestined* us to adoption as sons by Jesus Christ to Himself,
> according to the good pleasure of His will . . . (Eph. 1:4, 5)

> In whom also we have obtained an inheritance, being *predestined*
> according to the purpose of Him who works all things according
> to the counsel of His will . . . (Eph. 1:11)

> For whom He foreknew, He also *predestined* to be conformed
> to the image of His Son, that He might be the firstborn among
> many brethren. (Rom. 8:29, italics added)

If we are to be biblical, then, the issue is not whether we should have a doctrine of predestination or not, but what kind we should embrace. If the Bible is the Word of God, not mere human speculation, and if God Himself declares that there is such a thing as predestination, then it follows irresistibly that we must embrace some doctrine of predestination.

If we are to follow this line of thinking, then, of course, we must go one step further. It is not enough to have just any view of predestination. It is our duty to seek the correct view of predestination, lest we be guilty of distorting or ignoring the Word of God. Here is where the real struggle begins, the struggle to sort out accurately all that the Bible teaches about this matter.

My struggle with predestination began early in my Christian life. I knew a professor of philosophy in college who was a convinced Calvinist. He set forth the so-called "Reformed" view of predestination. I did not like it. I did not like it at all. I fought against it tooth and nail all the way through college.

I graduated from college unpersuaded of the Reformed or Calvinistic view of predestination only to go to a seminary that included on its staff the king of the Calvinists, John H. Gerstner. Gerstner is to predestination what Einstein is to physics or what Arnold Palmer is to golf. I would rather have challenged Einstein on relativity or entered into match play with Palmer than to take on Gerstner. But . . . fools rush in where angels fear to tread.

I challenged Gerstner in the classroom time after time, making a total pest of myself. I resisted for well over a year. My final surrender came in stages. Painful stages. It started when I began work as a student pastor in a church. I wrote a note to myself that I kept on my desk in a place where I could always see it.

> YOU ARE REQUIRED TO BELIEVE, TO PREACH,
> AND TO TEACH WHAT THE BIBLE SAYS IS TRUE,
> NOT WHAT YOU WANT THE BIBLE TO SAY IS TRUE.

The note haunted me. My final crisis came in my senior year. I had a three-credit course in the study of Jonathan Edwards. We spent the semester studying Edwards's most famous book, *The Freedom of the Will*, under Gerstner's tutelage. At the same time I had a Greek exegesis course in the book of Romans. I was the only student in that course, one on one with the New Testament professor. There was nowhere I could hide.

The combination was too much for me. Gerstner, Edwards, the New Testament professor, and above all the apostle Paul, were too formidable a team for me to withstand. The ninth chapter of Romans was the clincher. I simply could find no way to avoid the apostle's teaching in that chapter. Reluctantly, I sighed and surrendered, but with my head, not my heart. "Okay, I believe this stuff, but I don't have to like it!"

I soon discovered that God has created us so that the heart is supposed to follow the head. I could not, with impunity, love something with my head that I hated in my heart. Once I began to see the cogency of the doctrine and its broader implications, my eyes were opened to the graciousness of grace and to the grand comfort of God's sovereignty. I began to like the doctrine little by little, until it burst upon my soul that the doctrine revealed the depth and the riches of the mercy of God.

I no longer feared the demons of fatalism or the ugly thought that I was being reduced to a puppet. Now I rejoiced in a gracious Savior who alone was immortal, invisible, the only wise God.

They say there is nothing more obnoxious than a converted drunk. Try a converted Arminian. Converted Arminians tend to become flaming Calvinists, zealots for the cause of predestination. You are reading the work of such a convert.

My struggle has taught me a few things along the way. I have learned, for example, that not all Christians are as zealous about predestination as I am. There are better men than I who do not share my conclusions. I have learned that many misunderstand predestination. I have also learned the pain of being wrong.

When I teach the doctrine of predestination, I am often frustrated by those who obstinately refuse to submit to it. I want to scream, "Don't you realize you are resisting the Word of God?" In these cases I am guilty of at least one of two possible sins. If my understanding of predestination is correct, then at best I am being impatient with people who are merely struggling as I once did, and at worst I am being arrogant and patronizing toward those who disagree with me.

If my understanding of predestination is not correct, then my sin is compounded, since I would be slandering the saints who by opposing my view are fighting for the angels. So the stakes are high for me in this matter.

The struggle about predestination is all the more confusing because the greatest minds in the history of the church have disagreed about it. Scholars and Christian leaders, past and present, have taken different stands. A brief glance at church history reveals that the debate over predestination is not between liberals and conservatives or between believers and unbelievers. It is a debate among believers, among godly and earnest Christians.

It may be helpful to see how the great teachers of the past line up on the question.

"Reformed" View	*Opposing Views*
St. Augustine	Pelagius
St. Thomas Aquinas	Arminius
Martin Luther	Philip Melanchthon
John Calvin	John Wesley
Jonathan Edwards	Charles Finney

It must look like I am trying to stack the deck. Those thinkers who are most widely regarded as the titans of classical Christian scholarship fall heavily on the Reformed side. I am persuaded, however, that this is a fact of history that dare not be ignored. To be sure, it is possible that Augustine, Aquinas, Luther, Calvin, and Edwards could all be wrong on this matter. These men certainly disagree with each other on other points of doctrine. They are neither individually nor collectively infallible.

We cannot determine truth by counting noses. The great thinkers of the past can be wrong. But it is important for us to see that the Reformed doctrine of predestination was not invented by John Calvin. There is nothing in Calvin's view of predestination that was not earlier propounded by Luther and Augustine before him. Later, Lutheranism did not follow Luther on this matter but Melanchthon, who altered his views after Luther's death. It is also noteworthy that in his famous treatise on theology, *The Institutes of the Christian Religion*, John Calvin wrote sparingly on the subject. Luther wrote more about predestination than did Calvin.

The history lesson aside, we must take seriously the fact that such learned men agreed on this difficult subject. Again, that they agreed does not prove the case for predestination. They could have been wrong. But it gets our attention. We cannot dismiss the Reformed view as a peculiarly Presbyterian notion. I know that during my great struggle with predestination I was deeply troubled by the unified voices of the titans of classical Christian scholarship on this point. Again, they are not infallible, but they deserve our respect and an honest hearing.

Among contemporary Christian leaders we find a more balanced list of agreement and disagreement. (Keep in mind that we are speaking here in general terms and that there are significant points of difference among those on each side.)

"Reformed" View	Opposing Views
Francis Schaeffer	C. S. Lewis
Cornelius Van Til	Norman Geisler
Roger Nicole	John Warwick Montgomery
James Boice	Clark Pinnock
Philip Hughes	Billy Graham

I don't know where Bill Bright, Chuck Swindoll, Pat Robertson, and a lot of other leaders stand on this point. Jimmy Swaggart has made it clear that he considers the Reformed view a demonic heresy. His attacks on the doctrine have been less than sober. They do not reflect the care and earnestness of the men listed above in the "opposing" column. They are all great leaders whose views are worthy of our close attention.

My hope is that we will all continue to struggle. We must never assume that we have arrived. Yet there is no virtue in sheer skepticism. We look with a jaundiced eye at those who are always learning but never coming to a knowledge of the truth. God is delighted with men and women of conviction. Of course He is concerned that our convictions be according to truth. Struggle with me then as we embark upon the difficult but, I hope, profitable journey examining the doctrine of predestination.

TWO

⟨⟨⟩⟩

Predestination and the Sovereignty of God

A s we struggle through the doctrine of predestination, we must start with a clear understanding of what the word means. Here we encounter difficulties immediately. Our definition is often colored by our doctrine. We might hope that if we turn to a neutral source for our definition—a source like Webster's dictionary—we will escape such prejudice. No such luck. (Or should I say, no such providence.) Look at these entries in *Webster's New Collegiate Dictionary*.

> predestinate: *destined, fated, or determined beforehand; to foreordain to an earthly or eternal lot or destiny by divine decree.*

> predestination: *the doctrine that God in consequence of his foreknowledge of all events infallibly guides those who are destined for salvation.*

> predestine: *to destine, decree, determine, appoint, or settle beforehand.*

I am not sure how much we can learn from these dictionary definitions other than that Noah Webster must have been a Lutheran. What we can glean, however, is that predestination has something to do with the relationship of our ultimate destination and that something is done about that destination by somebody before we arrive there. The *pre* of predestination refers to time. Webster speaks of "beforehand." Destiny refers to the place we are going, as we see in the normal use of the word *destination*.

When I call my travel agent to book a flight, the question is soon raised: "What is your destination?" Sometimes the question is put more simply: "Where are you going?" Our destination is the place where we are going. In theology it refers to one of two places; either we are going to heaven or we are going to hell. In either case, we cannot cancel the trip. God gives us but two final options. One or the other is our final destination. Even Roman Catholicism, which has another place beyond the grave, purgatory, views that as an intermediate stop along the way. Their travelers ride the local while Protestants prefer the express route.

What predestination means, in its most elementary form, is that our final destination, heaven or hell, is decided by God not only before we get there, but before we are even born. It teaches that our ultimate destiny is in the hands of God. Another way of saying it is this: From all eternity, before we ever live, God decided to save some members of the human race and to let the rest of the human race perish. God made a choice—He chose some individuals to be saved unto everlasting blessedness in heaven and others He chose to pass over, to allow them to follow the consequences of their sins into eternal torment in hell.

This is a hard saying, no matter how we approach it. We wonder, "Do our individual lives have any bearing on God's decision? Even though God makes His choice before we are born, He still knows everything about our lives before we live them. Does He take that prior knowledge of us into account when He makes His decision?" How we answer that last question will determine whether our view of predestination is Reformed or not. Remember, we stated earlier that virtually all churches have *some* doctrine of predestination. Most churches agree that God's decision is made before we are born. The issue then rests upon the question, "On what basis does God make that decision?"

Before we set out to answer that, we must clarify one other point. Frequently, people think about predestination with respect to everyday questions about traffic accidents and the like. They wonder whether God decreed that the Yankees win the World Series or whether the tree fell on their car by divine edict. Even insurance contracts have clauses that refer to "acts of God."

Questions such as these are normally treated in theology under the broader heading of Providence. Our study focuses on predestination in the narrow sense, restricting it to the ultimate question of predestined salvation or damnation, what we call *election* and *reprobation*. The other questions are both interesting and important, but they fall beyond the scope of this book.

The Sovereignty of God

In most discussions about predestination, there is great concern about protecting the dignity and freedom of man. But we must also observe the crucial importance of the sovereignty of God. Though God is not a creature, He is personal, with supreme dignity and supreme freedom. We are aware of the ticklish problems surrounding the relationship between God's sovereignty and human freedom. We must also be aware of the close relationship between God's sovereignty and God's freedom. The freedom of a sovereign is always greater than the freedom of his subjects.

When we speak of divine sovereignty, we are speaking about God's author-ity and about God's power. As sovereign, God is the supreme authority of heaven and earth. All other authority is lesser authority. Any other authority that exists in the universe is derived from and dependent upon God's authority. All other forms of authority exist either by God's command or by God's permission.

The word *authority* contains within itself the word *author.* God is the author of all things over which He has authority. He created the universe. He owns the universe. His ownership gives Him certain rights. He may do with His universe what is pleasing to His holy will.

Likewise, all power in the universe flows from the power of God. All power in this universe is subordinate to Him. Even Satan is powerless without God's sovereign permission to act.

Christianity is not dualism. We do not believe in two ultimate equal pow-ers locked in an eternal struggle for supremacy. If Satan were equal to God, we would have no confidence, no hope of good triumphing over evil. We would be destined to an eternal standoff between two equal and opposing forces.

Satan is a creature. He is evil to be sure, but even his evil is subject to the sovereignty of God, as is our own evil. God's authority is ultimate; His power is omnipotent. He is sovereign.

One of my duties as a seminary professor is to teach the theology of the Westminster Confession of Faith. The Westminster Confession has been the central creedal document for historic Presbyterianism. It sets forth the classical doctrines of the Presbyterian Church.

Once, while teaching this course, I announced to my evening class that the following week we would study the section of the confession dealing with pre-destination. Since the evening class was open to the public, my students rushed to invite their friends for the juicy discussion. The next week the classroom was packed with students and guests.

I began the class by reading the opening lines from chapter 3 of the West-minster Confession: "God, from all eternity, did, by the most wise and holy counsel of His own will, freely, and unchangeably ordain whatsoever comes to pass."

I stopped reading at that point. I asked, "Is there anyone in this room who does not believe the words that I just read?" A multitude of hands went up. I then asked, "Are there any convinced atheists in the room?" No hands were raised. I then said something outrageous: "Everyone who raised his hand to the first question should also have raised his hand to the second question."

A chorus of groans and protests met my statement. How could I accuse someone of atheism for not believing that God foreordains whatever comes to pass? Those who protested these words were not denying the existence of God. They were not protesting against Christianity. They were protesting against Calvinism.

I tried to explain to the class that the idea that God foreordains whatever comes to pass is not an idea unique to Calvinism. It isn't even unique to Christianity. It is simply a tenet of theism—a necessary tenet of theism.

That God in some sense foreordains whatever comes to pass is a necessary result of His sovereignty. In itself it does not plead for Calvinism. It only declares that God is absolutely sovereign over His creation. God can foreordain things in different ways. But everything that happens must at least happen by His permission. If He permits something, then He must decide to allow it. If He decides to allow something, then in a sense He is foreordaining it. Who, among Christians, would argue that God could not stop something in this world from happening? If God so desires, He has the power to stop the whole world.

To say that God foreordains all that comes to pass is simply to say that God is sovereign over His entire creation. If something could come to pass apart from His sovereign permission, then that which came to pass would frustrate His sovereignty. If God refused to permit something to happen and it happened anyway, then whatever caused it to happen would have more authority and power than God Himself. If there is any part of creation outside of God's sovereignty, then God is simply not sovereign. If God is not sovereign, then God is not God.

If there is one single molecule in this universe running around loose, totally free of God's sovereignty, then we have no guarantee that a single promise of God will ever be fulfilled. Perhaps that one maverick molecule will lay waste all the grand and glorious plans that God has made and promised to us. If a grain of sand in the kidney of Oliver Cromwell changed the course of English history, so our maverick molecule could change the course of all redemption history. Maybe that one molecule will be the thing that prevents Christ from returning.

We've heard the story: For want of a nail the shoe was lost; for want of the shoe the horse was lost; for want of the horse the rider was lost; for want of the rider the battle was lost; for want of the battle the war was lost. I remember my distress when I heard that Bill Vukovich, the greatest car driver of his era, was killed in a crash in the Indianapolis 500. The cause was later isolated in the failure of a cotter pin that cost ten cents.

Bill Vukovich had amazing control of race cars. He was a magnificent driver. However, he was not sovereign. A part worth only a dime cost him his life. God doesn't have to worry about ten-cent cotter pins wrecking His plans.

There are no maverick molecules running around loose. God is sovereign. God is God.

My students began to see that divine sovereignty is not an issue peculiar to Calvinism, or even to Christianity. Without sovereignty God cannot be God. If we reject divine sovereignty then we must embrace atheism. This is the problem we all face. We must hold tightly to God's sovereignty. Yet we must do it in such a way so as not to violate human freedom.

At this point I should do for you what I did for my students in the evening class—finish the statement from the Westminster Confession. The whole statement reads as follows:

> God, from all eternity, did by the most wise and holy counsel
> of His own will, freely, and unchangeably ordain whatsoever
> comes to pass: *yet so, as thereby neither is God the author of sin, nor
> is violence offered to the will of the creatures;* nor is the liberty or
> contingency of second causes taken away, but rather established.
> (italics added)

Note that, while it affirms God's sovereignty over all things, the Confession also asserts that God does not do evil or violate human freedom. Human freedom and evil are under God's sovereignty.

God's Sovereignty and the Problem of Evil

Surely the most difficult question of all is how evil can coexist with a God who is both altogether holy and altogether sovereign. I am afraid that most Christians do not realize the profound severity of this problem. Skeptics have called this issue the "Achilles' Heel of Christianity."

I vividly remember the first time I felt the pain of this thorny problem. I was a freshman in college and had been a Christian for only a few weeks. I was playing Ping-Pong in the lounge of the men's dormitory when, in the middle of a volley, the thought struck me, *"If God is totally righteous, how could He have created a universe where evil is present? If all things come from God, doesn't evil come from Him as well?"*

Then, as now, I realized that evil was a problem for the sovereignty of God. Did evil come into the world against God's sovereign will? If so, then He is not absolutely sovereign. If not, then we must conclude that in some sense even evil is foreordained by God.

For years I sought the answer to this problem, scouring the works of theologians and philosophers. I found some clever attempts at resolving the problem but, as yet, have never found a deeply satisfying answer.

The most common solution we hear for this dilemma is a simple reference to man's free will. We hear such statements as, "Evil came into the world by man's free will. Man is the author of sin, not God."

Surely that statement squares with the biblical account of the origin of sin. We know that man was created with a free will and that man freely chose to sin. It was not God who committed sin, it was man. The problem still persists, however. From where did man ever gain the slightest inclination to sin? If he was created with a desire for sin, then a shadow is cast on the integrity of the Creator. If he was created with no desire for sin, then we must ask where that desire came from.

The mystery of sin is tied to our understanding of free will, man's state in creation, and God's sovereignty. The question of free will is so vital to our understanding of predestination that we will devote an entire chapter to the subject. Until then we will restrict our study to the question of man's first sin.

How could Adam and Eve fall? They were created good. We might suggest that their problem was the craftiness of Satan. Satan beguiled them. He tricked them into eating the forbidden fruit. We might suppose that the serpent was so slick that he utterly and completely fooled our original parents.

Such an explanation suffers from several problems. If Adam and Eve did not realize what they were doing, if they were utterly fooled, then the sin would have been all Satan's. But the Bible makes it clear that in spite of his craftiness the serpent spoke directly in challenge to the commandment of God. Adam and Eve had heard God issue His prohibition and warning. They heard Satan contradict God. The decision was squarely before them. They could not appeal to Satan's trickery to excuse them.

Even if Satan not only fooled but forced Adam and Eve to sin, we are still not free of our dilemma. If they could have rightfully said, "The devil made us do it," we would still face the problem of the devil's sin. Where did the devil come from? How did he manage to fall from goodness? Whether we are speaking of the Fall of man or the fall of Satan we still are dealing with the problem of good creatures becoming evil.

Again we hear the "easy" explanation that evil came through the creature's free will. Free will is a good thing. That God gave us free will does not cast blame on Him. In creation man was given an ability to sin and an ability not to sin. He chose to sin. The question is, "Why?"

Herein lies the problem. Before a person can commit an act of sin he must first have a desire to perform that act. The Bible tells us that evil actions flow from evil desires. But the presence of an evil desire is already sin. We sin because we are sinners. We were born with a sin nature. We are fallen creatures. But Adam and Eve were not created fallen. They had no sin nature. They were good creatures with a free will. Yet they chose to sin. Why? I don't know. Nor have I found anyone yet who does know.

In spite of this excruciating problem we still must affirm that God is not the author of sin. The Bible does not reveal the answers to all our questions. It does reveal the nature and character of God. One thing is absolutely unthinkable, that God could be the author or doer of sin.

But this chapter is about God's sovereignty. We are still left with the question that, given the fact of human sin, how does it relate to God's sovereignty? If it is true that in some sense God foreordains everything that comes to pass, then it follows with no doubt that God must have foreordained the entrance of sin into the world. That is not to say that God forced it to happen or that He imposed evil upon His creation. All that means is that God must have decided to allow it to happen. If He did not allow it to happen, then it could not have happened, or else He is not sovereign.

We know that God is sovereign because we know that God is God. Therefore we must conclude that God foreordained sin. What else can we conclude? We must conclude that God's decision to allow sin to enter the world was a good decision. This is not to say that our sin is really a good thing, but merely that God's allowing us to do sin, which is evil, is a good thing. God's allowing evil is good, but the evil He allows is still evil. God's involvement in all this is perfectly righteous. Our involvement in it is wicked. The fact that God decided to allow us to sin does not absolve us from our responsibility for sin.

A frequent objection we hear is that if God knew in advance that we were going to sin, why did He create us in the first place? One philosopher stated the problem this way: "If God knew we would sin but could not stop it, then He is neither omnipotent nor sovereign. If He could stop it but chose not to, then He is neither loving nor benevolent." By this approach God is made to look bad no matter how we answer the question.

We must assume that God knew in advance that man would fall. We also must assume that He could have intervened to stop it. Or He could have chosen not to create us at all. We grant all those hypothetical possibilities. Bottom line, we know that He knew we would fall and that He went ahead and created us anyway. Why does that mean He is unloving? He also knew in advance that He was going to implement a plan of redemption for His fallen creation that would include a perfect manifestation of His justice and a perfect expression of His love and mercy. It was certainly loving of God to predestine the salvation of His people, those the Bible calls His "elect" or chosen ones.

It is the nonelect that are the problem. If some people are not elected unto salvation then it would seem that God is not all that loving toward them. For them it seems that it would have been more loving of God not to have allowed them to be born.

That may indeed be the case. But we must ask the really tough question: Is there any reason that a righteous God ought to be loving toward a creature who hates Him and rebels constantly against His divine authority and holiness? The objection raised by the philosopher implies that God owes His love to sinful creatures. That is, the unspoken assumption is that God is obligated to be gracious to sinners. What the philosopher overlooks is that *if grace is obligated it is no longer grace.* The very essence of grace is that it is undeserved. God always reserves the right to have mercy upon whom He will have mercy. God may owe people justice, but never mercy.

It is important to point out once again that these problems arise for all Christians who believe in a sovereign God. These questions are not unique to a particular view of predestination.

People argue that God is loving enough to provide a way of salvation for all sinners. Since Calvinism restricts salvation only to the elect, it seems to require a less loving God. On the surface at least, it seems that a non-Calvinist view provides an opportunity for vast numbers of people to be saved who would not be saved in the Calvinist view.

Again, this question touches on matters that must be more fully developed in later chapters. For now let me say simply that, if the final decision for the salvation of fallen sinners were left in the hands of fallen sinners, we would despair of all hope that anyone would be saved.

When we consider the relationship of a sovereign God to a fallen world, we are faced with basically four options:

1. God could decide to provide no opportunity for anyone to be saved.
2. God could provide an opportunity for all to be saved.
3. God could intervene directly and insure the salvation of all people.
4. God could intervene directly and insure the salvation of some people.

All Christians immediately rule out the first option. Most Christians rule out the third. We face the problem that God saves some and not all. Calvinism answers with the fourth option. The Calvinist view of predestination teaches that God actively intervenes in the lives of the elect to make absolutely sure that they are saved. Of course the rest are invited to Christ and given an "opportunity" to be saved *if they want to.* But Calvinism assumes that without the intervention of God no one will ever want Christ. Left to themselves, no one will ever choose Christ.

This is precisely the point of dispute. Non-Reformed views of predestination assume that every fallen person is left with the capacity to choose Christ. Man is not viewed as being so fallen that it requires the direct intervention of God to the degree that Calvinism asserts. The non-Reformed views all leave it in man's power to cast the deciding ballot for man's ultimate destiny. In these views the best option is the second. God provides opportunities for all to be saved. But certainly the opportunities are not equal, since vast multitudes of people die without ever hearing the gospel.

The non-Reformed person objects to the fourth option because it limits salvation to a select group which God chooses. The Reformed person objects to the second option because he sees the universal opportunity for salvation *as not providing enough to save anybody.* The Calvinist sees God doing far more for the fallen human race through option four than through option two. The non-Calvinist sees just the reverse. He thinks that giving a universal opportunity, though it falls short of insuring the salvation of anyone, is more benevolent than insuring the salvation of some and not others.

The nasty problem for the Calvinist is seen in the relationship of options three and four. If God can and does choose to insure the salvation of some, why then does He not insure the salvation of all?

Before I try to answer that question, let me first point out that this is not just a Calvinist problem. Every Christian must feel the weight of this problem. We first face the question, "Does God have the power to insure the salvation of everyone?" Certainly it is within God's power to change the heart of every impenitent sinner and bring that sinner to Himself. If He lacks such power, then He is not sovereign. If He has that power, why doesn't He use it for everyone?

The non-Reformed thinker usually responds by saying that for God to impose His power on unwilling people is to violate man's freedom. To violate man's freedom is sin. Since God cannot sin, He cannot unilaterally impose His saving grace on unwilling sinners. To force the sinner to be willing when the sinner is not willing is to violate the sinner. The idea is that by offering the grace of the gospel God does everything He can to help the sinner get saved. He has the raw power to coerce men but the use of such power would be foreign to God's righteousness.

That does not bring much comfort to the sinner in hell. The sinner in hell must be asking, "God, if You really loved me, why didn't You coerce me to believe? I would rather have had my free will violated than to be here in this eternal place of torment." Still, the pleas of the damned would not determine God's righteousness if in fact it would be wrong of God to impose Himself on the will of men. The question the Calvinist asks is, "What is wrong with God creating faith in the heart of the sinner?"

God is not required to seek the sinner's permission for doing with the sinner what He pleases. The sinner didn't ask to be born in the country of his birth, to his parents, or even to be born at all. Nor did the sinner ask to be born with a fallen nature. All these things were determined by God's sovereign decision. If God does all this that affects the sinner's eternal destiny, what could possibly be wrong for him to go one more step to insure his salvation? What did Jeremiah mean when he cried, "O Lord, You have overwhelmed me and I am overwhelmed" (Jer. 20:7)? Jeremiah certainly did not invite God to overwhelm him.

The question remains. Why does God only save some? If we grant that God can save men by violating their wills, why then does He not violate everybody's will and bring them all to salvation? (I am using the word *violate* here not because I really think there is any wrongful violation but because the non-Calvinist insists on the term.)

The only answer I can give to this question is that I don't know. I have no idea why God saves some but not all. I don't doubt for a moment that God has the power to save all, but I know that He does not choose to save all. I don't know why.

One thing I do know. If it pleases God to save some and not all, there is nothing wrong with that. God is not under obligation to save anybody. If He chooses to save some, that in no way obligates Him to save the rest. Again the Bible insists that it is God's divine prerogative to have mercy upon whom He will have mercy.

The hue and cry the Calvinist usually hears at this point is "That's not fair!" But what is meant by fairness here? If by fair we mean equal, then of course the protest is accurate. God does not treat all men equally. Nothing could be clearer from the Bible than that. God appeared to Moses in a way that He did not appear to Hammurabi. God gave blessings to Israel that He did not give to Persia. Christ appeared to Paul on the road to Damascus in a way He did not manifest Himself to Pilate. God simply has not treated every human being in history in exactly the same manner. That much is obvious.

Probably what is meant by "fair" in the protest is "just." It does not seem just for God to choose some to receive His mercy while others do not receive the benefit of it. To deal with this problem we must do some close but very important thinking. Let us assume that all men are guilty of sin in the sight of God. From that mass of guilty humanity, God sovereignly decides to give mercy to some of them. What do the rest get? They get justice. The saved get mercy and the unsaved get justice. Nobody gets injustice.

Mercy is not justice. But neither is it injustice. Look at the following graphic:

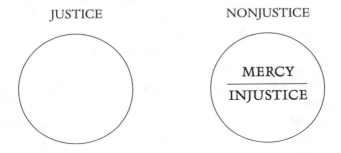

There is justice and there is nonjustice. Nonjustice includes everything outside of the category of justice. In the category of nonjustice we find two subconcepts, injustice and mercy. Mercy is a good form of nonjustice while injustice is a bad form of nonjustice. In the plan of salvation God does nothing bad. He never commits an injustice. Some people get justice, which is what they deserve, while other people get mercy. Again, the fact that one gets mercy does not demand that the others get it as well. God reserves the right of executive clemency.

As a human being I might *prefer* that God give His mercy to everyone equally, but I may not *demand* it. If God is not pleased to dispense His saving mercy to all men, then I must submit to His holy and righteous decision. God is never, never, never obligated to be merciful to sinners. That is the point we must stress if we are to grasp the full measure of God's grace.

The real question is why God is inclined to be merciful to anyone. His mercy is not required, yet He freely gives it to His elect. He gave it to Jacob in a way He did not give it to Esau. He gave it to Peter in a way He did not give it to Judas. We must learn to praise God both in His mercy and in His justice. When He executes His justice, He is doing nothing wrong. He is executing His justice according to His righteousness.

God's Sovereignty and Human Freedom

Every Christian gladly affirms that God is sovereign. God's sovereignty is a comfort to us. It assures us that He is able to do what He promises to do. But the bare fact of God's sovereignty raises one more big question. How is God's sovereignty related to human freedom?

When we stand before the question of divine sovereignty and human freedom, the "fight or flight" dilemma may confront us. We might try to fight our way into a logical solution of it or take a turn and run as fast as we can from it.

Many of us choose to flee from it. The flight takes different routes. The most common is simply to say that divine sovereignty and human freedom are contradictions that we must have the courage to embrace. We seek analogies that soothe our troubled minds.

As a college student I heard two analogies that gave me temporary relief, like a theological package of Rolaids:

Analogy 1—"God's sovereignty and human freedom are like parallel lines that meet in eternity."

Analogy 2—"God's sovereignty and human freedom are like ropes in a well. On the surface they seem to be separate, but in the darkness of the bottom of the well they come together."

The first time I heard these analogies I was relieved. They sounded simple yet profound. The idea of two parallel lines that meet in eternity satisfied me. It gave me something clever to say in the event that a hard-boiled skeptic asked me about divine sovereignty and human freedom.

My relief was temporary. I soon required a stronger dose of Rolaids. The nagging question refused to go away. *"How,"* I wondered, *"can parallel lines ever meet? In eternity or anywhere else?"* If the lines meet, then they are not ultimately parallel. If they are ultimately parallel, then they will never meet. The more I thought about the analogy, the more I realized that it did not solve the problem. To say that parallel lines meet in eternity is a nonsense statement; it is a blatant contradiction.

I don't like contradictions. I find little comfort in them. I never cease to be amazed at the ease with which Christians seem to be comfortable with them. I hear statements like, "God is bigger than logic!" or "Faith is higher than reason!" to defend the use of contradictions in theology.

I certainly agree that God is bigger than logic and that faith is higher than reason. I agree with all my heart and with all my head. What I want to avoid is a God who is smaller than logic and a faith that is lower than reason. A God who is smaller than logic would be and should be destroyed by logic. A faith that is lower than reason is irrational and absurd.

I suppose it is the tension between divine sovereignty and human freedom, more than any other issue, that has driven many Christians to claim contradictions as a legitimate element of faith. The idea is that logic cannot reconcile divine sovereignty and human freedom. The two defy logical harmony. Since the Bible teaches both poles of the contradiction we must be willing to affirm them both, in spite of the fact that they are contradictory.

God forbid! For Christians to embrace both poles of a blatant contradiction is to commit intellectual suicide and to slander the Holy Spirit. The Holy Spirit is not the author of confusion. God does not speak with a forked tongue.

If human freedom and divine sovereignty are real contradictions, then one of them, at least, has to go. If sovereignty excludes freedom and freedom excludes sovereignty, then either God is not sovereign or man is not free.

Happily, there is an alternative. We can keep both sovereignty and freedom if we can show that they are not contradictory.

At a human level we readily see that people can enjoy a real measure of freedom in a land ruled by a sovereign monarch. It is not freedom that is canceled out by sovereignty; it is *autonomy* that cannot coexist with sovereignty.

What is autonomy? The word comes from the prefix *auto* and the root *nomos*. *Auto* means "self." An automobile is something that moves itself. "Automatic" describes something that is self-acting.

The root *nomos* is the Greek word for "law." The word *autonomy* means, then, "self-law." To be autonomous means to be a law unto oneself. An autonomous creature would be answerable to no one. He would have no governor, least of all a sovereign governor. It is logically impossible to have a sovereign God existing at the same time as an autonomous creature. The two concepts are utterly incompatible. To think of their coexistence would be like imagining the meeting of an immovable object and an irresistible force. What would happen? If the object moved, then it could no longer be considered immovable. If it failed to move, then the irresistible force would no longer be irresistible.

So it is with sovereignty and autonomy. If God is sovereign, man cannot possibly be autonomous. If man is autonomous, God cannot possibly be sovereign. These would be contradictions.

One does not have to be autonomous to be free. Autonomy implies *absolute* freedom. We are free, but there are limits to our freedom. The ultimate limit is the sovereignty of God.

I once read a statement by a Christian who said, "God's sovereignty can never restrict human freedom." Imagine a Christian thinker making such a statement. This is sheer humanism. Does the law of God place restrictions on human freedom? Is God not permitted to impose limits on what I may choose? Not only may God impose moral limits upon my freedom, but He has every right at any moment to strike me dead if it is necessary to restrain me from exercising my evil choices. If God has no right of coercion, then He has no right of governing His creation.

It is better that we reverse the statement: "Human freedom can never restrict the sovereignty of God." That is what sovereignty is all about. If God's sovereignty is restricted by man's freedom, then God is not sovereign; man is sovereign.

God is free. I am free. God is more free than I am. If my freedom runs up against God's freedom, I lose. His freedom restricts mine; my freedom does not restrict His. There is an analogy in the human family. I have free will. My children have free wills. When our wills clash I have the authority to overrule their wills. Their wills are to be subordinate to my will; my will is not subordinate to theirs. Of course at the human level of the analogy we are not speaking in absolute terms.

Divine sovereignty and human freedom are often thought to be contradictions because on the surface they sound contradictory. There are some important distinctions that must be made and consistently applied to this question if we are to avoid hopeless confusion.

Let us consider three words in our vocabulary that are so closely related that they are often confused:

1. contradiction
2. paradox
3. mystery

1. *Contradiction.* The logical law of contradiction says that a thing cannot be what it is and not be what it is at the same time and in the same relationship. A man can be a father and a son at the same time, but he cannot be a man and not be a man at the same time. A man can be both a father and a son at the same time but not in the same relationship. No man can be his own father. Even when we speak of Jesus as the God/man, we are careful to say that, though He is God and man at the same time, He is not God and man in the same relationship. He has a divine nature and a human nature. They are not to be confused. Contradictions can never coexist, not even in the mind of God. If both poles of a genuine contradiction could be true in the mind of God, then nothing God ever revealed to us could possibly have any meaning. If good and evil, justice and injustice, righteousness and unrighteousness, Christ and Antichrist could all mean the same thing to God's mind, then truth of any kind would be utterly impossible.

2. *Paradox.* A paradox is an apparent contradiction that upon closer scrutiny can be resolved. I have heard teachers declare that the Christian notion of the Trinity is a contradiction. It simply is not. It violates no law of logic. It passes

the objective test of the law of contradiction. God is one in *essence* and three in *person*. There is nothing contradictory about that. If we said that God was one in essence and three in essence, then we would have a bona fide contradiction that no one could resolve. Then Christianity would be hopelessly irrational and absurd. The Trinity is a paradox, but not a contradiction.

Fogging things up even further is another term, *antinomy.* Its primary meaning is a synonym for contradiction, but its secondary meaning is a synonym for paradox. Upon examination, we see that it has the same root as *autonomy, nomos,* which means "law." Here the prefix is *anti,* which means "against" or "instead of." Thus the literal meaning of the term *antinomy* is "against law." What law do you suppose is in view here? The law of contradiction. The original meaning of the term was "that which violates the law of contradiction." Hence, originally and in normal philosophical discussion, the word *antinomy* is an exact equivalent of the word *contradiction.*

Confusion creeps in when people use the term *antinomy* not to refer to a genuine contradiction but to a paradox or apparent contradiction. We remember that a paradox is a statement that seems like a contradiction but actually isn't. In Great Britain, especially, the word *antinomy* is often used as a synonym for paradox.

I labor these fine distinctions for two reasons. The first is that if we are to avoid confusion we must have a clear idea in our minds of the crucial difference between a real contradiction and a seeming contradiction. It is the difference between rationality and irrationality, between truth and absurdity.

The second reason that it is necessary to state these definitions clearly is that one of the greatest defenders of the doctrine of predestination in our world today uses the term *antinomy.* I am thinking of the outstanding theologian, Dr. J. I. Packer. Packer has helped countless thousands of people come to a deeper understanding of the character of God, especially with regard to God's sovereignty.

I have never discussed this matter of Dr. Packer's use of the term *antinomy* with him. I assume he is using it in the British sense of *paradox.* I cannot imagine that he means to speak of actual contradictions in the Word of God. In fact, in his book *Evangelism and the Sovereignty of God,* he labors the point that there are no ultimate contradictions in the truth of God. Dr. Packer has not only been tireless in his defense of Christian theology, but has been equally tireless in his brilliant defense of the inerrancy of the Bible. If the Bible contained antinomies in the sense of real contradictions, that would be the end of inerrancy.

Some people actually do hold that there are real contradictions in divine truth. They think inerrancy is compatible with them. Inerrancy would then mean that the Bible inerrantly reveals the contradictions in God's truth. Of course a moment's thought would make clear that if God's truth is contradictory truth it is no truth at all. Indeed the very word *truth* would be emptied of meaning. If contradictions can be true we would have no possible way of discerning the difference between truth and a lie. This is why I am convinced that Dr. Packer uses antinomy to mean paradox and not contradiction.

3. *Mystery.* The term *mystery* refers to that which is true but which we do not understand. The Trinity, for example, is a mystery. I cannot penetrate the mystery of the Trinity or of the incarnation of Christ with my feeble mind. Such truths are too high for me. I know that Jesus was one person with two natures, but I don't understand how that can be. The same kind of thing is found in the natural realm. Who understands the nature of gravity, or even of motion? Who has penetrated the ultimate mystery of life? What philosopher has plumbed the depths of the meaning of the human self? These are mysteries. They are not contradictions.

It is easy to confuse mystery and contradiction. We do not understand either of them. No one understands a contradiction because contradictions are intrinsically unintelligible. Not even God can understand a contradiction. Contradictions are nonsense. No one can make sense out of them.

Mysteries are capable of being understood. The New Testament reveals to us things that were concealed and not understood in Old Testament times. There are things that once were mysterious to us that are now understood. This does not mean that everything that is presently a mystery to us will one day be made clear, but that many current mysteries will be unraveled for us. Some will be penetrated in this world. We have not yet reached the limits of human discovery. We know also that in heaven things will be revealed to us that are still hidden. But even in heaven we will not grasp fully the meaning of infinity. To understand that fully, one must himself be infinite. God can understand infinity, not because He operates on the basis of some kind of heavenly logic system, but because He Himself is infinite. He has an infinite perspective.

Let me state it another way: All contradictions are mysterious. Not all mysteries are contradictions. Christianity has plenty of room for mysteries. It has no room for contradictions. Mysteries may be true. Contradictions can never be true, neither here in our minds, nor there in God's mind.

The big issue remains. The grand debate that stirs the cauldron of controversy centers on the question, "What does predestination do to our free will?"

We will examine that issue in the next chapter.

Summary of Chapter 2

1. Definition of predestination. "Predestination means that our final destination, heaven or hell, is decided by God before we are even born."
2. God's sovereignty. God is supreme authority of heaven and earth.
3. God is supreme power. All other authority and power are under God.
4. If God is not sovereign, He is not God.
5. God exercises His sovereignty in such a way that it does no evil and violates no human freedom.
6. Man's first act of sin is a mystery. That God allowed men to sin does not reflect badly upon God.
7. All Christians face the difficult question of why God, who theoretically could save everybody, chooses to save some, but not all.
8. God does not owe salvation to anyone.
9. God's mercy is voluntary. He is not obligated to be merciful. He reserves the right to have mercy upon whom He will have mercy.

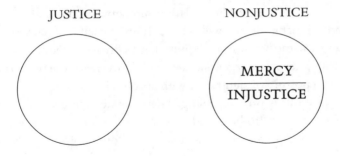

10. God's sovereignty and man's freedom are not contradictory.

THREE

❧

Predestination and Free Will

Predestination seems to cast a shadow on the very heart of human freedom. If God has decided our destinies from all eternity, that strongly suggests that our free choices are but charades, empty exercises in predetermined play-acting. It is as though God wrote the script for us in concrete, and we are merely carrying out His scenario.

To get a handle on the puzzling relationship between predestination and free will, we must first define free will. That definition itself is a matter of great debate. Probably the most common definition says *free will is the ability to make choices without any prior prejudice, inclination, or disposition*. For the will to be free it must act from a posture of neutrality, with absolutely no bias.

On the surface this is very appealing. There are no elements of coercion, either internal or external, to be found in it. Below the surface, however, lurk two serious problems. On the one hand, if we make our choices strictly from a neutral posture, with no prior inclination, then we make choices for no *reason*. If we have no reason for our choices, if our choices are utterly spontaneous, then our choices have no moral significance. If a choice just happens—it just pops out, with no rhyme or reason for it—then it cannot be judged good or bad. When God evaluates our choices, He is concerned about our motives.

Consider the case of Joseph and his brothers. When Joseph was sold into slavery by his brothers, God's providence was at work. Years later, when Joseph was reunited with his brothers in Egypt, he declared to them, "You meant evil against me; but God meant it for good" (Gen. 50:20). Here the motive was the decisive factor determining whether the act was good or evil. God's involvement in Joseph's dilemma was good; the brothers' involvement was evil. There was a reason why Joseph's brothers sold him into slavery. They had an evil motivation. Their decision was neither spontaneous nor neutral. They were jealous of their brother. Their choice to sell him was prompted by their evil desires.

The second problem this popular view faces is not so much moral as it is rational. If there is no prior inclination, desire, or bent, no prior motivation or reason for a choice, how can a choice even be made? If the will is totally neutral, why would it choose the right or the left? It is something like the problem encountered by Alice in Wonderland when she came to a fork in the road. She did not know which way to turn. She saw the grinning Cheshire cat in the tree. She asked the cat, "Which way should I turn?" The cat replied, "Where are you going?" Alice answered, "I don't know." "Then," replied the Cheshire cat, "it doesn't matter."

Consider Alice's dilemma. Actually she had four options from which to choose. She could have taken the left fork or the right fork. She also could have chosen to return the way she had come. Or she could have stood fixed at the spot of indecision until she died there. For her to take a step in any direction, she would need some motivation or inclination to do so. Without any motivation, any prior inclination, her only real option would be to stand there and perish.

Another famous illustration of the same problem is found in the story of the neutral-willed mule. The mule had no prior desires or equal desires in two directions. His owner put a basket of oats to his left and a basket of wheat on his right. If the mule had no desire whatsoever for either oats or wheat, he would choose neither and starve. If he had an exactly equal disposition toward oats as he had toward wheat, he would still starve. His equal disposition would leave him paralyzed. There would be no motive. Without motive there would be no choice. Without choice there would be no food. Without food soon there would be no mule.

We must reject the neutral-will theory not only because it is irrational but because, as we shall see, it is radically unbiblical.

Christian thinkers have given us two very important definitions of free will. We will consider first the definition offered by Jonathan Edwards in his classic work, *On the Freedom of the Will*.

Edwards defined the will as "the mind choosing." Before we ever can make moral choices we must first have some idea of what it is we are choosing. Our selection is then based upon what the mind approves or rejects. Our understanding of values has a crucial role to play in our decision making. My inclinations and motives as well as my actual choices are shaped by my mind. Again, if the mind is not involved, then the choice is made for no reason and with no reason. It is then an arbitrary and morally meaningless act. Instinct and choice are two different things.

A second definition of free will is "the ability to choose what we want." This rests on the important foundation of human desire. To have free will is to be able to choose according to our desires. Here desire plays the vital role of providing a motivation or a reason for making a choice.

Now for the tricky part. According to Edwards a human being is not only free to choose what he desires but he *must* choose what he desires to be able to choose at all. What I call *Edwards's Law of Choice* is this: "The will always chooses according to its strongest inclination at the moment." This means that every choice is free *and* every choice is determined.

I said it was tricky. This sounds like a blatant contradiction to say that every choice is free and yet every choice is determined. But "determined" here does not mean that some external force coerces the will. Rather it refers to one's internal motivation or desire. In shorthand the law is this: Our choices are determined by our desires. They remain our choices because they are motivated by our own desires. This is what we call *self-determination*, which is the essence of freedom.

Think for a minute about your own choices. How and why are they made? At this very instant you are reading the pages of this book. Why? Did you pick up this book because you have an interest in the subject of predestination, a desire to learn more about this complex subject? Perhaps. Maybe this book has been given to you to read as an assignment. Perhaps you are thinking, "I have no desire to read this whatsoever. I have to read it, and I am grimly wading through it to fulfill somebody else's desire that I read it. All things being equal I would never choose to read this book."

But all things are not equal, are they? If you are reading this out of some kind of duty or to fulfill a requirement, you still had to make a decision about fulfilling the requirement or not fulfilling the requirement. You obviously decided that it was better or more desirable for you to read this than to leave it unread. Of that much I am sure, or you would not be reading it right now.

Every decision you make is made for a reason. The next time you go into a public place and choose a seat (in a theater, a classroom, a church building), ask yourself why you are sitting where you are sitting. Perhaps it is the only seat available and you prefer to sit rather than to stand. Perhaps you discover that there is an almost unconscious pattern emerging in your seating decisions. Maybe you discover that whenever possible you sit toward the front of the room or toward the rear. Why? Maybe it has something to do with your eyesight. Perhaps you are shy or gregarious. You may think that you sit where you sit for no reason, but the seat that you choose will always be chosen by the strongest inclination you have at the moment of decision. That inclination may merely be that the seat closest to you is free and that you don't like to walk long distances to find a place to sit down.

Decision making is a complex matter because the options we encounter are often varied and many. Add to that that we are creatures with many and varied desires. We have different, often even conflicting, motivations.

Consider the matter of ice cream cones. Oh, do I have trouble with ice cream cones and ice cream sundaes. I love ice cream. If it is possible to be addicted to ice cream, then I must be classified as an ice cream addict. I am at least fifteen pounds overweight, and I am sure that at least twenty of the pounds that make up my body are there because of ice cream. Ice cream proves the adage to me, "A second on the lips; a lifetime on the hips." And, "Those who indulge bulge." Because of ice cream I have to buy my shirts with a bump in them.

Now, all things being equal, I would like to have a slim, trim body. I don't like squeezing into my suits and having little old ladies pat me on the tummy. Tummy patting seems to be an irresistible temptation for some folks. I know what I have to do to get rid of those excess pounds. I have to stop eating ice cream. So I go on a diet. I go on the diet because I want to go on the diet. I want to lose weight. I desire to look better. Everything is fine until someone invites me to Swenson's. Swenson's makes the greatest "Super Sundaes" in the world. I know I shouldn't go to Swenson's. But I like to go to Swenson's. When the moment of decision comes I am faced with conflicting desires. I have a desire to be thin and I have a desire for a Super Sundae. Whichever desire is greater at the time of decision is the desire I will choose. It's that simple.

Now consider my wife. As we prepare to celebrate our silver wedding anniversary, I am aware that she is exactly the same weight as she was the day we were married. Her wedding gown still fits her perfectly. She has no great problem with ice cream. Most eating establishments only carry vanilla, chocolate, and strawberry. Any of those make my mouth water, but they offer no enticement to my wife. Aha! But there is Baskin Robbins. They have pralines and cream ice cream. When we go to the mall and pass a Baskin Robbins, my wife goes through a strange transformation. Her pace decelerates, her hands get clammy, and I can almost detect the beginning of salivation. (That's salivation, not salvation.) Now she experiences the conflict of desires that assaults me daily.

We always choose according to our strongest inclination at the moment. Even external acts of coercion cannot totally take away our freedom. Coercion involves acting with some kind of force, imposing choices upon people that, if left to themselves, they would not choose. I certainly have no desire to pay the kind of income taxes that the government makes me pay. I can refuse to pay them, but the consequences are less desirable than paying them. By threatening me with jail the government is able to impose its will upon me to pay taxes.

Or consider the case of armed robbery. A gunman steps up to me and says, "Your money or your life." He has just restricted my options to two. All things being equal I have no desire to donate my money to him. There are far more worthy charities than he. But suddenly my desires have changed as a result of his act of external coercion. He is using force to provoke certain desires within me. Now I must choose between my desire to live and my desire to give him my money. I might as well give him the money, because if he kills me he will take my money anyway. Some people might choose to refuse, saying, "I would rather die than choose to hand this gunman my money. He'll have to take it from my dead body."

In either case, a choice is made. And it is made according to the strongest inclination at the moment. Think, if you can, of any choice you have ever made that was not according to the strongest inclination you had at the moment of decision. What about sin? Every Christian has some desire in his heart to obey Christ. We love Christ and we want to please Him. Yet every Christian sins. The hard truth is that at the moment of our sin we desire the sin more strongly than we desire to obey Christ. If we always desired to obey Christ more than we desired to sin, we would never sin.

Does not the apostle Paul teach otherwise? Does he not recount for us a situation in which he acts against his desires? He says in Romans, "The good that I would, I do not, and that which I would not, that I do" (Rom. 7:19, KJV). Here it sounds as if, under the inspiration of God the Holy Spirit, Paul is teaching clearly that there are times in which he acts against his strongest inclination.

It is extremely unlikely that the apostle is here giving us a revelation about the technical operation of the will. Rather, he is stating plainly what every one of us has experienced. We all have a desire to flee from sin. The "all things being equal" syndrome is in view here. All things being equal, I would like to be perfect. I would like to be rid of sin, just as I would like to be rid of my excess weight. But my desires do not remain constant. They fluctuate. When my stomach is full it is easy to go on a diet. When my stomach is empty my desire level changes. Temptations arise with the changing of my desires and appetites. Then I do things that, all things being equal, I would not want to do.

Paul sets before us the very real conflict of human desires, desires that yield evil choices. The Christian lives within a battlefield of conflicting desires. Christian growth involves the strengthening of desires to please Christ accompanied by the weakening of desires to sin. Paul called it the warfare between the flesh and the Spirit.

To say that we always choose according to our strongest inclination at the moment is to say that we always choose what we want. At every point of choice we are free and self-determined. To be self-determined is not the same thing as *determinism*. Determinism means that we are forced or coerced to do things by external forces. External forces can, as we have seen, severely limit our options, but they cannot destroy choice altogether. They cannot impose delight in things we hate. When that happens, when hatred turns to delight, it is a matter of persuasion, not coercion. I cannot be forced to do what I take delight in doing already.

The neutral view of free will is impossible. It involves choice without desire. That is like having an effect without a cause. It is something from nothing, which is irrational. The Bible makes it clear that we choose out of our desires. A wicked desire produces wicked choices and wicked actions. A godly desire produces godly deeds. Jesus spoke in terms of corrupt trees producing corrupt fruit. A fig tree does not yield apples and an apple tree produces no figs. So righteous desires produce righteous choices and evil desires produce evil choices.

Moral and Natural Ability

Jonathan Edwards made another distinction that is helpful in understanding the biblical concept of free will. He distinguished between *natural ability* and *moral ability*. Natural ability has to do with the powers we receive as natural human beings. As a human being I have the natural ability to think, to walk, to talk, to see, to hear, and, above all, to make choices. There are certain natural abilities that I lack. Other creatures may possess the ability to fly unaided by machines. I do not have that natural ability. I may desire to soar through the air like Superman, but I do not have this ability. The reason I cannot fly is not due to a moral deficiency in my character, but because my Creator has not given me the natural equipment necessary to fly. I have no wings.

The will is a natural ability given to us by God. We have all the natural faculties necessary to make choices. We have a mind and we have a will. We have the natural ability to choose what we desire. What, then, is our problem? According to the Bible the location of our problem is clear. It is with the nature of our desires. This is the focal point of our fallenness. Scripture declares that the heart of fallen man continually harbors desires that are only wicked (Gen. 6:5).

The Bible has much to say about the heart of man. In Scripture the heart refers not so much to an organ that pumps blood throughout the body as it does to the core of the soul, the deepest seat of human affections. Jesus saw a close connection between the location of man's treasures and the desires of his heart. Find a man's treasure map, and you have the highway of his heart.

Edwards declared that man's problem with sin lies with his moral ability, or lack thereof. Before a person can make a choice which is pleasing to God, he must first have a desire to please God. Before we can find God, we must first desire to seek Him. Before we can choose the good, we must first have a desire for the good. Before we can choose Christ, we must first have a desire for Christ. The sum and substance of the whole debate on predestination rests squarely at this point: Does fallen man, in and of himself, have a natural desire for Christ?

Edwards answers this question with an emphatic "No!" He insists that, in the Fall, man lost his original desire for God. When he lost that desire, something happened to his freedom. He lost the moral ability to choose Christ. In order to choose Christ, the sinner must first have a desire to choose Christ. Either he has that desire already within him or he must receive that desire from God. Edwards and all who embrace the Reformed view of predestination agree that if God does not plant that desire in the human heart nobody, left to themselves, will ever freely choose Christ. They will always and everywhere reject the gospel, precisely because they do not desire the gospel. They will always and everywhere reject Christ because they do not desire Christ. They will freely reject Christ in the sense that they will act according to their desires.

At this point I am not trying to prove the truth of Edwards's view. To do that requires a close look at the biblical view of man's moral ability or inability. We shall do that later. We must also answer the question, "If man lacks the moral ability to choose Christ, how can God ever hold him responsible to choose Christ? If man is born in a state of moral inability, with no desire for Christ, is it not then God's fault that men do not choose Christ?" Again I beg the reader for patience, with the promise that I will take up these very important questions soon.

Saint Augustine's View of Liberty

Just as Edwards made a crucial distinction between natural ability and moral ability, so Augustine before him made a similar distinction. Augustine got at the problem by saying that fallen man has a *free will* but lacks *liberty*. On the surface it seems like a strange distinction. How could anyone have a free will and still not have liberty?

Augustine was getting at the same thing that Edwards was. Fallen man has not lost his ability to make choices. The sinner still is able to choose what he wants; he can still act according to his desires. Yet, because his desires are corrupt, he does not have the royal liberty of those set free unto righteousness.

Fallen man is in a serious state of moral bondage. That state of bondage is called *original sin*.

Original sin is a very difficult subject that virtually every Christian denomination has had to face. The fall of man is so clearly taught in Scripture that we cannot construct a view of man without taking it into consideration. There are few, if any, Christians who argue that man is not fallen. Without acknowledging that we are fallen, we cannot acknowledge that we are sinners. If we do not acknowledge that we are sinners, we can hardly flee to Christ as our Savior. Admitting our fallenness is a prerequisite for coming to Christ.

It is possible to admit that we are fallen without embracing some doctrine of original sin, but only with severe difficulties in the process. It is no accident that almost every Christian body has formulated some doctrine of original sin.

At this point multitudes of Christians disagree. We agree that we must have a doctrine of original sin, but there remains great disagreement as to the concept of original sin and its extent.

Let us begin by stating what original sin is not. Original sin is not the first sin. Original sin does not refer specifically to the sin of Adam and Eve. Original sin refers to the *result* of the sin of Adam and Eve. Original sin is the punishment God gives for the first sin. It goes something like this: Adam and Eve sinned. That is the first sin. As a result of their sin humanity was plunged into moral ruin. Human nature underwent a moral fall. Things changed for us after the first sin was committed. The human race became corrupt. This subsequent corruption is what the church calls original sin.

Original sin is not a specific act of sin. It is a *condition* of sin. Original sin refers to a sin nature out of which particular sinful acts flow. Again, we commit sins because it is our nature to sin. It was not man's original nature to sin but, after the Fall, his moral nature changed. Now, because of original sin, we have a fallen and corrupt nature.

Fallen man, as the Bible declares, is born in sin. He is "under" sin. By nature we are children of wrath. We are not born in a state of innocence.

John Gerstner was once invited to preach at a local Presbyterian church. He was greeted at the door by the elders of the church, who explained that the order of worship for the day called for the administration of the sacrament of infant baptism. Dr. Gerstner agreed to perform the service. Then one of the elders explained a special tradition of the church. He asked Dr. Gerstner to present a white rose to each infant's parents before the baptism. Dr. Gerstner inquired about the meaning of the white rose. The elder replied, "We present the white rose as a symbol of the infant's innocence before God."

"I see," replied Dr. Gerstner. "And what does the water symbolize?"

Imagine the consternation of the elder when he tried to explain the symbolic purpose of washing away the sin of innocent babies. The confusion of this congregation is not unique. When we acknowledge that infants are not guilty of committing specific acts of sin, it is easy to jump to the conclusion that they are therefore innocent. This is a theological broad jump into a pile of swords. Though the infant is innocent of specific acts of sin, he is still guilty of original sin.

To understand the Reformed view of predestination it is absolutely necessary to understand the Reformed view of original sin. The two matters stand or fall (no pun intended) together.

The Reformed view follows the thinking of Augustine. Augustine spells out the state of Adam before the Fall and the state of mankind after the Fall. Before the Fall Adam was endowed with two possibilities: He had the ability to sin and the ability not to sin. After the Fall Adam had the ability to sin and the inability to not sin. The idea of the "inability to not" is a bit confusing to us because in English it's a double negative. Augustine's Latin formula was *non posse non peccare*. Stated another way, it means that after the Fall man was morally incapable of living without sin. The ability to live without sin was lost in the Fall. This moral inability is the essence of what we call original sin.

When we are born again, our bondage to sin is relieved. After we are made alive in Christ, we once again have the ability to sin and the ability to not sin. In heaven we will have the inability to sin.

Let's look at this with a chart:

Pre-Fall Man	Post-Fall Man	Reborn Man	Glorified Man
able to sin	able to sin	able to sin	
able to not sin		able to not sin	able to not sin
	unable to not sin		
			unable to sin

The chart shows that man before the Fall, after the Fall, and after being reborn is able to sin. Before the Fall he is able to not sin. This ability, the ability to not sin, is lost in the Fall. It is restored when a person is born again and continues in heaven. In creation man did not suffer from moral inability. Moral inability is a result of the Fall. To state it another way, before the Fall man was able to refrain from sinning; after the Fall man is no longer able to refrain from sinning. That is what we call original sin. This moral inability or moral bondage is overcome by spiritual rebirth. Rebirth liberates us from original sin. Before rebirth we still have a free will but we do not have this liberation from the power of sin, what Augustine called "liberty."

The person who is reborn can still sin. The ability to sin is not removed until we are glorified in heaven. We have the ability to sin, but we are no longer under the bondage of original sin. We have been set free. This of course does not mean that now we live perfect lives. We still sin. But we can never say that we sin because that is all our fallen natures have the power to do.

Jesus' View of Moral Ability

We have made a brief sketch of the views of Jonathan Edwards and St. Augustine on the matter of moral inability. I think they are helpful, and I am also persuaded that they are correct. Yet in spite of their authority as great theologians, neither of them can command from us our absolute submission to their teaching. They are both fallible. For the Christian, the teaching of Jesus is another matter. For us, and for anybody else as well if indeed Jesus is the Son of God, the teaching of Jesus must bind our consciences. His teaching on the question of man's moral ability is definitive.

One of the most important teachings of Jesus on this matter is found in the Gospel of John. "Therefore I have said to you that no one can come to Me unless it has been granted to him by My Father" (John 6:65).

Let us look closely at this verse. The first element of this teaching is a *universal negative*. The words *no one* are all-inclusive. They allow for no exception apart from the exceptions Jesus adds. The next word is crucial. It is the word *can*. This has to do with ability, not permission.

Who has not been corrected by a schoolteacher for confusing the words *can* and *may*? I used to have a teacher who never missed an opportunity to drill this point home. If I raised my hand and said, "Can I sharpen my pencil?" the response was always the same. She would smile and say, "I am sure that you *can*. You also *may* sharpen your pencil." The word *can* refers to ability; the word *may* refers to permission.

In this passage Jesus is not saying, "No one is allowed to come to Me. . . ." He is saying, "No one is *able* to come to Me. . . ."

The next word in the passage is also vital. "Unless" refers to what we call a *necessary condition*. A necessary condition refers to something that must happen before something else can happen.

The meaning of Jesus' words is clear. No human being can possibly come to Christ unless something happens that makes it possible for him to come.

That necessary condition Jesus declares is that "it has been granted to him by the Father." Jesus is saying here that the ability to come to Him is a gift from God. Man does not have the ability in and of himself to come to Christ. God must do something first.

The passage teaches at least this much: It is not within fallen man's natural ability to come to Christ on his own, without some kind of divine assistance. To this extent at least, Edwards and Augustine are in solid agreement with the teaching of our Lord. The question that remains is this: Does God give the ability to come to Jesus to all men? The Reformed view of predestination says no. Some other views of predestination say yes. But one thing is certain; man cannot do it on his own steam without some kind of help from God.

What kind of help is required? How far must God go to overcome our natural inability to come to Christ? A clue is found elsewhere in this same chapter. In fact, there are two other statements by Jesus that have direct bearing on this question.

Earlier in chapter 6 of John's Gospel, Jesus makes a similar statement. He says, "No one can come to Me unless the Father who sent Me draws him" (John 6:44). The key word here is *draw*. What does it mean for the Father to draw people to Christ? I have often heard this text explained to mean that the Father must woo or entice men to Christ. Unless this wooing takes place, no man will come to Christ. However, man has the ability to resist this wooing and to refuse the enticement. The wooing, though it is necessary, is not compelling. In philosophical language that would mean that the drawing of God is a necessary condition but not a sufficient condition to bring men to Christ. In simpler language it means that we cannot come to Christ without the wooing, but the wooing does not guarantee that we will, in fact, come to Christ.

I am persuaded that the above explanation, which is so widespread, is incorrect. It does violence to the text of Scripture, particularly to the biblical meaning of the word *draw*. The Greek word used here is *elk* . Kittel's *Theological Dictionary of the New Testament* defines it to mean to compel by irresistible superiority. Linguistically and lexicographically, the word means "to compel."

To compel is a much more forceful concept than to woo. To see this more clearly, let us look for a moment at two other passages in the New Testament where the same Greek word is used. In James 2:6 we read: "But you have dishonored the poor man. Do not the rich oppress you and drag you into the courts?" Guess which word in this passage is the same Greek word that elsewhere is translated by the English word *draw*. It is the word *drag*. Let us now substitute the word *woo* in the text. It would then read: "Do not the rich oppress you and *woo* you into the courts?"

The same word occurs in Acts 16:19. "But when her masters saw that their hope of profit was gone, they seized Paul and Silas and *dragged* them into the marketplace to the authorities." Again, try substituting the word *woo* for the word *drag*. Paul and Silas were not seized and then wooed into the marketplace.

I once was asked to debate the doctrine of predestination in a public forum at an Arminian seminary. My opponent was the head of the New Testament department of the seminary. At a crucial point in the debate we fixed our attention on the passage about the Father's drawing people. My opponent was the one who brought up the passage as a proof text to support his claim that God never forces anyone or compels them to come to Christ. He insisted that the divine influence on fallen man was restricted to drawing, which he interpreted to mean wooing.

At that point in the debate I quickly referred him to Kittel and to the other passages in the New Testament that translate the word *drag*. I was sure I had him. I was sure that he had walked into an insoluble difficulty for his own position. But he surprised me. He caught me completely off guard. I will never forget that agonizing moment when he cited a reference from an obscure Greek poet in which the same Greek word was used to describe the action of drawing water from a well. He looked at me and said, "Well, Professor Sproul, does one drag water from a well?" Instantly the audience burst into laughter at this startling revelation of the alternate meaning of the Greek word. I stood there looking rather silly. When the laughter died down I replied, "No sir. I have to admit that we do not drag water from a well. But, how do we get water from a well? Do we woo it? Do we stand at the top of the well and cry, 'Here, water, water, water'?" It is as necessary for God to come into our hearts to turn us to Christ as it is for us to put the bucket in the water and pull it out if we want anything to drink. The water simply will not come on its own, responding to a mere external invitation.

As crucial as these passages from John's Gospel are, they do not surpass in importance another teaching of Jesus in the same Gospel with respect to man's moral inability. I am thinking of the famous discussion that Jesus had with Nicodemus in John 3. Jesus said to Nicodemus, "Most assuredly, I say to you, unless one is born again, he cannot see the kingdom of God" (John 3:3). Two verses later Jesus repeats the teaching: "Most assuredly, I say to you, unless one is born of water and the Spirit, he cannot enter the kingdom of God."

Once again we encounter the pivotal word *unless*. Jesus is stating an emphatic necessary precondition for any human being's ability to see and to enter the kingdom of God. That emphatic precondition is spiritual rebirth. The

Reformed view of predestination teaches that before a person can choose Christ his heart must be changed. He must be born again. Non-Reformed views have fallen people first choosing Christ and then being born again. Here we find unregenerate people seeing and entering the kingdom of God. The moment a person receives Christ he is in the kingdom. One does not first believe, then become reborn, and then be ushered into the kingdom. How can a man choose a kingdom he cannot see? How can a man enter the kingdom without being first reborn? Jesus was pointing out Nicodemus' need to be born of the Spirit. He was still in the flesh. The flesh yields only flesh. The flesh, Jesus said, profits nothing. As Luther argued, "That does not mean a little something." Non-Reformed views have people responding to Christ who are not reborn. They are still in the flesh. For non-Reformed views the flesh not only profits something, it profits the most important thing a person could ever gain—entrance into the kingdom by believing on Christ. If a person who is still in the flesh, who is not yet reborn by the power of the Holy Spirit, can incline or dispose himself to Christ, what good is rebirth? This is the fatal flaw of non-Reformed views. They fail to take seriously man's moral inability, the moral impotency of the flesh.

A cardinal point of Reformed theology is the maxim: "Regeneration precedes faith." Our nature is so corrupt, the power of sin is so great, that unless God does a supernatural work in our souls we will never choose Christ. We do not believe in order to be born again; we are born again in order that we may believe.

It is ironic that in the same chapter, indeed in the same context in which our Lord teaches the utter necessity of rebirth to even see the kingdom, let alone choose it, non-Reformed views find one of their main proof texts to argue that fallen man retains a small island of ability to choose Christ. It is John 3:16: "For God so loved the world that He gave His only begotten Son, that whoever believes in Him should not perish but have everlasting life."

What does this famous verse teach about fallen man's ability to choose Christ? The answer, simply, is *nothing*. The argument used by non-Reformed people is that the text teaches that everybody in the world has it in their power to accept or reject Christ. A careful look at the text reveals, however, that it teaches nothing of the kind. What the text teaches is that everyone who believes in Christ will be saved. Whoever does A (believes) will receive B (everlasting life). The text says nothing, absolutely nothing, about who will ever believe. It says nothing about fallen man's natural moral ability. Reformed people and non-Reformed people both heartily agree that all who believe will be saved. They heartily disagree about who has the ability to believe.

Some may reply, "All right. The text does not *explicitly* teach that fallen men have the ability to choose Christ without being reborn first, but it certainly *implies* that." I am not willing to grant that the text even implies such a thing. However, even if it did, it would make no difference in the debate. Why not? Our rule of interpreting Scripture is that implications drawn from the Scripture must always be subordinate to the explicit teaching of Scripture. We must never, never, never reverse this to subordinate the explicit teaching of Scripture to possible implications drawn from Scripture. This rule is shared by both Reformed and non-Reformed thinkers.

If John 3:16 implied a universal natural human ability of fallen men to choose Christ, then that implication would be wiped out by Jesus' explicit teaching to the contrary. We have already shown that Jesus explicitly and unambiguously taught that no man has the ability to come to Him without God doing something to give him that ability, namely drawing him.

Fallen man is flesh. In the flesh he can do nothing to please God. Paul declares, "The fleshly mind is enmity against God; for it is not subject to the law of God, nor indeed *can* be. So then, those who are in the flesh *cannot* please God" (Rom. 8:7, 8).

We ask, then, "Who are those who are 'in the flesh'?" Paul goes on to declare: "But you are not in the flesh but in the Spirit, *if* indeed the Spirit of God dwells in you" (Rom. 8:9). The crucial word here is *if.* What distinguishes those who are in the flesh from those who are not is the indwelling of the Holy Spirit. No one who is not reborn is indwelt by God the Holy Spirit. People who are in the flesh have not been reborn. Unless they are first reborn, born of the Holy Spirit, they cannot be subject to the law of God. They cannot please God.

God commands us to believe in Christ. He is pleased by those who choose Christ. If unregenerate people could choose Christ, then they could be subject to at least one of God's commands, and they could at least do something that is pleasing to God. If that is so, then the apostle has erred here in insisting that those who are in the flesh can neither be subject to God nor please Him.

We conclude that fallen man is still free to choose what he desires, but because his desires are only wicked he lacks the moral ability to come to Christ. As long as he remains in the flesh, unregenerate, he will never choose Christ. He cannot choose Christ precisely because he cannot act against his own will. He has no desire for Christ. He cannot choose what he does not desire. His fall is great. It is so great that only the effectual grace of God working in his heart can bring him to faith.

Summary of Chapter 3

1. Free will is defined as "the ability to make choices according to our desires."

2. The concept of a "neutral free will," a will without prior disposition or inclination, is a false view of free will. It is both irrational and unbiblical.

3. True free will involves a kind of self-determination, which differs from coercion from an external force.

4. We struggle with choices, in part because we live with conflicting and changing desires.

5. Fallen man has the natural ability to make choices but lacks the moral ability to make godly choices.

6. Fallen man, as St. Augustine said, has "free will" but lacks "liberty."

7. Original sin is not the first sin but the sinful condition that is the *result* of Adam's and Eve's sin.

8. Fallen man is "unable to not sin."

9. Jesus taught that man is powerless to come to Him without divine aid.

10. Before a person will ever choose Jesus, he must first be born again.

FOUR

Adam's Fall and Mine

Another difficult question that shrouds the doctrine of predestination is the question of how our sinful nature can be inherited from Adam. If we are born with a fallen nature, if we are born in sin, if we are born in a state of moral inability, how can God hold us responsible for our sins?

We remember that original sin does not refer to the first sin but to the result of that first sin. The Scriptures speak repeatedly of sin and death entering the world through "one man's transgression." As a result of Adam's sin, all men are now sinners. The Fall was great. It had radical repercussions for the entire human race.

There have been many attempts to explain the relationship of Adam's fall to the rest of mankind. Some of the theories presented are quite complex and imaginative. Three theories, however, have emerged from the list as the most widely accepted. The first of these I will call the myth theory of the Fall.

The Myth Theory of the Fall

The myth theory of the Fall, as the name suggests, holds that there was no factual, historical fall. Adam and Eve are not considered historical persons. They are mythological symbols drawn to explain or represent the problem of man's corruption. The story of the Fall in the Bible is a kind of parable; it teaches a moral lesson.

According to this theory, the first few chapters of Genesis are mythological. There never was an Adam; there never was an Eve. The very structure of the story suggests parable or myth because it includes such elements as a talking serpent and such obviously symbolic objects as the tree of knowledge of good and evil.

The moral truth communicated by the myth is that people fall into sin. Sin is a universal problem. Everyone commits sin; no one is perfect. The myth points to a higher reality: Everyone is his own Adam. Every person has his own private fall. Sin is a universal human condition precisely because every person succumbs to his own private temptation.

The attractive elements of this theory are important. In the first place, this view absolves God entirely of any responsibility for holding future generations of people responsible for what one couple did. Here, no one can blame their parents or their Creator for their own sin. In this scheme, my fallenness is a direct result of my own fall, not of someone else's.

A second advantage of this view is that it escapes all need to defend the historical character of the beginning chapters of the Bible. This view suffers no anxiety from certain theories of evolution or from scientific disputes about the nature of creation. The factual truth of a myth never needs to be defended.

The disadvantages of this view, however, are more serious. Its most crucial failing is that it actually offers nothing by way of explanation for the universality of sin. If each one of us is born without a sinful nature, how do we account for the universality of sin? If four billion people were born with no inclination to sin, with no corruption to their nature, we would reasonably expect that at least some of them would refrain from falling. If our natural moral state is one of innocent neutrality, we would statistically expect that half of the human race would remain perfect. I grant that to account for one innocent person's fall presents an enormous intellectual problem. But when we compound that difficulty by the billions of people who have fallen, the problem becomes several billion times more difficult. We also grant that if one person created in the image of God could fall, then it is indeed possible that billions can likewise fall. It is the statistical probability here that is so astonishing. When we think of one person falling, that is one thing. But if everybody does it, without exception, then we begin to wonder why. We begin to wonder if man's natural state is all that neutral.

The standard reply of the advocates of the myth view is that people are not universally born in an idyllic environment like Eden. Society is corrupt. We are born into a corrupt environment. We are like Rousseau's "innocent savage" who is corrupted by the negative influences of civilization.

This explanation begs the question. How did society or civilization get corrupt in the first place? If everyone is born innocent, without a trace of personal corruption, we would expect to find societies that are no more than half corrupt. If birds of a feather flock together, we might find societies where all the corrupt people band together and other societies where no evil is present. Society cannot be a corrupting influence until it first becomes corrupt itself. To explain the fall of an entire society or civilization, one must face the difficulties we have already pointed out.

In another one of Jonathan Edwards's famous works, his treatise on original sin, he makes the important observation that because the sin of man is universal, even if the Bible said nothing about an original Fall of the human race, reason would demand such an explanation. Nothing screams more loudly about the fact that we are born in a state of corruption than the fact that we all sin.

Another thorny question that arises concerns the relationship of sin and death. The Bible makes it clear that death is not "natural" to man. That is, death is repeatedly said to have come into the world as a result of sin. If that is so, how do we account for the death of infants? If all men are born innocent, with no innate corruption, God would be unjust to allow as yet unfallen babies to die.

The mythological view of the Fall must also face the fact that it does radical violence to the teaching of Scripture. The view does more than merely interpret the opening chapters of the Bible as nonfactual. In so doing the view sets itself in clear opposition to the New Testament's view of the Fall. It would take intellectual gymnastics of the most severe sort to argue that the apostle Paul did not teach a historical Fall. The parallels that he draws between the first Adam and the second Adam are too strong to allow this, unless we argue that in Paul's mind Jesus was also a mythological character.

We grant that the Genesis account of the Fall has some unusual literary elements in it. The presence of a tree that does not follow the pattern of normal trees follows certain images of poetry. It is proper to interpret poetry as poetry and not as historical narrative. On the other hand, there are strong elements of historical narrative literature in Genesis 3. The setting of Eden is located in chapter 2 in the midst of four riverheads, including Pishon, Gihon, Hiddekel (or Tigris), and Euphrates.

We know that parables can be set in real historical settings. For example, the parable of the Good Samaritan is set in the geographical context of the road to Jericho. Therefore the mere presence of real historical rivers does not absolutely demand that we identify this section of Genesis as historical narrative.

There is another element of the text, however, that is more compelling. The account of Adam and Eve contains a significant genealogy. The Romans, with their penchant for mythology, may have no difficulty tracing their lineage to Romulus and Remus, but the Jews were surely more scrupulous about such matters. The Jews had a strong commitment to real history. In light of the vast difference between the Jewish view of history and the Greek view of history, it is unthinkable that Jewish people would include mythological characters in their own genealogies. In Jewish writing, the presence of genealogy indicates historical narrative. Note that the New Testament historian, Luke, includes Adam in the genealogy of Jesus.

It is much easier to account for a real tree serving as a focal point of a moral test and thereby being called a tree of the knowledge of good and evil than it is to accommodate genealogy to a parable or a myth. This of course could be done if other factors demanded it. But no such factors exist. There is no sound reason why we should not interpret Genesis 3 as historical narrative and multiple reasons why we should not treat it as parable or myth. To treat it as history is to treat it as the Jews did, including Paul and Jesus. To treat it otherwise is usually motivated by some contemporary agenda that has nothing to do with Jewish history.

The Realist View of the Fall

Remember the famous television series from the 1950s called *You Are There*? It took viewers, through the magic of television, to famous historical scenes. But in fact no electronic device has yet been invented to transport us back in time, H. G. Wells notwithstanding. We live in the present. Our only access to the past is through books, artifacts of archaeology, and the memories of ourselves and of others.

I remember teaching a course on the Bible that involved a brief study of Roman soldiers. I mentioned the Roman standard that carried the initials SPQR. I asked if anyone knew what those letters stood for. A dear friend who was in his seventies piped up, "*Senatus Populus Que Romanus*, 'The senate and the people of Rome.'" I smiled at my friend and said, "You are the only person in this room old enough to remember!"

None of us is old enough to carry memory images of the fall of Adam. Or are we? The realist view of the Fall contends that we are all old enough to remember the Fall. We should be able to remember it because we were really there.

Realism is not an exercise in a Bridey-Murphy kind of reincarnation. Rather, realism is a serious attempt to answer the problem of the Fall. The key concept is this: We cannot morally be held accountable for a sin committed by someone else. To be accountable we must have been actively involved somehow in the sin itself. Somehow we must have been present at the Fall. *Really* present. Hence the name *Realism*.

The realist view of the Fall demands some kind of concept of the pre-existence of the human soul. That is, before we were born, our souls must have already existed. They were present with Adam at the Fall. They fell along with Adam. Adam's sin was not merely an act for us; it was an act *with* us. We were there.

This theory seems speculative, perhaps even bizarre. Its advocates, however, appeal to two pivotal biblical texts as warrant for this view. The first is found in Ezekiel 18:2–4:

"What do you mean when you use this proverb concerning
the land of Israel, saying:
   'The fathers have eaten sour grapes,
   And the children's teeth are set on edge'?

"As I live," says the Lord GOD, "you shall no longer use this
proverb in Israel.

   "Behold, all souls are Mine;
   The soul of the father
   As well as the soul of the son is Mine;
   The soul who sins shall die."

Later in this chapter, Ezekiel writes:

   "Yet you say, 'Why should the son not bear the guilt of the
   father?' Because the son has done what is lawful and right, and
   has kept all My statutes and done them, he shall surely live.

   "The soul who sins shall die. The son shall not bear the
   guilt of the father, nor the father bear the guilt of the son.
   The righteousness of the righteous shall be upon himself,
   and the wickedness of the wicked shall be upon himself."
   (Ezek. 18:19, 20)

Here the realist finds a definitive text for his case. God clearly declares that
the son is not held guilty for the sins of his father. This would seem to pose
serious difficulties for the whole idea of people falling "in Adam."

The second pivotal text for realism is found in the New Testa-ment book
of Hebrews: "Even Levi, who receives tithes, paid tithes through Abraham, so
to speak, for he was still in the loins of his father when Melchizedek met him"
(Heb. 7:9, 10).

This text is part of a lengthy treatment by the author of Hebrews concerning the role of Christ as our great High Priest. The New Testament declares
that Jesus is both our king and our priest. It labors the fact that Jesus was from
the line of Judah, to whom the royal kingdom was promised. Jesus was a son
of David, who also was of the line of Judah.

The priesthood of the Old Testament was not given to Judah, but to the
sons of Levi. The Levites were the priestly line. We normally speak, therefore,
of the Levitical priesthood or the Aaronic priesthood. Aaron was a Levite. If this
is so, how could Jesus be a priest if he was not from the line of Levi?

This problem vexed some ancient Jews. The author of Hebrews argues that there was another priesthood mentioned in the Old Testament, the priesthood of the mysterious figure named Melchizedek. Jesus is said to be a priest of the order of Melchizedek.

This lengthy portion of Hebrews is not satisfied, however, merely to prove that there was another priesthood in the Old Testament besides the Levitical priesthood. The major point of the argument here is that the priesthood of Melchizedek was *superior* to the priesthood of Levi.

The author of Hebrews rehearses a bit of Old Testament history to prove his point. He calls attention to the fact that Abraham paid tithes to Melchizedek, not Melchizedek to Abraham. Melchizedek also blessed Abraham; Abraham did not bless Melchizedek. The point is this: In the relationship between Abraham and Melchizedek it was Melchizedek who served as the priest, not Abraham.

The key thought to the Jew is cited in verse 7: "Now beyond all contradiction the lesser is blessed by the better."

The author of Hebrews continues to weave the thread of his argument. He argues that, in effect, the father is superior to the son. That means that Abraham is ahead of Isaac in the patriarchal pecking order. In turn, Isaac is ahead of Jacob, and Jacob ahead of his sons, including his son Levi. If we carry this out, it means that Abraham is greater than his great-grandson Levi.

Now if Abraham is greater than Levi and Abraham subordinated himself to Melchizedek, then it means that the priest Melchizedek is greater than Levi and the entire line of Levi. The conclusion is clear. The priesthood of Melchizedek is a higher order of priesthood than the Levitical priesthood. This gives supreme dignity to the high priestly office of Christ.

It was not the chief concern of the author of Hebrews to explain the mystery of the fall of Adam with all this. Yet he says something along the way that the realists jump on to prove their theory. He writes that "Levi paid tithes through Abraham." Levi did this while he was "still in the loins of his father."

The realists see this reference to Levi doing something before he was even born as biblical proof for the concept of the preexistence of the human soul. If Levi could pay tithes while he was still in the loins of his father, that must mean that Levi in some sense already existed.

This treatment of this passage of Hebrews begs the question. The text does not explicitly teach that Levi really existed or preexisted in the loins of his father. The text itself calls it a "manner of speaking." The text does not demand that we leap to the conclusion that Levi "really" preexisted. The realists come to this text armed with a theory they did not find from the text and then read the theory into the text.

The argument from the text of Ezekiel also misses the point. Ezekiel was not giving a discourse on the fall of Adam. The Fall is not in view here. Rather, Ezekiel is addressing the commonplace excuse that men use for their sins. They try to blame someone else for their own misdeeds. That human activity has gone on since the Fall, but that is about all this passage has to do with the Fall. In the Fall Eve blamed the serpent, and Adam blamed both God and Eve for his own sin. He said, "The woman whom *You* gave to be with me, she gave me of the tree, and I ate" (Gen. 3:12).

Ever since, men have tried to pass the buck of their own guilt. Still, the realists argue, a principle is set forth in Ezekiel 18 that has bearing on the matter. The principle is that men are not held accountable for other people's sins.

To be sure, that general principle is set forth in Ezekiel. It is a grand principle of God's justice. Yet we dare not make it an absolute principle. If we do, then the text of Ezekiel would prove too much. It would prove away the Atonement of Christ. If it is never possible for one person to be punished for the sins of another, then we have no Savior. Jesus was punished for our sins. That is the very essence of the gospel. Not only was Jesus punished for our sins, but His righteousness is the meritorious basis for our justification. We are justified by an alien righteousness, a righteousness that is not our own. If we press Ezekiel's statement to the absolute limit when we read, "The righteousness of the righteous shall be upon himself, and the wickedness of the wicked shall be upon himself," then we are left as sinners who must justify themselves. That puts us all in deep weeds.

To be sure, the Bible speaks of God's "visiting" the iniquities of persons on the third and fourth generations. This refers to the "fall-out" or consequences of sin. A child may suffer from the consequences of his father's sin, but God does not hold him *responsible* for his father's sin.

The principle of Ezekiel allows for two exceptions: the Cross, and the Fall. Somehow we don't mind the exception of the Cross. It is the Fall that rankles us. We don't mind having our guilt transferred to Jesus or having His righteousness transferred to us; it is having the guilt of Adam transferred to us that makes us howl. We argue that if the guilt of Adam had never been transmitted to us then the work of Jesus would never have been necessary.

The Federal or Representative View of the Fall

For the most part, the federal view of the Fall has been the most popular among advocates of the Reformed view of predestination. This view teaches that Adam acted as a representative of the entire human race. With the test that God set before Adam and Eve, He was testing the whole of mankind. Adam's name means "man" or "mankind." Adam was the first human being created. He stands at the head of the human race. He was placed in the garden to act not only for himself but for all of his future descendants. Just as a federal government has a chief spokesman who is the head of the nation, so Adam was the federal head of mankind.

The chief idea of federalism is that, when Adam sinned, he sinned for all of us. His fall was our fall. When God punished Adam by taking away his original righteousness, we were all likewise punished. The curse of the Fall affects us all. Not only was Adam destined to make his living by the sweat of his brow, but that is true for us as well. Not only was Eve consigned to have pain in childbirth, but that has been true for women of all human generations. The offending serpent in the garden was not the only member of his species who was cursed to crawl on his belly.

When they were created, Adam and Eve were given dominion over the entire creation. As a result of their sin, the whole world suffered. Paul tells us: "For the creation was subjected to futility, not willingly, but because of Him who subjected it in hope; because the creation itself also will be delivered from the bondage of corruption into the glorious liberty of the children of God. For we know that the whole creation groans and labors with birth pangs together until now" (Rom. 8:20–22).

The whole creation groans as it awaits the full redemption of man. When man sinned, the repercussions of the sin were felt throughout the whole range of man's domain. Because of Adam's sin, not only do we suffer, but lions, elephants, butterflies, and puppy dogs also suffer. They did not ask for such suffering. They were hurt by the fall of their master.

That we suffer as a result of Adam's sin is explicitly taught in the New Testament. In Romans 5, for example, Paul makes the following observations:

"Through one man sin entered the world, and death through sin" (v. 12).

"By the one man's offense many died" (v. 15).

"Through one man's offense judgment came to all men, resulting in condemnation" (v. 18).

"By one man's disobedience many were made sinners" (v. 19).

There is no way to avoid the obvious teaching of Scripture that Adam's sin had dreadful consequences for his descendants. It is precisely because of the abundance of such biblical statements that virtually every Christian body has composed some doctrine of original sin linked to the fall of Adam.

We are still left with a big question. If God did in fact judge the entire human race in Adam, how is that fair? It seems manifestly unjust of God to allow not only all subsequent human beings but all of creation to suffer because of Adam.

It is the question of God's fairness that federalism seeks to answer. Federalism assumes that we were in fact represented by Adam and that such representation was both fair and accurate. It holds that Adam *perfectly* represented us.

Within our own legal system we have situations that, not perfectly but approximately, parallel this concept of representation. We know that if I hire a man to kill someone and that hired gunman carries out the contract, I can justly be tried for first-degree murder in spite of the fact that I did not actually pull the trigger. I am judged to be guilty for a crime someone else committed because the other person acted in my place.

The obvious protest that arises at this point is, "But we did not hire Adam to sin in our behalf." That is true. This example merely illustrates that there are *some* cases in which it is just to punish one person for the crime of another.

The federal view of the Fall still exudes a faint odor of tyranny. Our cry is, "No damnation without representation!" Just as people in a nation clamor for representatives to insure freedom from despotic tyranny, so we demand representation before God that is fair and just. The federal view states that we are judged guilty for Adam's sin because he was our fair and just representative.

Wait a minute. Adam may have represented us, but we did not choose him. What if the fathers of the American republic had demanded representation from King George and the king replied, "Of course you may have representatives. You will be represented by my brother!" Such an answer would have spilled even more tea in Boston Harbor.

We want the right to select our own representatives. We want to be able to cast our own vote, not have somebody else cast that vote for us. The word *vote* comes from the Latin *votum* which meant "wish" or "choice." When we cast our vote, we are expressing our wishes, setting forth our wills.

Suppose we would have had the total freedom to vote for our representative in Eden. Would that have satisfied us? And why do we want the right to vote for our representative? Why do we object if the king or any other sovereign wants to appoint our representatives for us? The answer is obvious. We want to be sure that our will is being carried out. If the king appoints my representative, then I will have little confidence that my wishes will be accomplished. I would fear that the appointed representative would be more eager to carry out the wishes of the king than my wishes. I would not feel fairly represented.

But even if we have the right to choose our own representatives, we have no guarantee that our wishes will be carried out. Who among us has not been enticed by politicians who promise one thing during an election campaign and do another thing after they are elected? Again, the reason we want to select our own representative is so that we can be sure we are accurately represented.

At no time in all of human history have we been more accurately represented than in the Garden of Eden. To be sure, we did not choose our representative there. Our representative was chosen for us. The one who chose our representative, however, was not King George. It was almighty God.

When God chooses our representative, He does so perfectly. His choice is an infallible choice. When I choose my own representatives, I do so fallibly. Sometimes I select the wrong person and am then inaccurately represented. Adam represented me infallibly, not because he was infallible, but because God is infallible. Given God's infallibility, I can never argue that Adam was a poor choice to represent me.

The assumption many of us make when we struggle with the Fall is that, had we been there, we would have made a different choice. We would not have made a decision that would plunge the world into ruin. Such an assumption is just not possible given the character of God. God doesn't make mistakes. His choice of my representative is greater than my choice of my own.

Even if we grant that indeed we were perfectly represented by Adam, we still must ask if it is fair to be represented at all with such high stakes. I can only answer that it pleased the Lord to do this. We know that the world fell through Adam. We know that in some sense Adam represented us. We know that we did not choose him to be our representative. We know that God's selection of Adam was an infallible selection. But was the whole process just?

I can only answer this question ultimately by asking another question—one the apostle Paul asked. "Is there unrighteousness in God?" The apostolic answer to this rhetorical question is as plain as it is emphatic. "God forbid!"

If we know anything at all about the character of God, then we know that He is not a tyrant and that He is never unjust. His structure of the terms of mankind's probation satisfied God's own righteousness. That should be enough to satisfy us.

Yet we still quarrel. We still contend with the Almighty. We still assume that somehow God did us wrong and that we suffer as innocent victims of God's judgment. Such sentiments only confirm the radical degree of our fallenness. When we think like this, we are thinking like Adam's children. Such blasphemous thoughts only underline in red how accurately we were represented by Adam.

I am persuaded that the federal view of the Fall is substantially correct. It alone of the three we have examined does justice to the biblical teaching of the fall of man. It satisfies me that God is not an arbitrary tyrant. I know that I am a fallen creature. That is, I know that I am a creature and I know that I am fallen. I also know that it is not God's "fault" that I am a sinner. What God has done for me is to redeem me from my sin. He has not redeemed me from His sin.

Though the federal representational view of the Fall is held by most Calvinists, we must remember that the question of our relationship to Adam's fall is not a problem unique to Calvinism. All Christians must struggle with it.

It is also vital to see predestination in light of the Fall. All Christians agree that God's decree of predestination was made before the Fall. Some argue that God first predestinated some people to salvation and others to damnation and then decreed the Fall to make sure that some folks would perish. Sometimes this dreadful view is even attributed to Calvinism. Such an idea was repugnant to Calvin and is equally repugnant to all orthodox Calvinists. The notion is sometimes called hyper-Calvinism. But even that is an insult. This view has nothing to do with Calvinism. Rather than hyper-Calvinism, it is anti-Calvinism.

Calvinism, along with other views of predestination, teaches that God's decree was made both *before* the Fall, and *in light of* the Fall. Why is this important? Because the Calvinistic view of predestination always accents the gracious character of God's redemption. When God predestines people to salvation, He is predestinating people to be saved whom He knows really *need* to be saved. They need to be saved because they are sinners in Adam, not because He forced them to be sinners. Calvinism sees Adam sinning by his own free will, not by divine coercion.

To be sure, God knew before the Fall that there would most certainly be a Fall and He took action to redeem some. He ordained the Fall in the sense that He chose to allow it, but not in the sense that He chose to coerce it. His predestinating grace is gracious precisely because He chooses to save people whom He knows in advance will be spiritually dead.

One final illustration may be helpful here. We bristle at the idea that God calls us to be righteous when we are hampered by original sin. We say, "But God, we can't be righteous. We are fallen creatures. How can You hold us accountable when You know very well we were born with original sin?"

The illustration is as follows. Suppose God said to a man, "I want you to trim these bushes by three o'clock this afternoon. But be careful. There is a large open pit at the edge of the garden. If you fall into that pit, you will not be able to get yourself out. So whatever you do, stay away from that pit."

Suppose that as soon as God leaves the garden the man runs over and jumps into the pit. At three o'clock God returns and finds the bushes untrimmed. He calls for the gardener and hears a faint cry from the edge of the garden. He walks to the edge of the pit and sees the gardener helplessly flailing around on the bottom. He says to the gardener, "Why haven't you trimmed the bushes I told you to trim?" The gardener responds in anger, "How do You expect me to trim these bushes when I am trapped in this pit? If You hadn't left this empty pit here, I would not be in this predicament."

Adam jumped into the pit. In Adam we all jumped into the pit. God did not throw us into the pit. Adam was clearly warned about the pit. God told him to stay away. The consequences Adam experienced from being in the pit were a direct punishment for jumping into it.

So it is with original sin. Original sin is both the consequence of Adam's sin and the punishment for Adam's sin. We are born sinners because in Adam all fell. Even the word *fall* is a bit of a euphemism. It is a rose-colored view of the matter. The word *fall* suggests an accident of sorts. Adam's sin was not an accident. He was not Humpty-Dumpty. Adam didn't simply slip into sin; he jumped into it with both feet. We jumped headlong with him. God didn't push us. He didn't trick us. He gave us adequate and fair warning. The fault is ours and only ours.

It is not that Adam ate sour grapes and our teeth are set on edge. The biblical teaching is that in Adam we all ate the sour grapes. That is why our teeth are set on edge.

Summary of Chapter 4

1. The pervasive, universal presence of human sin cannot be explained adequately by a myth.
2. Man's sinfulness cannot be explained by "society."
3. Society is made up of individual persons, who each must be a sinner before the society as a whole can be corrupt.
4. Realism also fails as an explanation because it involves a fanciful approach to Scripture.
5. The federal view of the Fall takes seriously the role Adam played as our representative.
6. Adam perfectly represented us not by virtue of his perfection but by virtue of God's perfect selection.
7. All Christians must have some view of the Fall.
8. God's saving grace is directed toward those whom He knows to be fallen creatures.

FIVE

Spiritual Death and Spiritual Life: Rebirth and Faith

R eformed theology is famous for a simple acrostic that was designed to sum-
marize the so-called Five Points of Calvinism. It spells the word TULIP.

T—*Total Depravity*
U—*Unconditional Election*
L—*Limited Atonement*
I—*Irresistible Grace*
P—*Perseverance of the Saints*

This acrostic has helped many people remember the distinctives of Reformed theology. Unfortunately, it has also caused great confusion and much
misunderstanding. The problem with acrostics is that the best terms we have for
ideas don't always start with letters that will spell neat little words. The acrostic
serves well as a memory device, but that is about all.

My first problem with the acrostic TULIP is with the first letter. *Total depravity* is a very misleading term. The concept of total depravity is often confused with
the idea of utter depravity. In Reformed theology total depravity refers to the idea
that our *whole humanity* is fallen. That is, there is no part of me that has not been
affected in some way by the Fall. Sin affects my will, my heart, my mind, and my
body. If Adam had never sinned, I suppose he would not have had the need to
wear bifocals when he reached middle age. In fact the very term *middle age* would
have been meaningless to him. Had he not sinned, Adam would not have died.
When one lives forever, where is middle age?

Total depravity also stresses the fact that sin reaches to the core of our
being. Sin is not a peripheral thing, a slight blemish that mars an otherwise

perfect specimen. Sin is radical in the sense that it touches the root (*radix*) of our lives.

Total depravity is not utter depravity. Utter depravity would mean that we are all as sinful as we possibly could be. We know that is not the case. No matter how much each of us has sinned, we are able to think of worse sins that we could have committed. Even Adolf Hitler refrained from murdering his mother.

Since total depravity is often confused with utter depravity, I prefer to speak of the "radical corruption" of man. That does mess up our acrostic. What in the world is a rulip? The concept of the radical character of sin is perhaps the most important concept for us to understand if we are going to make any sense out of the biblical doctrine of predestination. As I mentioned during our discussion of man's moral inability, this is the focal point of the entire debate.

I remember teaching a college class in theology. The class was made up of an interdenominational group of about twenty-five students. I asked at the beginning of the study on predestination how many students considered themselves Calvinists on the matter. Only one student raised his hand.

We started with a study of man's sinfulness. After I lectured for several days on the subject of man's corruption, I took another poll. I asked, "How many of you are persuaded that what you have just learned is in fact the Bible doctrine of human sinfulness?" Every hand went up. I said, "Are you sure?" They insisted that they were indeed sure. I gave a further warning. "Be careful now. This may come back to haunt you later in the course." No matter. They insisted that they were convinced.

At this point in the class I went to the corner of the chalkboard and wrote the date. Next to the date I wrote the figure *25*. I put a circle around this and added a note to the janitor to please refrain from erasing this portion of the board.

Several weeks later we began a study of predestination. When I got to the point of man's moral inability there were howls of protest. Then I went to the chalkboard and reminded them of the earlier poll. It took another two weeks to convince them that, if they really accepted the biblical view of human corruption, the debate about predestination for all intents and purposes was already over.

I shall, in brief, attempt to do the same thing here. I proceed with the same caution.

The Biblical View of Human Corruption

Let us begin our study of the degree of man's fallenness by looking at Romans 3. Here the apostle Paul writes:

"There is none righteous, no, not one;
There is none who understands;
There is none who seeks after God.
They have all gone out of the way;
They have together become unprofitable;
There is none who does good, no, not one." (Rom. 3:10–12)

Here we find a brief summation of the universality of human corruption. Sin is so pervasive that it captures everyone in its net. Paul uses words of emphasis to show that there are no exceptions to this indictment among fallen men. There is none righteous; there is none who does good.

The statement "There is none who does good, no, not one" flies in the face of our cultural assumptions. We grow up hearing that nobody is perfect and that to err is human. We are quite willing to acknowledge that none of us is perfect. That we are sinners is easy to admit; that none of us even does good is a bit much. Not one person in a thousand will admit that sin is this serious.

No one does good? How can that be? Every day we see rank pagans doing some good. We see them performing heroic acts of sacrifice, works of industry, prudence, and honesty. We see unbelievers scrupulously obeying the speed limits while cars whiz by them bearing bumper stickers that read, "Honk if you love Jesus."

Paul must be using hyperbole here. He must be intentionally exaggerating in order to make a point. Surely there are people who do good. No! The sober judgment of God is that no one does good, no, not one.

We stumble here because we have a relative understanding of what good is. Good is, indeed, a relative term. Something can only be judged good according to some sort of standard. We use the term as a comparison among men. When we say that a man is good, we mean that he is good compared with other men. But the ultimate standard for goodness, the standard by which we shall all be judged, is the law of God. That law is not God, but it comes from God and reflects the perfect character of God Himself. Judged against that standard, no one is good.

In biblical categories a good deed is measured in two parts. The first is in its outward conformity to the law of God. This means that, if God prohibits stealing, then it is good not to steal. It is good to tell the truth. It is good to pay our bills on time. It is good to assist people in need. Outwardly these virtues are performed every day. When we see them we quickly conclude that men do in fact do good things.

It is the second part of the measuring that gets us in trouble. Before God pronounces a deed "good" he considers not only the outward or external conformity to His law, but also the motivation. We look only at outward appearances; God reads the heart. For a work to be considered good, it must not only conform outwardly to the law of God, but it must be motivated inwardly by a sincere love for God.

We remember the Great Commandment to love the Lord our God with all our hearts, all our strength, and all our minds . . . and love our neighbors as much as we love ourselves. Every deed that we do should proceed from a heart that loves God totally.

From this perspective it is easy to see that no one does good. Our best works are tainted by our less than pure motives. No one among us has ever loved God with all of his heart or with all of his mind. There is a pound of flesh mixed in with all of our deeds, rendering them less than perfect.

Jonathan Edwards spoke of the concept of *enlightened self-interest*. Enlightened self-interest refers to that motivation we all feel to perform external righteousness and to restrain some evil impulses within ourselves. There are certain times and places where crime does not pay. Where the risk of punishment outweighs the possible reward of our misdeed, we may be inclined to refrain from it. On the other hand, we may win the applause of men by our virtuous acts. We may gain a pat on the head from our teacher or the respect of our peers if we do certain good deeds.

The whole world applauds recording artists when they band together to produce a special album with the proceeds to be used to relieve famine in Ethiopia. Applause rarely hurts the career of a stage performer, despite cynical statements that ethics and business do not mix. On the contrary, most of us have learned that ethics enhance our reputations in business.

I am not so cynical as to think that the gesture for Ethiopia by singers was done purely for personal applause or as a publicity stunt. Surely there were strong motives of compassion and care for starving people. On the other hand, I am not so naïve as to think that the motives were totally without self-interest. The compassion may far outweigh the self-interest, but no matter how minuscule, there was at least a grain of self-interest mixed in. There always is, in all of us. If we deny this I suspect that our very denials are motivated in part by self-interest.

We want to deny this allegation. We sense in our own hearts at times an overwhelming feeling of performing from duty alone. We like to think that we are truly altruistic. But no one ever flatters us more than we flatter ourselves.

The weight of our motives may at times lean heavily in the direction of altruism, but it is never perfectly there.

God does not grade on a curve. He demands perfection. None of us performs to that level. We do not do what God commands. Ever. Therefore the apostle is not indulging himself with hyperbole. His judgment is accurate. There is none who does good, no, not one. Jesus Himself reinforced this view in His discussion with the rich young ruler. "No one is good but One, that is, God" (Luke 18:19).

As troublesome as this indictment is, another element in the Romans passage may bring even more consternation to us, especially to evangelical Christians who talk and think to the contrary. Paul says, "There is none who seeks after God."

How many times have you heard Christians say, or have you heard the words from your own mouth, "So and so is not a Christian, but he's searching"? It is a common statement among Christians. The idea is that there are people all over the place who are searching for God. Their problem is that they just haven't been able to find Him. He is playing hide and seek. He is elusive.

In the Garden of Eden when sin came into the world, who hid? Jesus came into the world to *seek* and to save the lost. Jesus wasn't the one who was hiding. God is not a fugitive. We are the ones on the run. Scripture declares that the wicked flee when no man pursues. As Luther remarked, "The pagan trembles at the rustling of a leaf." The uniform teaching of Scripture is that fallen men are fleeing from God. There is none who seeks after God.

Why is it then, despite such clear biblical teaching to the contrary, that Christians persist in claiming that they know people who are searching for God but have not yet found Him? Saint Thomas Aquinas shed some light on this. Aquinas said that we confuse two similar yet different human actions. We see people searching desperately for peace of mind, relief from guilt, meaning and purpose to their lives, and loving acceptance. We know that ultimately these things can only be found in God. Therefore we conclude that since people are seeking these things they must be seeking after God.

People do not seek God. They seek after the *benefits that only God can give them.* The sin of fallen man is this: Man seeks the benefits of God while at the same time fleeing from God Himself. We are, by nature, fugitives.

The Bible tells us repeatedly to seek after God. The Old Testament cries, "Seek the Lord while He may be found" (Isa. 55:6). Jesus said, "Seek, and you will find; knock, and it will be opened to you" (Matt. 7:7). The conclusion we draw from these texts is that since we are called to seek after God it must mean that we, even in our fallen state, have the moral capacity to do that seeking.

But who is being addressed in these texts? In the case of the Old Testament it is the people of Israel who are called to seek the Lord. In the New Testament it is believers who are called to seek the kingdom.

We have all heard evangelists quote from Revelation: "I stand at the door and knock. If anyone hears My voice and opens the door, I will come in to him and dine with him, and he with Me" (Rev. 3:20). Usually the evangelist applies this text as an appeal to the unconverted, saying, "Jesus is knocking at the door of your heart. If you open the door He will come in." In the original saying, however, Jesus directed His remarks to the church. It was not an evangelistic appeal.

So what? The point is that seeking is something that unbelievers do not do on their own steam. *The unbeliever will not seek. The unbeliever will not knock.* Seeking is the business of believers. Edwards said, "The seeking of the kingdom of God is the chief business of the Christian life." Seeking is the result of faith, not the cause of it.

When we are converted to Christ, we use language of discovery to express our conversion. We speak of finding Christ. We may have a bumper sticker that reads I FOUND IT. These statements are indeed true. The irony is this: Once we have found Christ it is not the end of our seeking, but the beginning. Usually, when we find what we are looking for, it signals the end of our searching. But when we "find" Christ, it is the beginning of our search. The Christian life begins at conversion; it does not end where it begins. It grows; it moves from faith to faith, from grace to grace, from life to life. This movement of growth is prodded by a continual seeking after God.

There is one more insight in Romans 3 that we need to look at briefly. Not only does the apostle declare that no one seeks after God, but he adds the thought, "They have together become unprofitable." We must remember that here Paul is speaking of fallen men, natural men, unconverted men. This is a description of people who are still in the flesh.

What does Paul mean by unprofitable? Jesus earlier spoke of unprofitable servants. Profit has to do with positive values. The unconverted person, working in the flesh, achieves nothing of permanent value. In the flesh he may gain the whole world but he loses the thing of most value to himself, his own soul. The most valuable possession a person can ever have is Christ. He is the pearl of great price. To have Him is to have the greatest possible profit.

The person who is spiritually dead cannot, in his own flesh, gain the profit of Christ. He is described as one who has no fear of God before his eyes (Rom. 3:18). Those who are not righteous, who do no good, who never seek after God, who are altogether unprofitable, and who have no fear of God before their eyes, never incline their own hearts to Christ.

Quickening from Spiritual Death

The cure for spiritual death is the creation of spiritual life in our souls by God the Holy Spirit. A summary of this work is given to us in Ephesians:

> And you He made alive, who were dead in trespasses and sins, in which you once walked according to the course of this world, according to the prince of the power of the air, the spirit who now works in the sons of disobedience, among whom also we all once conducted ourselves in the lusts of our flesh, fulfilling the desires of the flesh and of the mind, and were by nature children of wrath, just as the others.

> But God, who is rich in mercy, because of His great love with which He loved us, even when we were dead in trespasses, made us alive together with Christ (by grace you have been saved), and raised us up together, and made us sit together in the heavenly places in Christ Jesus, that in the ages to come He might show the exceeding riches of His grace in His kindness toward us in Christ Jesus.

> For by grace you have been saved through faith, and that not of yourselves; it is the gift of God, not of works, lest any man should boast. For we are His workmanship, created in Christ Jesus for good works, which God prepared beforehand that we should walk in them. (Eph. 2:1–10)

Here we find a predestinarian passage *par excellence*. Notice that throughout this passage Paul places a heavy accent on the riches of God's grace. We must never shortchange this grace. The passage celebrates the newness of life that the Holy Spirit has created in us.

This work of the Spirit is sometimes called quickening. Rarely heard in ordinary speech, the term is almost exclusively used to describe an event that happens during a pregnancy. "Quickening" refers to the woman's first feeling of the life of the baby she is carrying in her womb.

What is here called quickening or being made alive is what is elsewhere called rebirth or regeneration. The term *regeneration*, as the word suggests, indicates a "generating again." To generate means to cause to happen or to begin. We think of the first book of the Bible, the book of beginnings, which is called Genesis. The prefix *re* means simply "again." Therefore the word *regeneration* means to begin something again. It is the new beginning of life that we are concerned with here, the beginning of spiritual life.

We note that this image of life is contrasted with an image of death. Fallen man is here described as being "dead in sin." In order for one who is dead to the things of God to come alive to God, something must be done *to* him and *for* him. Dead men cannot make themselves come alive. Dead men cannot create spiritual life within themselves. Paul makes it crystal clear here that it is God who makes alive; it is God who quickens us from spiritual death.

Fallen man is dead in sin. He is described here as being "by nature, a child of wrath." His fallen pattern is to "walk according to the course of this world." His allegiance is not to God but to the prince of the power of the air. Paul states that this is not merely the state of all the worst sinners but the former state of himself and of his brothers and sisters in Christ. ("Among whom also we all once conducted ourselves in the lusts of our flesh, fulfilling the desires of the flesh. . . .")

Most non-Reformed views of predestination fail to take seriously the fact that fallen man is spiritually dead. Other evangelical positions acknowledge that man is fallen and that his fallenness is a serious matter. They even grant that sin is a radical problem. They are quick to grant that man is not merely ill, but mortally ill, sick unto death. But he has not quite died yet. He still has one tiny breath of spiritual life left in his body. He still has a tiny island of righteousness left in his heart, a tiny and feeble moral ability that abides in his fallenness.

I have heard two illustrations from evangelists who plead for the repentance and conversion of their hearers. The first is an analogy of a person suffering from a terminal illness. The sinner is said to be gravely ill, on the very brink of death. He does not have it within his own power to cure himself of the disease. He is lying on his deathbed almost totally paralyzed. He cannot recover unless God provides the healing medicine. The man is so bad off that he cannot even stretch forth his arm to receive the medicine. He is almost comatose. God must not only offer the medicine, but God must put it on a spoon and place it by the dying man's lips. Unless God does all that, the man will surely perish. But though God does 99 percent of what is necessary, the man is still left with 1 percent. He must open his mouth to receive the medicine. This is the necessary exercise of free will that makes the difference between heaven and hell. The man who opens his mouth to receive the gracious gift of the medicine will be saved. The man who keeps his lips tightly clenched will perish.

This analogy *almost* does justice to the Bible and to Paul's teaching of the grace of regeneration. But not quite. The Bible does not speak of mortally ill sinners. According to Paul they are *dead*. There is not an ounce of spiritual life left in them. If they are to be made alive, God must do more than offer them medicine. Dead men will not open their mouths to receive anything. Their jaws are locked in death. Rigor mortis has set in. They must be raised from the dead. They must be new creations, crafted by Christ and reborn by His Spirit.

A second illustration is equally popular with those committed to evangelism. In this view fallen man is seen as a drowning man who is unable to swim. He has gone under twice and bobbed to the surface for the last time. If he goes under again, he will die. His only hope is for God to throw him a life preserver. God throws the lifeline and tosses it precisely to the edge of the man's outstretched fingers. All the man has to do to be saved is to grab hold. If he will only grab hold of the life preserver, God will tow him in. If he refuses the life preserver, he will certainly perish.

Again, in this illustration the utter helplessness of sinful man without God's assistance is emphasized. The drowning man is in a serious condition. He cannot save himself. However, he is still alive; he can still stretch forth his fingers. His fingers are the crucial link to salvation. His eternal destiny depends upon what he does with his fingers.

Paul says the man is dead. He is not merely drowning, he has already sunk to the bottom of the sea. It is futile to throw a life preserver to a man who has already drowned. If I understand Paul, I hear him saying that God dives into the water and pulls a dead man from the bottom of the sea and then performs a divine act of mouth-to-mouth resuscitation. He breathes into the dead man new life.

It is important to remember that regeneration has to do with new life. It is called the new birth or being born again. Much confusion exists about this matter. The new birth is closely linked in the Bible to the new life that is ours in Christ. Just as in natural biology there can be no life without birth, so in supernatural terms there can be no new life without a new birth.

Birth and life are closely connected, but they are not exactly the same thing. Birth is the beginning of the new life. It is a decisive moment. We understand that in normal biological terms. Every year we celebrate our birthdays. We are not like the queen in *Alice in Wonderland* who celebrated all of her "unbirthdays." Birth is a one-time experience. It may be celebrated but not repeated. It is a decisive moment of transition. A person is either born or not yet born.

So it is with spiritual rebirth. Rebirth produces new life. It is the beginning of new life, but it is not the total sum of the new life. It is the crucial point of transition from spiritual death to spiritual life. A person is never partially born again. He is either regenerate or he is not regenerate.

The clear biblical teaching of regeneration is that it is the work of God and the work of God alone. We cannot cause ourselves to be reborn. The flesh cannot produce the spirit. Regeneration is an act of *creation*. God does the creating.

In theology we have a technical term that may be helpful, *monergism*. It comes from two root words. *Mono* means "one." A monopoly is a business that has the market to itself. A monoplane is a single-winged aircraft. *Erg*, you may remember from grade school, refers to a unit of work. We get the common word *energy* from it.

Putting the parts together, we get the meaning "one working." When we say that regeneration is monergistic, we mean that only one party is doing the work. That party is God the Holy Spirit. He regenerates us; we cannot do it ourselves or even help Him with the task.

It may sound as if we are treating human beings like puppets. Puppets are made of wood. They can make no response. They are inert, lifeless. They are moved about by strings. But we are not talking about puppets. We are talking about humans who are spiritual corpses. These humans do not have hearts made of sawdust; they are made of stone. They are not manipulated by strings. They are biologically alive. They act. They make decisions, but never decisions for God.

When God regenerates a human soul, when He makes us spiritually alive, we make choices. We believe. We have faith. We cling to Christ. God does not believe for us. Faith is not monergistic.

Earlier we talked about the plight of fallen man and the status of his human will. We affirmed that though he is fallen he still has a free will in the sense that he can still make choices. His problem, which we defined as moral inability, is that he lacks a desire for Christ. He is indisposed and disinclined toward Christ. Unless or until man is inclined to Christ, he will never choose Christ. Unless he first desires Christ, he will never receive Christ.

In regeneration, God changes our hearts. He gives us a new disposition, a new inclination. He plants a desire for Christ in our hearts. We can never trust Christ for our salvation unless we first desire Him. This is why we said earlier that *regeneration precedes faith*. Without rebirth we have no desire for Christ. Without a desire for Christ we will never choose Christ. Therefore we conclude that before anyone ever will believe, before anyone *can* believe, God must first change the disposition of his heart.

When God regenerates us, it is an act of grace. Let us look again at Ephesians 2: "But God, who is rich in mercy, because of His great love with which He loved us, even when we were dead in trespasses, made us alive. . . ."

I have a sign on my desk that was embroidered for me by a woman in a church I once served. The sign reads simply, "But." When Paul rehearses fallen man's spiritual condition, it is enough to drive us to despair. Finally he gets to the magic word that makes us breathe a sigh of relief. But. Without it we are doomed to perish. The "but" captures the essence of the good news.

Paul says, "But God, who is rich in mercy. . . ." Notice that he does not say, "But man, who is rich in goodness." It is God alone who makes us alive. When does He do it? Paul does not leave us to guess. He says, ". . . when we were dead in trespasses." This is the amazing part of grace, that it is given to us when we are spiritually dead.

Paul concludes that it is a matter of grace and not a matter of works. His sterling summary is, "For by grace you have been saved through faith, and that not of yourselves, it is the gift of God." This passage should seal the matter forever. The faith by which we are saved is a gift. When the apostle says it is not of ourselves, he does not mean that it is not our faith. Again, God does not do the believing for us. It is our own faith but it does not originate with us. It is given to us. The gift is not earned or deserved. It is a gift of sheer grace.

During the Protestant Reformation there were three slogans that became famous. They are Latin phrases: *sola fide, sola gratia,* and *soli Deo gloria.* The three slogans belong together. They ought never to be divorced from one another. They mean, "by faith alone," "by grace alone," and "to God alone the glory."

Irresistible Grace?

Most Christians agree that God's work of regeneration is a work of grace. The issue that divides us is whether or not this grace is irresistible. Is it possible for a person to receive the grace of regeneration and still not come to faith?

The Calvinist answers with an emphatic "No!" but not because he believes that God's saving grace is literally irresistible. Again we run into a problem with the old acrostic TULIP. We have already changed the TULIP to RULIP and now we are going to have to change it some more. Now we will call it RULEP.

The term *irresistible grace* is misleading. Calvinists all believe that men can and do resist the grace of God. The question is, "Can the grace of regeneration fail to accomplish its purpose?" Remember that spiritually dead people are still biologically alive. They still have a will that is disinclined toward God. They will do everything in their power to resist grace. The history of Israel is the history of a hardhearted and stiff-necked people who resisted God's grace repeatedly.

God's grace is resistible in the sense that we can and do resist it. It is irresistible in the sense that it achieves its purpose. It brings about God's desired effect. Thus I prefer the term *effectual grace.*

We are speaking of the grace of regeneration. We remember that in regeneration God creates in us a desire for Himself. But when we have that desire planted in us, we will continue to function as we always have functioned, making our choices according to the strongest motivation at the moment. If God gives us a desire for Christ, we will act according to that desire. We will most certainly choose the object of that desire; we will choose Christ. When God makes us spiritually alive, we become spiritually alive. It is not merely the possibility of becoming spiritually alive that God creates. He creates spiritual life within us. When He calls something into being, it comes into being.

We speak of the *inward call* of God. The inward call of God is as powerful and effective as His call to create the world. God did not invite the world into existence. By divine mandate He called out, "Let there be light!" And there was light. It could not have been otherwise. The light *had* to begin to shine.

Could Lazarus have stayed in the tomb when Jesus called him out? Jesus cried, "Lazarus, come forth!" The man broke out of his grave clothes and came out of the tomb. When God creates, He exercises a power that only God has. He alone has the power to bring something out of nothing and life out of death.

Much confusion exists on this point. I remember the first lecture I ever heard from John Gerstner. It was on the subject of predestination. Shortly into his lecture Dr. Gerstner was interrupted by a student who was waving his hand in the air. Gerstner stopped and acknowledged the student. The student asked, "Dr. Gerstner, is it safe to assume that you are a Calvinist?" Gerstner answered, "Yes," and resumed his lecture. A few moments later a gleam of recognition appeared in Gerstner's eyes, and he stopped speaking in midsentence and asked the student, "What is your definition of a Calvinist?"

The student replied, "A Calvinist is someone who believes that God forces some people to choose Christ and prevents other people from choosing Christ." Gerstner was horrified. He said, "If that is what a Calvinist is, then you can be sure that I am not a Calvinist."

The student's misconception of irresistible grace is widespread. I once heard the president of a Presbyterian seminary declare, "I am not a Calvinist because I do not believe that God brings some people, kicking and screaming against their wills, into the kingdom, while He excludes others from His kingdom who desperately want to be there."

I was astonished when I heard these words. I did not think it possible that the president of a Presbyterian seminary could have such a gross misconception of his own church's theology. He was reciting a caricature which was as far away from Calvinism as one could get.

Calvinism does not teach and never has taught that God brings people kicking and screaming into the kingdom or has ever excluded anyone who wanted to be there. Remember that the cardinal point of the Reformed doctrine of predestination rests on the biblical teaching of man's spiritual death. Natural man does not want Christ. He will only want Christ if God plants a desire for Christ in his heart. Once that desire is planted, those who come to Christ do not come kicking and screaming against their wills. They come because they want to come. They now desire Jesus. They rush to the Savior. The whole point of irresistible grace is that rebirth quickens someone to spiritual life in such a way that Jesus is now seen in His irresistible sweetness. Jesus is irresistible to those who have been made alive to the things of God. Every soul whose heart beats with the life of God within it longs for the living Christ. All whom the Father gives to Christ come to Christ (John 6:37).

The term *effectual grace* may help to avoid some confusion. Effectual grace is grace that effects what God desires.

How does this view differ from other non-Reformed views of regeneration? The most popular alternate view rests upon the concept of prevenient grace.

Prevenient Grace

As the name suggests, prevenient grace is grace that "comes before" something. It is normally defined as a work that God does for everybody. He gives all people enough grace to respond to Jesus. That is, it is enough grace to make it *possible* for people to choose Christ. Those who cooperate with and assent to this grace are "elect." Those who refuse to cooperate with this grace are lost.

The strength of this view is that it recognizes that fallen man's spiritual condition is severe enough that it requires God's grace to save him. The weakness of the position may be seen in two ways. If this prevenient grace is merely external to man, then it fails in the same manner that the medicine and the life preserver analogies fail. What good is prevenient grace if offered outwardly to spiritually dead creatures?

On the other hand, if prevenient grace refers to something that God does within the heart of fallen man, then we must ask why it is not always effectual. Why is it that some fallen creatures choose to cooperate with prevenient grace and others choose not to? Doesn't everyone get the same amount?

Think of it this way, in personal terms. If you are a Christian you are surely aware of other people who are not Christians. Why is it that you have chosen Christ and they have not? Why did you say yes to prevenient grace while they said no? Was it because you were more righteous than they were? If so, then indeed you have something in which to boast. Was that greater righteousness something you achieved on your own or was it the gift of God? If it was something you achieved, then at the bottom line your salvation depends on your own righteousness. If the righteousness was a gift, then why didn't God give the same gift to everybody?

Perhaps it wasn't because you were more righteous. Perhaps it was because you are more intelligent. Why are you more intelligent? Because you study more (which really means you are more righteous)? Or are you more intelligent because God gave you a gift of intelligence He withheld from others?

To be sure, most Christians who hold to the prevenient grace view would shrink from such answers. They see the implied arrogance in them. Rather they are more likely to say, "No, I chose Christ because I recognized my desperate need for Him."

That certainly sounds more humble. But I must press the question. Why did you recognize your desperate need for Christ while your neighbor didn't? Was it because you were more righteous than your neighbor, or more intelligent?

The $64 question for advocates of prevenient grace is why some people co-operate with it and others don't. How we answer that will reveal how gracious we believe our salvation really is.

The $64,000 question is, "Does the Bible teach such a doctrine of prevenient grace? If so, where?"

We conclude that our salvation is of the Lord. He is the One who regenerates us. Those whom He regenerates come to Christ. Without regeneration no one will ever come to Christ. With regeneration no one will ever reject Him. God's saving grace effects what He intends to effect by it.

Summary of Chapter 5

1. Our salvation flows from a divine initiative. It is God the Holy Spirit who sets the captives free. It is He who breathes into us spiritual life and resurrects us from spiritual death.
2. Our condition before we are quickened is one of spiritual death. It is more severe than mere mortal illness. There is not an ounce of spiritual life in us until God makes us alive.
3. Without rebirth no one will come to Christ. All who are reborn do come to Christ. Those who are dead to the things of God stay dead to the things of God unless God makes them alive. Those whom God makes alive, come alive. Salvation is of the Lord.

SIX

Foreknowledge and Predestination

The vast majority of Christians who reject the Reformed view of predestination adopt what is sometimes called the prescient or foreknowledge (pre-science, prior knowledge) view of predestination. Briefly stated, this view teaches that from all eternity God knew how we would live. He knew in advance whether we would receive Christ or reject Christ. He knew our free choices before we ever made them. God's choice of our eternal destiny then was made on the basis of what He knew we would choose. He chooses us because He knows in advance that we will choose Him. The elect, then, are those who God knows will choose Christ freely.

In this understanding both the eternal decree of God and the free choice of man are left intact. In this view there is nothing arbitrary about God's decisions. There is no talk here of being reduced to puppets or of having our free wills violated. God is clearly absolved of any hint of wrongdoing. The basis for our ultimate judgment rests ultimately upon our decision for or against Christ.

There is much to commend this view of predestination. It is quite satisfying and has the benefits mentioned above. In addition it seems to have at least one strong biblical warrant. If we turn our attention again to Paul's letter to the Romans we read: "For whom He *foreknew*, He also *predestined* to be conformed to the image of His Son, that He might be the firstborn among many brethren. Moreover whom He predestined, these He also called; whom He called, these He also justified; and whom He justified, these He also glorified" (Rom. 8:29, 30, italics added).

This well-known passage in Romans has been called the Golden Chain of Salvation. We notice a kind of order here that begins with God's foreknowledge and is carried through to the glorification of the believer. It is crucial to the foreknowledge view that in this text God's foreknowledge comes *before* God's predestination.

I have great appreciation for the foreknowledge view of predestination. I once held it before I surrendered to the Reformed view. But I abandoned this view for several reasons. Not least is that I have become convinced that the foreknowledge view is not so much an explanation of the biblical doctrine of predestination as it is a denial of the biblical doctrine. It fails to include the whole counsel of God on the matter.

Perhaps the greatest weakness of the foreknowledge view is the text cited as its greatest strength. On closer analysis the passage in Romans cited above becomes a serious problem for the foreknowledge view. On the one hand those who appeal to it to support the foreknowledge view find too little. That is, the passage teaches less than the advocates of foreknowledge would like it to teach and yet teaches more than they want it to teach.

How can this be? First, the conclusion that God's predestination is determined by God's foreknowledge is not taught by the passage. Paul does not come out and say that God chooses people on the basis of His prior knowledge of their choices. That idea is neither stated nor implied by the text. All the text declares is that God predestines those whom He foreknows. No one in this debate disputes that God has foreknowledge. Even God could not choose people He didn't know anything about. Before He could choose Jacob He had to have some idea in His mind of Jacob. But the text does not teach that God chose Jacob on the basis of Jacob's choice.

In fairness it must be said that at least the order of foreknowledge-predestination that we find in Romans 8 is compatible with the foreknowledge view. It is the rest of the passage that creates difficulty.

Note the order of events in the passage. Foreknowledge—predestination—calling—justification—glorification.

The crucial problem here has to do with the relationship of calling and justification. What does Paul mean here by "calling"? The New Testament speaks of divine calling in more than one way. In theology we distinguish between God's *external* call and God's *internal* call.

We find God's external call in the preaching of the gospel. When the gospel is preached, everyone who hears it is called or summoned to Christ. But not everyone responds positively. Not everyone who hears the outward call of the gospel becomes a believer. Sometimes the gospel call falls upon deaf ears.

Now we know that only those who respond to the outward call of the gospel in faith are justified. Justification is by faith. But again, not everyone whose ears hear the outward preaching of the gospel responds in faith. Therefore we must conclude that not all who are called outwardly are justified.

But Paul says in Romans that those whom God calls, He justifies. Now, we grant that the Bible does not explicitly say that all those He calls He justifies. We are supplying the word *all*. Perhaps we are as guilty of reading something into the text that is not there as those who advocate the foreknowledge view.

When we supply the word *all* here, we are responding to an implication of the text. We are making an inference. Is it a legitimate inference to make? I think it is.

If Paul does not mean that all who are called are justified, the only alternative would be that *some* who are called are justified. If we supply the word *some* instead of the word *all* here, then we must supply it throughout the Golden Chain. Then it would read like this: "Some of those He foreknew, He also predestined. Some of those He predestined, He also called. Some of those He called, these He also justified. Some of those He justified, He also glorified."

This reading of the text leaves us with a theological monstrosity, a nightmare. It would mean that only some of the predestined ever hear the gospel and that only some of the justified are ultimately saved. These notions are utterly in conflict with what the rest of the Bible teaches on these matters.

Yet the foreknowledge view suffers an even bigger problem from the supplying of the word *some*. If God's predestination is based on His foreknowledge of how people will respond to the outward call of the gospel, how is it that only some of the predestined are even called? It would demand that God predestines some who are not called. If some of the predestined are predestined without being called, then God would not be basing His predestination on a prior knowledge of their response to His call. They could have no response to a call they never receive! God cannot have foreknowledge of a person's nonanswer to a noncall.

Whew! If we follow all of that, then we will see the conclusion screaming at us. Paul cannot be implying the word *some*. Rather, the Golden Chain necessarily implies the word *all*.

Let's review the bidding. If we supply the word *some* to the Golden Chain, the result is fatal to the foreknowledge view of predestination because it would have God predestinating some people who are not called. Since the view teaches that God's predestination is based upon God's foreknowledge of people's positive responses to the call of the gospel, then clearly the view collapses if some are predestined without a call.

The supplying of the word *all* is equally fatal to the foreknowledge view. This difficulty centers on the relationship of calling to justification. If all who are called are justified, then the passage could mean one of two things: (*A*) All who hear the gospel outwardly are justified; or (*B*) All who are called by God inwardly are justified.

If we answer with option *A*, then the conclusion we must reach is that everyone who ever hears the gospel is predestined to be saved. Of course the vast majority of those who hold the foreknowledge view of predestination also hold that not everyone who hears the gospel is saved. Some are universalists. They believe that everyone will be saved, whether they hear the gospel or not. But we must remember that the chief debate among evangelicals over predestination is not over the question of universalism. Both advocates of the Reformed view of predestination and advocates of the foreknowledge view agree that not everyone is saved. They agree that in fact there are people who hear the gospel outwardly (the external call of God) who do not respond in faith and who therefore are not justified. Option *A* is as repugnant to the advocates of the foreknowledge view as it is to the advocates of the Reformed view.

That leaves us with option *B*: all who are called inwardly by God are justified. What is the inward call of God? The outward call refers to the preaching of the gospel. Preaching is something that we do as human beings. The outward call can also be "heard" by reading the Bible. The Bible is the Word of God, but it comes to us in documents penned by human beings. In that sense it is external. No human being has the power to work inwardly on another human being. I cannot get inside a person's heart to work an immediate influence there. I can speak words which are outward. Those words may penetrate the heart, but I cannot make that happen by my own power. Only God can call a person inwardly. Only God can work immediately within the deepest chambers of the human heart to influence a positive response of faith.

So if option *B* is what the apostle means, then the implications are clear. If all whom God calls inwardly are justified and all whom God predestines are called inwardly, then it follows that God's foreknowledge concerns more than a mere prior awareness of the free decisions humans will make. To be sure, God does know from all eternity who will respond to the gospel and who will not. But such knowledge is not that of a mere passive observer. God knows from eternity whom he will inwardly call. All whom He inwardly calls He will also justify.

I said earlier that the Golden Chain teaches more than the foreknowledge view wants it to teach. It teaches that God predestines an inward call. All whom God predestines to be called inwardly will be justified. God is here doing something in the hearts of the elect to insure their positive response.

If option *B* is the correct understanding of the Golden Chain, then it is clear that God gives one kind of call to some people that He does not give to everyone. Since all who are called are justified and since not everyone is justified, then it follows that calling is a rather significant divine activity that some human beings receive and others do not.

Now we are forced back to a serious question not unlike our original question. Why is it that some are predestined to receive this call of God and others are not? Does the answer lie in man or in the purposes of God? An advocate of the foreknowledge view would have to answer that the reason God calls only some people inwardly is that He knows in advance who will respond positively to the inward call and who will not. Therefore He doesn't waste the inward call, He only gives it to those whom He knows will respond favorably to it.

How much power is there in God's inward call? Is there any advantage to receiving it? If it is only given to those whom God knows will respond to it in their own power, it would seem to be an inward influence without any *real* influence. If it does have any influence on the person who hears the outward call, then God is predestinating an advantage to some that He is withholding from others. If it has no influence on the human decision, then it is simply not an influence at all. If it is not an influence at all, then it is insignificant to salvation and a meaningless part of the Golden Chain.

It is crucial to remember that the inward call of God is given to people *before* they believe, *before* they respond in faith. If it influences the response in any way, then God is predestinating an advantage to the elect. If it does not influence the human decision, then what does it do? This dilemma is painful to the foreknowledge view, painful beyond relief.

The Reformed View of Predestination

In contrast with the foreknowledge view of predestination, the Reformed view asserts that the ultimate decision for salvation rests with God and not with man. It teaches that from all eternity God has chosen to intervene in the lives of some people and bring them to saving faith and has chosen not to do that for other people. From all eternity, without any prior view of our human behavior, God has chosen some unto election and others unto reprobation. The ultimate destiny of the individual is decided by God before that individual is even born and without depending ultimately upon the human choice. To be sure, a human choice is made, a free human choice, but the choice is made because God first chooses to influence the elect to make the right choice. The basis for God's choice does not rest in man but solely in the good pleasure of the divine will.

In the Reformed view of predestination God's choice precedes man's choice. We choose Him only because He has first chosen us. Without divine predestination and without the divine inward call, the Reformed view holds that nobody would ever choose Christ.

This is the view of predestination that rankles so many Christians. This is the view that raises serious questions about man's free will and about God's fairness. This is the view that provokes so many angry responses and charges of fatalism, determinism, and so on.

The Reformed view of predestination understands the Golden Chain as follows: From all eternity God foreknew His elect. He had an idea of their identities in His mind before He ever created them. He not only foreknew them in the sense of having a prior idea of their personal identities, but He also foreknew them in the sense of foreloving them. We must remember that when the Bible speaks of "knowing" it often distinguishes between a simple mental awareness of a person and a deep intimate love of the person.

The Reformed view believes that all whom God has thus foreknown He has also predestined to be inwardly called, to be justified, and to be glorified. God sovereignly brings to pass the salvation of His elect and only of His elect.

Summary of Chapter 6

1. Foreknowledge is not a valid explanation of predestination.
2. It makes redemption ultimately a human work.
3. Predestination is sidestepped and rendered virtually empty of significance.
4. The Golden Chain shows that our justification depends upon God's calling.
5. God's calling rests upon a prior predestination.
6. Without predestination there is no justification.
7. It is not our future choices, however, that induce God to choose us.
8. It is God's sovereign decision on our behalf.

~⁊⊙⊱~

SEVEN

Double, Double, Toil and Trouble: Is Predestination Double?

D ouble predestination. The very words sound ominous. It is one thing to contemplate God's gracious plan of salvation for the elect. But what about those who are not elect? Are they also predestined? Is there a horrible decree of reprobation? Does God destine some unfortunate people to hell?

These questions immediately come to the fore as soon as double predestination is mentioned. Such questions make some declare the concept of double predestination out of bounds. Others, while believing in predestination, declare emphatically that they believe in *single* predestination. That is, while believing that some are predestined to salvation, there is no need to suppose that others are likewise predestined to damnation. In short, the idea is that some are predestined to salvation, but everyone has an opportunity to be saved. God makes sure that some make it by providing extra help, but the rest of mankind still has a chance.

Though there is strong sentiment to speak of single predestination only, and to avoid any discussion of double predestination, we must still face the questions on the table. Unless we conclude that every human being is predestined to salvation, we must face the flip side of election. If there is such a thing as predestination at all, and if that predestination does not include all people, then we must not shrink from the necessary inference that there are two sides to predestination. It is not enough to talk about Jacob; we must also consider Esau.

Equal Ultimacy

There are different views of double predestination. One of these is so frightening that many shun the term altogether, lest their view of the doctrine be confused with the scary one. This is called the equal ultimacy view.

Equal ultimacy is based on a concept of symmetry. It seeks a complete balance between election and reprobation. The key idea is this: Just as God intervenes in the lives of the elect to create faith in their hearts, so God equally intervenes in the lives of the reprobate to create or work unbelief in their hearts. The idea of God's actively working unbelief in the hearts of the reprobate is drawn from biblical statements about God hardening people's hearts.

Equal ultimacy is *not* the Reformed or Calvinist view of predestination. Some have called it hyper-Calvinism. I prefer to call it sub-Calvinism or, better yet, anti-Calvinism. Though Calvinism certainly has a view of double predestination, the double predestination it embraces is not one of equal ultimacy.

To understand the Reformed view of the matter we must pay close attention to the crucial distinction between *positive* and *negative* decrees of God. Positive has to do with God's active intervention in the hearts of the elect. Negative has to do with God's passing over the nonelect.

The Reformed view teaches that God positively or actively intervenes in the lives of the elect to insure their salvation. The rest of mankind God leaves to themselves. He does not create unbelief in their hearts. That unbelief is already there. He does not coerce them to sin. They sin by their own choices. In the Calvinist view the decree of election is positive; the decree of reprobation is negative.

Hyper-Calvinism's view of double predestination may be called *positive-positive predestination*. Orthodox Calvinism's view may be called *positive-negative predestination*. Let us view it in chart form:

Calvinism	Hyper-Calvinism
positive-negative	positive-positive
asymmetrical view	symmetrical view
unequal ultimacy	equal ultimacy
God passes over the reprobate	God works unbelief in the hearts of the reprobate

The dreadful error of hyper-Calvinism is that it involves God in coercing sin. This does radical violence to the integrity of God's character.

The primary biblical example that might tempt one toward hyper-Calvinism is the case of Pharaoh. Repeatedly we read in the Exodus account that God hardened Pharaoh's heart. God told Moses ahead of time that He would do this:

> You shall speak all that I command you. And Aaron your brother shall speak to Pharaoh, that he must send the children of Israel out of his land. And I will harden Pharaoh's heart, and multiply My signs and My wonders in the land of Egypt. But Pharaoh will not heed you, so that I may lay My hand on Egypt and bring My armies and My people, the children of Israel, out of the land of Egypt by great judgments. And the Egyptians shall know that I am the LORD, when I stretch out My hand on Egypt and bring out the children of Israel from among them. (Exod. 7:2–5)

The Bible clearly teaches that God did, in fact, harden Pharaoh's heart. Now we know that God did this for His own glory and as a sign to both Israel and Egypt. We know that God's purpose in all of this was a redemptive purpose. But we are still left with a nagging problem. God hardened Pharaoh's heart and then judged Pharaoh for his sin. How can God hold Pharaoh or anyone else accountable for sin that flows out of a heart that God Himself hardened?

Our answer to that question will depend on how we understand God's act of hardening. How did He harden Pharaoh's heart? The Bible does not answer that question explicitly. As we think about it, we realize that basically there are only two ways He could have hardened Pharaoh's heart: actively or passively.

Active hardening would involve God's direct intervention within the inner chambers of Pharaoh's heart. God would intrude into Pharaoh's heart and create fresh evil in it. This would certainly insure that Pharaoh would bring forth the result that God was looking for. It would also insure that God is the author of sin.

Passive hardening is a totally different story. Passive hardening involves a divine judgment upon sin that is already present. All that God needs to do to harden the heart of a person whose heart is already desperately wicked is to "give him over to his sin." We find this concept of divine judgment repeatedly in Scripture.

How does this work? To understand it properly, we must first look briefly at another concept, God's *common grace*. This refers to that grace of God that all men commonly enjoy. The rain that refreshes the earth and waters our crops falls upon the just and the unjust alike. The unjust certainly do not deserve such benefits, but they enjoy them anyway. So it is with sunshine and rainbows. Our world is a theater of common grace.

One of the most important elements of common grace we enjoy is the restraint of evil in the world. That restraint flows from many sources. Evil is restrained by policemen, laws, public opinion, balances of power, and so on. Though the world we live in is filled with wickedness, it is not as wicked as it possibly could be. God uses the means mentioned above as well as other means to keep evil in check. By His grace He controls and bridles the amount of evil in this world. If evil were left totally unchecked, then life on this planet would be impossible.

All that God has to do to harden people's hearts is to remove the restraints. He gives them a longer leash. Rather than restricting their human freedom, He increases it. He lets them have their own way. In a sense He gives them enough rope to hang themselves. It is not that God puts His hand on them to create fresh evil in their hearts; He merely removes His holy hand of restraint from them and lets them do their own will.

If we were to determine the most wicked, the most diabolical men of human history, certain names would appear on almost everyone's list. We would see the names of Hitler, Nero, Stalin, and others who have been guilty of mass murder and other atrocities. What do these people have in common? They were all dictators. They all had virtually unlimited power and authority within the sphere of their domains.

Why do we say that power corrupts and absolute power corrupts absolutely? (We know that this has no reference to God but only to the power and corruption of men.) Power corrupts precisely because it raises a person above the normal restraints that restrict the rest of us. I am restrained by conflicts of interest with people who are as powerful or more powerful than I am. We learn early in life to restrict our belligerence toward those who are bigger than we are. We tend to enter into conflicts selectively. Discretion tends to take over from valor when our opponents are more powerful than we.

Pharaoh was the most powerful man in the world when Moses went to see him. About the only restraint there was on Pharaoh's wickedness was the holy arm of God. All God had to do to harden Pharaoh further was to remove His arm. The evil inclinations of Pharaoh did the rest.

In the act of passive hardening, God makes a decision to remove the restraints; the wicked part of the process is done by Pharaoh himself. God does no violence to Pharaoh's will. As we said, he merely gives Pharaoh *more* freedom.

We see the same kind of thing in the case of Judas and with the wicked men whom God and Satan used to afflict Job. Judas was not a poor innocent victim of divine manipulation. He was not a righteous man whom God forced to betray Christ and then punished for the betrayal. Judas betrayed Christ because Judas wanted thirty pieces of silver. As the Scriptures declare, Judas was a son of perdition from the beginning.

To be sure, God uses the evil inclinations and evil intentions of fallen men to bring about His own redemptive purposes. Without Judas there is no Cross. Without the cross there is no redemption. But this is not a case of God coercing evil. Rather it is a glorious case of God's redemptive triumph over evil. The evil desires of men's hearts cannot thwart God's sovereignty. Indeed they are subject to it.

When we study the pattern of God's punishment of wicked men, we see a kind of poetic justice emerging. In the final judgment scene of the book of Revelation we read the following: "He who is unjust, let him be unjust still; he who is filthy, let him be filthy still; he who is righteous, let him be righteous still; he who is holy, let him be holy still" (Rev. 22:11).

In God's ultimate act of judgment, He gives sinners over to their sins. In effect, He abandons them to their own desires. So it was with Pharaoh. By this act of judgment, God did not blemish His own righteousness by creating fresh evil in Pharaoh's heart. He established His own righteousness by punishing the evil that was already there in Pharaoh.

This is how we must understand double predestination. God gives mercy to the elect by working faith in their hearts. He gives justice to the reprobate by leaving them in their own sins. There is no symmetry here. One group receives mercy. The other group receives justice. No one is a victim of injustice. None can complain that there is unrighteousness in God.

Romans 9

The most significant passage in the New Testament that concerns double predestination is found in Romans 9.

> For this is the word of promise: "At this time I will come and Sarah shall have a son." And not only this, but when Rebecca also had conceived by one man, even by our father Isaac (for the children not yet being born, nor having done any good or evil, that the purpose of God according to election might stand, not of works but of Him who calls), it was said to her, "The older shall serve the younger." As it is written, "Jacob I have loved, but Esau I have hated."
>
> What shall we say then? Is there unrighteousness with God? Certainly not! For He says to Moses, "I will have mercy on

whomever I will have mercy, and I will have compassion on
whomever I will have compassion."

So then it is not of him who wills, nor of him who runs, but of
God who shows mercy. For the Scripture says to Pharaoh, "Even
for this same purpose I have raised you up, that I might show
My power in you, and that My name might be declared in all the
earth." Therefore He has mercy on whom He wills, and whom
He wills He hardens. (Rom. 9:9–18)

In this passage we have the clearest biblical expression we can find for the
concept of double predestination. It is stated without reservation and without
ambiguity. "Therefore He has mercy on whom He wills, and whom He wills
He hardens." Some people get mercy, others get justice. The decision for this
is in the hand of God.

Paul illustrates the double character of predestination by his reference to
Jacob and Esau. These two men were twin brothers. They were carried in the
same womb at the same time. One received the blessing of God and one did
not. One received a special portion of the love of God, the other did not. Esau
was "hated" by God.

The divine hatred mentioned here is not an expression of an insidious attitude of malice. It is what David earlier called a "holy hatred" (Ps. 139:22). Divine
hatred is not malicious. It involves a withholding of favor. God is "for" those
whom He loves. He turns His face against those wicked people who are not the
objects of His special redemptive favor. Those whom He loves receive His mercy.
Those whom He "hates" receive His justice. Again, no one is treated unjustly.

Why did God choose Jacob and not Esau? Did God foresee in Jacob some
righteous act that would justify this special favor? Did God look down the cor-
ridors of time and see Jacob making the right choice and Esau making the
wrong choice?

If this is what the apostle intended to teach, it would not have been difficult to make the point clear. Here was Paul's golden opportunity to teach
a foreknowledge view of predestination, had he wanted to. It seems strange
indeed that he does not take such an opportunity. But this is no argument from
silence. Paul does not remain mute on the subject. He labors the opposite point.
He emphasizes the fact that God's decision was made before the birth of these
twins and without a view to their future actions.

Paul's phrase in verse 11 is crucial. "For the children not yet being born, nor
having done any good or evil, that the purpose of God according to election
might stand, not of works but of Him who calls." Why does the apostle say

this? The accent here is clearly on the work of God. It emphatically denies that election is a result of the work of man, foreseen or otherwise. It is the purpose of God according to His election that is in view here.

If Paul meant that election is based on some foreknown human decision, why did he not say so? Instead he declares that the decree was made before the children were born and before they had done any good or evil. Now we grant that a foreknowledge view of predestination realizes that the divine decree was made prior to birth. But that view insists that God's decision was based on His knowledge of future choices. Why doesn't Paul make that point here? All he says is that the decree was made before birth and before Jacob and Esau had done any good or evil.

We grant that in this passage Paul does not come right out and say that God's decision was not based on their future good or evil. But he did not need to say that. The implication is clear in light of what he does say. He places the accent where it belongs, on the purpose of God and not on the work of man. The burden here is on those who want to add the crucial qualifying notion of foreseen choices. The Bible doesn't add it here or anywhere.

The point is this: If Paul believed that God's predestination was based on foreseen human choices, this was the context in which to spell it out.

We must go a step further. Though Paul is silent about the question of future choices here, he does not remain so. In verse 16 he makes it clear. "So then it is not of him who wills, nor of him who runs, but of God who shows mercy." This is the *coup de grace* to Arminianism and all other non-Reformed views of predestination. This is the Word of God that requires all Christians to cease and desist from views of predestination that make the ultimate decision for salvation rest in the will of man. The apostle declares: It is *not* of him who wills. The non-Reformed views must say that it *is* of him who wills. This is in violent contradiction to the teaching of Scripture. This one verse is absolutely fatal to Arminianism.

It is our duty to honor God. We must confess with the apostle that our election is not based on our wills but on the purposes of the will of God.

Paul raises two rhetorical questions in this passage that we must consider. The first is, "What shall we say then? Is there unrighteousness in God?" Why does Paul anticipate this question? No one raises that question to an Arminian. If our election is ultimately based on human decisions, there is no need to raise such an objection.

It is to the biblical doctrine of predestination that this question is raised. It is to predestination based on God's sovereign purpose, on His decision without a view to Jacob or Esau's choices, that prompts the outcry, "God is not fair!" But the outcry is based on a superficial understanding of the matter. It is the protest of fallen man complaining that God is not gracious enough.

How does Paul answer the question? He is not satisfied by merely saying, "No, there is no unrighteousness in God." Rather, his answer is as emphatic as he can make it. He says, "Certainly not!" or, "God forbid!" depending on the translation you are reading.

The second objection Paul anticipates is this: "You will say to me then, 'Why does He still find fault? For who has resisted His will?' " Again we wonder why the apostle anticipates this objection. This is another objection never raised against Arminianism. Non-Reformed views of predestination don't have to worry about handling questions like this. God would obviously find fault with people whom He knew would not choose Christ. If the ultimate basis for salvation rests in the power of human choice, then the blame is easily fixed and Paul would not have to wrestle with this anticipated objection. But he wrestles with it because the biblical doctrine of predestination demands that he wrestle with it.

How does Paul answer this question? Let us examine his reply:

> But indeed, O man, who are you to reply against God? Will the thing formed say to him who formed it, "Why have you made me like this?" Does not the potter have power over the clay, from the same lump to make one vessel for honor and the other for dishonor? What if God, wanting to show His wrath and to make His power known, endured with much longsuffering the vessels of wrath prepared for destruction, and that He might make known the riches of His glory on the vessels of mercy, which He had prepared beforehand for glory, even us whom He called, not of the Jews only, but also of the Gentiles? (Rom. 9:20–24)

This is a heavy answer to the question. I must confess that I struggle with it. My struggle, however, is not over whether the passage teaches double predestination. It clearly does that. My struggle is with the fact that this text supplies ammunition for the advocates of equal ultimacy. It sounds like God is actively making people sinners. But that is not required by the text. He does make vessels of wrath and vessels of honor from the same lump of clay. But if we look closely at the text we will see that the clay with which the potter works is "fallen" clay. One batch of clay receives mercy in order to become vessels of honor. That mercy presupposes a clay that is already guilty. Likewise God must "endure" the vessels of wrath that are fit for destruction because they are guilty vessels of wrath.

Again the accent in this passage is on God's sovereign purpose and not upon man's free and good choices. The same assumptions are operating here that are operating in the first question.

The Arminian Reply

Some Arminians will reply to my treatment of this text with indignation. They agree that the passage teaches a strong view of divine sovereignty. Their objection will focus at another point. They will insist that Paul is not even talking about the predestination of individuals in Romans 9. Romans 9 is not about individuals but about God's electing of nations. Paul is here talking about Israel as God's chosen people. Jacob merely represents the nation Israel. His very name was changed to Israel and his sons became the fathers of the twelve tribes of Israel.

That God favored Israel over other nations is not in dispute. It was out of Israel that Jesus came. It was out of Israel that we received the Ten Commandments and the promises of the covenant with Abraham. We know that salvation is of the Jews.

That much is indeed true of Romans 9. We must consider, however, that in the electing of a nation God elected individuals. Nations are made up of individuals. Jacob was an individual. Esau was an individual. Here we see clearly that God sovereignly elected individuals as well as a nation. We must hasten to add that Paul *extends* this treatment of election beyond Israel in verse 24 when he declares: "even us whom He called, not of the Jews only, but also of the Gentiles."

Unconditional Election

Let us return for a moment to our famous acrostic, TULIP. We have already quarreled with the *T* and the *I* and changed it to RULEP. Though I prefer the term *sovereign election* to *unconditional election*, I will not damage the acrostic further. If we changed it to RSLEP it wouldn't even rhyme with TULIP.

Unconditional election means that our election is decided by God according to His purpose, according to His sovereign will. It is not based upon some foreseen condition that some of us meet and others fail to meet. It is not based on our willing or on our running, but upon the sovereign purpose of God.

The term *unconditional election* can be misleading and grossly abused. I once met a man who never darkened the door of a church and who showed no evidence of being a Christian. He made no profession of faith and was engaged in no Christian activity. He told me that he believed in unconditional election. He was confident that he was elect. He did not have to trust Christ, he did not have to repent, he did not have to be obedient to Christ. He declared that he was elect and that was enough. No further conditions for salvation were necessary for him. He was, in his opinion, saved, sanctified, satisfied, and Sanforized.

We must be careful to distinguish between conditions that are necessary for salvation and conditions that are necessary for election. We often speak of election and salvation as if they were synonymous, but they are not exactly the same thing. Election is *unto* salvation. Salvation in its fullest sense is the complete work of redemption that God accomplishes in us.

There are all sorts of conditions that must be met for someone to be saved. Chief among them is that we must have faith in Christ. Justification is by faith. Faith is a necessary requirement. To be sure, the Reformed doctrine of predestination teaches that all the elect are indeed brought to faith. God insures that the conditions necessary for salvation are met.

When we say that election is unconditional, we mean that the original decree of God by which He chooses some people to be saved is not dependent upon some future condition in us that God foresees. There is nothing in us that God could foresee that would induce Him to choose us. The only thing He would foresee in the lives of fallen creatures left to themselves would be sin. God chooses us simply according to the good pleasure of His will.

Is God Arbitrary?

That God chooses us not because of what He finds in us, but according to His own good pleasure, gives rise to the charge that this makes God arbitrary. It suggests that God makes His selection in a whimsical or capricious manner. It seems like our election is the result of a blind and frivolous lottery. If we are elect, then it is only because we are lucky. God pulled our names out of a celestial hat.

To be arbitrary is to do something for no reason. Now, it is clear that there is no reason found *in us* for God to choose us. But that is not the same as saying that God has no reason in Himself. God doesn't do anything without a reason. He is not capricious or whimsical. God is as sober as He is sovereign.

A lottery is intentionally left up to chance. God does not operate by chance. He knew whom He would select. He foreknew and foreloved His elect. It was not a blind draw because God is not blind. Yet we still must insist that it was nothing that He foreknew, foresaw, or foreloved in us that was the decisive reason for His choice.

Calvinists do not generally like to speak of luck. Instead of wishing people "good luck," we prefer to say, "Providential blessings." Yet if we were to speak of our "lucky day," we would mark that day in eternity when God decided to choose us.

Let us turn our attention to Paul's teaching on this matter in Ephesians:

> Blessed be the God and Father of our Lord Jesus Christ, who has blessed us with every spiritual blessing in the heavenly places in Christ, just as He chose us in Him before the foundation of the world, that we should be holy and without blame before Him in love, having predestined us to adoption as sons by Jesus Christ to Himself, according to the good pleasure of His will, to the praise of the glory of His grace, by which He has made us accepted in the Beloved. (Eph. 1:3–6)

According to the good pleasure of His will. This is the apostolic statement that seems to suggest divine arbitrariness. The chief culprit is the word *pleasure*. In our vocabulary the word *pleasure* is often charged with the meaning of wild, reckless abandon. Pleasure is that which feels good, something that has sensual and emotional overtones. We are aware of vices that bring wicked pleasure to us.

When the Bible speaks of God's pleasure, the term is not used in such a frivolous manner. Here pleasure means simply "that which is pleasing." God predestines us according to what pleases Him. The Bible speaks of God's *good* pleasure. God's good pleasure must never be mistaken for an evil pleasure. What pleases God is goodness. What pleases us is not always goodness. God never takes pleasure in wickedness. There is nothing wicked about the good pleasure of His will. Though the reason for choosing us does not lie in us but in the sovereign divine pleasure, we may rest assured that the sovereign divine pleasure is a good pleasure.

We remember also what the apostle instructed the Philippian Christians. He said to them: ". . . work out your own salvation with fear and trembling; for it is God who works in you both to will and to do for His good pleasure" (Phil. 2:12, 13).

In this passage Paul is not teaching that election is a joint enterprise between God and man. Election is exclusively the work of God. It is, as we have seen, *monergistic*. Paul is speaking here about the outworking of our salvation that follows our election. He is specifically referring here to the process of our sanctification. Sanctification is not monergistic. It is *synergistic*. That is, it demands the cooperation of the regenerate believer. We are called to work to grow in grace. We are to work hard, resisting sin unto blood if necessary, pummeling our bodies if that is what it takes to subdue them.

We are called to this sober work of sanctification by a divine summons. The work is to be carried out in a spirit of fear and trembling. Our sanctification is not a casual matter. We do not approach it in a cavalier manner, saying simply, "Let go and let God." God does not do it all for us.

Neither, however, does God leave us to work out our own salvation by ourselves, in our own strength. We are comforted by His sure promise to be working in us both to do and to will what is pleasing to Him.

I recently heard a sermon by the great Scottish preacher, Eric Alexander, in which he stressed that God is working in us for *His* good pleasure. Paul does not say that God is working in us for *our* good pleasure. We are not always entirely pleased by what God is doing in our lives. Sometimes we experience a conflict between the purpose of God and our own purpose. I never choose to suffer on purpose. Yet it may well be within the sovereign purpose of God that I suffer. He promises us that by His sovereignty all things work together for good for those who love Him and are called according to His purpose.

My purposes do not always include God's good. I am a sinner. Fortunately for us, God is not a sinner. He is altogether righteous. His purposes are always and everywhere righteous. His purposes work for my good, even when His purposes are in conflict with my purposes. Perhaps I should say, *especially* when His purposes are in conflict with my purposes. What pleases Him is good for me. That is one of the most difficult lessons Christians ever learn.

Our election is unconditional except for one thing. There is one requirement we must meet before God will ever elect us. To be elect we must first be sinners.

God does not elect righteous people unto salvation. He does not need to elect righteous people unto salvation. Righteous people do not need to be saved. Only sinful people are in need of a savior. Those who are whole have no need of a physician.

Christ came to seek and to save people who were really lost. God sent Him into the world not only to make our salvation possible, but to make it sure. Christ has not died in vain. His sheep are saved through His sinless life and His atoning death. There is nothing arbitrary in that.

Summary of Chapter 7

1. Not all men are predestined to salvation.
2. There are two aspects or sides to the question. There are those who are elect and those who are not elect.
3. Predestination is "double."
4. We must be careful not to think in terms of equal ultimacy.
5. God does not create sin in the hearts of sinners.

6. The elect receive mercy. The nonelect receive justice.
7. No one receives injustice at the hands of God.
8. God's "hardening of hearts" is itself a just punishment for sin that is already present.
9. God's choice of the elect is sovereign, but not arbitrary.
10. All of God's decisions flow from His holy character.

~&~

EIGHT

Can We Know
That We Are Saved?

The ministry of Evangelism Explosion keys its presentation of the gospel upon two crucial questions. The first is, "Have you come to the place in your spiritual life where you know *for sure* that when you die you will go to heaven?" Experienced workers say the vast majority of people answer this question in the negative. Most people are not sure of their future salvation. Many, if not most, raise serious doubts about whether such assurance is even possible.

When I was in seminary, a poll was taken of my classmates. Of that particular group of seminarians approximately 90 percent said that they were not sure of their salvation. Many expressed anger at the question, seeing in it a kind of implied presumptuousness. It seems arrogant to some people even to talk about assurance of salvation.

To be sure, stating our assurance of salvation may be an act of arrogance. If our confidence in our salvation rests in a confidence in ourselves, it is an act of arrogance. If we are sure we are going to heaven because we think we deserve to go to heaven, then it is unspeakably arrogant.

With respect to the assurance of salvation there are basically four kinds of people in the world. (1) There are people who are not saved who know that they are not saved. (2) There are people who are saved who do not know that they are saved. (3) There are people who are saved who know that they are saved. (4) There are people who are not saved who "know" that they are saved.

It is the last group that throws a monkey wrench into the works. If there are people who are *not* saved who "know" that they are saved, how can the people who *are* saved know that they really are saved?

To answer that question we must first ask another question. Why do some people have a false assurance of their salvation? Actually it is relatively easy. False assurance stems chiefly from false understanding of what salvation requires or entails.

Suppose, for example, that a person is a universalist. He believes that everybody is saved. If that premise is correct, then the rest of his logical deduction is easy. His reasoning goes like this:

Everybody is saved.
I am a body.
Therefore I am saved.

Universalism is far more prevalent than many of us realize. When my son was five years old, I asked him the two questions from Evangelism Explosion. He answered the first question in the affirmative. He was sure that when he died he would go to heaven. I proceeded then to the second question. "If you were to die tonight and God said to you, 'Why should I let you into my heaven?' What would you answer?" My son did not hesitate. He answered immediately, "Because I'm dead!"

By the time my son was five years old he already had received a message loud and clear. The message was that everyone who dies goes to heaven. His doctrine of justification was not justification by faith alone. It was not even justification by works, or a combination of faith and works. His doctrine was much simpler; he believed in justification by death. He had a false assurance of his salvation.

If universalism is widespread in our culture, so is the concept of justification by works. In a statistical survey of over a thousand people who were asked the same question I asked my son, over 80 percent of them gave an answer that involved some sort of "works righteousness." People said things like, "I have gone to church for thirty years," "I have perfect attendance in Sunday school," or "I have never done any serious harm to anybody."

I learned one thing clearly in my experience in evangelism: The message of justification by faith alone has not penetrated our culture. Multitudes of people are resting their hopes for heaven on their own good works. They are quite willing to admit that they are not perfect, but they assume that they are good enough. They have done "their best" and that, they tragically assume, is good enough for God.

I remember a student protesting to John Gerstner about a grade he received on a term paper. He punctuated his complaint by saying, "Dr. Gerstner, I did my best." Gerstner looked at him and said softly, "Young man, you have *never* done your best."

Surely we do not believe that we have done our best. If we review our performance for the last twenty-four hours, we will know that we have not done our best. It is not necessary to review our entire lives to see how specious such a statement is.

Yet even if we granted what we never in fact would grant, that people do their best, we know that even that is not good enough. God requires perfection to get into his heaven. We either find that perfection in ourselves or we find it somewhere else, in someone else. If we think we can find it in ourselves, we delude ourselves and the truth is not in us.

We see then that it is quite easy to have a false sense of security about our salvation. But what if we do have a proper understanding of what salvation requires, does that guarantee that we will avoid a false assurance of salvation?

By no means. The devil himself knows what is required for salvation. He knows who the Savior is. He understands the intellectual part of salvation better than we do. But he does not put his personal trust in Christ for his salvation. He hates the Jesus who is the Savior.

We can have a proper understanding of what salvation is and still delude ourselves about whether or not we meet the requirements of salvation. We may think that we have faith when in fact we have no faith. We may think that we are believing in Christ, but the Christ we embrace is not the biblical Christ. We may think that we love God, but the God we love is an idol.

Do we love a God who is sovereign? Do we love a God who sends people to hell? Do we love a God who demands absolute obedience? Do we love a Christ who will say to some on the last day, "Depart from Me, I never knew you"? I am not asking whether we love this God and this Christ perfectly; I am asking whether we love this God and this Christ at all.

One of my all-time favorite anecdotes is told by Dr. James Montgomery Boice. Dr. Boice tells of a mountain climber who slipped from his moorings and was about to plunge thousands of feet to his death. In panic he grabbed a scrawny bush that was growing out of a rock on the side of the mountain. It momentarily broke his fall, but it was slowly coming out of its place by the roots. The climber looked to heaven and cried, "Is there anybody up there who can help me?" A deep bass voice was heard from the sky. "Yes, I will help you. Trust me. Let go of the bush." The climber looked into the cavern below and cried once more, "Is there anyone *else* up there who can help me?"

It is possible that the God we believe in is "someone else." I have often spoken to staff persons associated with Young Life, the ministry that has an outstanding mission to teenagers. The strength of Young Life is at the same time its greatest danger. Young Life has a frighteningly high rate of youngsters who make professions of faith and later repudiate that profession.

Young Life has done an outstanding job of relating to teenagers. They are masters at making the gospel attractive. The danger is, however, that Young Life is so attractive, so neat, that young people can be converted to Young

Life and never deal with the biblical Christ. That in no way is intended as a criticism of Young Life. I am not suggesting that we should therefore seek to make the gospel unattractive. We do enough of that already. It is only to point out what we all must be reminded of, that people can respond to us, or to our group, as a substitute for Christ, and thereby gain a false assurance of salvation.

From a biblical standpoint we must realize that it is still not only possible for us to have a genuine assurance of our salvation, but that it is our *duty* to seek such assurance. If assurance is possible and if it is commanded, it is not arrogant to seek it. It is arrogant not to seek it.

The apostle Peter writes: "Therefore, brethren, be even more diligent to make your calling and election sure, for if you do these things you will never stumble; for so an entrance will be supplied to you abundantly into the everlasting kingdom of our Lord and Savior Jesus Christ" (2 Pet. 1:10, 11).

Here we see the mandate to make our election sure. To do so requires diligence. We have a pastoral concern here. Peter links assurance with freedom from stumbling. One of the most important factors that contribute to a Christian's spiritual growth, a consistent spiritual growth, is the assurance of salvation. There are many Christians who are indeed in a state of salvation who lack assurance. To be lacking in assurance is a grave hindrance to spiritual growth. The person who is not sure of his state of grace is exposed to doubts and terrors in his soul. He lacks an anchor for his spiritual life. His uncertainty makes him tentative in his walk with Christ.

Not only is it important that we gain authentic assurance, but it is important that we gain it early in our Christian experience. It is a key element in our growth toward maturity. Pastors need to be aware of that and assist their flocks in the diligent search for assurance.

I never know for sure whether another person I meet is elect or not. I cannot see into other people's souls. As human beings our view of others is restricted to outward appearances. We cannot see the heart. The only person who can know for sure that you are elect is you.

Who can know for sure that he is not elect? Nobody. You may be certain that at this moment you are not in a state of grace. You cannot know for certain that tomorrow you will not be in a state of grace. There are multitudes of elect people walking around who are as yet unconverted.

Such a person might say, "I don't know if I am elect or not and I am not the least bit concerned about it." There can hardly be any greater folly. If you do not yet know if you are elect, I can think of no more urgent question to answer.

If you are not sure, you would be well advised to make sure. Don't ever assume that you are not elect. Make your election a matter of certainty.

The apostle Paul was sure of his election. He frequently used the term *we* when he spoke of the elect. He said toward the end of his life:

> For I am already being poured out as a drink offering, and the time of my departure is at hand. I have fought the good fight, I have finished the race, I have kept the faith. Finally, there is laid up for me the crown of righteousness, which the Lord, the righteous Judge, will give to me on that Day, and not to me only but also to all who have loved His appearing. (2 Tim. 4:6–8)

Earlier in the same epistle he declared: "For this reason I also suffer these things; nevertheless I am not ashamed, for I know whom I have believed and am persuaded that He is able to keep what I have committed to Him until that Day" (2 Tim. 1:12).

How can we, like Paul, have true assurance, assurance that is not spurious? True assurance is grounded in the promises of God for our salvation. Our assurance comes first of all from our trust in the God who makes these promises. Secondly, our assurance is enhanced by the *inward evidence* of our own faith. We know that we could never have any true affection for Christ if we were not reborn. We know that we could not be reborn if we were not elect. A knowledge of sound theology is vital to our assurance. If we have a correct understanding of election, that understanding will help us interpret these inward evidences.

I know inwardly that I do not love Christ totally. But at the same time I do know that I love Him. I rejoice inwardly at the thought of His triumph. I rejoice inwardly at the thought of His coming. I will His exaltation. I know that none of these sentiments that I find in myself could possibly be there if it were not for grace.

When a man and woman are in love we assume that they are aware of it. A person is usually able to discern whether or not he or she is in love with another person. This comes from an inward assurance.

In addition to the inward evidence of grace, there is also outward evidence. We should be able to see visible fruit of our conversion. The outward evidence, however, may also cause our lack of assurance. We can see the abiding sin in our lives. Such sin does not do much for our assurance. We see ourselves sinning and we ask ourselves, "How can I do these things if I really love Christ?"

To have assurance we must make a sober analysis of our lives. It is not much use to compare ourselves with others. We will always be able to find others who are more advanced in their sanctification than we are. We may also be able to find others who are less advanced. No two people are ever at exactly the same point in their spiritual growth.

We must ask ourselves if we see any real change in our behavior, any real outward evidence of grace. This is a precarious process because we can lie to ourselves. It is a difficult task to perform, but by no means impossible.

We have one more vital method of reaching assurance. We are told in Scripture about the internal witness of the Holy Spirit. Paul states that "the Spirit Himself bears witness with our spirit that we are children of God" (Rom. 8:16).

The chief means by which the Spirit testifies to us is through His Word. I never have greater assurance than when I am meditating on the Word of God. If we neglect this means of grace, it is difficult to have any lasting or strong assurance of our salvation.

One Reformed theologian, A. A. Hodge, gives the following list of distinctions between true assurance and false assurance:

True Assurance	False Assurance
begets unfeigned humility	begets spiritual pride
leads to diligence in holiness	leads to slothful indulgence
leads to honest self-examination	avoids accurate evaluation
leads to desire for more intimate fellowship with God	is cold toward fellowship with God

Assurance of salvation can be augmented or diminished. We can increase our assurance or we can decrease it. We can even lose it altogether, at least for a season. There are many things that can cause our assurance to slip away from us. We can grow negligent in our preserving of it. The diligence to which we are called to make our election sure is an ongoing diligence. If we become smug in our assurance and begin to take it for granted, we run the risk of losing that assurance.

The greatest peril to our continued assurance is a fall into some serious and gross sin. We know the love that covers a multitude of sins. We know that we do not have to be perfect to have assurance of salvation. But when we fall into special sorts of sins, our assurance is shaken brutally. David's sin of adultery caused him to tremble in terror before God. If we read his prayer of confession in Psalm 51, we can hear the lament of a man who is struggling to regain his assurance. After Peter cursed and denied Christ and Christ's eyes fell upon him, what was the state of Peter's assurance?

We all experience periods of spiritual coldness in which we feel as though God has totally removed the light of His countenance from us. The saints have called it the "dark night of the soul." There are times when we feel as though God has abandoned us. We think that He no longer hears our prayers. We do not feel the sweetness of His presence. At times like these, when our assurance is at a low ebb, we must incline ourselves toward Him with all of our might. He promises us that, if we will draw near to Him, He in turn will come near to us.

Finally, we may be shaken in our assurance if we are exposed to great suffering. A serious illness, a painful accident, a loss of a loved one to death may disturb our assurance. We know that Job cried out, "Though He slay me, yet will I trust Him." That was the cry of a man in pain. He said that he was sure that his Redeemer lived, but I am certain that Job had his moments when doubts assailed him.

Again it is the Word of God that comforts us in times of trial. Our tribulations have the ultimate effect not of destroying our hope but of establishing it. Peter wrote:

> Beloved, do not think it strange concerning the fiery trial which is to try you, as though some strange thing happened to you; but rejoice to the extent that you partake of Christ's sufferings, that when His glory is revealed, you may also be glad with exceeding joy. (1 Pet. 4:12, 13)

When we are attentive to the promises of God, our suffering may be used to increase our assurance rather than diminish it. We need not have a crisis of faith. Our faith may be strengthened through suffering. God promises that our suffering will not merely result ultimately in joy, but in *exceeding* joy.

Can We Lose Our Salvation?

We have already stated that it is possible to lose our assurance of salvation. That does not mean, however, that we lose the salvation itself. We are moving now to the question of eternal security. Can a justified person lose his justification?

We know how the Roman Catholic Church has answered that question. Rome insists that the grace of justification can in fact be lost. The sacrament of penance, which demands confession, was established for this very reason. Rome calls the sacrament of penance the "second plank of justification for those who have made shipwreck of their souls."

According to Rome, saving grace is destroyed in the soul when a person commits a "mortal" sin. Mortal sin is so called because it has the power to kill grace. Grace can die. If it is destroyed by mortal sin, it must be restored through the sacrament of penance or the sinner himself finally perishes.

The Reformed faith does not believe in mortal sin in the way Rome does. We believe that all sins are mortal in the sense that they deserve death but that no sin is mortal in the sense that it destroys the grace of salvation in the elect. (Later, we will consider the "unpardonable sin" about which Jesus warned.)

The Reformed view of eternal security is called the "perseverance of the saints," the *P* in TULIP. The idea here is, "Once in grace, always in grace." Another way of stating it is, "If you have it, you never lose it; if you lose it, you never had it."

Our confidence in the perseverance of the saints does not rest upon our confidence in the saints' ability, in themselves, to persevere. Again, I would like to modify the acrostic TULIP slightly. Same letter, new word. I prefer to speak of the *preservation* of the saints.

The reason true Christians do not fall from grace is that God graciously keeps them from falling. Perseverance is what we do. Preservation is what God does. We persevere because God preserves.

The doctrine of eternal security or perseverance is based on the promises of God. A few of the key biblical passages are listed below:

> Being confident of this very thing, that He who has begun a good work in you will complete it until the day of Jesus Christ. (Phil. 1:6)

> My sheep hear My voice, and I know them, and they follow Me. And I give them eternal life, and they shall never perish; neither shall anyone snatch them out of My hand. My Father, who has given them to Me, is greater than all; and no one is able to snatch them out of My Father's hand. (John 10:21–29)

> Blessed be the God and Father of our Lord Jesus Christ, who according to His abundant mercy has begotten us again to a living hope through the resurrection of Jesus Christ from the dead, to an inheritance incorruptible and undefiled and that does not fade away, reserved in heaven for you, who are kept by the power of God through faith for salvation ready to be revealed in the last time. (1 Pet. 1:3–5)

> For by one offering He has perfected forever those who are being sanctified. (Heb. 10:14)

Who shall bring a charge against God's elect? It is God who justifies. Who is he who condemns? It is Christ who died, and furthermore is also risen, who is even at the right hand of God, who also makes intercession for us. Who shall separate us from the love of Christ? Shall tribulation, or distress, or persecution, or famine, or nakedness, or peril, or sword? As it is written: "For Your sake we are killed all day long; we are accounted as sheep for the slaughter." Yet in all these things we are more than conquerors through Him who loved us. For I am persuaded that neither death nor life, nor angels nor principalities nor powers, nor things present nor things to come, nor height nor depth, nor any other created thing, shall be able to separate us from the love of God which is in Christ Jesus our Lord. (Rom. 8:33–39)

We see from these passages that the ground for our confidence in perseverance is the power of God. God promises to finish what He starts. Our confidence does not rest in the will of man. This difference between the will of man and the power of God separates Calvinists from Arminians. The Arminian holds that God elects persons to eternal life only on the condition of their voluntary cooperation with grace and perseverance in grace until death, as foreseen by Him.

The Roman Catholic Church, for example, has decreed the following: "If anyone says that a man once justified cannot lose grace and therefore that he who falls and sins never was truly justified, let him be accursed" (Council of Trent 6/23).

Protestant Arminians made a similar statement: "Persons truly regenerate, by neglecting grace and grieving the Holy Spirit with sin, fall away totally, and at length finally, from grace into eternal reprobation" (*see* Conference of Remonstrants 11/7).

A chief argument given by Arminians is that it is inconsistent with man's free will for God to "force" his perseverance. Yet the Arminians themselves believe that believers will not fall from grace in heaven. In our glorified state God will render us incapable of sinning. Yet the glorified saints in heaven are still free. If preservation and free will are consistent conditions in heaven, they cannot possibly be inconsistent conditions here on earth. The Arminians again try to prove too much with their view of human freedom. If God can preserve us in heaven without destroying our free will, He can preserve us on earth without destroying our free will.

We are able to persevere only because God works within us, with our free wills. And because God is at work in us, we are certain to persevere. The decrees of God concerning election are immutable. They do not change, because He does not change. All whom He justifies He glorifies. None of the elect is ever lost.

Why then does it seem to us that many people do fall away from grace? We have all known people who made zealous starts with the Christian faith only to repudiate their faith later. We have heard of great Christian leaders who have committed gross sins and scandalized their profession of faith.

The Reformed faith readily acknowledges that people make professions of faith and then repudiate them. We know that Christians "backslide." We know that Christians are capable of and do in fact commit gross and heinous sins.

We believe that true Christians can fall seriously and radically. We do not believe that they can fall *totally* and *finally*. We observe the case of King David, who was guilty not only of adultery but of conspiracy in the death of Uriah, Bathsheba's husband. David used his power and authority to make sure Uriah was killed in battle. In essence David was guilty of murder in the first degree, premeditated and with malice aforethought.

David's conscience was so seared, his heart so hardened, that it required nothing less than direct confrontation with a prophet of God to bring him to his senses. His subsequent repentance was as deep as his sin. David sinned radically but not totally and finally. He was restored.

Consider the record of two famous persons in the New Testament. Both of them were called by Jesus to be disciples. Both of them walked beside Jesus during His earthly ministry. Both of them betrayed Jesus. Their names are Peter and Judas.

After Judas betrayed Christ, he went out and committed suicide. After Peter betrayed Christ, he repented and was restored, emerging as a pillar of the early church. What was the difference between these two men? Jesus predicted that both of them would betray him. When He finished speaking with Judas, He said to him, "What you have to do, do quickly."

Jesus spoke differently to Peter. He said to him: "Simon, Simon! Indeed, Satan has asked for you, that he may sift you as wheat. But I have prayed for you, that your faith should not fail; and when you have returned to Me, strengthen your brethren" (Luke 22:31, 32).

Notice carefully what Jesus said. He did not say *if* but *when*. Jesus was confident that Peter would return. His fall would be radical and serious, but not total and final.

It is clear that Jesus' confidence in Peter's return was not based on Peter's strength. Jesus knew that Satan would sift Peter like wheat. That is like saying that Peter was a "piece of cake," "duck soup," for Satan. Jesus' confidence was based upon the power of Jesus' intercession. It is from the promise of Christ that He would be our great High Priest, our Advocate with the Father, our Righteous Intercessor, that we believe that we will persevere. Our confidence is in our Savior and our Priest who prays for us.

The Bible records a prayer that Jesus offered for us in John 17. We ought to read this great high priestly prayer frequently. Let us examine a portion of it:

> . . . keep through Your name those whom You have given Me,
> that they may be one as We are. While I was with them in the
> world, I kept them in Your name. Those whom You gave Me I
> have kept; and none of them is lost except the son of perdition,
> that the Scripture might be fulfilled. (vv. 11, 12)

Again we read:Father, I desire that they also whom You gave Me may be with Me where I am, that they may behold My glory which You have given Me; for You loved Me before the foundation of the world. (v. 24)

Our preservation is a trinitarian work. God the Father keeps and preserves us. God the Son intercedes for us. God the Holy Spirit indwells and assists us. We are given the "seal" and the "earnest" of the Holy Spirit (2 Tim. 2:19; Eph. 1:14; Rom. 8:23). These images are all images of a divine guarantee. The seal of the Spirit is an indelible mark like the waxed imprint of a monarch's signet ring. It indicates that we are His possession. The earnest of the Spirit is not identical to earnest money that is paid in modern real estate transactions. Such earnest money may be forfeited. In biblical terms the earnest of the Spirit is a down payment with a promise to pay the rest. God does not forfeit His earnest. He does not fail to finish the payments He began. The first fruits of the Spirit guarantee that the last fruits will be forthcoming.

An analogy of God's work of preservation may be seen in the image of a father holding onto his small child's hand as they walk together. In the Arminian view the safety of the child rests in the strength of the child's grip on the father's hand. If the child lets go, he will perish. In the Calvinist view the safety of the child rests in the strength of the father's grip on the child. If the child's grip fails, the father's grip holds firm. The arm of the Lord does not wax short.

Still we ask why it seems that some people do in fact fall away totally and finally. Here we must echo the words of the apostle John: "They went out from us, but they were not of us; for if they had been of us, they would have continued with us; but they went out that they might be made manifest, that none of them were of us" (1 John 2:19).

We repeat our aphorism: If we have it, we never lose it; if we lose it, we never had it. We recognize that the church of Jesus Christ is a mixed body.

There are tares that live side by side with the wheat; goats that live side by side with sheep. The parable of the sower makes it plain that people can experience a false conversion. They may have an appearance of faith, but that faith may not be genuine.

We know people who have been "converted" many times. Every time there is a church revival, they go to the altar and get "saved." One minister told of a man in his congregation who had been "saved" seventeen times. During a revival meeting the evangelist made an altar call for all who wanted to be filled with the Spirit. The man who had been converted so often made his way toward the altar again. A woman from the congregation shouted, "Don't fill him, Lord. He leaks!"

We all leak to some degree, but no Christian is totally and finally of God's Spirit. Those who become "unconverted" were never converted in the first place. Judas was a son of perdition from the beginning. His conversion was spurious. Jesus did not pray for his restoration. Judas did not lose the Holy Spirit, because he never had the Holy Spirit.

Of course there is nothing wrong with repeated calls to commitment to Christ. We may visit the altar many times or respond to invitations repeatedly and not be exactly sure which of the responses was truly genuine. Two benefits of repeated responses to evangelistic calls are to strengthen our assurance of salvation and to deepen our commitment to Christ.

Biblical Warnings about Falling Away

Probably the strongest arguments the Arminians offer against the doctrine of the perseverance of the saints are drawn from the manifold warnings in Scripture against falling away. Paul, for example, writes: "But I discipline my body and bring it into subjection, lest, when I have preached to others, I myself should become disqualified" (1 Cor. 9:27).

Paul elsewhere speaks of men who have been apostate: "And their message will spread like cancer. Hymenaeus and Philetus are of this sort, who have strayed concerning the truth, saying that the resurrection is already past; and they overthrow the faith of some" (2 Tim. 2:17, 18).

These passages suggest that it is possible for believers to be "disqualified" or to have their faith "overthrown." It is important, however, to see how Paul concludes his statement to Timothy. "Nevertheless the solid foundation of God stands, having this seal: 'The Lord knows those who are His,' and 'Let everyone who names the name of Christ depart from iniquity' " (v. 19).

Peter also speaks of washed sows wallowing again and dogs who return to their vomit, comparing them to people who have turned away after being instructed in the way of righteousness. These are false converts whose natures have never been changed (2 Pet. 2:22).

Hebrews 6

The text that contains the most solemn warning against falling away is also the most controversial regarding the doctrine of perseverance. It is found in Hebrews 6:

> For it is impossible for those who were once enlightened, and have tasted the heavenly gift, and have become partakers of the Holy Spirit, and have tasted the good word of God and the powers of the age to come, if they fall away, to renew them again to repentance, since they crucify again for themselves the Son of God, and put Him to open shame. (vv. 4–6)

This passage strongly suggests that believers can and do fall away, totally and finally. How are we to understand it?

The full meaning of the passage is difficult for several reasons. The first is that we do not know for sure what issue of apostasy was involved in this text, since we are not certain of either the author or the destination of Hebrews. There were two burning issues in the early church that easily could have provoked this dire warning.

The first issue was the problem of the so-called *lapsi*. The *lapsi* were those people who during severe persecution did not keep the faith. Not every church member went to the lions singing hymns. Some broke down and recanted their faith. Some even betrayed their comrades and collaborated with the Romans. When the persecutions died down, some of these former collaborators repented and sought readmission to the church. How they were to be received was no small controversy.

The other burning issue was that provoked by the Judaizers. The destructive influence of this group is dealt with in several parts of the New Testament, most notably in the book of Galatians. The Judaizers wanted to profess Christ and at the same time enforce the Old Testament cultic ceremonies. They insisted, for example, on ceremonial circumcision. I believe that it was the Judaizer heresy that the author of Hebrews was concerned with.

A second problem is to identify the nature of people who are being warned against falling away in Hebrews. Are they true believers or are they tares growing among the wheat? We must remember that there are three categories of people we are concerned with here. There are (1) believers, (2) unbelievers in the church, and (3) unbelievers outside of the church.

The book of Hebrews draws several parallels with Old Testament Israel, especially with those in the camp who were apostates. Who are these people in Hebrews? How are they described? Let us list their attributes:

1. once enlightened
2. tasted the heavenly gift
3. partakers of the Holy Spirit
4. tasted the good Word of God
5. cannot be renewed again to repentance

At first glance this list certainly appears to describe true believers. However it may also be describing church members who are not believers, people who have made a false profession of faith. All of these attributes may be possessed by nonbelievers. The tares who come to church every week hear the Word of God taught and preached and thus are "enlightened." They participate in all of the means of grace. They join in the Lord's Supper. They partake of the Holy Spirit in the sense that they enjoy the nearness of His special immediate presence and His benefits. They have even made a kind of repentance, at least outwardly.

Many Calvinists thereby find a solution to this passage by relating it to nonbelievers in the church who repudiate Christ. I am not entirely satisfied by that interpretation. I think this passage may well be describing true Christians. The most important phrase for me is "renew again to repentance." I know there is a false kind of repentance that the author elsewhere calls the repentance of Esau. But here he speaks of renewal. The new repentance, if it is renewed, must be like the old repentance. The renewed repentance of which he speaks is certainly the genuine kind. I assume therefore that the old was likewise genuine.

I think the author here is arguing in what we call an *ad hominem* style. An *ad hominem* argument is carried out by taking your opponent's position and carrying it to its logical conclusion. The logical conclusion of the Judaizer heresy is to destroy any hope of salvation.

The logic goes like this. If a person embraced Christ and trusted in His atonement for sin, what would that person have if he went back to the covenant of Moses? In effect he would be repudiating the finished work of Christ. He would once again be a debtor to the law. If that were the case, where would he turn for salvation? He has repudiated the cross; he couldn't turn to that. He would have no hope of salvation, because he would have no Savior. His theology does not allow a finished work of Christ.

The key to Hebrews 6 is found in verse 9. "But, beloved, we are confident of better things concerning you, yes, things that accompany salvation, though we speak in this manner."

Here the author himself notes that he is speaking in an unusual manner. His conclusion differs from those who find here a text for falling away. He concludes with a confidence of *better things* from the beloved, things that accompany salvation. Obviously falling away does not accompany salvation. The author does not say that any believer actually does fall away. In fact he says the opposite, that he is confident they will not fall away.

But if no one falls away, why even bother to warn people against it? It seems frivolous to exhort people to avoid the impossible. Here is where we must understand the relationship of perseverance to preservation. Perseverance is both a grace and a duty. We are to strive with all our might in our spiritual walk. Humanly speaking, it is possible to fall away. Yet as we strive we are to look to God who is preserving us. It is impossible that He should fail to keep us. Consider again the analogy of the child walking with his father. It is possible that the child will let go. If the father is God, it is not possible that He will let go. Even given the promise of the Father not to let go, it is still the duty of the child to hold on tightly. Thus the author of Hebrews warns believers against falling away. Luther called this the "evangelical use of exhortation." It reminds us of our duty to be diligent in our walk with God.

Finally, with respect to perseverance and preservation, we must look to the promise of God in the Old Testament. Through the prophet Jeremiah, God promises to make a new covenant with His people, a covenant that is everlasting. He says: "And I will make an everlasting covenant with them, that I will not turn away from doing them good; but I will put My fear in their hearts so that they will not depart from Me" (Jer. 32:40).

Summary of Chapter 8

1. We conclude that assurance of our salvation is vital to our spiritual lives. Without it our growth is retarded and we are assailed with crippling doubts.

2. God calls us to make our election sure, to find the comfort and strength that God offers in assurance. In Romans 15 Paul declares that it is God who is the source or fountainhead of our perseverance and encouragement (v. 5) and of our hope (v. 13). Finding our assurance is both a duty and a privilege.

3. No true believer ever loses his salvation. To be sure, Christians fall at times seriously and radically, but never fully and finally. We persevere, not because of our strength but because of God's grace that preserves us.

Questions and Objections Concerning Predestination

There remain several problems and issues surrounding predestination that we must at least touch upon.

Is Predestination Fatalism?

A frequent objection raised against predestination is that it is a religious form of fatalism. If we examine fatalism in its literal sense, we see that it is as far removed from the biblical doctrine of predestination as the east is from the west. Fatalism literally means that the affairs of men are controlled either by whimsical subdeities (the Fates) or more popularly by the impersonal forces of chance.

Predestination is based neither on a mythical view of goddesses playing with our lives nor upon a view of destiny controlled by the chance collision of atoms. Predestination is rooted in the character of a personal and righteous God, a God who is the sovereign Lord of history. That my destiny would ultimately be in the hands of an indifferent or hostile force is terrifying. That it is in the hands of a righteous and loving God is quite another matter. Atoms have no righteousness in them; they are at best amoral. God is altogether holy. I prefer that my destiny be with Him.

The great superstition of modern times is focused on the role given to chance in human affairs. Chance is the new reigning deity of the modern mind. Chance inhabits the castle of the gods. Chance is given credit for the creation of the universe and the emergence of the human race from the slime.

Chance is a shibboleth. It is a magic word we use to explain the unknown. It is the favorite power of causality for those who will attribute power to anything or anyone but God. This superstitious attitude toward chance is not new. We read of its attraction very early in biblical history.

We remember the incident in Jewish history when the sacred ark of the covenant was captured by the Philistines. On that day death visited the house of Eli and the glory departed from Israel. The Philistines were jubilant over their victory, but they soon learned to rue the day. Wherever they took the ark, calamity befell them. The temple of Dagon was humiliated. The people were devastated by tumors. For seven months the ark was shuttled between the great cities of the Philistines with the same catastrophic results in each city.

In desperation the kings of the Philistines took counsel together and decided to send the ark back to the Jews with a ransom as well, to mollify the wrath of God. Their final words of counsel are noteworthy:

> Then take the ark of the LORD and set it on the cart; and put
> the articles of gold which you are returning to Him as a trespass
> offering in a chest by its side. Then send it away, and let it go.
> And watch: if it goes up the road to its own territory, to Beth
> Shemesh, then He has done us this great evil. But if not, then we
> shall know that it is not His hand that struck us; it was by chance
> that it happened to us. (1 Sam. 6:8, 9)

We have already noted that chance can do nothing because it is nothing. Let me elaborate. We use the word *chance* to describe mathematical possibilities. For example, when we flip a coin we say that it has a fifty/fifty chance to come up heads. If we call heads on the toss and it turns up tails, we might say that our luck was bad and that we missed our chance.

How much influence does chance have on the toss of a coin? What makes the coin turn up heads or tails? Would the odds change if we knew which side the coin started on, how much pressure was exerted by the thumb, how dense the atmosphere was, and how many revolutions the coin made in the air? With this knowledge, our ability to predict the outcome would far exceed fifty/fifty.

But the hand is faster than the eye. We can't measure all these factors in the normal tossing of the coin. Since we can reduce the possible outcome to two, we simplify matters by talking about chance. The point to remember, however, is that chance exercises absolutely no influence on the coin toss. Why not? As we keep saying, chance can do nothing because it *is* nothing. It is *no thing*. Before something can exert power or influence it must first be something. It must be some kind of entity, either physical or nonphysical. Chance is neither. It is merely a mental construct. It has no power because it has no being. It is nothing.

To say that something has happened by chance is to say that it is a coincidence. This is simply a confession that we cannot perceive all the forces and causal powers that are at work in an event. Just as we cannot see all that is happening in a coin toss with the naked eye, so the complex affairs of life are also beyond our exact ability to penetrate. So we invent the term *chance* to explain them. Chance really explains nothing. It is merely a word we use as shorthand for our ignorance.

I recently wrote on the subject of cause and effect. A professor of philosophy wrote to me complaining of my naïve understanding of the law of cause and effect. He chided me for failing to take into account "uncaused events." I thanked him for his letter and said that I would be happy to grapple with his objection if he would write back and provide just one example of an uncaused event. I am still waiting. I will wait forever, because even God cannot have an uncaused event. Waiting for an uncaused event is like waiting for a square circle.

Our destinies are not controlled by chance. I say that dogmatically with all the bluster I can manage. I know that my destiny is not controlled by chance, because I know that nothing can be controlled by chance. Chance can control nothing because it is nothing. What are the chances that the universe was created by chance or that our destinies are controlled by chance? Not a chance.

Fatalism finds its most popular expression in astrology. Our daily horoscopes are compiled on the basis of the movements of the stars. People in our society know more about the twelve signs of the zodiac than they do about the twelve tribes of Israel. Yet Reuben has more to do with my future than Aquarius, Judah more than Gemini.

Doesn't the Bible Say That God Is Not Willing that Any Should Perish?

The apostle Peter clearly states that God is not willing that any should perish. "The Lord is not slack concerning His promise, as some count slackness, but is longsuffering toward us, not willing that any should perish but that all should come to repentance" (2 Pet. 3:9).

How can we square this verse with predestination? If it is not the will of God to elect everyone unto salvation, how can the Bible then say that God is not willing that any should perish?

In the first place we must understand that the Bible speaks of the will of God in more than one way. For example, the Bible speaks of what we call God's *sovereign efficacious will*. The sovereign will of God is that will by which God brings things to pass with absolute certainty. Nothing can resist the will of God in this sense. By His sovereign will He created the world. The light could not have refused to shine.

The second way in which the Bible speaks of the will of God is with respect to what we call His *preceptive will*. God's preceptive will refers to His commands, His laws. It is God's will that we do the things He mandates. We are capable of disobeying this will. We do in fact break His commandments. We cannot do it with impunity. We do it without His permission or sanction. Yet we do it. We sin.

A third way the Bible speaks of the will of God has reference to God's disposition, to what is pleasing to Him. God does not take delight in the death of the wicked. There is a sense in which the punishment of the wicked does not bring joy to God. He chooses to do it because it is good to punish evil. He delights in the righteousness of His judgment but is "sad" that such righteous judgment must be carried out. It is something like a judge sitting on a bench and sentencing his own son to prison.

Let us apply these three possible definitions to the passage in 2 Peter. If we take the blanket statement, "God is not willing that any should perish," and apply the sovereign efficacious will to it, the conclusion is obvious. No one will perish. If God sovereignly decrees that no one should perish, and God is God, then certainly no one will ever perish. This would then be a proof text not for Arminianism but for universalism. The text would then prove too much for Arminians.

Suppose we apply the definition of the preceptive will of God to this passage. Then the passage would mean that God does not *allow* anyone to perish. That is, He forbids the perishing of people. It is against His law. If people then went ahead and perished, God would have to punish them for perishing. His punishment for perishing would be more perishing. But how does one engage in more perishing than perishing? This definition will not work in this passage. It makes no sense.

The third alternative is that God takes no delight in the perishing of people. This squares with what the Bible says elsewhere about God's disposition toward the lost. This definition could fit this passage. Peter may simply be saying here that God takes no delight in the perishing of anyone.

Though the third definition is a possible and attractive one to use in resolving this passage with what the Bible teaches about predestination, there is yet another factor to be considered. The text says more than simply that God is not willing that any should perish. The whole clause is important: "but is longsuffering toward us, not willing that any should perish but that all should come to repentance."

What is the antecedent of *any*? It is clearly *us*. Does *us* refer to all of us humans? Or does it refer to us Christians, the people of God? Peter is fond of speaking of the elect as a special group of people. I think what he is saying here is that God does not will that any of us (the elect) perish. If that is his meaning, then the text would demand the first definition and would be one more strong passage in favor of predestination.

In two different ways the text may easily be harmonized with predestination. In no way does it support Arminianism. Its only other possible meaning would be universalism, which would then bring it into conflict with everything else the Bible says against universalism.

What Is the Unpardonable Sin?

In our discussions on assurance of salvation and the perseverance of the saints, we touched on the question of the unforgivable sin. The fact that Jesus warns against the committing of a sin that is unforgivable is beyond dispute. The questions we must face then are these: What is the unforgivable sin? Can Christians commit this sin?

Jesus defined it as blasphemy against the Holy Spirit:

> Therefore I say to you, every sin and blasphemy will be forgiven men, but the blasphemy against the Spirit will not be forgiven men. Anyone who speaks a word against the Son of Man, it will be forgiven him; but whoever speaks against the Holy Spirit, it will not be forgiven him, either in this age or in the age to come. (Matt. 12:31, 32)

In this text Jesus does not provide a detailed explanation of the nature of this dreadful sin. He declares that there is such a sin and gives an ominous warning about it. The rest of the New Testament adds little in the way of further explanation. As a result of this silence, there has been much speculation about the unforgivable sin.

Two sins have been frequently mentioned as candidates for the unforgivable sin: adultery and murder. Adultery is chosen on the grounds that it represents a sin against the Holy Spirit because the body is the temple of the Holy Spirit. Adultery was a capital crime in the Old Testament. The reasoning is that, since it deserved the death penalty and involved a violation of the temple of the Holy Spirit, this must be the unpardonable sin.

Murder is chosen for similar reasons. Since man is created in the image of God, an attack upon the human person is considered an attack upon God Himself. To slay the image-bearer is to insult the One whose image is borne. Likewise murder is a capital sin. We add to this the fact that murder is a sin against the sanctity of life. Since the Holy Spirit is the ultimate "life force," to kill a human being is to insult the Holy Spirit.

As attractive as these theories may be to speculators, they have not gained the consent of most biblical scholars. A more popular view has to do with the final resistance to the Holy Spirit's application of Christ's work of redemption. Final unbelief is then seen as the unpardonable sin. If a person repeatedly, fully, and finally repudiates the gospel, then there is no hope of future forgiveness.

What all three of these theories lack is a serious consideration of the meaning of blasphemy. Blasphemy is something that we do with our mouths. It deals with what we say out loud. Certainly it can also be done with the pen, but blasphemy is a *verbal* sin.

The Ten Commandments include a prohibition against blasphemy. We are forbidden to make frivolous or irreverent use of the name of God. In God's eyes the verbal abuse of His holy name is a serious enough matter to make it to His top-ten list of commands. This tells us that blasphemy is a serious matter in God's sight. It is a heinous sin to blaspheme any member of the Godhead.

Does this mean that anyone who has ever abused the name of God has no possible hope of forgiveness, now or ever? Does it mean that if a person curses once, using the name of God, that he is doomed forever? I think not.

It is crucial to note in this text that Jesus makes a distinction between sinning against Him (the Son of Man), and sinning against the Holy Spirit. Does this mean that it is okay to blaspheme the first person of the Trinity and the second person of the Trinity, but to insult the third person is to cross the boundaries of forgiveness? This hardly makes sense.

Why then would Jesus make such a distinction between sinning against Himself and against the Holy Spirit? I think the key to answering this question is the key to the whole question of the blasphemy against the Holy Spirit. That key is found in the context in which Jesus originally gave His severe warning.

In Matthew 12:24 we read: "But when the Pharisees heard it they said, 'This fellow does not cast out demons except by Beelzebub, the ruler of the demons.' " Jesus responds with a discourse about a house divided against itself and the foolishness of the idea that Satan would work to cast out Satan. His warning about the unpardonable sin is the conclusion of this discussion. He introduces His severe warning with the word *therefore.*

The situation runs something like this: The Pharisees are being repeatedly critical of Jesus. Their verbal attacks upon Him get more and more vicious. Jesus had been casting out demons "by the Finger of God," which means by the Holy Spirit. The Pharisees sink so low as to accuse Jesus of doing His holy work by the power of Satan. Jesus warns them. It is as if He were saying: "Be careful. Be really careful. You are coming perilously close to a sin for which you cannot be forgiven. It is one thing to attack Me, but watch yourselves. You're treading on holy ground here."

We still wonder why Jesus made the distinction between sinning against the Son of Man and sinning against the Spirit. We notice that even from the cross

Jesus pled for the forgiveness of those who were murdering Him. On the day of Pentecost Peter spoke of the horrible crime against Christ committed in the crucifixion, yet still held out hope for forgiveness to those who had participated in it. Paul says, "But we speak the wisdom of God in a mystery, the hidden wisdom which God ordained before the ages for our glory, *which none of the rulers of this age knew; for had they known, they would not have crucified the Lord of glory*" (1 Cor. 2:7, 8; italics added).

These texts indicate an allowance of sorts for human ignorance. We must remember that when the Pharisees accused Jesus of working by the power of Satan they did not yet have the benefit of the fullness of God's disclosure of the true identity of Christ. These charges were made *before* the Resurrection. To be sure, the Pharisees *should* have recognized Christ, but they did not. Jesus' words from the cross are important: "Father, forgive them, for they *know not* what they do."

When Jesus gave the warning and distinguished between blasphemy against the Son of Man and blasphemy against the Holy Spirit, it was at a time when He had not yet been made fully manifest. We note that this distinction tends to fall away after the Resurrection, Pentecost, and the Ascension. Note what the author of Hebrews declares:

> For if we sin willfully after we have received the knowledge of the truth, there no longer remains a sacrifice for sins, but a certain fearful expectation of judgment, and fiery indignation which will devour the adversaries. Anyone who has rejected Moses' law dies without mercy on the testimony of two or three witnesses. Of how much worse punishment, do you suppose, will he be thought worthy who has trampled the Son of God underfoot, counted the blood of the covenant by which he was sanctified a common thing, and insulted the Spirit of grace? (Heb. 10:26–29)

In this passage the distinction between sinning against Christ and against the Spirit falls away. Here, to sin against Christ is to insult the Spirit of grace. The key is in the willful sin *after* we have received the knowledge of the truth.

If we take the first line of this text as an absolute, none of us has a hope of heaven. We all sin willfully after we know the truth. A specific sin is in view here, not each and every sin. I am persuaded that the specific sin in view here is the blasphemy against the Holy Spirit.

I agree with the New Testament scholars who conclude that the unforgivable sin is to blaspheme Christ *and* the Holy Spirit by saying Jesus is a devil when you know better. That is, the unforgivable sin cannot be done in ignorance. If a person knows with certainty that Jesus is the Son of God and then declares with his mouth that Jesus is of the devil, that person has committed unpardonable blasphemy.

Who commits such a sin? This is a sin common to devils and to totally degenerate people. The devil knew who Jesus was. He could not plead ignorance as an excuse.

One of the fascinating facts of history is the strange way in which unbelievers speak of Jesus. The vast majority of unbelievers speak of Jesus with great respect. They may attack the church with great hostility but still speak of Jesus as a "great man." Only once in my life have I heard a person say out loud that Jesus was a devil. I was shocked to see a man stand in the middle of the street shaking his fist toward heaven and screaming at the top of his lungs. He cursed God and used every obscenity he could utter in attacking Jesus. I was equally shocked only hours later when I saw the same man on a stretcher with a bullet hole in his chest. It was self-inflicted. He died before morning.

Even that dreadful sight did not drive me to the conclusion that the man had actually committed the unpardonable sin. I had no way of knowing if he was ignorant of Christ's true identity or not.

Saying that Jesus is a devil is not something we see many people do. It is, however, possible for people to know the truth of Jesus and sink this low. One does not need to be born again to have an intellectual knowledge of the true identity of Jesus. Again, the unregenerate demons know who He is.

What of Christians? Is it possible for a Christian to commit the unforgivable sin and thereby lose his salvation? I think not. The grace of God makes it impossible. In ourselves we are capable of any sin, including blasphemy against the Holy Spirit. But God preserves us from this sin. He preserves us from full and final fall, guarding our lips from this horrible crime. We perform other sins and other kinds of blasphemy, but God in His grace restrains us from committing the ultimate blasphemy.

Did Jesus Die for Everyone?

One of the most controversial points of Reformed theology concerns the *L* in TULIP. *L* stands for *limited atonement*. It has been such a problem of doctrine that there are multitudes of Christians who say they embrace most of the doctrines of Calvinism but get off the boat here. They refer to themselves as four-point Calvinists. The point they cannot abide is limited atonement.

I have often thought that to be a four-point Calvinist one must misunderstand at least one of the five points. It is hard for me to imagine that anyone could understand the other four points of Calvinism and deny limited atonement. There always is the possibility, however, of the happy inconsistency by which people hold incompatible views at the same time.

The doctrine of limited atonement is so complex that to treat it adequately demands a full volume. I have not even given it a full chapter in this book because a chapter cannot do it justice. I have thought about not mentioning it altogether because the danger exists that to say too little about it is worse than saying nothing at all. But I think the reader deserves at least a brief summary of the doctrine, and so I will proceed—with the caution that the subject requires a much deeper treatment than I am able to provide here.

The issue of limited atonement concerns the question, "For whom did Christ die? Did He die for everybody or only for the elect?" We all agree that the value of Jesus' atonement was great enough to cover the sins of every human being. We also agree that His atonement is truly offered to all men. Any person who places his trust in the atoning death of Jesus Christ will most certainly receive the full benefits of that atonement. We are also confident that anyone who responds to the universal offer of the gospel will be saved.

The question is, "For whom was the Atonement *designed?*" Did God send Jesus into the world merely to make salvation *possible* for people? Or did God have something more definite in mind? (Roger Nicole, the eminent Baptist theologian, prefers to call limited atonement "definite atonement," disrupting the acrostic TULIP as much as I do.)

Some argue that all limited atonement means is that the benefits of the Atonement are limited to believers who meet the necessary condition of faith. That is, though Christ's atonement was sufficient to cover the sins of all men and to satisfy God's justice against all sin, it only *effects* salvation for believers. The formula reads: Sufficient for all; efficient for the elect only.

That point simply serves to distinguish us from universalists who believe that the Atonement secured salvation for everyone. The doctrine of limited atonement goes further than that. It is concerned with the deeper question of the Father's and the Son's *intention* in the cross. It declares that the mission and death of Christ was restricted to a limited number—to His people, His sheep. Jesus was called "Jesus" because He would save His people from their sins (Matt. 1:21). The Good Shepherd lays down His life for the sheep (John 10:15). Such passages are found liberally in the New Testament.

The mission of Christ was to save the elect. "This is the will of the Father who sent Me, that of all He has given Me I should lose nothing, but should raise it up at the last day" (John 6:39). Had there not been a fixed number contemplated by God when He appointed Christ to die, then the effects of Christ's death would have been uncertain. It would be possible that the mission of Christ would have been a dismal and complete failure.

Jesus' atonement and His intercession are joint works of His high priesthood. He explicitly excludes the nonelect from His great high priestly prayer. "I do not pray for the world but for those whom You have given Me" (John 17:9). Did Christ die for those for whom He would not pray?

The essential issue here concerns the nature of the Atonement. Jesus' atonement included both *expiation* and *propitiation*. Ex-piation involves Christ's removing our sins "away from" (*ex*) us. Pro-pitiation involves a satisfaction of sin "before or in the presence of" (*pro*) God. Arminianism has an atonement that is limited in value. It does not cover the sin of unbelief. If Jesus died for all the sins of all men, if He expiated all our sins and propitiated all our sins, then everybody would be saved. A potential atonement is not a real atonement. Jesus *really* atoned for the sins of His sheep.

The biggest problem with definite or limited atonement is found in the passages that the Scriptures use concerning Christ's death "for all" or for the "whole world." The world for whom Christ died cannot mean the entire human family. It must refer to the universality of the elect (people from every tribe and nation) or to the inclusion of Gentiles in addition to the world of the Jews. It was a Jew who wrote that Jesus did not die merely for *our* sins but for the sins of the whole world. Does the word *our* refer to believers or to believing Jews?

We must remember that one of the cardinal points of the New Testament concerned the inclusion of the Gentiles in God's plan of salvation. Salvation was *of* the Jews but not restricted to the Jews. Wherever it is said that Christ died for all, some limitation must be added or the conclusion would have to be universalism or a mere potential atonement.

Christ's atonement was real. It effected all that God and Jesus intended by it. The design of God was not and cannot be frustrated by human unbelief. The sovereign God sovereignly sent His Son to atone for His people.

Our election is in Christ. We are saved by Him, in Him, and *for* Him. The motive for our salvation is not merely the love God has for us. It is especially grounded in the love the Father has for the Son. God insists that His Son will see the travail of His soul and be satisfied. There never has been the slightest possibility that Christ could have died in vain. If man is truly dead in sin and in bondage to sin, a mere potential or conditional atonement not only *may have* ended in failure but most certainly *would have* ended in failure. Arminians have no sound reason to believe that Jesus did not die in vain. They are left with a Christ who tried to save everybody but actually saved nobody.

What Does Predestination Do to the Task of Evangelism?

This question raises grave concerns about the mission of the church. It is particularly weighty for evangelical Christians. If personal salvation is decided in advance by an immutable divine decree, what is the sense or urgency of the work of evangelism?

I will never forget the terrifying experience of being quizzed on this point by Dr. John Gerstner in a seminary class. There were about twenty of us seated in a semicircle in the classroom. He posed the question: "All right, gentlemen, if God has sovereignly decreed election and reprobation from all eternity, why should we be concerned about evangelism?" I breathed a sigh of relief when Gerstner started his interrogation on the left end of the semicircle since I was sitting in the last seat on the right. I took comfort in the hope that the question would never get around to me.

The comfort was short-lived. The first student replied to Gerstner's query, "I don't know, sir. That question has always plagued me." The second student said, "It beats me." The third just shook his head and dropped his gaze toward the floor. In rapid succession the students all passed on the question. The dominoes were falling in my direction.

"Well, Mr. Sproul, how would you answer?" I wanted to vanish into thin air or find a hiding place in the floorboards, but there was no escape. I stammered and muttered a reply. Dr. Gerstner said, "Speak up!" In tentative words I said, "Well, Dr. Gerstner, I know this isn't the answer you are looking for, but one small reason we should still be concerned about evangelism is that, well, uh, you know, after all, Christ does command us to do evangelism."

Gerstner's eyes started to flame. He said, "Ah, I see, Mr. Sproul, one *small* reason is that your Savior, the Lord of glory, the King of kings has so commanded it. A small reason, Mr. Sproul? Is it barely significant to you that the same sovereign God who sovereignly decrees your election also sovereignly commands your involvement in the task of evangelism?" Oh how I wished I'd never used the word *small*. I got Gerstner's point.

Evangelism is our duty. God has commanded it. That should be enough to end the matter. But there is more. Evangelism is not only a duty; it is also a privilege. God allows us to participate in the greatest work in human history, the work of redemption. Hear what Paul says about it. He adds a chapter 10 to his famous chapter 9 of Romans:

For "whoever calls upon the name of the LORD shall be saved."
How then shall they call on Him in whom they have not

believed? And how shall they believe in Him of whom they have not heard? And how shall they hear without a preacher? And how shall they preach unless they are sent? As it is written:

"How beautiful are the feet of those who preach the gospel
    of peace,
Who bring glad tidings of good things!" (Rom. 10:13–15)

We notice the logic of Paul's progression here. He lists a series of necessary conditions for people to be saved. Without sending there are no preachers. Without preachers there is no preaching. Without preaching there is no hearing of the gospel. Without the hearing of the gospel there is no believing of the gospel. Without the believing of the gospel there is no calling upon God to be saved. Without the calling upon God to be saved there is no salvation.

God not only foreordains the *end* of salvation for the elect, He also foreordained the *means* to that end. God has chosen the foolishness of preaching as the means to accomplish redemption. I suppose He could have worked out His divine purpose without us. He could publish the gospel in the clouds using His holy finger in skywriting. He could preach the gospel Himself, in His own voice, shouting it from heaven. But that is not His choice.

It is a marvelous privilege to be used by God in the plan of redemption. Paul appeals to an Old Testament passage when he speaks of the beauty of the feet of those who bring good tidings and publish peace.

How beautiful upon the mountains
Are the feet of him who brings good news,
Who proclaims peace,
Who brings glad tiding of good things,
Who proclaims salvation,
Who says to Zion,
"Your God reigns!"
Your watchmen shall lift up their voices,
With their voices they shall sing together;
For they shall see eye to eye
When the LORD brings back Zion.
Break forth into joy, sing together,
You waste places of Jerusalem!
For the LORD has comforted His people,
He has redeemed Jerusalem. (Isa. 52:7–9)

In the ancient world, news of battles and other crucial events was carried by runners. The modern marathon race is named after the Battle of Marathon because of the endurance of the messenger who carried the news of the outcome home to his people.

Lookouts were posted to watch for the approaching messengers. Their eyes were sharp and trained to the subtle nuances of the strides of the approaching runners. Those bearing bad news approached with heavy feet. Those runners bearing good news approached swiftly, with feet sprinting through the dust. Their strides revealed their excitement. For the watchmen the sight of a runner approaching rapidly in the distance with his feet skimming over the mountain was a gorgeous vision to behold.

So the Bible speaks of the beauty of the feet of those who bring us good news. When my daughter was born and the doctor came to the waiting room to announce it, I wanted to hug him. We are favorably inclined to those who bring us good tidings. I will always have a special place in my affections for the man who first told me of Christ. I know that it was God who saved me and not that man, but I still appreciate the man's role in my salvation.

To lead people to Christ is one of the greatest personal blessings that we ever enjoy. To be a Calvinist takes no joy away from that experience. Historically, Calvinists have been strongly active in evangelism and world mission. We need only point to Edwards and Whitefield and the Great Awakening to illustrate this point.

We have a meaningful role to play in evangelism. We preach and we proclaim the gospel. That is our duty and our privilege. But it is God who brings the increase. He does not need us to accomplish His purpose, but He is pleased to use us in the task.

I once met a traveling evangelist who said to me, "Give me any man alone for fifteen minutes, and I will get a decision for Christ." Sadly, the man really believed his own words. He was convinced that the power of conversion rested solely in his powers of persuasion.

I don't doubt that the man was basing his claim on his past track record. He was so overbearing that I am sure there were multitudes who made decisions for Christ within fifteen minutes of being alone with him. Sure, he could make good his promise to produce a decision in fifteen minutes. What he couldn't guarantee was a conversion in fifteen minutes. People would make decisions just to get away from him.

We must never underestimate the importance of our role in evangelism. Neither must we overestimate it. We preach. We bear witness. We provide the outward call. But God alone has the power to call a person to Himself inwardly.

I do not feel cheated by that. On the contrary, I feel comforted. We must do our job, trusting that God will do His.

Conclusion

At the beginning of this book I related a bit of my own personal pilgrimage concerning the doctrine of predestination. I mentioned the earnest and long-term struggle it involved. I mentioned that I was finally brought into submission to the doctrine reluctantly. I was first brought to a conviction of the truth of the matter before I took any delight in it.

Let me close this book by mentioning that soon after I awoke to the truth of predestination I began to see the beauty of it and taste its sweetness. I have grown to love this doctrine. It is most comforting. It underlines the extent to which God has gone in our behalf. It is a theology that begins and ends with grace. It begins and ends with doxology. We praise a God who lifted us from spiritual deadness and makes us walk in high places. We find a God who is "for us," giving us the courage to withstand those who may be against us. It makes our souls rejoice to know that all things are working together for our good. We delight in our Savior who truly saves us and preserves us and intercedes for us. We marvel at His craftsmanship and in what He has wrought. We skip and kick our heels when we discover His promise to finish in us what He has started in us. We ponder mysteries and bow before them, but not without doxology for the riches of grace He has revealed:

> Oh, the depth of the riches both of the wisdom and knowledge
> of God! . . . For of Him and through Him and to Him are all
> things, to whom be glory forever. Amen. (Rom. 11:33, 36)

PLEASING GOD

R. C. SPROUL

For Chuck Green
and
Dale and Joyce Linder,
People who love to please God

Contents

Preface

"This is My beloved Son, in whom I am well pleased" (Matt. 3:17).

There are three occasions in the New Testament when God speaks audibly from heaven: Jesus' baptism (Matt. 3:17; Mark 1:11; Luke 3:22), the Transfiguration (Matt. 17:5; Mark 9:7; Luke 9:35), and Jesus' address after the triumphal entry (John 12:28). On the first two of these occasions God declares that He is pleased with His Son. What higher approval could a man enjoy than to know that what he has done is pleasing to God? Every Christian should have a passion to please God. We are to delight in honoring Him. It is our own greatest pleasure to please our Redeemer. We all begin the Christian life with the intention of living in such a way as to please God. But we encounter obstacles along the way. We meet with conflicts between what pleases us and what pleases God.

We need help in overcoming these obstacles. In a real way the Christian life is often a struggle. We gain ground and then slip backward. There is such a thing as backsliding. Sometimes the slide seems as if it is greased with the slickest substance the devil can use. But as children who totter at the top of a sliding board, fearful to move, we have a heavenly Father who guards the edge of the board and who waits at the bottom of the slide to catch us in His arms.

This book is intended as a practical guide for Christian living. It is not a weighty scholarly volume. It is an attempt to provide help for the struggle in which we are involved.

The book was suggested by my editor, Dr. Wendell Hawley, who has a profound concern for helping Christians who are struggling to please God.

Special thanks for this book go to Dr. Hawley and to my secretary, Mrs. Maureen Buchman, who assisted in its preparation. Again, special thanks to my most ruthless editor, my wife, Vesta, who wields a cruel red pen.

Orlando 1987

ONE

※

Tender Grace

I see men like trees, walking" (Mark 8:24). What a strange experience. Walking trees are not a normal sight for normal people. But the man who saw "walking trees" was a man in transition. He was at an intermediate stage between total blindness and full clarity of vision. He was, as we shall see, a representative of all Christians in their progress toward pleasing God.

When the Bible records the miracle healings wrought by Jesus, the healings are usually instantaneous and complete. Jesus did not partially raise Lazarus from the dead. The man with the withered arm did not recover in stages. In most other miracles, the person was changed instantly.

So the episode recorded in Mark's Gospel is unusual. It records the healing of a blind man in two stages:

> And they came to Bethsaida. And they brought a blind man
> to Him, and entreated Him to touch him. And taking the
> blind man by the hand, He brought him out of the village;
> and after spitting on his eyes, and laying His hands upon
> him, He asked him, "Do you see anything?" And he looked
> up and said, "I see men, for I am seeing them like trees,
> walking about." Then again He laid His hands upon his eyes;
> and he looked intently and was restored, and began to see
> everything clearly. (Mark 8:22–25, NASB)

This is a story of the power and the grace of Christ. It is a story of *tender grace.* When Jesus was approached by people concerned about the plight of the blind man, the first act He performed was to "take the blind man by the hand." Holding his hand, Jesus led the man out of town.

Picture the scene. The Son of God surely had the power to heal the man on the spot. Instead, Jesus led him away from the crowd. He ministered to him in private. The blind man was not a spectacle for the curious to gaze upon. Our Lord directed the man's steps. Never in his life did the blind man have so secure a guide. There was no danger of falling, no menace of tripping. He was being led by the hand of Christ.

Had Jesus' act of tenderness ended at that point, I'm sure it would have been enough. The blind man could tell the story to his life's end. "He touched me!" he could exclaim, and he would have savored the experience forever. But Jesus was not finished. He took the next step.

When they were away from the crowd Jesus did something that could offend our sensibilities. He spit on the man's eyes. Now, to have someone spit in our eye is to experience a shameful, degrading insult. But the purpose of Jesus was not to insult, but to heal. He touched the man and asked him if he could see anything.

It was at this point that the man began to see men as walking trees. He saw what any blind man would give anything to see. His vision was dim, blurred—but he could see. Moments earlier he could see nothing. His eyes were useless. He lived in perpetual darkness. But now, suddenly, he could discern moving forms. He could detect the difference between light and shadow. A new world was opening before him. No longer would he require that someone lead him by the hand. He could throw away his cane.

Jesus was not finished. He applied a second touch. With the second touch the things that were blurred came into sharp focus. Now the man could clearly distinguish between trees and men. Now he saw trees standing still, their branches swaying gently in the breeze. He saw men as men, walking. He could discern the difference between short men and tall men, fat men and thin men, young men and old men. He was beginning to recognize the minute facial characteristics that provoke recognition of distinctive personal identities. Perhaps he could have done it before by means of touch. Possibly he could have run his fingers over a person's face and recognized certain people. He surely would not have noticed the unique sounds of different people's voices. But now he could keep his hands in his pockets and still know who was standing before him. The first face he saw clearly was the face of Christ. For him it was the beginning of the blessed vision.

Though the Bible doesn't say so, it appears certain that his eyes were not the only part of the man that was healed. With the touch of Christ comes also the healing of the heart. His heart of stone had been changed to a heart of flesh, pulsating anew with spiritual life.

The story of this healing was not intended as just a parable of the Christian's spiritual renewal. The event was a real miracle in space and time, a prodigious display of the power of Christ. But it serves us well as a parallel of spiritual renewal.

The Bible uses the metaphor of blindness to describe our fallen estate. We are all men born blind. We enter this world in a state of spiritual darkness. We do not see the things of the kingdom of God. By nature we have scales upon our eyes, cataracts so thick that we cannot even perceive men as trees, walking. It requires a special act of tender grace for us to see the kingdom of God.

The Beginning: Regeneration

The act of grace by which our eyes are opened to the things of God is *regeneration*, spiritual rebirth. It is an act that only God can perform. We are no more able to regenerate ourselves than a blind man is able to see by a sheer act of the will. A blind man can decide to see, but he cannot see unless his eyes are healed.

Regeneration does not take place in stages. It is instantaneous. It is accomplished by one touch of the Holy Spirit upon our souls. It is a sovereign work, a thoroughly effective work accomplished by the immediate power of the omnipotence of God. Only God can bring something out of nothing and life out of death. Only God can quicken the human soul.

When God quickens a human soul, He does it *immediately*. When I say "immediately" I do not mean immediate with respect to time, though indeed it happens spontaneously. I mean by the term that He does it directly without *means*, without the use of secondary causes. (The Latin word *immediatus* actually meant "without intermediary.")

When I am sick I do two things. I pray and I take my medicine. I ask that God will bring healing to me by means of the medicine. I ask God to guide the doctor's hands, to guide the means of healing by His special providence.

Yet when Jesus healed the blind man, He did not use any indirect means. No medicine was necessary. Jesus could heal by the sound of His voice. I am puzzled by the narrative at one point. Why did Jesus spit upon the man's eyes? Why did He have him bathe in the pool of Siloam? Obviously the power was not in the spit or in the water of the pool. On other occasions Jesus dispensed with such devices. His power was direct and immediate.

So it is with our regeneration. We are required to be bathed with the water of baptism. But the water in the baptismal pool does not contain a magic elixir to redeem human souls. The water is a sign that points beyond itself to the living water that makes us alive. It is an outward, concrete symbol of the healing power of God.

There is another parallel, however, in the story of the healing of the blind man. Though we are regenerated instantly by the sovereign power of God and are transferred immediately from the kingdom of darkness into the kingdom of light, our sanctification is indeed in stages.

When we are born again we see men as trees, walking. Our spiritual vision is clouded. We do not see all things in sharp spiritual focus. Our vision is still clouded by ongoing sin. There will come a day when all remnants of our old nature will be destroyed. There will come a day when our hearts will be so purified that Christ's beatitude will be fulfilled: "Blessed are the pure in heart, for they shall see God" (Matt. 5:8). This is what many Christians in the Middle Ages called the "beatific vision."

The work of perfecting our spiritual state is called *glorification*. Glorification does not take place in this life. We must wait for heaven for our sanctification to be complete. Now, though we see what we could not see before, we still see through a glass darkly.

In this life we need the second touch of Christ. Indeed we require a third, fourth, fifth, and continual touch. Though the scales are removed from our eyes, we still need to be led by the hand of Jesus.

Regeneration is the beginning of a journey. It is a journey with successes and failures, with growth amidst stumbling. At times the progress seems painfully slow, but progress is there. It is a movement to sharper focus—a life that begins with a touch of tender grace that moves toward more grace.

Sisyphus was the tragic hero of an ancient Greek myth. Because he had offended the gods he was doomed to an everlasting hell of repeated and constant frustration. His task was to push a huge boulder up a steep hill. It took all of his strength to move the rock.

Every time he reached the top, the boulder rolled over and crashed once more to the bottom. Sisyphus' task required that he race to the bottom to start all over again. His task was never finished. No final progress was achieved.

Sometimes Christians feel like Sisyphus. Progress seems so slow in the Christian life that it feels like we are walking in place, spinning our wheels, doubling our efforts and gaining no ground.

The image that captures the torture of the damned is the image of the circle. The circle goes round and round with no beginning and no end—merely endless repetition.

Consider the punishment of Samson. After he revealed the secret of his strength to his traitorous lover, Delilah, he was captured by the Philistines. His dreadful disgrace is summarized by one verse in the Bible: "Then the Philistines seized him and gouged out his eyes; and they brought him down to Gaza and bound him with bronze chains, and he was a grinder in the prison" (Judg. 16:21, NASB).

I don't really know what a grinder in a Philistine prison did. I do remember how the job was depicted by Hollywood. I have vague memories of an old film about Samson. Victor Mature played the mighty man of Israel. The scene that sticks in my mind is that of the blinded Samson replacing an ox on the wheel of a grinding machine. The ox was yoked to a lever that turned the gears of the machine as the ox plodded around in a circle, wearing a rut in the ground. I can see Victor Mature with vacant eyes, his muscles glistening with sweat, walking around and around in an endless cycle of toil, getting nowhere, only digging the rut of his path deeper and deeper.

That is the brutal image of the circle.

The Continuation: Sanctification

But the Christian life is not futile like that. It does not follow the pattern of the circle. The image of the Christian life is a line. It has a beginning, a middle, and an end. There is an end goal of glory. The God who started all things in the beginning has a goal for His people. We reach ahead for the day when we hear Christ say, "Come, My beloved, enter the kingdom which My Father has prepared for you."

With the apostle Paul we say, "Forgetting what lies behind and reaching forward to what lies ahead, I press on toward the goal for the prize of the upward call of God in Christ Jesus" (Phil. 3:13, NASB). In the Christian life there is an *upward call*. One does not move upward in a circle. We are on a line that is going somewhere. It is moving forward. In a word, there is *progress* to the Christian life.

We remember the classic of Christian literature written by John Bunyan, *The Pilgrim's Progress*. The pilgrim is the Christian who moves toward heaven. His progress is made slow and cumbersome by the weight he carries on his back. He faces obstacles at every turn. He is threatened by the Slough of Despond. He is tripped up by the likes of Mr. Worldlywise.

Bunyan understood the many temptations and pitfalls that stand in the path of every Christian. But he also understood two vitally important truths about the Christian life: We are pilgrims, and we make progress.

A pilgrim is one who is on a journey. His travels take him to strange places. He is a person on the move. Like the Old Testament Hebrew, a Christian pilgrim lives in tents. He is a seminomad. He is never so at home in this world that he completely settles in. Life is always a frontier for him. The water he drinks is never stagnant. Like Abraham, the father of the faithful, he searches for a better country whose Builder and Maker is God. All of God's people are pilgrims and sojourners on the earth.

All Christians make progress. Progress is made certain by the indwelling Holy Spirit who refuses to allow us to stand still. Oh, we try to stand still. We even regress. Like the disciples, we hide in our upper rooms, huddled in fear. But Jesus will not allow us to stay there.

No one is born a Christian. By nature we are flesh. The Christian life begins with the work of the Holy Spirit in rebirth. The term "born-again Christian" is almost a misnomer. It is a redundancy. It is a kind of theological stuttering. If one is born again, then he is a Christian. If he is a Christian, then he is born again. There are no nonborn-again Christians and no born-again non-Christians. To be reborn is to be born into Christ by the Holy Spirit. This is a prerequisite for the Christian life. It is also the genesis, the beginning of the Christian life.

Everyone starts the Christian life the same way: We all start by being born again. Our experiences of rebirth may differ, but the fact of rebirth is necessary for all of us.

It is important for us to understand that no two Christians begin their Christian walk with the same baggage. Some people are born again at five years old, some at fifty-five. Some come to faith from a well-disciplined background, others from a life of riotous and unbridled wildness. We struggle with different sins. We carry mixed and matched luggage.

Some of us know the day and the hour we were converted. Others have no distinct recollection of when we were reborn. Billy Graham speaks of a meeting held by Mordecai Ham where he met Christ. Ruth Graham can't pinpoint within five years the date of her conversion. Some people weep at conversion, others are giddy with joy.

It is a grave mistake to insist that everybody display the same outward signs of conversion that we experienced. Those with a sudden and dramatic conversion experience tend to be suspicious of those who cannot name the day and the hour. Those whose experience is less dramatic may wonder about the emotional stability of those who cite a sudden experience.

Here we must honor the work of the Holy Spirit, who convicts people in different ways at different times. The ultimate question we face is not *when* we were converted or *where* we were converted. The only real question is whether we *are* converted. If we are born of the Spirit, then we are brothers and sisters to all who are in Christ.

Paul tells us: "For by grace you have been saved through faith; and that not of yourselves, it is the gift of God; not as a result of works, that no one should boast. For we are His workmanship, created in Christ Jesus for good works, which God prepared beforehand that we should walk in them" (Eph. 2:8–10, NASB).

At this point we are all equal. None of us has converted ourselves. Rebirth is the work of God. We are the workmanship or the craftsmanship of Christ. Christ is the master craftsman. His workmanship is neither dull nor monotonous.

When He redeems us He does not destroy our identity nor our individuality. Each Christian is a distinctive work of art fashioned by Christ. Each redeemed person is literally a masterpiece.

Jesus does not fashion His art on an assembly line. His work of molding and shaping is done with infinite care and patience. We've seen the bumper sticker that reads, "Please be patient with me; God is not finished with me yet."

Sanctification is a process. It is a gradual process. Run for your life from those who promise you instant sanctification. There is a poisonous doctrine—one that dies hard in Christian circles—called the doctrine of perfectionism. It teaches that some people have already attained spiritual perfection in this world. They promise a "second work of grace," a "second blessing" of instant sanctification. From such teachers turn away.

I was a Christian for only a few months when I met my first preacher of instant sanctification. He offered to lay hands on me and pray that I receive the second blessing. I found the idea very attractive. The most serious frustration I experienced in my new Christian life was that I was still sinning. I had experienced profound victory in some parts of my life, but other areas seemed very stubborn. I was already acutely aware of the ongoing warfare between the flesh and the Spirit.

I prayed with the preacher for instant sanctification. It didn't work. The second blessing eluded me. Martin Luther, who spent so much of his early life trying to be completely righteous, had said, "If ever a man could get to heaven through monkery [faithfully living the monastic life], it was I." I was thinking that if ever a man could get the second blessing by seeking it, it was I.

The preacher was convinced that my sin was blocking my efforts to gain release from my sin. I was caught in the most vicious of circles. What the minister was actually saying to me was that if I was going to get rid of my sin I had to first get rid of my sin. In other words, all I needed before I could get the second blessing was the second blessing.

Finally, another minister helped me out of this hopeless dilemma. I soon realized that the idea of a second blessing that would give me instant sanctification was a pious fraud.

Since that experience I have met two people who claimed they had attained perfect sanctification. Their Christian lives were tragic. For people to convince themselves that they have already achieved spiritual perfection, they must do one or both of two things: They must so reduce the demands of God's law to such a low level that they can obey them, or they must radically inflate their own assessment of their spiritual performance.

Either of these steps is deadly. To reduce the demands of God's law is to do violence against the holiness of God. To inflate one's own self-assessment to the point of self-delusion is an extreme form of pride.

Sanctification requires far more than a quick experience of the laying on of hands. Rebirth is instantaneous. Justification is instantaneous. *But sanctification is a lifelong process.* It involves a diligent struggle against a multitude of obstacles. It is like the journey of Bunyan's pilgrim, filled with pitfalls and laden with perils. It is a journey that takes us through the dark night of the soul, through the valley of the shadow of death, and through the wilderness of temptation.

The journey has but one guarantee: Christ promises to go with us and to bring us out the other side. Our Lord finishes what He starts. He does not abort His handiwork in the middle of its creation. He does not leave us staring at walking trees.

No, the Lord is intensely interested in our welfare and our maturing. He wants us to learn more and more about God and how to please God. He wants us to find joy in pleasing God. He wants us to change, like the healed blind man, so that our vision clears, so that we grow in how we perceive the world and how we act in it. Growth and change in such perception means learning more and more about what pleases the holy God. The growth in pleasing God is sanctification, and that is what this book is all about.

TWO

❦

The Goal of Christian Living

I once read the following definition of a fanatic: "A fanatic is a person who, having lost sight of his goal, redoubles his effort to get there." The fanatic runs around frantically getting nowhere. He is a basketball player without a basket, a tennis player without a net, a golfer without a green.

For a Christian to make progress in sanctification, in learning to please God, he must have a clear idea of what his goal is. Though the Bible makes that goal clear, it is one that is easily forgotten.

What is the goal? Jesus stated it this way: "Seek first the kingdom of God and His righteousness, and all these things shall be added to you" (Matt. 6:33).

Let us examine the elements of this charge. First, Jesus said that we must *seek*. To seek something requires effort. It involves a diligent search. It is like the woman who lost a coin and swept every nook and cranny of the house to find it. Seeking is not accomplished by taking a nap. It involves work. Persistent work. We do not sit back and wait for God to drop it in our laps.

We all know the story of the Greek mathematician Archimedes who discovered his famous principle of specific gravity while taking a bath. He shouted, "Eureka, I have found it." We also know the legend of Isaac Newton's discovering the law of gravity while sitting under an apple tree when an apple fell on his head. These flashes of insight that befell Archimedes and Newton were merely the culmination of years of diligent quest. Their achievements were not a matter of luck. It is said that Thomas Edison experimented with over a thousand different substances before he finally discovered one that would act as a suitable filament for the electric light. Not much luck, but much work. So is it with us in our learning to please God.

We are to seek the kingdom of God and God's righteousness. We notice that Jesus says that we are to seek these things *first*. The New Testament word that is used here for *first* is the Greek word *protos*, which does not mean simply first in a series of many things. Rather the word carries the force of *priority*. A more accurate translation of the concept would be, "Seek ye first, *above all else,* the kingdom of God and His righteousness."

Seek the kingdom. Seek righteousness. These are the priorities of the Christian life.

Seeking the Kingdom of God

What does it mean to seek the kingdom of God? There is much confusion about spiritual seeking in the Christian world. We frequently hear this comment out of the mouths of Christians: "My friend is not a Christian, but he's seeking."

What is the non-Christian seeking? One thing we know he is not seeking. He is not seeking God. Paul declares, "There is none who seeks after God" (Rom. 3:11). The unbeliever never, never, never seeks God. The unbeliever is a fugitive from God. The natural pattern for man is to run from Him, to hide from Him. Jesus came to seek and to save the lost. He is the Seeker; we are the ones who are running. In man's sinful state he may look for answers to life's puzzles, but he does not seek God.

Why then does it so often seem to us that unbelievers are seeking God? We observe them. They are seeking happiness, peace of mind, relief from guilt, a meaningful life, and a host of other things that we know only God can give them. But they are not seeking God. They are seeking the *benefits* of God. Natural man's sin is precisely this: He wants the benefits of God without God Himself.

I belabor this point for this reason: Seeking after God is a Christian enterprise. The seeking of God *begins* at conversion. Though we may proclaim to the world that we "found it," the finding of God is, ironically, the beginning of seeking after God. To seek God is a lifelong pursuit. The seeking after God is what Jonathan Edwards called "the main business of the Christian life."

To seek God's kingdom is to fulfill the last command of Jesus as well as the crucial petition of the Lord's Prayer: "Your kingdom come. Your will be done on earth as it is in heaven."

The last question His disciples asked Jesus was, "Lord, will You at this time restore the kingdom to Israel?" (Acts 1:6). Just moments before Jesus departed this planet in His glorious ascension, His students pressed Him with one last question. The question was about the kingdom. Jesus answered the question first with a mild rebuke and then with a command: "You shall be witnesses to Me" (Acts 1:8).

We are called to seek the kingdom by bearing witness to the kingdom. We are to seek to show the world what the kingdom of God looks like. For the kingdom to come on earth as it is in heaven means that loyal children of the King do the King's will here and now. We bear witnesses to God's kingdom by serving God's King. This is the will of God. This is what pleases Him. There is a reason why Jesus links the coming of the kingdom with the doing of the will of God. "Your kingdom come. Your will be done" belong together. They are two sides of the same coin. The kingdom comes on earth where God's will is done on earth.

The conclusion we reach is this: The great overarching goal of the Christian life is *obedience to the King*. And He is pleased when we obey.

Seeking Righteousness

The quest for the kingdom is linked with the quest for the righteousness of God. It is the kind of righteousness displayed by Jesus Himself. Jesus' life was a blaze of righteousness. He was the Lamb without blemish, the Son of whom the Father was well pleased. The Scriptures say of Him that zeal for His Father's house consumed Him (John 2:17). His meat and His drink was to do the will of His Father (John 4:34). Jesus was not only Incarnate God but was also the supreme man of righteousness. We cannot possibly imitate His deity, but we are to imitate His single-minded devotion to obedience, His commitment to pleasing God.

When I first became a Christian I was introduced to the priorities of the Christian community. I learned quickly that it was expected of me that I have a daily devotion time, a time reserved for Bible reading and prayer. I was expected to go to church. I was expected to have a kind of piety that was evident by not cursing, not drinking, not smoking, and the like. I had no idea that biblical righteousness went far beyond these things. However, like most new Christians, I learned to emphasize such things. My personal letters took on a new pattern of language. They began to sound like pages from New Testament epistles. I soon learned to use Christian jargon in my everyday speech. I didn't "tell" anybody anything, I "shared" it with them. Every good fortune was a "blessing," and I found I could hardly speak without sprinkling my sentences with spiritual platitudes.

Soon, however, I found that there was more to the Christian life than daily devotions and sanctified words. I realized that God wanted more. He wanted me to grow in my faith and obedience, to go beyond milk to the meat. I also discovered that Christian jargon was an almost meaningless form of communication, both to non-Christians and Christians alike. I found myself more interested in echoing a subculture's lingo than in finding true godliness.

My error was this: I was confusing spirituality with righteousness. I also discovered that I was not alone in this. I was caught up with a crowd who confused the means with the end. Spirituality can be a cheap substitute for righteousness.

Over the years I've had many young Christians ask me how to be more spiritual or more pious. Rare has been the earnest student who said, "Teach me how to be righteous." "Why," I wondered, "does anybody want to be spiritual? What is the purpose of spirituality? What use is there in piety?"

Spirituality and piety are not ends in themselves. In fact they are worthless *unless* they are means to a higher goal. The goal must go beyond spirituality to righteousness.

Spiritual disciplines are vitally necessary to achieve righteousness. Bible study, prayer, church attendance, evangelism, are necessary for Christian growth, but they cannot be the final goal. I cannot achieve righteousness without spirituality. But it is possible to be "spiritual," at least on the surface, without attaining righteousness.

Jesus was a man of prayer. His prayer life was intense and powerful. He was a man of vast knowledge of the Scriptures. He obviously mastered the Word of God. He was spiritual. But His spirituality ultimately showed itself by authentic righteousness. So His spirituality was not merely a surface thing. His inner life displayed itself in outward obedience, obedience even unto death.

What is righteousness? The simplest answer to that question is this: *Righteousness is doing what is right in the sight of God.* This is a simple definition that is far more complex under the surface. To be righteous is to do everything that God calls us to do. The demands of true righteousness are so great and so many that none of us ever in this world achieves it perfectly. It involves following the whole counsel of God.

There are times when Scripture provides a simple summary of true righteousness. There are occasions when God reduces the vast sum of commandments to a few that capture the essence of true righteousness. Let us examine a few of those summaries.

Micah's Summary

In the book of the prophet Micah we read this summary statement on holy living: "He has told you, O man, what is good; and what does the LORD require of you but to do justice, to love kindness, and to walk humbly with your God?" (Mic. 6:8, NASB).

Justice, kindness (or loyal love), and humility. This triad is not easy to achieve. God wants me to care about the weighty matters of justice and mercy.

He enjoys the companionship of humble saints. He promises to add grace to the humble and to resist the proud.

Charles Colson had recently been released from prison after spending time incarcerated for his part in the Ellsberg paper incident. Though not part of the Watergate scandal, Colson was linked to the episode that brought about the downfall of Richard Nixon. Colson was speaking on a university campus and was being heckled unmercifully by some anti-Nixon students. One of the students interrupted Colson's speech by shouting, "Hey, Colson, why did you stick by Nixon?"

Colson stopped his speech and looked at the heckler. He replied, "Because he was my friend."

With that answer the audience erupted in spontaneous applause. Though the audience despised the Watergate scandal and all that it involved, they appreciated a kind of loyalty that would allow a man to go to jail for the sake of friendship.

When Micah speaks of "kindness" he uses the Hebrew word for "loyal love." It is the kind of love God has for His children. It is a steadfast love, a love that endures. It is the kind of love that lasts. Though God hardly approves of everything His children do, He stands by them. That's a priority of Christian love.

My children do not have to earn my love. They can disappoint me, frustrate me, and even anger me, but their failures do not disqualify them from my love. The Prodigal Son's father never stopped loving him. I cannot always give my permission but I must always give my love. To endure in love is to imitate how God loves us even when we fail.

Loyalty. Kindness. These qualities are what makes it possible for Christians to keep moving in spite of our sin. To be a loyal friend requires more than blind acceptance. It requires patience, long-suffering, gentleness, the kind of fruit that flows from the Holy Spirit. It is because Christ is loyal to us that we are motivated to show that same kind of loyalty to others.

Jesus' Summary

Jesus summarized the Christian life in the simplest summation of all: "Just as you want men to do to you, you also do to them likewise" (Luke 6:31). This we call the Golden Rule—the law of gold, a gold more precious than diamonds and rubies. Any child can recite the Golden Rule, but to make it an active part of daily living is no mean feat.

I hate petty criticism. I do not enjoy the company of nitpickers. Judgmental people are difficult for me to enjoy. I cannot control how such people relate to me, but I can learn from them. From everyone who hurts me I can learn what kinds of things are hurtful. Chances are that what hurts me is the same kind of behavior that hurts other people. Therefore, I can learn what not to do to others.

Our response to petty criticism is often to retaliate in kind, instead of in kindness. This is where the Golden Rule touches life. Here is where Jesus spoke of not returning evil for evil. Doing to others what we want others to do to us is simply a matter of kindness. It involves being thoughtful and considerate. But it is more than mere politeness. It is doing what is right. It is doing what pleases God.

Righteousness means right living. It means treating people right. It means living with personal integrity. A righteous person is one whom we can trust. His integrity is consistent. It is not for sale. A righteous person is moral without being moralistic. He is pious without being pietistic. He has a sense of concern for other people's feelings. He wants to treat people right because he has the overarching desire to please a loving God.

James's Summary

The author of the Letter of James was probably the blood brother of Jesus. He was called "James the Just" or "James the Righteous" in the early church. His summary of true righteousness may be shocking to some Christians: "This is pure and undefiled religion in the sight of our God and Father, to visit orphans and widows in their distress, and to keep oneself unstained by the world" (James 1:27, NASB).

True religion means visiting orphans and widows. Why does James say this? He understood that true righteousness is *people-oriented*. Our prayers are worthless if they do not result in the care of people. In the ancient world the orphan and the widow were almost helpless in society. They had financial stress, legal impotency, and, above all, the emotional stress of the pain of loneliness.

We now have government programs to aid orphans and widows financially. They have some legal rights. But the estate of widowhood or orphanhood is still not pleasant. They—and all other people who are lonely and helpless—still need the outreach of love. Societal institutions may change, but the requirement to show compassion to those in need stays the same. Piety without compassion is a lie. It turns the Golden Rule into rust.

We please the loving God when we obey the Golden Rule. We please Him when we pursue justice and mercy and when we practice loyal love. We please Him when we treat others as we wish to be treated. We please Him when we reach out to the forgotten and the downtrodden. These, rules of Scripture for righteous living, weigh far more than concerns about a "spiritual" life that precludes drinking, smoking, and cursing.

Righteousness has rules, but it is more than rules. If we care for rules without caring for people, we have missed the goal of righteousness. The scriptural rules come from God precisely because He cares about people.

We need rules to be righteous, but they must be the right rules. They must be God's rules. We may accept no substitutes. In God's Word we find adequate rules for pleasing God with a righteous life. And if we abide by those rules, we are not goal-less fanatics, but true children of the King.

꩜

THREE

Beware the Leaven of the Pharisees

B eware!" This is an ominous warning. It is the warning Caesar heard that made his bones tremble: "Caesar! Beware the Ides of March!" It is the warning the sailor Ishmael heard from the waterfront prophet before he signed on with the crew of the *Pequod* to join Ahab in his maniacal quest for Moby Dick.

The simple sign "Beware of the Dog!" is enough to give a burglar pause. The word *beware* posts a warning that stops us in our tracks, a caveat that conjures up visions of a menace that can quickly destroy or hurt us.

It was this word that Jesus used to startle His followers into vigilance against a deadly danger. "Beware the leaven of the Pharisees" (Luke 12:1, NASB). Jesus put up a signpost for the church, a divine call to heed the threat of a poison that could be swallowed by the unsuspecting. He warned of wolves in sheep's clothing, of rapacious killers that disguised themselves under the cloak of gentle spirituality.

The danger is one that kills by small doses. It is injected in seemingly harmless amounts, but it is potent in its full impact. "A little leaven leavens the whole lump," He said (1 Cor. 5:6).

Jesus' words are a warning against allowing in an infectious element that can ruin the whole Christian life. It is something that rises from a small beginning. The warning is coupled with another frightening caveat. Jesus said, "Unless your righteousness exceeds the righteousness of the scribes and Pharisees, you will by no means enter the kingdom of heaven" (Matt. 5:20).

If we fail to heed a "Beware of the Dog" sign, we may get bitten on the leg and get our pants ripped. But this warning of Jesus involves far more than a loss of some blood or a patch of our trousers. It means the loss of the kingdom of God.

What is this dreaded leaven of the Pharisees? In a word, it is the leaven of *hypocrisy*. It is the leaven of a false kind of righteousness. It is the leaven of deception, a masquerade of righteousness that is a substitute for the real thing.

"Unless your righteousness *exceeds* . . ." The word *unless* introduces a necessary condition for something else that follows. Here Jesus warns that our righteousness absolutely must surpass the righteousness of the scribes and Pharisees or we will miss the kingdom.

This warning is one of the most neglected warnings Jesus ever pronounced. It is lightly dismissed by the modern Christian, who sees no real threat in it. After all, what do we have to worry about? We view the Pharisees as the treacherous, corrupt group of unprincipled men who actually plotted the murder of Christ. What could be more diabolical than that? Surely it is a small thing for any lover of Christ to surpass Jesus' most hostile enemies in righteousness. The Pharisees have become the symbol of corruption to us. At first glance it would appear that the weakest Christian should have no problem in surpassing the Pharisees in righteousness.

We might offer an easy answer to Jesus' warning. We might ask, "What do we have to worry about?" As Christians we are justified by faith. By faith we receive the righteousness of Christ Himself. Surely Christ's righteousness surpasses the righteousness of the Pharisees. If we have the righteousness of Christ, what do we need to worry about?

The easy answer is nothing! To be sure, if we truly have faith in Christ we do possess His righteousness. We are declared to be justified by God. The kingdom is ours. Nothing could be more certain than the fact that all who possess the righteousness of Christ will surely inherit the kingdom of God. Nothing more is required than the righteousness of Christ. No righteousness can possibly exceed that righteousness with which the Christian is cloaked by faith. In this sense the hymn writer was correct: "He's all I need."

That's the easy answer. The deeper question, however, still remains. How do I know I have the saving righteousness of Christ? Can I not deceive myself into thinking I have the real thing when in fact my faith is fraudulent? Just because a person claims to believe in Christ is no guarantee that he has saving faith. It is by our fruits that we demonstrate the reality of our faith. We know that God is pleased with those who truly honor Christ. We feel just as certain that He is not pleased when men blithely use the name but avoid any real life-affecting commitment to Him. This is the scary part of Jesus' warning.

Both the Warning and the Dog

There are homeowners who post signs saying "Beware of the Dog" when in fact they don't own a dog. They claim a dog when there is no dog. The warning has no reality to back it up. Jesus had harsh words to say about people who used words but had no reality to back them up. His words are a real threat to those whose righteousness is not genuine.

A local newspaper told an anecdote about a burglar who stalked the neighborhood watching for homes left unguarded by people leaving for vacation. He watched as a family loaded their suitcases into their car and departed. He waited until dark and then approached the front door and rang the bell. There was no answer. The burglar neatly picked the lock and let himself in. He called into the darkness, "Is anybody home?" He was stunned when he heard a voice in reply, "I see you, and Jesus sees you." Terrified, the burglar called out, "Who's there?" Again the voice came back, "I see you, and Jesus sees you." The burglar switched on his flashlight and aimed it in the direction of the voice. He was instantly relieved when his light revealed a caged parrot reciting the refrain, "I see you, and Jesus sees you." The burglar laughed out loud and switched on the lights. Then he saw it. Beneath the parrot's cage was a huge Doberman pinscher. Then the parrot said, "Attack, Jesus, attack!"

Jesus has the quintessential Doberman. His bite is worse than his bark. Jesus is really righteous, and so should His followers be. The sign "Beware of the Dog" points to a clear reality in His case. The words are not empty. There is a real dog on the premises, and He makes the sign very meaningful.

Beware of the Dog—a notice that is only valid if there is really a dangerous dog present. "We Christians, God's beloved children, have Christ's righteousness"—a valid statement only if we are truly aiming for righteousness. No pretense, just reality.

The fruit of our righteousness must exceed the pretense of righteousness displayed by the scribes and the Pharisees. On the surface the Pharisees achieved a high level of righteousness. Their righteousness was external. It was only an outward show. But their outward show was a brilliant display of virtue. It fooled a lot of people. Most tragically, it fooled the Pharisees themselves. They actually were able to convince themselves that they had the real thing. "Abraham is our father," they said (John 8:39). They claimed to be loyal to Moses. They were convinced they were in the kingdom. But they were not pleasing to God, who hates pretense.

Let us examine the level of righteousness the Pharisees achieved. We begin by noting that the Pharisees began as a kind of Puritan reform movement in Israel. There were no Pharisees in the Old Testament. They came into being in the period between the close of the Old Testament and the advent of the New Testament. They originated as a group of men who were concerned about the inroads of paganism into the Jewish nation.

Israel was being secularized. The Jews were moving away from fidelity and obedience to the covenant God had made with their fathers. The Pharisees were called Pharisees because the word meant "separated ones." These men separated themselves from the trends toward paganism. They devoted themselves to the zealous pursuit of righteousness. They were almost fanatical in their drive to obey God. Their concern for godliness was neither casual nor superficial. They were seriously acting to please God.

The origin of Pharisaism was noble. But their movement soon degenerated into a kind of external pietism that was rooted in self-righteousness. They began to trust in their own good works, so that when their Savior came they not only missed His salvation but they plotted against Him. Their fatal error was this: They did not think they needed Christ. They thought they could please God without accepting the Redeemer He sent.

What were the Pharisees like in Jesus' day? What follows is a brief sketch of the marks of the first-century Pharisees.

The Pharisees Were Evangelistic

Jesus said to the Pharisees, "You travel over land and sea to make one proselyte, and when he is won, you make him twice as much a son of hell as yourselves" (Matt. 23:15).

Imagine the evangelistic zeal of people who would cross land and sea for one convert. This is missionary outreach of a higher order.

I hate to travel. I wish God would let me confine my ministry to my hometown. But I am required to travel great distances to carry out my work. When I am invited to speak, however, I usually consider the potential size of my audience before agreeing to travel. So far, I have not crossed the United States in order to preach to one person. I stand ashamed by the goal of the Pharisees in this regard.

They were evangelists. But Jesus marked them as evangelists of hell. They shame us in their zeal even as Mormons shame Christians and as communists tend to be more zealous for their cause than we do for ours.

But the warning is clear. Even though Christians are called to the evangelistic and missionary enterprise, the mere fact that we are involved in such work is no guarantee that we have exceeded the righteousness of the Pharisees. We should be alarmed if we are not zealous for evangelism and missions, but if we are, that does not in and of itself prove that our faith is genuine.

The Pharisees Were Tithers

On one occasion Jesus acknowledged that the Pharisees were scrupulous in their giving patterns. They did not fail to pay their tithes. Jesus noted this in the midst of proclaiming a curse upon them: "Woe unto you, scribes and

Pharisees, hypocrites! For you pay tithe of mint and anise and cumin, and have neglected the weightier matters of the law: justice and mercy and faith" (Matt. 23:23).

The Pharisees fell into the trap of majoring in minors. Their priorities were reversed. Outward became more important than inward. They exalted minor matters to a high level in order to obscure their failure to be faithful in more important matters. But at least they paid their tithes.

In Israel the tithe was usually paid in terms of produce or livestock. The first fruits of their crops and herds were returned to the Lord. That the Pharisees were scrupulous about tithing is seen in Jesus' recognition that they even tithed from their mint and cumin. That would be comparable to a modern person who kept such strict accounts of tithing that when he finds a dime on the street he makes sure that he returns a penny to the Lord.

We could take a few lessons about tithing from the Pharisees. The latest survey I saw indicated that of those church members who identified themselves as "evangelical" only 4 percent were tithers. If the survey is accurate, it would mean that 96 percent of evangelical Christians regularly and systematically rob God. In this area our righteousness falls short of the Pharisees. We might protest and say, "But we pay attention to the big things. We might not tithe but we are concerned about justice and mercy."

For the most part such protests are as hollow as they sound. We are called to be faithful in little things before we graduate to the big things. Even if it were true that we are so busy doing the big things that we have overlooked little things like tithing, it would not excuse us for robbing God.

On the other hand, if we are part of the small group who does tithe, we would have nothing of which to boast. We would simply be doing what it is our duty to do. Tithing itself would be nothing greater than what the Pharisees did with scrupulosity.

Let me say again that we need to beware not only of the leaven of the Pharisees, but also to beware of judging the Pharisees too harshly. In their desire to please God they overemphasized the small (and visible) acts of righteousness. How tempting for us to so underplay these small acts that we end up neglecting both small and great matters. And if we neglect all, we are no more pleasing to God than were the Pharisees.

The Pharisees Were Men of Prayer

Jesus spoke of the Pharisees' pattern of prayer. They enjoyed making a public display of their piety. They assumed a reverent posture and offered eloquent prayers. They knew nothing of the kind of wrestling with God that characterized David's prayer life. Where David's pillow was wet with his tears, the pillows of the Pharisees were dry as a bone. And they had no prayer closet because a human audience could not fit in one.

The Pharisees' piety was external. They were like the farmer in the story of a pig with a wooden leg:

> A man and his wife returned home from church and enjoyed a Sunday supper. After dinner they decided to go for a ride in the country. During their leisurely tour the husband was startled to see a pig with a wooden leg in a pasture by the road. "Look at that!" he said to his wife. "There's a pig with a wooden leg!"
>
> The man was amazed that a farmer would be so humane as to provide a wooden leg for his wounded pig. He insisted that they stop at the farmhouse and inquire about the circumstances that led to his porcine prosthesis. He knocked at the farmer's door and introduced himself to the farmer.
>
> "I'm sorry to bother you, sir, but I am intrigued about the pig you have with a wooden leg. Would you mind telling me how it came about?"
>
> "Not at all," said the farmer. "A few months back my grandchildren were here for a visit. One afternoon they wandered into a pasture where our bull was grazing. The bull charged them in fury. The pig noticed the danger and put himself between the children and the bull and headed the bull off. That pig saved my grandchildren's lives. The very next day one of the children fell in the farm pond and was drowning. That pig dove into the water and saved her life.
>
> "So you see," said the farmer, "the pig is almost like family to us. That's why it has a wooden leg. I just couldn't bring myself to eat that pig all at one time!"

So much for the humane farmer. He wasn't *too* devoted to the heroic pig, but he at least wanted to *appear* grateful. The wooden leg symbolized, to passersby, the farmer's humaneness, but the passersby did not know the whole story. His concern for the pig was as deep as the Pharisees' real love for prayer. But at least the Pharisees prayed. They heaped up vain repetitions, but they at least went through the motions. Some of us have prayer lives that are so barren that we neglect even the motions of prayer. We displease God by hypocritical prayer, but we displease Him as well by our failure to pray.

The Pharisees Read Their Bibles

Jesus rebuked the Pharisees by saying: "You search the Scriptures, for in them you think you have eternal life" (John 5:39). The Pharisees were learned in theology. They could recite chapter and verse of their Bible, the Old Testament. (They would have been champions in the "sword drills" so dear to Sunday school teachers!) But they missed the heart and soul of the Word of God.

But at least the Pharisees were diligent in searching the Scriptures. Many Christians never read the Bible. They have good intentions of reading it some day, but in the meantime they put it off. When theological disputes arise, they may quote a text here and there, but there are few who embark upon a diligent *search* of Scriptures. We go to Bible studies where we have enjoyable fellowship, neat discussions, and tasty snacks. Often we do everything at Bible studies except study, and often when we do study, the word *superficial* seems to apply.

Jesus loved the Word of God. It was His meat and His drink. He calls His people to be diligent students of Scripture. But He demands more than the acquisition of Bible knowledge. We must have a sound doctrine of the Bible. But even this is not enough. The righteousness that pleases Him is a righteousness that proceeds from being doers of His Word and not hearers only.

Evangelism. Tithing. Prayer. Bible study. These are but a few of the rigorous activities of the scribes and the Pharisees. In all these things they excelled. But their activity was almost solely external. They were hypocrites. They went through the outward motions of piety, but their hearts were far from God. They kept the letter of the law but killed the spirit of the law.

The Scriptures warn us that man looks at outward appearances but God looks on the heart (1 Sam. 16:7). This is not to say that God cares only for the spirit of the law and not the letter. We cannot excuse external disobedience by appealing to a warm heart within. The Christian life that pleases God is one that is both internal and external. Authentic righteousness keeps the spirit and the letter. That kind of obedience exceeds the scribes' and the Pharisees'. It is the kind of obedience to which we are called.

FOUR

Battle with the World

Martin Luther spoke of a threefold battle in the Christian life. The Christian is locked in combat with the world, the flesh, and the devil. These are formidable opponents. They do not always fight fairly. It is a gang attack. The tactics of the enemy are devious. Satan is the master of the sneak attack. The flesh is an enemy within, a saboteur who undermines the Spirit.

In living to please a righteous God, we do constant battle with these enemies. Part of the process of sanctification is fighting with and—if we are truly growing—frequently triumphing over these foes. Every sensitive believer knows only too well how difficult it can be to win a victory against such formidable opposition.

In this chapter we will examine the first of the three enemies, the world. The world spirit, the value systems of a fallen creation, may be distinguished from the flesh and the devil but not separated from them. The flesh is part of the fallen world and the devil is the prince of this world.

We live in this world. We are part of the world. We are to a certain degree products of this world. And the world is our battlefield. The war is not contained in a European theater or Pacific theater. The world includes our own hometown. Wherever we live and move in this world, we are still engaged in combat. There is no demilitarized zone. The whole planet is fallen. The whole creation groans in travail waiting for redemption.

We live in a world injured by tooth, claw, and fang. We look forward to a new world where the wolf will lie down with the lamb and the child will play safely by the nest of the rattlesnake. But right now we do not invite wolves to act as shepherds of our sheep.

When I first moved to Florida, I quickly became aware of the danger of poisonous snakes. The dreaded eastern diamondback rattler thrives side by side with the menacing cottonmouth, or water moccasin. I was concerned for the safety of our grandchildren playing in our backyard. At the edge of my property I had a clump of palmetto palms that were overgrown with high grass and weeds. I was determined to clear the area lest it become a breeding ground for lethal reptiles.

As I began the task of clearing away the brush, my eye caught a sudden movement at the base of a palmetto. I was mesmerized by the appearance of a snake. It was beautiful—slender, graceful, marked with vividly colored rings of black, yellow, and red. The snake slithered away from me, appearing harmless. It looked like a living necklace, the kind of trinket that would surely attract the interest of an inquisitive child. But it was a coral snake, the most beautiful and most deadly of North American reptiles. I reacted in haste, moving quickly to destroy it.

Once the coral snake was dead, I put it in a jar and took it inside the house. There I showed it to the children and explained to them the danger the snake represented.

The world is filled with serpents of all varieties. The serpent that beguiled our first parents is still at large. The venom of untamed creatures can spoil our garden. The world is indeed the habitat of devouring dragons.

The Seduction of This World

The world is a seducer. It seeks to attract our attention and our devotion. It remains so close at hand, so visible, so enticing. It eclipses our view of heaven. What is seen vies for our attention. It entices our eyes lest we look up for a better country whose Builder and Maker is God. It pleases us—much of the time, anyway—and, alas, we often live our lives to please it. And that is where conflict ensues, for pleasing the world so seldom overlaps with pleasing God.

The divine call we receive is this: "Do not be conformed to this world" (Rom. 12:2). But the world wants us to be partners with it. We are urged to participate in the fullness of it. It presses upon us with the ultimate peer pressure.

Remember the anxiety we all experienced as teenagers? Our self-worth, our esteem, was measured by one magic word, a single all-encompassing standard: *popularity*. I remember going to a department store in Pittsburgh to buy shoes. I was in the sixth grade. My mother sat me down in the shoe department. While the clerk was showing me shoes, he asked me about my school. I blurted out, "I'm the most popular boy in my class!"

My mother was horrified. She lectured me on the virtue of humility. She explained that my boast was in the poorest of taste. No matter. What mattered to me was whether my words were true or not. I wanted to think I was the most popular boy in class. For my sixth-grade mind that was the central issue of life. Oh, to be sure, I wanted my parents to love me and my sister to be proud of me, but the end-all of my existence was popularity.

There was a price tag for popularity. I had to conform. I had to be "with-it." I had to wear the right clothes, learn how to comb my hair properly, know the lyrics to the right popular songs. To prove my masculinity I had to perform the proper rituals. I had to accept dares. I had to prove that I could "swipe" a magazine or a chocolate bar from the drugstore without being caught. I had to join in evening capers that involved being chased by the police. I had to commit pranks to harass my teachers. I had to learn the art of senseless vandalism. I cleaned out Mrs. Daughbert's onion patch and I didn't even like onions. I stole old Nick Green's grapes from his grapevine while Nick himself was busy picking grapes in the very next row. I learned how to copy Linda Huffington's homework and then pass it on to my buddies. These and many more antics were all part of the price for the mystique of popularity.

But that sort of thing passes with the passing of adolescence. Or does it? The games change. The tests are different. The price tags are different, for things are more expensive. But the stakes are the same. I still want to be popular.

In ninth grade I discovered a new way to be popular. Sports. I was the captain of the basketball team. My world pivoted on that axis. The Pittsburgh *Post Gazette* did not cover our games. I did not make the cover of *Sport* magazine. But in my little world I was a hero. When we won, I heard the cheerleaders: "Sproul, Sproul, he's our man, if he can't do it, nobody can."

I loved the days at school following the nights when our team won. As we walked the halls to change classes, every student smiled at me and called me by name. In the lunchroom the seventh-grade girls asked me to autograph their napkins. When we won. But *only* when we won.

When we lost it was different. I lowered my head in the halls to avoid the angry stares. I let tears escape from my eyes and stain my pillow as I tried to fall asleep with the sound of boos still in my ears. I didn't go to the drugstore after the games we lost.

I learned very early not to trust the cheers of the crowd. But I never learned to disdain them. They remain a seductive force in my life. I still struggle to please men. I still struggle with the mystique of popularity. I still hate to be booed.

To be "conformed" to this world is to be *with* (Latin *con*) the *forms* or *structures* of this world. It means doing the popular thing. The conflict is this: What is popular with men is not always popular with God. To be pleasing to God is not always to be pleasing to men. Sometimes we must choose whom we will please. That is a daily struggle in the Christian life.

In every generation, every culture there is a dominant prevailing spirit. The Germans coined a word for it, *zeitgeist*, a term that joins two common ideas together. *Zeit* is the German word for "time." *Geist* is the German word for "spirit." So *zeitgeist* means "spirit of the time" or "spirit of the age."

The contemporary *zeitgeist* in which the Christian lives is one of secularism. The emphasis is on this world, on this time. Little attention is given to things that are above and beyond this world. Eternity is rarely considered, save for brief moments at a graveside. What counts is the here and now. To live for the moment, for the gusto of the present, is the spirit of this world.

The secular spirit of this world has its own modern trends and emphases, but in its essence it is not new. Every generation has its own form of secularism. We are earthbound creatures. Our focus is on this world.

The same was true in Jesus' day. He repeatedly called His disciples to look beyond the present. He lifted our gaze to the eternal. "Store up treasures in heaven," He said. He called us to weigh the matters in the balance of eternity. "What is a man profited if he gains the whole world, and loses his own soul?" (Matt. 16:26).

The world or the soul? Please the world or please God? This is the issue of every generation. To be conformed to this world is to risk the loss of one's eternal soul. The world places little value on the soul. A body in the hand is worth two souls in the bush, according to the *zeitgeist* of our generation. The world spirit invites us to play now and pay later, though the emphasis is on the now. This is the popular way to go.

For the Christian to resist the seduction of this world he must risk going against the tide. He must be willing to risk the loss of pleasing men to gain pleasing God. Hence Jesus said, "Blessed are you when they shall revile and persecute you, and say all kinds of evil against you falsely for My sake. Rejoice and be exceedingly glad, for great is your reward in heaven" (Matt. 5:11, 12).

The key words in this beatitude are "for My sake." The nonconformity we are called to is not simply nonconformity for nonconformity's sake. Anyone can call attention to himself by being a maverick. It is the "for My sake" that separates cheap nonconformity from the genuine article. There is no virtue in being "out of it" indiscriminately. Our nonconformity must be *selective*. It must be at the points that matter.

It is easy to trivialize nonconformity. We can reduce this to simplistic externals as the Pharisees did. Authentic nonconformity rests upon transformation. The apostle Paul adds a positive mandate to the negative prohibition. He said, "Do not be conformed to this world, but be transformed by the renewing of your mind" (Rom. 12:2).

It is the prefix that must be changed. The prefix "con-" ("with") must yield to the prefix "trans-," which means "across," "beyond," or "over." It is not enough for Christians to drop out of society. The call to transformation does not mean withdrawal from the world. We need no more monasteries. We are to go beyond the forms of this world. We are to effect changes in the world. The perspective of Jesus is beyond the forms of this world. We neither surrender to the world nor flee from the world. We are to penetrate the world with a new and different spirit.

There is a timeworn Christian saying that has become a cliché through its use: "We are to be in the world, but not *of* the world." To be *of* the world is to be worldly. It is to conform to this world. To drop out of the world is to be a nonconformist without transformation.

The theater of God's redemption is this world. It is to this world that God came in Christ. Christ refused to allow His disciples to hide in an upper room with the doors locked by reason of fear. No booths were allowed to be built on the mountain of Transfiguration. We are called to be Christ's witnesses in Jerusalem, Judea, Samaria, and to the ends of the earth. Jerusalem is in this world. Judea is in this world. Samaria is in this world. The ends of the earth are still on this earth. So we should not flee this world. But, oh, how many Christians try to do so. And in doing so, they may actually be displeasing the God who wants the world to be redeemed, not escaped.

The Evangelical Flight

A great movement is sweeping the United States. The Christian parochial school has arisen as an alternative to secular public education. Christians are no longer satisfied to have their children educated by the secular state. The government has no zeal in inculcating a Christian worldview in public education. The state prefers to remain "neutral" with respect to the things of God. In the attempt at religious "neutrality," the schools educate children as if there were no God or as if God is not relevant to reading, writing, and arithmetic. But Christians know that there is little difference between an irrelevant God and no God at all.

The God of Christianity is the Creator of the whole world. He is sovereign over everything He creates. He is sovereign over the church *and* the state. He is sovereign over theology and over biology. So a "neutral" educator is an unvarnished myth. Every teacher and every curriculum has a viewpoint. Every teacher and every curriculum has a value system. Either God is integral to that viewpoint or He isn't. There is no neutrality with God. He is either acknowledged or He is ignored. Either way, a viewpoint is expressed.

More and more Christian parents are realizing that training a child in the things of God is a sacred duty. They are taking advantage of the limited freedom that remains in America for alternative education to the so-called neutral system. It means paying double, for the tax-collector still demands that we underwrite the state schools. Then we must pay again for our own educational system. It is hard to fault dedicated parents for putting forth so much effort—and money—to educate their children in an environment where pleasing God is a high priority.

But it is not good enough for schools to be mere nonconformists. The Christian school movement can be, and often is, merely a new form of monastic retreat, an attempt at insulation from the world with no witnessing to it. If we wish to please God, we must keep ourselves stainless, but we must do more than withdraw.

Some people have raised questions about just what makes Christian schools distinctively Christian. Merely teaching Bible classes or having prayer in classes does not make a school Christian. It is the perspective of the curriculum that counts. God must be acknowledged in every field of inquiry. And we must still study the world if we are to be effective witnesses in the world.

Recently, I received a telephone call from the headmaster of a Christian high school. He was facing a crisis that threatened to destroy his school. The senior English class included John Steinbeck's *The Grapes of Wrath* on its required reading list. Several parents were outraged by the selection and demanded that the book be removed from the list. Steinbeck's work was too "worldly" for the parents' taste. They did not want their children exposed to this type of literature. The parents insisted that only *Christian* literature be read in the course.

"What shall I do?" asked the headmaster. "How can we have an authentic course in American literature if we delete all non-Christian books from our reading list?"

The answer is simple. The school cannot have an authentic course in American literature if non-Christian books are excluded. If a student is to become knowledgeable of American literature, he cannot completely bypass Steinbeck or Hemingway or a host of other authors who are not Christian. Authentic Christian education is not "hot house" education. For a student to understand the major themes of the literature that shapes the American culture, he must be able to study them. What better environment to study the world's perspective than a school that acknowledges and honors God? To ignore such literature is to ignore some of the beauties of the world—and, yes, there are many—and to give ammo to critics who accuse Christians of being anti-intellectual and backward.

The apostle Paul was versed in worldly literature. At Mars Hill, as he debated with pagan philosophers, he quoted from the writings of pagan poets. (See Acts 17:28, where Paul quotes the poet Epimenides.) Paul did that not because he was worldly, but because he was educated. No one ever loved the Scriptures more than Paul, except for Jesus. Yet Paul found the time to read other things as well.

Augustine, bishop of Hippo in Africa, ministered to the church by virtue of his background in Neoplatonic philosophy. The great medieval theologian Thomas Aquinas answered the worldly philosophers of his day. John Calvin quoted Cicero almost as frequently as he quoted Augustine. Jonathan Edwards, who liked the writings of the philosopher John Locke, engaged the continental atheists with his pen. Those men were acutely aware of worldly philosophy and sought to defeat it with Christian truth. They did not retreat into an isolationist posture. At times, though they maintained a distinctively Christian stance, they quoted with approval the words of unbelievers.

There are risks involved in exposing our children to pagan thought. My own son was reading Aldous Huxley at age twelve. But he was reading him with my supervision. We discussed the ideas of the pagan philosophers together. We tried to examine the antithesis that exists between the perspective of this world and the perspective of the Word of God.

Some will reply: "But doesn't the Bible say that we must 'beware of vain philosophy'?" (Col. 2:8). Indeed it does. But to be able to beware of something we must first be *aware* of it. Authentic Christian education is not intimidated by worldly philosophers. We are confident that Christian truth goes beyond it. It triumphs over it. We need not flee from the enemy, nor do we need to compromise with the enemy. But it is to our advantage to understand how the enemy thinks.

I recently spoke with an executive of a Christian college. He made an unsettling remark: "The contemporary student has two options, a Christian education or a good education." The remark was not made in a spirit of cynicism. Rather, it was an expression of deep concern that Christian education not be satisfied with low standards of excellence. Many bright young Christians have gone to secular schools because they believed that they could receive a better all-around education there. Regrettably, their decisions have some basis in fact, although, thankfully, there are many excellent Christian colleges around.

God demands a transformed mind. This is a mind that views the world from a different perspective. We still study pagan philosophers. But we learn to "read with a comb"—that is, we have a value system that gives us the ability to be *critical* of what we study. Here the word *critical* does not mean coming with a negative spirit. It means to be cautious, to be discerning. The truth of God is the grid by which we are to evaluate the teaching of this world.

The call to transformation is a call to the renewal of the mind. The new mind comes from a deep study of God's perspective. That does demand a mastery of sacred Scripture. The Scriptures reveal the mind of God. The more we understand the mind of God, the less threatened we will be by Ernest Hemingway or Jean-Paul Sartre.

We can also learn something from the world. Not all of God's revelation is found in Scripture. God also reveals Himself in nature and in human culture. All truth is God's truth. Though in general the worldly philosophers are false prophets, not everything they say is false. Truth can be found anywhere. We can discover elements of truth in the writings of pagans. The nuggets of truth gleaned from them may be difficult to find, but they are there and we can benefit from them. Most books of sermon illustrations quote from unbelievers as well as from believers.

The world is an obstacle to our sanctification. But it can also be an ally if we approach it from the right perspective. This is still my Father's world. He does not despise it. He loves it enough to redeem it. He visits it. He does not abandon it, neither does He surrender it. At this point we must be imitators of God, seeking to approach the world in the same manner as He does. The goal is transformation.

We must learn how to live with the world and in the world as God's people. Martin Luther described a pattern of Christian growth that is helpful. He said that when a person is first converted to Christ he goes through a period of withdrawal from and renunciation of the world. The new convert in a real sense is "finished with the world." The old patterns of conformity must be set aside. There is a period of withdrawal during which we immerse ourselves in the things of God. Before Paul was sent out as the apostle to the Gentiles, he first spent time in retreat in Arabia. Moses was in the wilderness, alone with God before he was sent to Pharaoh's court.

This period of withdrawal is both normal and healthy. But, as Luther insisted, we do not reach spiritual maturity until we are able to reenter the world, to embrace it, not as we once did in all its worldliness—but to embrace it as the arena of redemption. It is our place of labor. It is the place God made and to which Christ came. We do not give up on the world. In all of its fallenness, it is still our Father's world.

We must learn to claim it for Him. Not by conformity, not by yielding to its seduction, but by witnessing to it and transforming it. This can be accomplished without fear if we come to the world with minds that are renewed.

A renewed mind is essential in pleasing God. The God who desires our sanctification also desires that we shine like stars in a fallen world. We do this best when we understand this world and its values. When we understand—when we begin to perceive the world as God perceives it—then we can act with good conscience in renewing a marred creation. And in this we please the Creator and Redeemer.

FIVE

꧁꧂

The Battle with the Flesh

"he spirit indeed is willing, but the flesh is weak" (Matt. 26:41). This sentiment expresses a deep struggle that is a reality for every child of God. The
New Testament speaks of a warfare between flesh and spirit. The flesh is part
of Luther's triad of enemies, the world, the flesh, and the devil.

What then is the "flesh" of which Scripture speaks? What is there about the
flesh that can lead a believer away from a God-centered, God-pleasing life?

The Flesh—Physical or Fallen?

When we use the word *flesh* we usually mean our physical nature. On the one
hand, flesh refers to the substance that composes our bodies. We speak of "flesh
tones," of people appearing "in the flesh," of "suntanned flesh," of "flushed
flesh," of "flesh and blood," and of kinsfolk who are "my own flesh."

Because our human flesh is something physical, we are tempted to see the
biblical struggle between flesh and spirit as referring to a war between the body
and the soul. But this is misleading. In biblical terms, *flesh* sometimes refers to
the body and sometimes to something else. We will try to sort out the different
ways in which the Bible speaks of flesh.

In the New Testament we find two Greek words that are often translated
by the English word *flesh*. Those two Greek words are *soma* and *sarx*. The word
soma is normally used to refer to the physical body. (We have the word *psychosomatic* as an integral part of the English language. It combines the words for
flesh or body—*soma*—and mind—*psyche*.) Normally the word *soma* in the Greek
New Testament carries no connotation of sinfulness or fallenness. It is simply
the word used to refer to the physical body.

It is a different story with the Greek word *sarx*. Sometimes the word clearly
refers to the physical body, but at other times it means something else. It can
either refer simply to the physical flesh (just as *soma* does), or it can refer to
man's fallen nature.

When the Gospel of John declares, "The Word became flesh, and dwelt
among us" (John 1:14), it does not mean that the Word became fallen. It simply
means that the eternal Logos, the Word, took upon Himself a human nature.

The Word becomes *incarnate*. Likewise, Paul speaks of his kinsmen "according to the flesh" (Rom. 9:3). Here he is referring not to all of fallen humanity, but to his own ethnic group, the Jews. Paul's fleshy kinsmen are his fellow Israelites. The apostle speaks in the same manner as we do in describing our earthly relatives, our "own flesh."

But there are special times in the Bible that *sarx* is used to refer specifically to our fallen nature. Here *sarx* describes our corruption, which is by no means limited to our bodies. The whole man is fallen. Sin infects every aspect of our existence. By nature we have a "fleshly mind" (Col. 2:18). Neither the mind nor the flesh is any less fallen than the other. They are both geared toward pleasing ourselves, not pleasing God.

A Mind of Flesh

A "mind of flesh" does not refer simply to "evil thoughts about physical vices." The mind of flesh is a mind that involves a "mind-set" against God. It is the mind of a fallen humanity that does not want God in its thoughts. It is the mind of a person who is not guided by the Holy Spirit.

Paul expounds about an ongoing warfare between the flesh (*sarx*) and the Spirit (*pneuma*). The contrast in Galatians 5:16–21 is not between man's spirit and man's flesh, but between the life led by the Spirit, the Holy Spirit, and the life that serves the flesh, man's fallen nature.

> I say then: Walk in the Spirit, and you shall not fulfill the
> lust of the flesh. For the flesh lusts against the Spirit, and
> the Spirit against the flesh; and these are contrary to one
> another, so that you do not do the things that you wish.
> But if you are led by the Spirit, you are not under the law.
> Now the works of the flesh are evident, which are: adultery,
> fornication, uncleanness, licentiousness, idolatry, sorcery,
> hatred, contentions, jealousies, outbursts of wrath, selfish
> ambitions, dissensions, heresies, envy, murders, drunkenness,
> revelries, and the like; of which I tell you beforehand, just
> as I also told you in time past, that those who practice such
> things will not inherit the kingdom of God.

Here we see the stark contrast between flesh and Spirit. This is not a conflict between body and soul but between the old man who is driven by his fallen sinful nature and the new man indwelt by the Spirit of God. Here the Spirit and the flesh are opposed. They are in irreconcilable conflict. The flesh of our fallen nature resists the dominion of the Holy Spirit in our lives. The flesh takes offense at the Spirit and seeks to overcome it.

Likewise the Spirit is the enemy of the flesh. It wills what the flesh abhors. It wills righteousness. It seeks the fruit of the Spirit.

The contrast is seen vividly by two lists. The second list is well-known to Christians. It is the list of the fruit of the Spirit: love, joy, peace, and of such like. Our attention for the present, however, is on the first list. This list includes the work of the flesh.

As we examine the list of the works of the flesh one element is striking to us. The list includes sins that involve our bodies *and* sins that are of a more nonphysical character. In the list we find fornication and drunkenness. These are sins we commit with our physical appetites and bodily functions. Yet in this same list we find references to envy, jealousy, idolatry, and the like.

To be sure, when we are guilty of envy and jealousy, our bodies are involved. We don't do anything without our bodies. But envy is not a physical exercise. It involves a kind of mental attitude. It involves our minds, our thinking processes. We may use our bodies in acts of idolatry. We may physically bow down before an idol. But the essence of idolatry is not found in physical gestures but in the inward attitude of the heart.

We conclude then that when the New Testament speaks of flesh (*sarx*) in direct contrast to the Spirit (*pneuma*), the primary reference of the flesh is not to our physical bodies but to our fallen sinful nature that includes the whole man. It is the conflict of two styles of living—the life of the flesh, which is controlled by the impulse to sin, and the life of the Spirit, which leads us into righteousness, into pleasing God.

Controlled by the Spirit

This point is crucial to grasp lest we fall into the deadly error of thinking that righteousness consists chiefly in external physical acts. The kingdom of God involves much more than eating and drinking. If we focus merely on externals, we risk the trap of Pharisaism, which measures righteousness by outward, tangible actions. A saccharine smile can conceal an envious heart. A polite gesture can hide a jealous spirit. The Holy Spirit seeks to clean up our whole lives, both outwardly and inwardly.

At the same time we must guard against the opposite error of reducing righteousness to the internal realm. We can fool ourselves into thinking that all that matters is our inward attitude. As long as our spirit is right, it doesn't matter how we perform outwardly. This is an insidious form of self-deception. By it people seek to justify all sorts of sin. We say to ourselves that "love" justifies adultery. The teenager excuses his fornication by saying that it was committed in love.

It is also important to understand that though *flesh* does not exclusively refer to physical sins or inclinations, it does include them. They are powerful physical forces in our lives that are tainted by and influenced by our fallen sinful natures. Physical desires are often excruciatingly difficult to tame. These desires are not constant. They come in waves of varying degrees of intensity. It is easy to resolve to go on a diet *after* the dinner. It is another thing to go on a diet *before* dinner when hunger pangs are assaulting our wills.

The Spirit seeks to teach us self-control. We are called by God to harness our physical desires, to keep them in check. The desire to eat is, in itself, no sin. It is a normal physical function of our bodies. Yet when that desire runs out of control, we allow gluttony to enter our lives.

The sexual impulse is also a natural appetite that is not wrong in itself. God provides marriage as a context in which sexual expression is not only permitted, but it is commanded. We have both conjugal rights and conjugal responsibilities. Outside of marriage we are to abstain from sexual activities. God invented sex. God built the body with a complex of nerve endings that are highly susceptible to physical arousal.

It is possible that God could have made us with the ability to procreate without physical pleasure. He could likewise have made us with the ability to eat food without the added benefit of the pleasures of taste. But the Creator chose a more excellent way. Sex with all of its physical delight is a gift of God. But the gift comes to us with divine restrictions in its use. Sin is the abuse of the divine gift. It is using the gift in a manner God does not allow.

I once heard a man who was tragically involved in adultery declare, "My sexual organ has no conscience." He was excusing his physical behavior on the grounds that he was not personally responsible for what his body did. I explained that his sexual organ *did* have a conscience—his own mind. Our bodies are an integral part of ourselves. My whole body is to be governed by my mind. My mind is to be governed by the law of God.

There are involuntary physical impulses. We do not cause our hearts to beat on rhythm by our ethical ideas. But not all of our bodily activities are involuntary. We are called by God to control our sexual behavior. We may not be able to control our awareness of what is sexually desirable, but we can control what to do about it.

Luther once observed some aspects of the question of lust. Lust is not noticing that a woman is sexually attractive. Lust is born when we turn a simple awareness into a preoccupied fantasy. When we invite sexual thoughts into our minds and nurture them, we have passed from simple awareness into lust. Luther put it this way: "We cannot help it if birds fly over our heads. It is another thing if we invite them to build nests in our hair."

Self-control is the rule of sexual activity. We are responsible to God for our sexual behavior. The Scriptures declare, "But fornication and all uncleanness or covetousness, let it not even be named among you, as is fitting for saints" (Eph. 5:3). This absolute prohibition has been attacked by every subtle excuse known to man. The psychiatrists tell us that fornication among red-blooded youths is natural and normal. They are partly correct in their assessment. It is natural in the sense that by nature we are inclined to such activity. It is normal by virtue of the high statistical frequency of it. We could say that fornication is natural to normal *fallen* humanity. But so is lying. God forbids both.

It may be extremely difficult for a person to remain chaste, particularly in a culture where sexual taboos have been lifted and our senses are bombarded daily by erotic stimuli. But the Law of God is clear. He says, "No!" He calls us to self-control even in the midst of a fallen culture.

Consider for a moment the plight of the person with a homosexual orientation. This person suffers from a serious dilemma. God simply does not permit sexual acts between men and men or between women and women. Just as a heterosexual person is commanded to refrain from sexual activity outside of marriage, so the homosexual person is likewise called to chastity. God gives no provision for homosexual marriage. The homosexual is called to the same chastity as a single heterosexual person is called. Chastity pleases God, even if it seems initially unpleasant to our bodies.

Sexual chastity is difficult to achieve because of the weakness of the flesh. But it is possible to achieve, and God commands us to achieve it. If we fail, we are guilty of sin. Though we must be patient with those who fall into sin, we do no one a service by changing the standards of God and bringing them down to our own feeble levels of performance. It is scandalous to God for us to seek to change His standards and call good evil and evil good.

The flesh is an ally with the world. It seeks its justification not from the righteousness of Christ but from the standards of this world. The flesh is allied with the world and the world is allied with Satan. Here the enemy seeks our destruction by calling us away from the Spirit to surrender to the flesh.

But the Spirit is the believer's ally. How sad that every day we are reminded of our minds' and bodies' alliance with this fallen world while we forget that the children of God also have the Spirit to help them. In a world where the flesh seems to rule human activity, the Spirit is still present, enabling God's people to please Him.

✦✦✦

SIX

The Devil

The world, the flesh, the devil. Of this triad of enemies, the most formidable foe we have is the devil. Satan is not merely our enemy: He is our archenemy. He is called the prince of darkness, the father of lies, the accuser of the brethren, and the beguiling serpent.

The apostle Paul warns us that our battle against the devil's forces transcends the visible and tangible elements of this world: "We do not wrestle against flesh and blood, but against principalities, against powers, against the rulers of the darkness of this age, against spiritual hosts of wickedness in the heavenly places" (Eph. 6:12). That is, in our lives of trying to please a holy God, we are warring against not only our own petty desires but some fearsome, terrifying forces.

The first point we must understand in combatting the devil is that there really is a devil out there. In many segments of society, and even of the church, the concept of a personal devil is regarded as primitive mythology. I remember asking a class of students who were studying Western philosophy this question: "How many of you believe in a real personal devil?" In this class of thirty students, three indicated that they believed the devil was real. The other twenty-seven indicated that they considered the devil a myth.

I then asked the class, "How many of you believe in the existence of God?" To my surprise, all thirty indicated that they believed in God. I proceeded to my next question: "How many of you would be willing to define God as a spiritual being who has the ability to influence men for good?" They all were willing to allow the definition.

Then I asked, "Why is it that you affirm the existence of a spiritual being who has the ability to influence for good, but you deny the existence of a spiritual being who can influence us to evil?"

The basic response I got was this: "Modern science has made it impossible for educated people to believe in the devil." I questioned this point by asking, "What discovery of modern science has made the idea of Satan no longer credible? Is it the second law of thermodynamics? Is it the laws that govern nuclear fusion or fission? What is it?"

At first my question was met with stony silence. No one could point to a specific scientific discovery that applied. Finally one student said, "The idea of a devil seems to fit in the category of ghosts and goblins. How can anyone believe in a sinister fellow in a red flannel suit with cloven hoofs, horns, and a pitchfork?"

The student was not responding to the biblical image of the devil. His idea of Satan was a caricature. His devil was a fugitive from a Halloween party.

Satan the Proud and Powerful

Where did the idea of a red-flanneled, pitchfork-bearing devil come from? The roots of this grotesque caricature of Satan are found in the Middle Ages. It was popular sport in medieval days to mock the devil by describing him in ludicrous terms. There was a method in this madness. The medieval church believed in the reality of Satan. It was aware that Satan was a fallen angel who suffered from an overdose of pride. Pride was Satan's supreme weakness. To resist Satan, that proud but fallen creature, required fierce combat. The combat focused on Satan's most vulnerable point, his pride. The theory was this: Attack Satan at his point of weakness and he will flee from us.

What better way to attack Satan's pride than to depict him as a cloven-hoofed court jester in a red suit? These silly images of Satan were intentional caricatures. Unfortunately, later generations responded to the caricatures as if they were intended to be the real thing.

The biblical view of Satan is far more sophisticated than the caricature. The biblical images include that of an "angel of light" (2 Cor. 11:14). The "angel of light" image indicates Satan's clever ability to manifest himself *sub species boni* (under the appearances of good). Satan is subtle. He is beguiling. The serpent in the garden was described as "crafty" (Gen. 3:1). Satan does not appear as a fool. He is a beguiling counterfeit. He speaks with eloquence. His appearance is stunning. The prince of darkness wears a cloak of light.

A second image we have of Satan is that of a roaring lion who goes about seeking whom he will devour (1 Pet. 5:8). Notice that the same figure that is used for Christ, the *lion*, is used by Satan, the archetype of the Antichrist. The antilion devours. The Lion of Judah redeems.

With both allusions to the lion we find a symbol of strength, though with Satan it is an evil, demonic strength. His strength is no match for Christ, but it is a strength that is certainly superior to ours. He is not as strong as Christ, but he is stronger than we are.

There are two frequent ways that Satan deceives us. On the one hand, he will seek to have us *underestimate* his strength. On the other hand, there are times that he seeks to have us *overestimate* his strength. In either event he deceives us and can trip us up.

The pendulum of popular belief about Satan tends to swing between two extremes. On one side, there are those who believe that he doesn't exist at all, or if he does exist, he is a mere impersonal evil "force," sort of a collective evil that finds its origin in the sin of society. On the other side, there are those who have a preoccupied fixation, a cultic focus of attention upon him that diverts their gaze from Christ.

Either way Satan gains some ground. If he can persuade people that he does not exist, he can work his wiles without being detected or resisted. If he can get people to become preoccupied with him, he can lure them into the occult.

Peter underestimated Satan. When Jesus warned Peter about his impending betrayal, Peter protested, saying, "Lord, I am ready to go with You, both to prison and to death" (Luke 22:33). Peter was overconfident. He underestimated the strength of the adversary. Moments before Jesus had warned him about the strength of Satan, but Peter rejected the warning. Jesus said, "Simon, Simon! Indeed, Satan has asked for you, that he may sift you as wheat" (Luke 22:31).

Peter's protests notwithstanding, he became as putty in the hands of Satan. It was as easy for Satan to seduce Peter as it is to sift wheat in a sieve. In common jargon it was as if Jesus said to Peter, "Peter, you are a piece of cake. You are no match for the formidable strength of the devil."

Even so, Satan's power over us is limited. He may be stronger than we are, but we have a champion who can and does defeat him. The Scripture declares, "Greater is He who is in you than he who is in the world" (1 John 4:4, NASB). James adds these words: "Therefore submit to God. Resist the devil and he will flee from you" (James 4:7). When we resist the roaring lion in the power of the Holy Spirit, he runs away with his tail between his legs.

Satan sifted Peter, but his victory was temporary. With the warning Jesus gave came also the consolation: "But I have prayed for you, that your faith should not fail; and when you have returned to Me, strengthen your brethren" (Luke 22:32). Jesus predicted both the fall and the restoration of Peter.

To underestimate Satan is to suffer from the pride that goes before destruction. To overestimate him is to grant him more honor and respect than he deserves.

Satan is a creature. He is finite and limited. He is subordinate to God. Christianity never embraces an ultimate dualism of equal and opposite power. Satan is stronger than men but no match for God. He has no divine attributes. His knowledge may exceed ours, but he is not omniscient. His strength may be greater than ours, but he is not omnipotent. He may have a wider sphere of influence than we have, but he is not omnipresent.

Satan cannot be at more than one place at one time. He is a space-time creature who is limited, as are all angels good or bad, by space and time. Chances are that in your whole lifetime you will never experience a direct, immediate encounter with Satan himself. You might encounter one of his junior-grade lieutenants or one of his host of disciples, but he is likely to spend his time and space in bigger targets than you or me. Even in his concentrated attack on Jesus, Satan departed from him "for a season" (Luke 4:13).

Too Much Concern with Devils?

In our day there has been a renewal of interest in the work of Satan. Hollywood has given us *The Exorcist* and *The Omen* and a host of other films to whet our appetite for the occult. Within Christian circles there has arisen a new concern for ministries of deliverance. Some of these deliverance ministries have developed a bizarre and radically unbiblical view of demon possession and deliverance.

For example, we hear that we can recognize the departure of a demon from a human soul by a manifest sign that is linked to the particular point of bondage. We have people saying that particular demons cause particular sins. There is, they say, a demon of alcohol, a demon of depression, a demon of tobacco, and so on. I have listened to tapes from well-known deliverance ministers (whose names I will not mention, to protect the guilty) in which they teach the signs of departure of the demon. A sigh, for example, indicates the departure of the demon of tobacco. Since the tobacco demon enters with the inhaling of smoke, he leaves us with an audible exhale. Likewise vomiting may be the sign of the departure of the demon of alcohol. There are demons for every conceivable sin. Not only must each one of these demons be exorcized, but there are necessary procedures to keep them from returning on a daily basis.

I know of no polite way to respond to this kind of teaching. It is unmitigated nonsense. Nowhere in sacred Scripture is there to be found the slightest hint of this kind of demonic diagnosis. These teachings cross the line into the sphere of magic and result in serious harm to believers who are duped by them. Sadly, too much concern with Satan and demons means that we focus less of our attention on Christ. That must please Satan, though it certainly is not pleasing to God.

The Scriptures indicate that Satan can oppress us, assault us, tempt us, slander us, and accuse us. But a Christian who is indwelt by the Holy Spirit cannot be possessed by a demon. Where the Spirit of the Lord is, there is liberty. If a person indwelt by the Holy Spirit can at the same time be sovereignly controlled by an evil spirit, then our redemption is defeated.

All this emphasis on Satan and demons tends to distract us from another very real menace, our own sin. Yes, there is a devil. There are real demons. But there is also the reality of sin. Satan may be our accomplice in our ongoing sin, but we cannot pass the blame and responsibility for our sin to a controlling demon. We do not have to be possessed by a devil to get drunk. There is enough abiding wickedness in us to do it all by ourselves. We can never say, "The devil made me do it." We can say that we are tempted or incited or seduced by Satan, but not that we are controlled or coerced by him.

There are two serious problems with the view that our sins are the result of controlling demons. The first is that we yield to the temptation to take no personal responsibility for our sin. How can we be responsible if in fact we are not able to resist? Second, we are lured into thinking that we are powerless without the aid of the deliverance minister. We are encouraged to think that we are not really guilty and that we are actually helpless without a minister with special powers of deliverance. This negates the entire biblical concept of sanctification. It is surely unbiblical to teach that we cannot lead lives pleasing to God unless some so-called expert on deliverance enters into the battle. Therefore, I say with all urgency that believers must turn away from those who teach such things. Indeed run, for your very spiritual lives.

The Tempter and Adam

What then does Satan do to us? There are two chief activities with which Satan directs his power against us. These primary activities are temptation and accusation. We will look closely at accusation in the next chapter. Our concern here is his work as the tempter.

Satan's work of temptation is seen most dramatically in the Genesis account of the fall of Adam and Eve and in the wilderness testing of Jesus. Some startling parallels and contrasts may be observed in these two episodes.

In the Garden of Eden, the serpent approaches Eve with an innocuous-sounding question: "Has God indeed said, 'You shall not eat of every tree in the garden'?" (Gen. 3:1).

On the surface the question sounds silly. Satan assumes a pose of amazement, as if he is surprised by the severity of God's rules and prohibitions. "Did God really say that you are not allowed to eat of any of the trees of the Garden?" The question involved an obvious distortion. Eve was quick to set the devil straight: "We may eat the fruit of the trees of the garden; but of the fruit of the tree which is in the midst of the garden, God has said, 'You shall not eat it, nor shall you touch it, lest you die' " (Gen. 3:2, 3).

God had given Adam and Eve free use of the garden—with one exception. One tree was placed off limits. The rest were fully available. Yet Satan asked, "Did God say you couldn't eat from any of the trees?" Here we see the subtlety of the serpent. His thinly veiled suggestion is that if God places one limit on human freedom, he has taken away freedom altogether. The serpent's question was more than a question. It was an accusation against the fairness and kindness of God.

We see a parallel with our children's response to prohibitions. If our children ask permission to do ten things and for the first nine we say yes, but on the tenth we say no, the standard complaint is, "You never let us do anything!" Adults are much the same way.

Satan's question is an indirect assault on the integrity of God. He moves quickly from an indirect attack to a frontal assault. When Eve sets the record straight and declares that only one tree is forbidden with the divine warning of death, Satan boldly declares: "You will not surely die. For God knows that in the day you eat of it your eyes will be opened, and you will be like God, knowing good and evil" (Gen. 3:4, 5).

Here the temptation is wrapped in a bold-faced lie: "You will not die." The serpent declares a clear contradiction of what God said. Satan accuses God of lying. "You won't die. God says you will die, but I say you will not."

The issue is, who is telling the truth? Jesus called Satan "a liar, and the father of lies" (John 8:44, NASB). Satan's chief device of temptation is to attack the truth of God. Not only does Satan accuse God of lying, but he provides Eve with a reason for God's lie. He charges God with a kind of divine jealousy. God does not want Adam and Eve's eyes to be opened. He wants to keep His level of knowledge to Himself. He does not want to share His deity. He is afraid that the fruit of the tree will make Adam and Eve divine. His prohibition is both unfair and selfish.

Now Satan launches an all-out attack on the integrity of God. He is suggesting that Adam and Eve have a *right* to the tree. God's rules are unfair. Man has an inalienable right to do what he pleases, even if it is not pleasing to God.

This was not the last time in history such a temptation was placed before man. The same diabolical train of thought takes place in the human mind every day. Every time I sin, I sin because I want to do what I want to do rather than what God wants me to do. Deep within our hearts we harbor the treacherous thought that God's laws are not fair.

The Tempter and Christ

Now consider the temptation of Christ. First, let us note the differences between the circumstances of the test of Adam and Eve and that of Jesus. Adam's temptation took place in the midst of paradise. He had the comfort of human fellowship. He had a full stomach. A gourmet feast was there for the taking. Adam had every creature comfort available.

By contrast Christ was alone. In solitude he faced the worst natural elements. The Judean wilderness was the habitat of scorpions, scrub brush, and a few birds. Devoid of human companionship, Jesus faced a temptation after forty days with no food. He had no fruit to eat, no trees from which to choose.

In spite of this stark contrast of circumstances, there was a striking similarity of the temptation. The same issue was at stake, the trustworthiness of the Word of God. The devil approached Jesus and said, "If You are the Son of God, command this stone to become bread" (Luke 4:3). Notice that Satan did not say, "*Since* You are the Son of God. . . ." The accent was on the first word: "*If* You are the Son of God. . . ."

Why the *if*? What were the last words Jesus had heard before the Spirit drove Him into the wilderness to be tested? The heavens had opened at Jesus' baptism and God spoke audibly saying, "You are My beloved Son; in You I am well pleased" (Luke 3:22).

The subtle suggestion of Satan by using the word *if* was this: "Are You sure You are the Son of God? If You are so beloved of God, what are You doing here? Is this how God treats His Son in whom He is well pleased? Perhaps we need to make sure that You are the Son of God. You're hungry, aren't You? It shouldn't require much power from the very Son of God to change a few stones into bread. What harm will that do?".

Jesus was quick to reply. Of course He was hungry, but His hunger for righteousness was greater than His hunger for bread. His meat and His drink was to do the will of the Father. He said, "Man shall not live by bread alone, but by every word of God" (Luke 4:4).

Jesus saw through the subtlety of Satan's words. In Jesus' mind there was no "if." God had said that He was His Son. Jesus lived by the Word of God. Adam was enticed to deny the truthfulness of what God said. Jesus was not moved from it.

Satan changed his tactics with Jesus. He showed Him all the kingdoms of this world. He said to Jesus, "All this authority I will give You, and their glory; for this has been delivered to me, and I give it to whomever I wish. Therefore, if You will worship before me, all will be Yours" (Luke 4:6, 7).

Power and glory. These were the enticements. Satan was armed with this maxim: "Every man has his price." But he was unable to find a price for Jesus. This was the man without a price. This was the man who later would ask, "What shall it profit a man if he gains the whole world, and loses his own soul?" (Mark 8:36).

Jesus replied to Satan, "Get behind Me, Satan! For it is written, 'You shall worship the LORD your God, and Him only you shall serve' " (Luke 4:8). Again the issue was the same: obedience to the Word of God. What Satan offered could only be accepted by Jesus if He was willing to negotiate the Word of God. Jesus repelled Satan with Holy Scripture. "It is written . . . ," said Jesus. He quoted from Deuteronomy. Obviously Jesus had more regard for the Pentateuch than many of our contemporaries. He had moments before declared that men must live by every word that comes from God. Then He cited a specific word that cannot be broken.

It was Satan's turn to quote the Bible. Again he used the word *if.*

> If You are the Son of God, throw Yourself down from here.
> For it is written:

> "He shall give His angels charge over You,
> To keep You,"

and

> "In their hands they shall bear You up,
> Lest You dash Your foot against a stone." (Luke 4:9–11)

Satan was not above citing Scripture. His, however, was a distorted hermeneutic. He twisted Scripture by setting Scripture against Scripture. He appealed to the Bible as his source to justify sin. He did radical violence to the Holy Spirit.

It was as if Satan had said, "Okay, Jesus, You say You believe the Scripture. Then prove it! Put God to the test. Throw Yourself down and see if the angels will catch You."

Jesus replied, "It has been said, 'You shall not tempt the LORD your God' " (Luke 4:12).

What Jesus was saying is clear. "I know the promises of God. But don't try to tempt me with a promise that is circumscribed by a prohibition. The Bible also says that we must not put God to the test (Deut. 6:16). I don't need to jump off the pinnacle of the temple to know that the angels are caring for Me. God has declared it and I am confident that what He has declared is true."

The irony of this reply is found in Matthew's Gospel: "Then the devil left Him, and behold, angels came and ministered to Him" (Matt. 4:11).

The Temptation to Unbelief

In both cases of temptation, with Adam and with Jesus, the issue focused on the trustworthiness of God's Word. If Satan can cast doubt on the veracity of God's Word, the stage is set for our fall. Failure to believe what God says is the foundation of all sin. Once the truth of God is set aside, we have nothing to restrain us from doing what is right in our own eyes. Doing our "own thing" is the very essence of disobedience. And when we keep our attention focused on what is right in our own eyes, we cannot possibly be committed to pleasing God.

Why is unbelief a sin? To refuse to believe God is to be guilty of slandering His righteous character. It is to assume that either God does not know what He is talking about or that what He says is in fact evil. Either way we assault His divine integrity. Either His omniscience or His righteousness is brought into question.

But isn't blind faith a weakness? Indeed it is. There is a great difference between faith and credulity. Credulity is gullibility, naïveté. It is based on superstition and irrational prejudice. To believe something with no reason for believing is not a virtue. But God does not require that. He asks us to believe in that which He utters in the fullness of light and with consummate evidence. He does not ask us to believe in a Resurrection without first bringing Jesus forth from the grave.

He does ask us to trust Him for the future, but such trust is not blind. It rests upon God's perfect track record. He has demonstrated over and over that His promises are certain. Indeed, if we were asked to put our unquestioned trust in a man who has been repeatedly convicted of fraud, whose promises are constantly broken, who is a notorious liar and cheat, such trust would be incredulous.

But God is not a man. He is guilty of none of those things. We dare not transfer to God the same lack of integrity that we find in ourselves.

The Roman Catholic Church has a concept that is worth our attention. It is the idea of a *fides implicitum*. This means simply that the believer is to give the church an implicit faith, or to trust the church implicitly because the church as an institution that teaches Christian doctrine is considered infallible.

Indeed, if the church were infallible it would be right and proper to grant it an implicit faith. Whatever or whoever is infallible deserves such trust. I don't believe that the Roman Catholic Church or any church is infallible. But God is infallible. To Him we owe a *fides implicitum*.

If Satan can destroy our implicit trust in God, then his goal of seduction is achieved. We fall to the temptation of unbelief. Adam fell. He did not believe God. Jesus, the second Adam, lived by the Word of God. His trust in the Father could not be shaken. He did not yield to the tempter.

Before Jesus' temptation, He had heard the voice of the Father, who declared His approval of the Son: "I am well pleased." We can feel certain that God was also well pleased at Jesus' victory in the temptation. Jesus chose well between the word of Satan the liar and the Word of God. He cast His lot with trust and belief instead of selfish doubt and skepticism. Both then and now God takes pleasure in His children when they trust.

❧

SEVEN

Satan as Accuser

A s powerful as Satan is in his work of temptation, he is also formidable in his work of accusation. In the last chapter we looked at how we please God by resisting Satan the tempter. Here we will look at how, at times when we do sin, we please God by throwing ourselves on His mercy instead of listening to the taunts of Satan the accuser.

The Sinister Accuser

As an accuser of God's people, Satan can disguise himself as the Holy Spirit and bury us in a quagmire of moral confusion. He can make us feel good when we should feel guilty and make us feel guilty when we should be at peace.

Zechariah records an incident that displays the accusation of Satan:

> Then he showed me Joshua the high priest standing before the Angel of the LORD, and Satan standing at his right hand to oppose him. And the LORD said to Satan, "The LORD rebuke you, Satan! The LORD who has chosen Jerusalem rebuke you! Is this not a brand plucked from the fire?"

> Now Joshua was clothed with filthy garments, and was standing before the Angel.

> Then He answered and spoke to those who stood before Him, saying, "Take away the filthy garments from him." And to him He said, "See I have removed your iniquity from you, and I will clothe you with rich robes."

> And I said, "Let them put a clean turban on his head." So they put a clean turban on his head, and they put the clothes on him. And the Angel of the LORD stood by.

> Then the Angel of the LORD admonished Joshua, saying,
> "Thus says the LORD of hosts: If you will walk in My ways, and
> if you will keep My command, then you shall also judge My
> house, and likewise have charge of My courts; I will give you
> places to walk among these who stand here." (Zech. 3:1–7)

Joshua was clad in filthy garments. As he stood in the presence of God, Satan called attention to his clothes. The enemy accused Joshua before the Lord. Indeed his clothes were dirty. Satan picked on a vulnerable spot. But the Lord defended His elect. "Is not this a brand plucked from the fire?"

Every Christian is a brand plucked from the fire. The salvaged brand is rescued from the inferno. After it is removed from the center of the flames, the heat can no longer destroy it. It may smolder for a few moments, but it survives.

A smoldering brand is filthy. It makes black marks on whoever handles it. Its charred surface is covered with tar and soot.

That is who we are. The redeemed of God who are snatched from the flames by the hand of the Lord are still covered with ashes. We remain streaked with charcoal. We remain blemished with soot. We are redeemed, but not totally sinless. Satan is quick to call attention to the dirt. He wants us to be more conscious of our own sin than of God's mercy.

Satan's accusations are met by a divine reprimand: "The LORD who has chosen Jerusalem rebuke you!" God stops the mouth of Satan. Christ is our attorney who rises to our defense. As Satan prosecutes us, Christ stands before the bench and declares, "Objection, your honor! This is one of My brands snatched from the fire." God replies from the throne of judgment, "Objection sustained!" The tongue of the accuser is silenced in the courtroom of the Almighty.

The Lord's angel removed Joshua's filthy garments and clothed him with rich robes. A clean turban was placed upon his head. This is how Christ clothes His redeemed. We are clothed in His righteousness so that we need not be embarrassed in the presence of God.

The right clothing can be so important. Recently I attended a reception for the governor of Florida. It was a black-tie affair and my invitation came at the last minute. I rushed to the tuxedo rental agency to order my outfit. The clerk put a rush order in but declared that my tuxedo might not arrive in time. That night I dreamed that I appeared at the reception without a tuxedo. I was the only person present who was improperly dressed. I awoke in a cold sweat and was instantly relieved that it was only a bad dream.

It is one thing to commit a social faux pas by being improperly dressed in front of the governor. It is quite another to show up in the presence of God dressed in filth. Rightly do we fear being poorly dressed in the throne room of God.

But God has His own private tuxedo shop. The clothes He puts on us are not rented. They are given to us permanently. To be sure, they conceal ragged undergarments, but we are properly covered. Once we are attired in these clothes, we will never again suffer embarrassment. These garments never wear out; they never go out of style.

It was God who made the first suit of clothes. The first recorded act of divine mercy was God's providing clothing to cover Adam and Eve's nakedness. He had mercy on their shame and stooped to minister to their embarrassment (Gen. 3:21). He continues to provide garments for His beloved but sin-stained people.

Zechariah records that after the Lord removed Joshua's iniquity and put him in clean clothes He admonished him—that is, He reprimanded him in a kind, loving way. In this short episode Joshua experienced both the accusation of Satan and the admonishment of God. This is not unlike what we experience as Christians. When we sin we can receive both the accusation of Satan and the conviction of the Holy Spirit.

What is the difference? The goal of Satan's accusation is to harm us. He wants to drive us away from God. The goal of the Spirit's conviction is to turn us from sin. He wants our awareness of sin to bring us close to God. Satan would have us perish in our guilt. The Spirit seeks to save us from our guilt. They both may call attention to the same sin. But their goals are radically different.

The Sweet Conviction

Satan's accusations drive us to despair, but there is something sweet about the conviction of the Holy Spirit. When He brings our guilt to our attention, He brings also the consolation of forgiveness and restoration.

Consider the experience of the prodigal son. After he had wasted his inheritance and was reduced to the ignominy of feeding swine, he reached the depths of coveting the pods that the pigs ate. Then, the Scripture declares, "He came to himself" (Luke 15:17).

To come to oneself is to awaken to one's desperate plight. It is to have a revival of conscience. The segment of the conscience that had been temporarily dormant is suddenly awakened. It is as though one awakens from a moral slumber. What follows is authentic remorse coupled with a resolve to cease from wickedness. The parable expresses it this way:

> But when he came to himself, he said, "How many of my
> father's hired servants have bread enough and to spare, and I
> perish with hunger! I will arise and go to my father, and will
> say to him, 'Father, I have sinned against heaven and before
> you, and I am no longer worthy to be called your son. Make
> me like one of your hired servants.' " And he arose and came
> to his father. But when he was still a great way off, his father
> saw him and had compassion, and ran and fell on his neck
> and kissed him. (Luke 15:17–20)

Here we see the kind of result that follows from the conviction of God the Holy Spirit. When the Spirit convicts us of sin, He leads us to repentance and restoration. The initial awakening to the reality of guilt may be painful, but it does not lead us to despair. Rather, it leads us back to the Father, who is eager to embrace us. The Father kills the fatted calf, clothes us with His finest robe, puts shoes on our blistered feet, and adorns our hand with the family ring. Certainly this parable makes it clear that nothing is more pleasing to God than our sincere sorrowing over sin and turning from it.

The Spirit's conviction is liberating. It is kind and gentle. The judgment is coupled with compassion. The welcome sign is vividly displayed for those with contrite hearts. It is a time not for bitter retribution but for godly merriment. There is rejoicing among the angels and delight in the heart of God. Observe the gladness of the father in the parable: " 'And bring the fatted calf here and kill it, and let us eat and be merry; for this my son was dead and is alive again; he was lost and is found." And they began to be merry" (Luke 15:23, 24).

The goal of Satan's accusation is not restoration but destruction. The last thing he wants to see is repentance. There is no joy among his lieutenants when a sinner comes to himself and quits his sin. Rather, Satan wants us to surrender to sin. He wants everybody in the pigpen. His torment aims at making the sinner bitter and hostile toward God. He wants the sinner to feel sorry for himself and to blame God for his plight. He would have hoped that while the son was busy cursing the pigs he would also curse God. He wanted to hear the prodigal say, "My father did not provide enough of an inheritance. God is not fair to allow me to be starving with pigs."

The attitude of Satan is mirrored in the attitude of the elder son:

> Now his older son was in the field. And as he came and
> drew near to the house, he heard music and dancing. So

he called one of the servants and asked what these things
meant. And he said to him, "Your brother has come, and
because he has received him safe and sound, your father
has killed the fatted calf." But he was angry and would not
go in. (Luke 15:25–28)

Here we see anger and jealousy toward the father's mercy. This was Satan's
attitude toward Job. It is the devil's mentality that seeks to accuse rather than
forgive. This is why a judgmental spirit is unbecoming to a Christian. It is why
the apostle Paul speaks so strongly of the strength we find in the stronghold of
Christ: "Who shall bring a charge against God's elect? It is God who justifies.
Who is he who condemns? It is Christ who died, … who is even at the right hand
of God, who also makes intercession for us" (Rom. 8:33, 34).

Paul's questions are rhetorical. When he asks, "Who will bring a charge
against God's elect?" he is saying, "Nobody dare!" To accuse one whom God
has justified is to insult the gospel. To condemn one for whom Christ died and
for whom Christ intercedes is as foolish as it is wicked.

Our defense against the accusation of Satan is the gospel. He despises the
gospel. He denies the gospel. He wants us to seek our justification somewhere
other than in our Christ, who clothes us with His perfect righteousness. Satan
will lay charges against us. He will condemn us. He will shout into our ears that
our garments are filthy, that we are too sinful to ever be pleasing to a righteous
God. But in Christ we say, "Begone, slanderer—who shall bring a charge against
God's elect? My Savior has covered me. He has taken away my iniquity. He prays
for me at this very moment. Cover your ears, devil, lest you hear the intercession of Christ for me. Christ is my righteousness. His merit is mine. Nothing
can separate me from His love."

We please God when we resist temptation and do not sin. Certainly part
of our maturing in the Lord is to do this more and more. But we do sin, again
and again, and as we grow in the Lord we become even more conscious of how
many ways we can find to sin against God and others. But part of our growth is
becoming more and more sure of God's acceptance of us. He does not save us
because of our spotless lives, but because we are clothed in Christ's righteous
garments. Our awareness of our sin is painful indeed, but it is a sweet pain that
drives us into the arms of the loving Father. We please Him when we do not
leave His side, as Satan the tempter would have us do. We also please Him when
we return to Him, something Satan the accuser does his best to prevent. When
Satan whispers to the believer, "You, with all your sin, can't be pleasing to God,"
the believer replies, "Ah, but I am. To God be the glory."

EIGHT

✤

Fear and Guilt Paralysis

During the troubled era of the Roosevelt administration the president rallied the nation with his famous utterance, "We have nothing to fear but fear itself." President Franklin Delano Roosevelt understood that fear is a powerful force. It can paralyze people and hold them tightly in bondage.

Fear takes many forms. It may include a fear of bodily harm, a fear of failure, or a fear of success with the responsibilities and expectations that accompany it. We hear the expression, "I was frozen with fear." To be frozen with fear refers to the paralysis by which the normal flow of things is arrested as ice jams lock the normal flow of a river.

We are a phobic people. A recent study listed the top ten phobias of American people. The list included fear of death (thanatophobia), fear of heights (acrophobia), fear of narrowly confining spaces (claustrophobia), the fear of strangers (xenophobia), and several others. At the top of the list was the fear of public speaking. I can relate to that one. A hollow sinking feeling attacks the stomach. The hands become clammy. The throat muscles tense. It can become so severe that people "freeze" when they are called upon to speak. The memory fails. The mind goes blank. The mouth opens but no words come forth. Perhaps the root of this fear is simply the fear of saying or doing something foolish. Ironically, the fear itself produces just that effect.

No one wants to do something stupid in front of a crowd. The pressure in front of large groups can be tremendous. The athlete knows the dread of "choking" under such pressure. Recently a reporter interviewed a contestant in a golf tournament who was winning until the final holes. Suddenly the player's game fell apart and his score skyrocketed. In the press tent a reporter asked, "What happened out there?" The golfer replied simply, "I choked."

It was refreshing to hear this candid reply. The reporter was accustomed to hearing other explanations such as, "I lost my concentration," or, "I was distracted by a camera shutter clicking," or, "My ball took a strange bounce into a hazard." Normally professional athletes do not respond by saying, "I choked."

But even the most accomplished performers choke. They all know what it feels like. Fear comes over them in such a way as to grip their muscles in a vise.

The smooth flow of the golf swing becomes stiff and jerky, with disastrous results.

What causes choking? The obvious answer is the fear of losing, of failing to achieve a much sought-after goal. The fear of being humiliated by playing badly may be the exact force that causes bad play.

But the fear may be more complex. Many athletes have a real fear of winning. If one wins he rises into a new status. A new level of expectation and its pressures is reached. Also, a person might actually feel guilty for winning, thinking that he does not deserve to be victorious. Here there is an unspoken connection of fear with a nagging feeling of guilt. More about guilt in a moment.

Fear of Change

For the moment, let us consider the factor of fearing a change in our status. We tend to be comfortable with the level of achievement we have attained. If we slip below that level, we experience a loss of confidence and self-esteem. That disturbs our comfort level. But if we rise above our normal achievement level, that is also discomforting. We are cast into strange and foreign waters. We are not sure what to expect. We are in a new zone of responsibility.

We have comfort zones in all sorts of areas. The comfort zone goes beyond sports. We have an economic comfort zone, an academic comfort zone, a social comfort zone, and so on. We also have a spiritual comfort zone. Too much change coming too quickly can be traumatic to the point of paralysis. We can handle change, but we don't wish to handle too much. And we also tend to become satisfied with the status quo. That can prevent the professional athlete—and the Christian—from striving too hard.

We speak of being "well-adjusted." What does that mean? To adjust is to respond to some kind of change in our lives. The child that moves from junior high school to high school must adjust. The single person who gets married must adjust. The businessman who gets a promotion must adjust. We admire people who can adapt creatively and productively to new situations. Perhaps we admire adaptation because we know how difficult it can be. Adjustments are not easy because they involve a change in our comfort zone.

Yet every Christian is called to change. We are commanded to move ahead in our spiritual progress. God is not inert, and He refuses to allow us to be. But with change comes the element of fear. Consider the example of Abraham:

> Now the LORD had said to Abram: "Get out of your country,
> from your kindred and from your father's house, to a land

that I will show you. I will make you a great nation; I will
bless you and make your name great; and you shall be a
blessing. I will bless those who bless you, and I will curse
him who curses you; and in you all the families of the earth
shall be blessed."

So Abram departed as the LORD had spoken to him, and Lot
went with him. And Abram was seventy-five years old when
he departed from Haran. (Gen. 12:1–4)

God called Abraham to move. He had to leave his comfort zone. He had to
leave his town, his nation, and his family. He had to leave his roots, his security,
and his familiar territory. He was ten years past the retirement age. He was an
old dog who was expected to learn new tricks.

God's call to Abraham was a call to greatness. "I will make you a great nation" was the promise. The author of Hebrews commented later on Abraham's
response to this fearful call:

By faith Abraham obeyed when he was called to go out
to the place which he would afterward receive as an
inheritance. And he went out, not knowing where he was
going. By faith he sojourned in the land of promise as in a
foreign country, dwelling in tents with Isaac and Jacob, the
heirs with him of the same promise; for he waited for the
city which has foundations, whose builder and maker is
God. . . . Therefore from one man, and him as good as dead,
were born as many as the stars of the sky in multitude—
innumerable as the sand which is by the seashore.

These all died in faith, not having received the promises, but
having seen them afar off were assured of them, embraced
them, and confessed that they were strangers and pilgrims
on the earth. (Heb. 11:8–13)

Abraham became a pilgrim. He was a man on the move out of obedience to a divine call. The same may be said of Moses, of Joshua, of David, of
Paul, and especially of Christ. They went where God told them to go. They
did what God told them to do, though that entailed a certain lack of security.
Likewise the Christian is called to forgo a feeling of security in this world—
though the ultimate security (the love of God) is a more than adequate com-
pensation for that.

The Linking of Fear and Guilt

But how does this relate to guilt? As I mentioned, there is often a close but subtle link between fear and guilt. Both have a fierce power to paralyze. Both can make us halt—or even retreat—in our spiritual journey. Both can keep us from reaching out to God. Both can distract us from the great goal of pleasing God.

Though we can distinguish between fear and guilt, we cannot always separate them. Frequently, paralyzing fear is a direct result of unresolved guilt. The ultimate fear is the fear of punishment at the hands of God. We are frightened by social rejection, parental disapproval, and peer judgment. We may be afraid of the sheriff or the IRS. But the most fearful thing is to fall into the hands of the living God. Though many people do not acknowledge it, they are afraid that their lives have angered the Creator of the universe. Consciousness of sin seems to be universal, and Christian and pagan alike know, or sense, that Almighty God is not pleased at our failings.

I once was invited by a psychiatrist to join him in his practice as a regular consultant. He was not particularly a religious man, but he said, "A great many of my patients need a priest more than they need a doctor. Many of them suffer from problems that at root are tied up with guilt."

To be a psychiatrist requires a lengthy term of academic study. A psychiatrist must first learn medicine and qualify as an M.D. before going on to his specialty. Yet with all his years of academic training, he receives little or no education in theology.

Guilt is ultimately a theological problem. Without a thorough knowledge of theology, the psychiatrist is seriously hampered in dealing with guilt-ridden people. He cannot, unless he is a believer, understand that guilt is something very real, for real human beings do feel guilt over their acts and attitudes.

Sadly, so many people pay to have professional therapists listen to their woes, while the therapists may have little or no understanding of sin and guilt. Problems that appear to be mainly physiological may have deep roots in human guilt. Many marriage counselors counsel people who face problems of sexual dysfunction that threaten the marital union. Problems of so-called "frigidity" and "impotence" are *always* rooted in some form of guilt or fear. Assuming that the problem is merely a "mechanical failure" is very unfair to the patient.

God is loving and forgiving. God is also the Creator and Sustainer of the universe. He is a force to be reckoned with. Even people who have only rudimentary ideas about God seem to sense that God (even if they no longer use the word *God*) is a moral being who is disappointed at our troubled world. This powerful Being is intimidating for both pagan and believer. We remember Moses' and the Israelites' response to the presence of God at Sinai. So terrifying was it that the people could not endure His presence, and Moses himself was led to exclaim, "I am exceedingly afraid and trembling" (Heb. 12:21).

Though modern man seems to do everything in his power to insulate himself from any thoughts about the terror of God, he is not able to erase such fears entirely from his conscience. The pagan still trembles at the rustling of a leaf; the wicked still flee when no man pursues. There remains a nagging, mostly unspoken fear, that God is crouched, lying in wait for us, ready to pounce upon us at any moment. We are still afraid of things that go bump in the night.

Recently the elders of our local church went on a weekend retreat for fun and fellowship. They arrived at a country home on a Friday night. The event featured four-wheel-drive buggies that the elders revved up for a midnight frolic. There were not enough buggies to go around, so one enterprising elder joined the frolic by climbing aboard a riding lawn mower. He drove slowly into the night to join the others. Suddenly he let out a scream of fear. He saw the shadow of something looming up behind him and felt the ominous touch of some foreign object against his neck. Then he screamed. As his friends rushed to his aid, they fell over laughing at the sight of their friend frozen in terror. He was firmly in the grasp of the grass-catcher attachment that had risen in the night to attack him. Perhaps our eternal fear of the dark is at root the fear of God, a God who will (we fear) eventually cause our sins to catch up with us.

No one dares turn his back on God. We know that He sees our every move, that He notes our every thought. The fear of punishment at His hands can never be eradicated by those stricken with guilt.

In considering guilt we must be careful to distinguish between guilt and guilt *feelings*. Guilt feelings are subjective. They arise from within us. We can feel guilty even when there is no guilt. Guilt, however, is objective. It involves a real state of affairs. Whenever we sin we incur guilt. Guilt involves a debtor relationship to God. It is tied to sin.

The Westminster Catechism defines sin as "Any want of conformity to, or transgression of the Law of God." This is a masterful definition. It captures both sins of omission and sins of commission. When we fail to conform to the Law of God, we fall short of what God requires. We do not do what God commands. That is a sin of omission. When we transgress the Law of God, we do what God forbids. This is a sin of commission.

Facing Real Guilt

Either way, by omission or commission, if we violate the Law of God we incur guilt. That guilt is real and objective. It is also devastating. Appropriate guilt feelings may or may not accompany guilt. We know that guilt feelings make us uncomfortable. We employ numerous devices to rid ourselves of those feelings. We excuse ourselves. We rationalize. We shift the blame to other people or to our circumstances. We blame society. We blame our environment. We blame our parents. We appeal to everything we can to escape the pain of personal responsibility. We use every kind of avoidance mechanism, because our guilt is indeed great. It is too much to handle, and unless we cope with it in the right way—appealing to the saving work of Christ—we spend valuable time and energy in running from guilt.

We have learned how to harden our hearts. We can lose the capacity to blush. Jeremiah declared the word of God to Judah: "You have had a harlot's forehead; you refuse to be ashamed" (Jer. 3:3).

Here we see the refusal to repent linked to the squashing of guilt feelings. The people of Judah protested their innocence while they continuously violated the Law of God. By repeated sin they acquired the forehead of a harlot. That is, they forgot how to be ashamed.

But the lack of guilt feelings does not excuse real guilt. A man on trial for murder would find his defense flimsy indeed if all he said was, "But I don't feel guilty." There are psychopathic killers who feel no remorse for their crimes. The lack of remorse, however, does not excuse their deeds.

A sad commentary on contemporary life is the frequency with which counselors seek to relieve people's guilt problems by focusing on the removal of guilt feelings. To relieve guilt, people are told that they are victims of their environment and of the oppressive moral standards of outmoded religion. This applies not only to non-Christians, but to Christians as well. Many Christians, living with a burdensome guilt over past or present sins, tell their woes to therapists who say, in effect, "Considering the life you've had to lead, no wonder you've behaved in this way. As long as you understand that, there is no real problem." But it isn't true, is it? Explaining the problem does not eliminate the problem. Guilt only disappears when we are made right with God. That rightness is available at any time, for we serve a forgiving God. But He does not force His children to ask His forgiveness. They do so willingly, or they torment themselves with guilt that the therapists cannot explain away.

I was approached by a distressed college girl who was engaged to be married. She explained that she had been sexually involved with her fiancé and was feeling guilty about it. She related to me that she had gone to her school counselor who told her, "The reason you feel guilty is because you have been a victim of a Victorian ethic or a Puritan taboo. You need to understand that your behavior is perfectly normal. It is a healthy part of mature self-expression and of preparation for marriage."

The girl then said to me, "But Professor Sproul, I still feel guilty!" I said, "Perhaps the reason you feel guilty is because you *are* guilty. The prohibition for fornication was not invented by Queen Victoria, nor was it the creation of the Puritans. It is God who forbids fornication. When we break the laws of God we incur real guilt. The only remedy I know for real guilt is real forgiveness."

I explained to the young woman that the price tag for real forgiveness is real repentance. Real repentance is what the individual must do himself. No one else can repent for me. I cannot repent for anyone else. I encouraged the woman to get alone with God, to go before Him on her knees. Without me. Without the counselors. Then I promised her—indeed, I guaranteed her—that in God's sight her guilt would be removed and that she would once again be a virgin in God's sight. Then she would be free of the fear and paralysis that come in the wake of guilt.

As Christians we must examine our lives. We must ask ourselves two basic questions: At what point am I paralyzed in my spiritual growth? Why am I paralyzed? Chances are that if we can answer these two questions accurately, we can identify those areas of fear and guilt that are in need of resolution. The grace of God—especially the grace of forgiveness—is the most potent force available to us to be freed from paralysis.

God does not want us paralyzed. He wants us to feel so secure in Him that we need have no real fear of the world and its obstacles. He wishes us to be conscious of our sins, but He takes no joy in our being immobilized by guilt. God is, like any good human parent, eager to lead us out of a life of fear and guilt so that we are free to do what is right and pleasing. What freedom is offered to us! Freedom *from* guilt, freedom *from* fear, freedom *to* serve and please God with everything we are. No therapist in the world can offer us such a life.

NINE

❧❧❧

Real Forgiveness

W e have seen the paralyzing force of unresolved guilt. The reality of guilt is a cumbersome burden for anyone to carry about with him. We remember the dreadful weight that the hero of *The Pilgrim's Progress* dragged through his travels. We remember the awful "body of death" of which the apostle Paul spoke. Those who saw the Hollywood movie *The Mission* recall the graphic torture the penitent mercenary soldier bore as he climbed a mountain weighted down with a bundle of armor.

To cast off this burden is to know the sweetness of relief. To hear what Isaiah heard—"Your sins are forgiven"—is to hear the music of freedom. For centuries Roman Catholics have experienced a moment of relief in the confessional as the priest pronounced the words, *Te Absolvo*—"I forgive you."

In Roman Catholicism, confession belongs to the sacrament of penance. This sacrament was repudiated by the vast majority of Protestant churches during the Reformation. As a result, many Protestants look at the Roman Catholic practice of confession with a jaundiced eye. We hear the continuing protest expressed in words like, "Why should I confess my sins to a priest? Christ is the High Priest. I can confess my sins to Him directly. I don't need an earthly priest!" Is this realistic, or are we just justifying an anti-Catholic prejudice?

It is a sad fact of church history that most Protestants do not know what it is they are protesting. The passing of time has dimmed the classic point of protest. What is left is a somewhat ambiguous prejudice against Rome that focuses on trivial matters.

Penance and Protestantism

To put the debate in perspective, let us look briefly at the historical issues that provoked the Reformers. The Reformation was triggered by an abuse centering on the sacrament of penance. Penance was seen by Rome as a necessary step for restoring saving grace to those who had committed a mortal sin. Rome calls the sacrament of penance the "second plank of justification for those who have made shipwreck of their souls."

Why the "second plank of justification"? In Roman theology the first plank of justification is found in the sacrament of baptism. By baptism justifying grace is infused into the human soul. A baptized person remains in a state of grace until or unless that person commits a mortal sin. A mortal sin is called "mortal" because it kills or destroys saving grace. A person who commits a mortal sin is in need of being justified again. The new justification comes through the sacrament of penance.

The sacrament of penance has several parts to it. It includes confession, contrition, priestly absolution, and works of satisfaction. The Roman Catholic Church defines penance not so much as a feeling as an activity. It is something a person *does*. Traditional biblical texts that Protestant Bibles translate *repent* are translated by the words "do penance" in Catholic versions of Scripture.

The Reformation controversy centered on one aspect of penance, the aspect of *works of satisfaction*. In modern terms it works like this. A person comes to the privacy of the confessional and tells the priest his sins. The person prays the prayer of confession and awaits the priest's words of absolution. Then the priest prescribes a penance to perform. The penitent may be required to say so many "Hail Marys" or "Our Fathers" or other ritual prayers. At times more rigorous and demanding penalties are required. These are the works of satisfaction. They "satisfy" the demands of God and make it fitting or "congruous" for God to restore justification to the penitent.

During the Middle Ages the act of almsgiving was seen as a legitimate form of doing penance. The church was very careful to point out that salvation was not for sale. One cannot "purchase" forgiveness by giving money to the poor or to the church. Yet almsgiving motivated by a genuine spirit of repentance and love for God was a fitting work of satisfaction.

A serious problem with this erupted in the sixteenth century. Rome was involved in a massive building program with the construction of St. Peter's Basilica. The church authorized papal indulgences for sins for those who made contributions to the project out of sincere and godly motives. (An indulgence was remission of temporal or purgatorial punishment for sins committed.)

In Germany, William Tetzel, an unscrupulous representative of Rome, began to sell indulgences, particularly to uneducated peasants, as if these indulgences could be received without the proper attitude. In other words, for paying a fee a person could receive remission for sins. There was no need for genuine repentance nor for penitential acts of charity. The chief salesman, the monk Tetzel, provoked the wrath of Martin Luther for cheapening the system of penance. The famous Ninety-five Theses were posted in response to these abuses.

The indulgence controversy opened Pandora's box. The debate led to a full-scale issue of the whole question of justification. Ultimately Luther declared the doctrine of justification by faith alone. He attacked the sacrament of penance at the point of works of satisfaction.

Luther argued that the total satisfaction offered for our sins was performed by Christ. No person can add to that satisfaction. No human can supplement the merit of Jesus by any form of human merit, including the so-called "congruous merit" (*meritum de congruo*) that can be gained by works of satisfaction. Justifying grace is offered freely to all who genuinely confess their sins and embrace Christ by faith.

Luther considered other issues as "trifles" compared with the central issue of justification by faith alone. He called justification by faith alone "the article upon which the individual believer stands or falls."

As a result, most Protestant Christians no longer have a confessional. We almost never hear from human beings the audible words *Te Absolvo*.

Protestants are often rankled by the idea of a human priest saying, "I forgive you." In Rome's defense we must point out that by no means does the church intend to declare that a priest has the intrinsic right to forgive sins. In Rome's view the priest is carrying out the authority Jesus gave to His apostles when He said, "If you forgive the sins of any, they are forgiven them" (John 20:23). This is not far removed from what Protestant ministers do when they declare the "Assurance of Pardon" from the pulpit on Sunday morning.

The Burning Need for Assurance

Sadly, many Protestants do not feel an assurance of forgiveness for their sins. They are plagued by persistent guilt feelings. We live as if the Cross never happened. We harbor a lingering, nagging feeling that somehow the Atonement of Jesus is not enough to cover our sins. Grace is something other people need. We want to atone for our own sins. We think that we must somehow make up for our guilt.

I once spoke with a woman who said to me, "How can I receive forgiveness for my sins? I have prayed and prayed to God for forgiveness for my sins, but I still feel guilty."

The woman was seeking theological advice. She looked at me as if she expected me to come up with some secret, esoteric device to grant her full assurance of her forgiveness. I replied, "I think you need to pray for forgiveness one more time."

My answer not only disappointed her; it clearly annoyed her. She said, "Didn't you hear what I said? I've prayed repeatedly. What good will praying one more time do?"

I answered, "This time I want you to ask God to forgive you for your arrogance."

Now she was really angry. "Arrogance! What do you mean arrogance? I've humbled myself time and again in prayer. Why is that arrogance?"

I explained that God has declared that if we confess our sins to Him He will forgive us of our sins: "If we confess our sins, He is faithful and just to forgive us our sins and to cleanse us from all unrighteousness" (1 John 1:9).

Just as there is a crucial difference between guilt and guilt feelings, so there is a similar difference between forgiveness and feelings of forgiveness. Guilt is objective; guilt feelings are subjective. Forgiveness is objective; feelings of forgiveness are subjective.

If God declares a person forgiven, that person is truly, objectively, really and fully forgiven. Forgiveness is now a reality. If the warm feelings of peace of mind flow out of the reality of forgiveness, that is a sweet and wonderful bonus. But it is not the final test of forgiveness.

This is a two-edged sword. A person can manufacture feelings of forgiveness when they are not forgiven. I've heard numerous people tell me that God has given them "peace" about doing things God clearly forbids. I've heard people say that God gave them peace of mind to commit adultery. Such statements must certainly grieve the Spirit.

God gives forgiveness freely to the repentant. But He never grants license for sin. He is not the author of peace to the impenitent. That peace is a false peace, a lying peace.

I asked the woman to pray for forgiveness for her arrogance for this reason: God has promised to forgive our sins if we truly repent and turn to Him in confession. God's promises are faithful. It is arrogant for us to refuse to forgive anyone whom God forgives, including ourselves. Consider the words of Paul: "Who are you to judge another's servant? To his own master he stands or falls. Indeed, he shall be made to stand, for God is able to make him stand" (Rom. 14:4).

Here the apostle warns against judging other people whom Christ has received. If we are not permitted to judge others whom God has forgiven, how much less are we permitted to judge ourselves when God has forgiven us?

When God forgives a person, that person is forgiven whether we feel the forgiveness or not. The sensuous Christian lives by his feelings. The spiritual Christian lives by the Word of God. If God declares that I am forgiven, then it is sheer arrogance for me to refuse to forgive myself.

Perhaps the woman I was counseling did not feel forgiven because she doubted the truthfulness of God's promise. Perhaps it was something else. Perhaps she was reacting against grace. Again, grace is all right for other people, but she was too proud to accept it for herself. She wanted to *earn* her forgiveness. She did justification the old-fashioned way, the Smith-Barney method: she wanted to *earn* it.

Jesus told a short parable that is easy for us to understand with our minds but is difficult for us to get in our bloodstream:

> And which of you, having a servant plowing or tending sheep,
> will say to him when he has come in from the field, "Come
> at once and sit down to eat"? But will he not rather say to
> him, "Prepare something for my supper, and gird yourself
> and serve me till I have eaten and drunk, and afterward you
> will eat and drink"? Does he thank that servant because he
> did the things that were commanded him? I think not. So
> likewise you, when you have done all those things which you
> are commanded, say, "We are unprofitable servants. We have
> done what was our duty to do." (Luke 17:7–10)

We are unprofitable servants. If we did every single thing that God has commanded us to do, we would have nothing of which to boast. Perfect obedience to Him is our duty. We have no claim to extra merit.

The fact is, we have not done everything He has commanded us to do. So how can we possibly make it up? If we did everything we were commanded and were still unprofitable servants, how could we possibly be profitable in our shortcomings? We simply cannot. That is why grace is absolutely necessary for all of us.

We are debtors who cannot pay our debts. We are like the unjust steward who when he was called into account cried out within himself, "What shall I do? For my master is taking the stewardship away from me. I cannot dig; I am ashamed to beg" (Luke 16:3).

That is our dilemma. We cannot dig and we are ashamed to beg. But beg we must. That is all a debtor who cannot pay can do.

We live by grace. We walk by forgiveness. We rejoice in the certainty that when we confess our sins God promises to forgive them.

Forgiving and Forgetting

The Bible tells us that when God forgives us, He removes our sins from us as far as the east is from the west:

> He has not dealt with us according to our sins,
> Nor punished us according to our iniquities.

For as the heavens are high above the earth,
So great is His mercy toward them who fear Him.
As far as the east is from the west,
So far has He removed our transgressions from us.
(Ps. 103:10–12)

When God forgives us of our sins, He casts them into the Sea of Forgetfulness. Jeremiah declares the promise: "For I will forgive their iniquity, and their sin I will remember no more" (Jer. 31:34). What does the Bible mean when it says that God will no longer remember our sins? In what way does God forgive and forget? We must be careful to note that these expressions use human figures of speech as a manner of speaking. We must not jump to the conclusion that the Almighty, Omniscient, Immutable God suddenly has a lapse in His memory. God knows everything about my life. He is very much aware of every sin I have ever committed. When He blots out my transgression, it is not that He actually loses all knowledge of it. Rather He blots it out of the record book. He treats me as if I had not sinned. He covers my sin with the righteousness of Christ.

The forgetting of God is a relational forgetting. That is, He remembers it no more *against* me. When God forgives me of my sin, He doesn't hold it against me. He bears no grudges. He harbors no lingering hostility. My relationship with Him is totally and completely restored. He does for me what He promised in the book of Isaiah: " 'Come now, and let us reason together,' says the LORD: 'Though your sins are like scarlet, they shall be as white as snow; though they are red like crimson, they shall be as wool' " (Isa. 1:18).

Forgiving Other People

One of the most terrifying elements of the Lord's Prayer is the petition "Forgive us our debts, as we forgive our debtors" (Matt. 6:12). We tend to be far more ungenerous in forgiving others than God is in forgiving us. If God were to be as reluctant to forgive us as we are in forgiving those who sin against us, we would be in serious trouble.

As Christians we are forgiven people. We are likewise called to be forgiving people. The key to forgiving others is found in Jesus' teaching: "Take heed to yourselves. If your brother sins against you, rebuke him; and if he repents, forgive him. And if he sins against you seven times in a day, and seven times in a day returns to you, saying, 'I repent,' you shall forgive him. And the apostles said to the Lord, 'Increase our faith' " (Luke 17:3–5).

Much confusion exists about the Christian's responsibility to forgive others. Two major issues need clarification. They are: Whom are we required to forgive? What does forgiveness entail?

On the question of whom we must forgive, there is a widespread misunderstanding in Christian circles. Somehow, somewhere, the idea gained currency that Christians are under obligation to grant unqualified, unilateral forgiveness to anyone who sins against them. For example, if a person attacks my character unjustly, it is assumed that I must simply absorb the grievance and forgive that person immediately.

Where did such an idea originate? Perhaps a clue may be found in the example of Jesus as well as in some of His teaching. We see Jesus praying for the forgiveness of His executioners while He was on the cross. "Father, forgive them for they do not know what they do" (Luke 23:34). We hear Jesus teach in the Sermon on the Mount, "Blessed are the merciful: for they shall obtain mercy" (Matt. 5:7). Again He declares, "But I tell you not to resist an evil person. But whoever slaps you on your right cheek, turn the other to him also" (Matt. 5:39).

Jesus clearly sets forth an ethic of charity. We are called to be forbearing, patient, and long-suffering toward those who abuse us. Jesus commands us to be willing to go the second mile. A spirit of contentiousness, bitterness, argumentativeness, and belligerence has no place in the kingdom of God.

When Jesus tells us to "turn the other cheek," He is using a Jewish idiom that involves bearing insults. We notice in the text that Jesus said that if someone smites us on the *right* cheek we are to turn the other cheek. This is usually understood to mean that if someone hits us on one side of the face we should offer the other side as well. The saying seems to teach that we have no right to self-defense if we are physically attacked. We must be doormats to anyone who wants to beat up on us.

How far do we take this? Does the text imply that if someone kidnaps our daughter we should offer the kidnapper our son as well? I think not. Think about the words Jesus uses. He speaks of hitting on the *right cheek*. Suppose you are standing in front of someone, face to face, and that person wants to hit you on your right cheek. How can that be accomplished? It can be done one of two ways. Either the person must strike you with his left hand or the person must hit you with the back of his right hand. The vast majority of people are right-handed. A right-handed person does not normally attack with the left hand (unless they have a highly trained left hook).

In Jewish idiom, to be struck on the right cheek has reference to an insulting slap of the back of the right hand. In the Middle Ages it was the sign of a challenge to a duel. A person might take off his glove and hit you with the glove by a backhanded slap. It is the ancient idiom of the insult. In all probability Jesus' hearers understood Him to mean that if a person insults you, you are not to respond in kind. We are not to return evil for evil. The central focus is on peaceful restraint and nonviolent responses to verbal abuse. During His trial Jesus was mocked and slapped, and though He could have called on legions of angels to assist Him, He chose to bear the insults in silence. He blessed those who cursed Him and did good to them who hated Him. In a word, He showed love toward His enemies.

How Far to Forgive

Yet all of this does not nullify the fact that biblical law has manifold provision for the seeking of justice in the case of wrongful injury. Virtually every Christian church has some provision to deal with grievances within the church by the valid use of church courts. There are also provisions for the use of civil courts to settle serious disputes.

Our preliminary conclusion is this: If we are sinned against we *may* exercise unilateral forgiveness, but it is not an absolute obligation in every circumstance. Here we see the crucial distinction between *may* and *must*. We notice in Jesus' extended teaching on forgiveness in Luke 17 that He says, "If your brother sins against you, rebuke him: and if he repents, forgive him." Here the one who sins is a brother. It is possible that this mandate does not apply to everyone who sins against us. We are to treat all people as *neighbors*, but not everyone is a *brother*. A brother has specific reference to a fellow Christian.

At least in the case of being sinned against by a fellow Christian we have specific instructions. The first is to *rebuke* the brother. We are not thereby commanded to bear all sins in silence. Jesus gives clear expression to rebuke or admonish the guilty party. What follows is of central importance. Jesus says, "And if he repents, forgive him." Here we see a conditional clause, "if he repents." Presumably if the brother does not repent we are under no obligation to grant unilateral forgiveness. Just as God requires repentance from us before He grants forgiveness, we may exact the same requirement.

Of course we *may* choose to forgive someone who does not repent, but that is not the same thing as saying that we *must* forgive the impenitent person. However, if the condition of repentance is met, then we are under obligation to grant forgiveness. If the brother repents then we *must* forgive him. Refusal to forgive a repentant person is itself a sin that requires forgiveness.

When I was in seminary I was a student minister in a small church. I insulted the daughter of a woman who was a pillar of the church. The daughter was deeply offended. I went to her and apologized profusely. She refused to forgive me. I went two more times and apologized literally in tears. Still she refused to forgive me.

It came time for my monthly meeting with the minister who was appointed moderator of our session. He was my pastoral supervisor. He was an eighty-five-year-old retired missionary who had spent fifty years in the interior of China, five years of that in a communist prison camp. He was a man of extraordinary godliness. I went to him with deep embarrassment for the mess I had made of my first pastoral experience. I told him what I had done. He listened carefully and then replied calmly, "Young man, you have made two serious mistakes. The first is obvious. You should not have insulted the daughter. The second mistake is this: You should not have apologized three times. After the first apology, the ball was in her court. If she refused to forgive you, she is heaping coals of fire upon her own head."

There was wisdom in the old saint's words. If we sin against a person, we must repent, and then it is over for us. Likewise, if our brother repents of a sin against us, we must forgive. But that leads us to the next important consideration. What does forgiveness involve?

We have already seen that when God forgives us He no longer holds our sin against us. He forgets it insofar as He remembers it no more against us. This, however, does not preclude restitution. Restitution is not the same thing as works of satisfaction in the Roman Catholic sacrament of penance. Restitution means paying what we owe.

For example, if I steal money from my employer and then repent of my theft, it is not enough for me simply to confess my sin and apologize. I must also return the money and pay whatever penalties are involved. Zacchaeus understood this principle of restitution when he declared to Jesus: "Look, Lord, I give half of my goods to the poor; and if I have taken anything from anyone by false accusation, I restore fourfold" (Luke 19:8).

When I repent I must still pay what I owe. It means being willing to accept the consequences of my actions and attending penalties. We distinguish between earthly or temporal guilt and heavenly or eternal guilt. If I break the earthly law and ask God to forgive me, I may receive His eternal pardon but still face the penalties of my temporal guilt.

The old Hollywood gangster movies often portrayed execution scenes in which a convict walked the "last mile" to the gallows or the electric chair in the company of a priest who was intoning prayers for forgiveness. The image of the noose side by side with the Bible seemed radically inconsistent.

Yet the Bible calls for real penalties to be enacted against lawbreakers, even against penitent, confessing lawbreakers. The civil magistrate may temper justice with mercy, but he is not required by God to waive all penalties in the case of a penitent criminal. The repentant person pleases God with his contriteness, but society has a right to demand that justice be done.

Forgiveness and Repeated Sins

How does forgiveness apply to situations where the marriage vows have been broken? Let us suppose that a man commits adultery and his sin is discovered. He confesses his guilt, indicates deep shame and remorse, and asks his wife to forgive him. What is the wife's moral duty in such a circumstance?

The question has both a simple answer and a complex one. First the simple answer. Jesus requires us to forgive those who sin against us who repent of their sin. Therefore, the wife *must* forgive her penitent husband.

The complex question is this: What does such forgiveness entail? A related question is this: May the wife forgive her husband and still divorce him?

On the surface it may seem absurd to even ask such a question. It would seem that forgiveness would exclude any thought of divorce. But it is not that simple. There are basically three approaches taken to the question of divorce in the case of the penitent adulterer.

Approach 1: There are many Christians who are persuaded that divorce is never justifiable on any grounds whatsoever. For this group the solution is easy. The wife may not divorce her husband even if he is not repentant.

Approach 2: This approach allows for divorce on the grounds of adultery. It takes the position that if the man is unrepentant the wife may justly divorce him. But if the man repents, then it is the duty of the wife to forgive him and stay married to him.

Approach 3: This view also recognizes the right of divorce in the case of adultery. It does not demand divorce in the case of adultery but permits it. Here the view is that even if the husband repents, the wife may justly exercise her right of divorce. She must forgive her husband and must receive him as a brother in Christ. But she is not required to stay married to him. The forfeiture of marital rights are seen as part of the civil penalties that may be invoked in the crime.

Although such issues are exceedingly difficult to resolve, one thing is clear: Forgiveness does not necessarily mean that no penalties or restitution follow. By forgiveness is meant a maintaining of a personal relationship without estrangement. It also means that the sin is not rehashed in the personal relationship.

In Luke 17 Jesus says that if your brother trespasses against you seven times in a day and repents seven times in a day—"You shall forgive him."

Jesus does not allow for "three strikes and you're out." If my brother sins against me, repents, is forgiven, and then does exactly the same thing, I may not say to him, "That's two!"

I may not keep a scorecard of offenses. If I forgive the first transgression and put it aside by forgiving my brother, I am promising to hold it against him no longer. If he sins again I must say, "That's one!" because the first sin has no bearing on the second.

Now that is a tall order. It is particularly in the realm of repeated sins that we find the greatest difficulty in being merciful. We have a saying—"Fool me once, shame on you. Fool me twice, shame on me."

To forgive the same offense twice is exceedingly difficult. To forgive seven times pushes our ability to be gracious to the extreme. It is no wonder that the disciples responded to Jesus' command by saying, "Increase our faith" (Luke 17:5).

Forgiveness for Former Sins

Can a Christian be forgiven for sins committed before conversion? The obvious answer is yes. If the answer were no, we would still be under the curse of God's judgment. But the Atonement of Christ is made for all of our sins.

The answer to the next question will not find such widespread agreement. Is a Christian responsible for sins committed prior to conversion? Again, on the surface it would appear that the obvious answer to the question is yes. The whole principle of restitution would apply.

Those who answer no usually do so in a particular context based on a particular argument. Again, the context is marriage and divorce. Suppose a man divorces his wife illegitimately, that is, without biblical grounds. Five years later he is converted to Christ. He falls in love with a Christian woman and wants to marry her. How does the church respond? Is the man required to seek reconciliation with his former wife or may he move freely into a new marriage?

Those who argue that the man is free to move into a new marriage without any obligation to his former wife often argue this point on the grounds that the man is a "new creature" in Christ. Being born anew, the man has no responsibility for what he did before conversion because the man was not the same man then.

This is a woeful distortion of biblical principle. Though indeed I am a new creation in Christ, it is "I," R. C. Sproul, who is a new creation. R. C. Sproul may be born again, but there is a personal continuity between the new R. C. Sproul and the old R. C. Sproul. The new R. C. Sproul is still required to pay the old R. C. Sproul's debts.

Imagine this scenario. At four o'clock in the afternoon, Mr. Smith robs his employer of ten thousand dollars. At five o'clock in the afternoon Mr. Smith is converted to Christ. May he now keep the money? On the contrary. Far from conversion eliminating a person's obligations, it actually increases them. A reborn man should be all the more scrupulous in his willingness to pay his debts and make full restitution wherever possible.

Full restitution is an integral part of full repentance. It is the mark of true repentance. True repentance is necessary for true forgiveness. If our goal is full and complete forgiveness, we must be willing to offer full and complete repentance. If our goal is to please God, we must repent. We may see the price tag as high. In fact, here we find the real meaning of "cheap grace." The value of full forgiveness is infinite. Compared to the benefits we receive in full forgiveness, the price tag of repentance is outrageously cheap. There is no greater bargain to be found in this world than the bargain of forgiving grace.

The forgiving God we serve is pleased when we gratefully accept His forgiveness. He is also pleased when we are willing to act as adults and make amends for the sins we have committed against others. If we read the New Testament correctly, it seems the kingdom of God is composed of responsible and forgiven people.

TEN

The Carnal Christian

We have seen that guilt and fear are dreadful burdens to carry through life. The sweetness of the gospel is found in these words: "Behold, this has touched your lips; your iniquity is taken away, and your sin purged" (Isa. 6:7). The hot coal touching the stricken Isaiah's lips symbolized the power of the forgiving God to raise up a guilt-ridden soul.

When God removes our iniquity, when He takes away our iniquity from us, we experience a liberation unlike anything the world can match. No windfall profit, no military victory, no election results, no romance or job promotion can liberate the spirit of man as much as one sentence from God: "Your sins are forgiven."

The apostle Paul once used a vivid and almost crude word picture to describe the awful burden of guilt: "O wretched man that I am! Who will deliver me from this body of death?" (Rom. 7:24).

I say that this word picture borders upon crudeness because of the source of the phrase "body of death." There was a tradition in many ancient cultures whereby a person guilty of cold-blooded murder was forced to go about chained to the body of his victim. Imagine being bound to a decaying corpse. Having to drag a dead body around while it underwent the process of putrefaction was enough to drive men mad.

It is a fitting analogy of the Christian life. Our old nature is crucified with Christ. The old man is under a death sentence. We are to reckon it already dead in Christ. The Christian is a new creation, made alive by the Holy Spirit.

But herein is our dilemma. The old man may be declared dead, but we are not altogether free of him. We still carry around that old nature of wretchedness with us. It is as though that corpse does not know that it has died.

I once explained the dilemma like this: Our old nature is like a chicken with its head cut off. It runs wildly around the barnyard, flapping its wings and squawking all over the place. My image worked well until a farmer politely reminded me that once a chicken's head is cut off it no longer has the capacity to squawk!

Chickens without heads may not squawk, but our old nature squawks like mad. It creates a ruckus like no dead thing should be able to do. In a word, the old man continues to incite us to sin. That is why the Christian life requires daily trips to the throne of grace for a fresh and vital experience of forgiveness.

It is a source of irritation for me to hear preachers proclaim, "Come to Jesus, and all your problems will be over!" It is a zealous proclamation of the gospel that simply is not true. In one sense life doesn't begin to get complicated until one becomes a Christian. When we are born of the Spirit, we are born anew into a fierce struggle between the old man and the new man. It is the struggle a person faces when they have a renewed and sensitized conscience.

The old life was one of consistent disobedience. It is the life Paul described to the Ephesians:

> And you He made alive, who were dead in trespasses and
> sins, in which you once walked according to the course
> of this world, according to the prince of the power of the
> air, the spirit who now works in the sons of disobedience,
> among whom also we all once conducted ourselves in the
> lusts of our flesh, fulfilling the desires of the flesh and of
> the mind, and were by nature children of wrath, just as the
> others. (Eph. 2:1–3)

This passage shows the consistent pattern of disobedience that characterizes the unregenerate life. Life has one course, the course of this world. It has one master, Satan, the prince of the power of the air. Augustine once declared that a man is like a horse. The horse is either ridden by Satan or by the Spirit of God. The image is helpful except for one thing. In the Christian life we are not as consistent as we were when we were ridden by Satan alone. To be sure, Satan has been thrown off our backs and the Spirit is now in the saddle. But Satan still does everything in his power to clutch at the reins. The horse still veers from side to side. He rears up and bucks, trying to throw the new master from the saddle. We are still whinnying in rebellion, seeking to have our noses stroked by our old master.

Paul put it this way:

> For we know that the law is spiritual, but I am carnal, sold
> under sin. For what I am doing, I do not understand. For
> what I will to do, that I do not practice; but what I hate, that

I do. If, then, I do what I will not to do, I agree with the law
that it is good. But now, it is no longer I who do it, but sin
that dwells in me. For I know that in me (that is, in my flesh)
nothing good dwells; for to will is present with me, but how
to perform what is good I do not find. For the good that I
will to do, I do not do; but the evil I will not to do, that I
practice. (Rom. 7:14–19)

The Antinomian View

Romans 7 is the subject of much controversy. The first concerns the concept
of the so-called carnal Christian. There is a widespread notion within evangelical Christianity that there are two distinctive types of Christians. There is the
carnal Christian and the spiritual Christian. The carnal Christian is a believer
who does not have Christ on the throne of his life and thereby lives a pattern
of constant disobedience. Then there is the "Spirit-filled" Christian whose life
is characterized by a life of obedience and spiritual devotion. Here Christ reigns
on the throne of the Christian life.

This distinction is fraught with peril. The peril has two faces, both of which
are ugly distortions of the truth. The first distortion is that of the ancient heresy
of antinomianism. Antinomianism means literally "anti-lawism." The song of
the antinomian is this: "Free from the law, O blessed condition; I can sin all I
want and still have remission!" This distortion rests upon a false view of grace
and forgiveness. It includes the idea that a person can receive Christ as Savior
but not as Lord. It assumes a faith without obedience, a faith with no fruit of
good works. This is precisely the kind of "dead faith" of which James writes, a
faith that is no faith, a faith that can never please God.

Here the carnal Christian is one who is said to believe in Christ but lives
a life of consistent carnality, giving no evidence of the fruit of the Spirit. This
represents a fatal contradiction in terms. Such a person may not be called a
carnal Christian. He must be considered a carnal non-Christian. If a person
manifests a life of pure and consistent carnality, he is no Christian. He has not
the Spirit of Christ living in him. It is a flat impossibility to be born of the Spirit
and have no change in one's life. A Christian with no fruit is simply not a Christian. Antinomianism is the spirit of lawlessness that reigns in the children of
disobedience. The "faith" of a carnal Christian is no faith. It cannot justify the
ungodly. It cannot be pleasing to God.

We remember that justification by faith alone is not by a faith that is alone.
The central affirmation of all Protestantism is that we are justified by faith and
not by works. But the instant that true justifying faith is present in the life of

the believer, the person begins to change. That change will be evidenced in a life that moves to obedience. Good works necessarily flow out of true faith. The works do not justify us. It is the righteousness of Christ that justifies us. But if the works do not follow, it is proof positive that we do not have genuine faith and are therefore still unjustified people.

In the antinomian sense there is no such thing as a carnal Christian. The concept is as perilous as it is self-contradictory. The peril is this: People begin to think that all that is required to be saved is a *profession* of faith. But the Bible warns us that people can honor Christ with their lips while their hearts are far from Him. They can say they have faith without having what they claim to have: "What does it profit, my brethren, if someone says he has faith but does not have works? Can faith save him?" (James 2:14).

James answers his own question by declaring emphatically that such a faith is dead and can save no one.

We conclude then that although we are required to profess our faith, the mere profession of faith is not enough to save us. We must possess what we profess. It is the *possession* of saving faith that justifies us, not the mere *profession* of it.

The Perfectionist View

The second ancient heresy of the distinction between two types of Christians, carnal and Spirit-filled, is the heresy of perfectionism. Here the error is in the opposite direction from antinomianism. Perfectionism teaches that there is a class of Christians who achieve moral perfection in this life. To be sure, credit is given to the Holy Spirit as the agent who brings total victory over sin to the Christian. But there is a kind of elitism in perfectionism, a feeling that those who have achieved perfection are somehow greater than other Christians. The "perfect" ones do not—officially—take credit for their state, but smugness and pride have a way of creeping in.

The peril of perfectionism is that it seriously distorts the human mind. Imagine the contortions through which we must put ourselves to delude us into thinking that we have in fact achieved a state of sinlessness.

Inevitably the error of perfectionism breeds one, or usually two, deadly delusions. To convince ourselves that we have achieved sinlessness, we must either suffer from a radical overestimation of our moral performance or we must seriously underestimate the requirements of God's law. The irony of perfectionism is this: Though it seeks to distance itself from antinomianism, it relentlessly and inevitably comes full circle to the same error.

To believe that we are sinless, we must annul the standards of God's Law. We must reduce the level of divine righteousness to the level of our own performance. We must lie to ourselves both about the Law of God and about our own obedience. To do that requires that we quench the Spirit when He seeks to convict us of sin. Persons who do that are not so much Spirit-filled as they are Spirit-quenchers.

One of the true marks of our ongoing sanctification is the growing awareness of how far short we fall of reaching perfection. Perfectionism is really antiperfectionism in disguise. If we think we are becoming perfect, then we are far from becoming perfect.

I once encountered a young man who had been a Christian for about a year. He boldly declared to me that he had received the "second blessing" and was now enjoying a life of victory, a life of sinless perfection. I immediately turned his attention to Paul's teaching on Romans 7. Romans 7 is the biblical death blow to every doctrine of perfectionism. My young friend quickly replied with the classic agreement of the perfectionist heresy, namely, that in Romans 7 Paul is describing his former unconverted state.

I explained to the young man that it is exegetically impossible to dismiss Romans 7 as the expression of Paul's former life. We examined the passage closely and the man finally agreed that indeed Paul was writing in the present tense. His next response was, "Well, maybe Paul was speaking of his present experience, but he just hadn't received the second blessing yet."

I had a difficult time concealing my astonishment at this spiritual arrogance. I asked him pointedly, "You mean that you, at age nineteen, after one year of Christian faith, have achieved a higher level of obedience to God than the apostle Paul enjoyed when he was writing the Epistle to the Romans?"

To my everlasting shock the young man replied without flinching, "Yes!" Such is the extent to which persons will delude themselves into thinking that they have achieved sinlessness.

I spoke once with a woman who claimed the same "second blessing" of perfectionism who qualified her claim a bit. She said that she was fully sanctified into holiness so that she never committed any willful sins. But she acknowledged that occasionally she still committed sins, though never willfully. Her present sins were unwillful.

What in the world is an unwillful sin? All sin involves the exercise of the will. If an action happens apart from the will it is not a moral action. The involuntary beating of my heart is not a moral action. All sin is willful. Indeed, the corrupt inclination of the will is of the very essence of sin. There is no sin without the willing of sin. The woman was excusing her own sin by denying that she had willed to commit the sin. The sin just sort of "happened." It was the oldest self-justification known to man: "I didn't mean to do it!"

In one strand of the Wesleyan tradition there is another type of qualified perfectionism. Here the achievement of perfection is limited to a perfected *love*. We may continue to struggle with certain moral weaknesses, but at least we can receive the blessing of a perfected love. But think on this a moment. If we received the blessing of a love that was absolutely perfect, how then would we ever commit any kind of sin? If I ever loved God perfectly, I would will only obedience to Him. How could a creature who loved God perfectly ever sin against Him at all?

Someone might answer: "We could still sin against Him in ignorance." But the perfect love with which we are called to love God is a perfect love of our minds as well as our hearts. If we perfectly loved God with all of our minds, from whence could this ignorance flow? One who loves God *perfectly* with the mind is perfectly diligent in studying and mastering the Word of God. The perfectly loving mind perceives correctly the light into our paths. A perfectly loving mind doesn't make errors in understanding Scripture.

But could we not still make mistakes because our minds are less than perfect? I ask why our minds are less than perfect. It is not because we lack brains or the faculty of thinking. Our thinking is clouded because our hearts are clouded. Take away the cloud from our hearts and our minds are illumined by the clear light of God.

A perfect love would yield perfect obedience. The only perfected love this world has ever seen was the love of Christ, who exhibited perfect obedience. Jesus loved the Father perfectly. He sinned not at all, either willfully or in ignorance.

The Biblical View

In Romans 7:14, Paul declares: "I am carnal, sold under sin." Does this mean that Paul was a carnal Christian? Did Paul receive Christ as Savior and not as Lord? To ask such foolish questions is to answer them. The world has never seen a more Spirit-filled Christian than the apostle Paul. Yet he said, "I am carnal."

When Paul declares that he is carnal, he is expressing the ongoing struggle in the Christian life between the old man and the new man, the warfare that goes on between the flesh and the Spirit. He summarizes his struggle with these words:

> For I delight in the law of God according to the inward
> man. But I see another law in my members, warring against
> the law of my mind, and bringing me into captivity to the
> law of sin which is in my members. O wretched man that I
> am! Who will deliver me from this body of death? I thank

God—through Jesus Christ our Lord! So then, with the mind
I myself serve the law of God, but with the flesh the law of
sin. (Rom. 7:22–25)

We notice that Paul ends this expression of personal struggle with doxology. He utters praise and thanksgiving to God through Christ for the deliverance that we have in the inward man.

In the popular booklet published by Campus Crusade for Christ called "The Holy Spirit Booklet" (or, affectionately, the "Bird Book" because of the image of the dove that adorns its cover), mention is made of distinction between the carnal Christian and the Spirit-filled Christian. On the surface it appears as if Dr. Bill Bright is teaching an absolute distinction between two kinds of Christians. I am confident, however, that is not the intention of the booklet or of its author. Rather, in a pastoral way, Dr. Bright is discussing the classical struggle here between the flesh and the Spirit that every genuine Christian faces. The point of the booklet is to call us to exercise the power of the Holy Spirit in our lives in order to keep the evil tendencies of the old man in check. The old man is to be put to death daily. Victory comes in the Christian life by keeping our eyes upon the Spirit who is to reign over our possessions. Here the struggle is transcended as we look to Christ, the Author and Finisher of our faith.

All Christians are "carnal" insofar as we continue to struggle with the old nature of flesh. But no true Christian is carnal in the sense that the flesh totally dominates his life. If the carnal aspect were in total dominion, we would know that we were still unregenerate. We are called to live a Spirit-filled life in order to be victorious over the old man. It is precisely because of the residual power of sin that we need the filling of the Holy Spirit. We please God by asking for this holy filling. He is pleased with us—not when we express our joy at our "perfect" state—but when we express our need of Him and our dissatisfaction with the "body of death" that, thanks be to Him, is steadily growing less important in the Christian's life.

ELEVEN

The Sin of Pride

Karl Barth once declared that fallen man has three primary or basic sins from which all other sins proceed. These three sins include pride (*hubris*), slothfulness, and dishonesty. Whether Barth is correct in his evaluation is arguable, but there is no doubt that this triad of vices is indeed formidable. They raise their ugly heads in a multitude of ways, bringing to ruin our efforts to achieve true godliness.

In this chapter we will consider the first of the three, pride. Perhaps the classic biblical quotation on pride is this oft-quoted section from Proverbs:

> Pride goes before destruction,
> And a haughty spirit before a fall.
> Better to be of a humble spirit with the lowly,
> Than to divide the spoil with the proud. (Prov. 16:18, 19)

Pride goes before destruction. Destruction is a description of collapse. People can be moving forward, building empires or reputations, riding high. It all collapses when pride undermines a sound foundation. The plaintive cry of the fallen is "I am ruined." It is a dreadful cry, a mournful whimper of those who make a wreck of their lives.

One morning I had a humorous experience with pride. At the break of dawn my wife and I went to the supermarket. As we pulled into the parking lot, Vesta said to me, "I hope you don't expect me to get out of the car. I have some pride, you know." Vesta was reluctant to leave the car because of her pre-dawn appearance. She was wearing sweatpants, a man's large sweatshirt, and no makeup. She had not yet combed her hair. "I have some pride, you know," she said. I looked at her and with a mischievous grin said, "I have one question." "What's that?" she asked. Looking at her attire, I said, "Why?"

She was ready to hit me over the head with a book. She proved Luther's famous quote he once made concerning his beloved wife, Katy Von Bora: "If God wanted me to have a meek woman, He'd have to hew one out of stone!"

But the kind of pride Vesta was declaring was not the pride of which the Bible speaks. There is nothing evil in "taking pride in your work" or in wanting to "look your best." These matters are simple concerns of human dignity. There is no sin in wanting to do a quality job. The striving after excellence is a virtue, not a vice. To feel good about one's work is to achieve the sense of satisfaction of a job well done. God Himself looked at the work of His own hands and said, "That's good." Here the deity was not puffed up in arrogance on the way to His own divine destruction.

Proverbs links pride with a haughty spirit, a spirit of insufferable arrogance. The arrogant have a cocky stance about them. We all recognize it when we see it. We remember the warning from Scripture about those things that are repugnant to God:

> These six things the LORD hates,
> Yes, seven are an abomination to Him:
> A proud look. . . . (Prov. 6:16, 17)

The destructive pride born of arrogance is evident in the most destructive episode in human history. This event is not referred to simply as "a" fall but is described as "the" Fall, the fall of the entire human race.

In the Garden of Eden the first sin was a sin of pride. The temptation of the serpent came with these words: "You will be like God" (Gen. 3:5). It is one thing to strive for excellence. It is another to seek equal status with God.

The lust for power and dominance among men knows no limits. We are vulnerable to the temptation to achieve status above all men. We want to be able to declare our opinions without the need to defend them. "Because I say so" is an argument that ultimately is valid only for God.

The temptation to be like God is greater than we think. We resist being subject to law. We squirm when we are placed under too much authority. We love to be free—free of restraints, free of accountability.

The Quest for Autonomy

Freedom is indeed a precious commodity. But our freedom has limits. The fact is we are under restraints and we are accountable. We are ultimately answerable to God. We are simply not permitted to do everything we want to do.

Recently I was riding in a car with a friend. We found ourselves traveling the wrong direction on a city street. A sign at the intersection read, "No U-Turn." My friend promptly made a U-turn and proceeded in the other direction. When I voiced a protest at this lawless action he said to me, "R. C., you can't be intimidated by a metal sign."

This was the expression of a "scofflaw." I thought at once of the biblical mandate to obey the civil magistrates. Certainly there are times when civil laws seem to reflect bureaucratic incompetence more than justice, but we are still called to avoid the complex of lawlessness. My obedience to law is not rendered to a metal sign. It is to be offered to Christ as an indication of my willingness to be in subjection to the authorities He establishes.

Obviously there are times when Christians not only may but must disobey the civil authorities, but such civil disobedience requires a just and necessary reason. We may not disobey the law willy-nilly simply because the law inconveniences us. To do so is to set ourselves above the law, which is a symptom of destructive pride.

Our quest to be like God is a quest to be above law. It is the quest for autonomy. Autonomy means literally "self-law." A person who seeks to be utterly autonomous is a person who seeks to be a law unto himself. He is answerable to no one.

We must be careful here. To avoid autonomy does not mean that we seek to be under tyranny. There are authority structures set down in Scripture that define appropriate lines of accountability. Children are to submit to their parents, employees to employers, the sheep to their shepherd, students to their teachers, and so on. We all are unavoidably cast into some type of human relationships in which we must either exercise authority or submit to it.

We must be wary of tyrants in disguise who seek to place us under authority where God has left us free. It is not arrogant for parents to refuse to submit to the authority of their children or for teachers to refuse to submit to their students. That is not being "accountable"; it is being manipulated.

I am fearful of people who are forever talking about being "accountable." The concept can be an insidious device of manipulation, a favorite tool of control managers who want to extend their own authority beyond valid limits.

I once talked to a man who owned his own business. He remarked, "I hold my board meetings in the shower." What he meant was this: As president and owner of his company, he was at the apex of authority in the organization. He was the boss. The buck stopped with him. This did not mean that he was a man without accountability. He was accountable to his bank. He was accountable to the law of his community and state. He was accountable to his elders and pastor in his church. He was accountable ultimately to God. But he was not under the authority of his secretary. She was under his authority, at the office.

It is important for the Christian to know precisely what authority he is under and then to be subject to that authority with a willing spirit. Part of my vows of ordination to the ministry require that I take a solemn oath before God to be in subjection to the authority of my church. We acknowledge that the church cannot bind my conscience. Only God can bind my conscience. If I have a conscientious objection to the rule of my church in which I face the dilemma of obeying the church or obeying God, then I must obey God. If my disobedience to the church is of such magnitude as to disturb the peace and unity of the church, then it is my duty to withdraw from that body in peace.

The same applies to working relationships. I am to be in subjection to my authorities unless I am constrained by conscience to disobey. If such disobedience is intolerable to my employer, then I must seek work elsewhere.

When we find ourselves in such tension, we must be careful to search our hearts and make sure our objection is really motivated by a godly conscience. It is easy to camouflage a prideful resistance with a spiritual cloak of hypocrisy.

The Quest for Status

There is no occasion more painful to our pride than when we are treated beneath our dignity. We work to achieve certain levels of human respect. We want to be treated with a level of dignity commensurate with our status. Status seeking seems to be an integral dimension of American life. But it is by no means limited to America. It is a human phenomenon. The chief of a primitive tribe of natives is as jealous to guard the extra feathers in his bonnet as the manager is to guard his key to the executive washroom.

When I enrolled in the Free University of Amsterdam, I was given an instruction booklet on the proper protocol for formal titles of my professors. If the professor was from an upper-class family, he was to be addressed as "very well-born." If he had a graduate degree, he was "very well-learned." If he was ordained, he was "highly worthy." The string of titles was at best cumbersome. Two lines of print were necessary to address an envelope to some of these titled men. Woe to the student who failed to use the proper title.

I thought this system of titles was one of the silliest things I had ever encountered. It came down to status of cars on the highway. Volkswagens were expected to yield the right of way to Mercedes. I once witnessed a truck pull up beside a bicyclist at a stoplight. The truck slowly nudged over toward the bicycle until the driver intentionally nudged the bike over to the ground because the cyclist would not yield the right of way to the truck.

This obsession with status is, alas, contagious. After I lived in this culture for a time, I received a letter in the mail addressed to De Heer Sproul. I was miffed. "De Heer!" I was worthy of far more titles than that! I felt like I was being addressed as "occupant." Then it suddenly dawned on me that I was getting caught up in the status game.

I would like to report that my flirtation with status seeking ended in Amsterdam. But it didn't. Just recently I was in a shopping mall with my son. We stopped to browse in a jewelry store. I found myself looking enviously at a display of Rolex watches. I said to my son, "I sure would like to have a Rolex watch."

My son registered shock. "Gee, Dad," he said, "I can understand wanting to spend money on things that could bring some comfort to your life, but why would you want to buy something just for status?"

I was stung by his words. I was ready to launch into a speech about aesthetics. I wanted to say, "It's just a matter of beauty. I like beautiful things." The speech would have been a half-truth. I do like beautiful things. I love art. But I knew in my heart of hearts that the Rolex did not fit that category for me. My son was right. I was taken with the name "Rolex" and what it represents. It was a matter of status, and I was not too "proud" of myself for the realization.

The great hymn of *kenosis* (self-emptying) in Philippians 2 speaks to this issue. Hear the words of the apostle Paul: "Let nothing be done through selfish ambition or conceit, but in lowliness of mind let each esteem others better than himself. Let each of you look out not only for his own interests, but also for the interests of others" (Phil. 2:3, 4).

This introduction to the hymn is a hard saying. We are preoccupied with the issue of self-esteem. Yet here we are called to esteem others better than ourselves. This is precisely the opposite of our normal patterns. We usually want to think of ourselves as better than others. We want other people to esteem us as better than themselves.

This is part of the primordial temptation to be as gods. In the film *Hoosiers*, actor Gene Hackman, playing the role of a new coach in a small Indiana town, responds to the charge that too much importance is being given to basketball in the school. His antagonist complains that basketball players are being treated as gods. Hackman replies, "Don't you understand that men would kill to be treated like God for just a few minutes?"

That is self-esteem run amok. It is self-esteem tottering on the brink of destruction. It is the opposite of the lowliness of mind to which we are called.

True Humility

Such a high calling to humility might easily be dismissed as an idealistic abstract ethic with no real example in concrete life. But Paul doesn't leave it in an abstract realm. He moves quickly to the hymn that celebrates the supreme example of lowliness of mind as it was displayed in the life of Christ:

> Let this mind be in you which was also in Christ Jesus, who,
> being in the form of God, did not consider it robbery to
> be equal with God, but made Himself of no reputation,
> taking the form of a servant, and coming in the likeness of
> men. And being found in appearance as a man, He humbled
> Himself and became obedient to the point of death, even
> the death of the cross. Therefore God also has highly exalted
> Him and given Him the name which is above every name.
> (Phil. 2:5–9)

We are called to share the mind of Christ. He emptied Himself in the Incarnation. He did not empty Himself of His deity or any of His divine attributes. He emptied Himself of His *status*. He set aside His prerogatives as God. He was willing to be treated beneath the level of His dignity. This example of the man with the highest dignity ever possessed by a human shames every other human who sets pride above obedience.

We remember King Saul. Saul was selected by God to be the first king of Israel. The king of Israel was not to be given autonomous authority. He was subject to the divine King's law. No earthly monarch could supplant the ultimate ruler of the nation, Yahweh. Yahweh was the Jews' God and King.

Saul got off to a good beginning, but soon he grew puffed up with his own importance. He took to himself the prerogatives of the priest and supplanted the role of Samuel (1 Sam. 13:9). He grew more selfish and arrogant. His jealousy reached a peak when the people began to praise the exploits of the young David with the song: "Saul has slain his thousands, and David his ten thousands" (1 Sam. 18:7). What follows is a history of Saul's pathetic dementia.

Saul's life ended in tragedy. After being severely wounded in battle with the Philistines, Saul took his own life by falling upon his sword. His enemies cut off his head and hung his body on a wall as a public spectacle.

David lamented the death of Saul and instructed the children of Judah to learn the Song of the Bow:

> The beauty of Israel is slain on your high places!
> How the mighty have fallen!
> Tell it not in Gath.
> Proclaim it not in the streets of Ashkelon. (2 Sam. 1:19, 20)

Throughout the song the mournful refrain is repeated: "How the mighty have fallen."

The life of Saul is a clear example of the Proverb: Pride goes before destruction and a haughty spirit before a fall. Mighty power begets mighty pride. Mighty pride begets a mighty fall.

The lure of status is powerful. It looms as a dreadful obstacle to Christian growth. We are all so vulnerable to it. No one wants to live like Rodney Dangerfield. We all crave the respect of others. Sigmund Freud once told the story of a schoolboy who was expelled from school for misbehavior. He stood outside the classroom and threw pebbles against the windows. Finally the principal went outside and confronted the boy: "Why are you throwing pebbles against the windows?" he asked. The boy replied, "I just wanted everyone to know that I'm still here."

We all carry pebbles in our pockets. We want to save "face." We want to keep our self-esteem intact. We fear humiliation. Our pride is a powerful force.

During the Cuban missile crisis of the early 1960s, President Kennedy demanded the removal of Russian military rockets from Cuba. The United States dispatched vessels to Cuba. At the same time Nikita Khrushchev ordered the Soviet fleet toward Cuba.

The world held its breath. Walter Cronkite gave hourly bulletins on the progress of the Soviet fleet. The military powers seemed on a headlong course toward Armageddon. At the last moment Russia blinked. The Soviet ships veered off and returned home. It was a great triumph for Kennedy. It was a total disgrace for Khrushchev, ultimately leading to his fall from power.

Then what happened? Kennedy had demanded on-site inspections in Cuba. Khrushchev refused, and Kennedy withdrew his demand. When the press asked President Kennedy why he had backed down on the demand he said, "We have won the dispute. It was important to give the Soviet premier a graceful exit."

Kennedy's diplomacy was directed toward preserving some of Khrushchev's pride. He did not want to back the premier into a corner where he had no dignity left. I shudder to think what could have happened had Kennedy been less sensitive. The pride issue in that confrontation might have led to the very destruction of the world.

What place does pride have in the Christian life? None. In a fallen world, premiers and presidents must play their games of face-saving and exhibition of status. We know that this is the way the world works. But we hark back to the hymn in Philippians 2, where Paul exalts the humility of Christ while telling the Philippian Christians to imitate their Lord. Obedience, humility, the steady withering of pride and arrogance—these things appear foolish in a world that values status and esteem. But we have it on good authority that pleasing the Ruler of the universe means holding to values different from the world's. He certainly gave us the supreme example of what it means to live humbly. He did not just teach us to shun pride—He showed us how.

TWELVE

⟣⟨⟢

The Sin of Slothfulness

God is a God of work. The Bible's first description of God gives us a glimpse of God in the act of creation. He is the original and supreme producer. He is the fountainhead of all productivity.

Because the curse of the fall of man stresses unpleasant aspects of work, many have jumped to the conclusion that work itself is part of man's curse. But we see that before sin entered the world man and woman were given a task to perform by their Creator.

As soon as God created man, He planted a garden eastward in Eden. God made the trees grow there in abundance. Then God gave man the responsibility to take care of the garden: "Then the LORD God took the man and put him in the garden of Eden to tend and keep it" (Gen. 2:15).

At this point there were no thorns, briars, and weeds in the garden. Imagine taking care of a garden where there were no weeds. Adam's gardening chores were the fun type—pruning, picking the fruit, trimming, and the like. He didn't have to fight the never-ending battle with weeds. There were no thorns to get stuck between his fingernail and his skin. He could take care of the daily chores, have the assurance of a full yield of fruit, and never work up a drop of sweat. Before the Fall, God was pleased to have man working in the garden. It was a pleasant work, pleasant for man to do, and pleasant for the Creator to watch.

Once sin came into the world, everything changed. Caring for a garden became a matter of difficult labor. Here is the curse of Adam:

> Cursed is the ground for your sake; in toil you shall eat of it
> all the days of your life. Both thorns and thistles it shall bring
> forth for you, and you shall eat the herb of the field. In the
> sweat of your face you shall eat bread till you return to the
> ground, for out of it you were taken; for dust you are, and to
> dust you shall return. (Gen. 3:17–19)

Here are the elements of the curse: thorns, thistles, sweat, and death. Here is the origin of the triad of human pain: blood, sweat, and tears. Yet, as we shall see, the curse is not work itself. After the Fall, as before, work is a divine mandate. God is pleased to see His human creature working.

Man the Worker

When we consider our humanity we usually define ourselves as *homo sapiens*, "man the wise" or "man the thinking animal." We point to our thought patterns as our most distinctive characteristic.

Karl Marx wasn't satisfied with that definition. He preferred another Latin name—*homo faber*. This is "man the maker" or "man the worker." Marx was convinced that labor is so integral to human life that the very definition of man is tied to his labor. In other words, work is not a curse. It is something that to an enormous degree defines who we are and brings (or *should* bring) satisfaction and meaning.

At that point Marx was not completely wrong. When we meet people for the first time, we usually go through a three-step routine. We ask each other three questions: "What is your name?" "Where do you live?" and "What do you do?" Name, address, occupation—these are the three factors that define a person in our culture.

What we do is bound up with our total self-identity. How we do what we do is equally important. We are constantly being judged on our performance at our jobs. In one sense we are all like the major-league baseball player whose batting average changes with each fresh turn at the bat. If the player's average slips below a certain point, his job is in jeopardy. His livelihood is tied to his job. All of us face the trials of the relationship of life and labor. We must work to live, and, more than just working, we must perform reasonably well.

Yet work is to have a higher purpose than self-preservation. With Adam we are all called by God to be productive. We are called to bear fruit. To be productive and fruit-bearing people we must be willing to work with dedication.

A refusal to work is a refusal to participate in one of the most fundamental human duties. We groan at times under the burden of the curse, but the thorns, briars, and sweat do not excuse us from our vocation.

The very word *vocation* comes from the Latin *vocare*, "to call." Our vocation is a calling; it is a calling from God. To shirk our vocation is to run from our duty. We must work.

Sloth and Poverty

Sloth is the enemy of productivity. The slothful person not only injures himself but is a burden to society. Not only does the slothful person fail to add to the productivity of his society, but he begins to live off other people's labor. This is the antisocial dimension of sloth—the lazy person expects to be cared for by the diligent.

The society's responsibility toward the handicapped does not carry over to the able-bodied. The Bible has much to say about the poor and the church's responsibility toward the poor. We err grievously, however, if we fail to distinguish among the various types of poor people mentioned in Scripture. Scripture distinguishes among at least *four* types of poverty.

Poverty as a Result of Calamity: There are those who are poor because they have been the victims of some catastrophe. They have been rendered incapable of productivity by disease, injury, flood, or some other natural disaster. To these people the Christian is called to open his heart in loving assistance. We are responsible to bring relief to these stricken people.

Poverty as a Result of Oppression: Some people experience poverty as a result of being victims of unjust people of power. They may be victimized by theft, extortion, or brutality. Perhaps they have been sold into slavery and have been treated as animals. Perhaps they are orphans and widows who are being exploited.

These people's oppressors cause God to thunder in anger. He will not tolerate the oppression and exploitation of the weak. The history of Israel as a nation began when God heard the groans of an enslaved people and demanded of the pharaoh of Egypt, "Let My people go!"

Poverty for the Kingdom's Sake: There are those who are poor because they choose to be poor. They voluntarily divest themselves of worldly goods. They are the Mother Teresas of this world who resolve to live at a bare subsistence level in order to provide more relief to the needy. Although this lifestyle is by no means required by God, it nevertheless evokes a certain delight in God. This kind of poverty is noble. Its virtuous motivation is indeed noteworthy.

Therefore, we see three distinct groups of poor people who are by no means under the judgment of God. It is the fourth group that provokes God's wrath. It is the fourth group whose poverty is an expression and consequence of their sin.

Poverty Because of Sloth: This fourth category of the poor does not awaken the compassion of God. On the contrary, God's wrath is kindled against the indolent. Note the words of Proverbs:

> Go to the ant, you sluggard!
> Consider her ways and be wise,
> Which, having no captain,
> Overseer or ruler,

> Provides her supplies in the summer,
> And gathers her food in the harvest.
> How long will you slumber, O sluggard?
> When will you rise from your sleep?
> A little sleep, a little slumber,
> A little folding of the hands to sleep—
> So shall your poverty come on you like a robber,
> And your need like an armed man. (Prov. 6:6–11)

"Just a little nap, forty winks. I'll do it tomorrow." Play now, work later is the creed of the sluggard. The ant, by contrast, prepares for the winter in the summer. Her storehouses are full when the bitter weather comes.

Again the Proverbs speak:

> He who deals with a slack hand becomes poor,
> But the hand of the diligent makes one rich.
> He who gathers in summer is a wise son,
> But he who sleeps in harvest is a son who causes shame.
> (Prov. 10:4, 5)

The wisdom literature of the Old Testament abounds with references to slothfulness. Let us note merely a few passages in passing:

> He who is slothful in his work
> Is a brother to him who is a great destroyer. (Prov. 18:9)

> A slothful man buries his hand in the bowl,
> And will not so much as bring it to his mouth again. (Prov. 19:24)

> The desire of the slothful kills him,
> For his hands refuse to labor. (Prov. 21:25)

> The slothful man says, "There is a lion outside!
> I shall be slain in the streets!" (Prov. 22:13)

> Because of laziness the building decays,
> And through idleness of hands the house leaks. (Eccles. 10:18).

Such views are not limited to the Old Testament. The same negative judgment toward slothfulness is found in the New Testament. In the parable of the talents, the master speaks harshly to the unprofitable servant: "You wicked and lazy servant, you know that I reap where I have not sown, and gather where I have not scattered seed" (Matt. 25:26).

Perhaps the strongest indictment against the slothful anywhere in Scripture is found in Paul's Second Letter to the Thessalonians: "For even when we were with you, we commanded you this: If anyone will not work, neither shall he eat. For we hear that there are some who walk among you in a disorderly manner, not working at all, but are busybodies" (2 Thess. 3:10, 11).

No work, no food, is the apostle's mandate. Paul describes those who refuse to work as busybodies.

It is a strange term to use for malingerers. (Perhaps a more current word would be *loafers*.) Those who refused to work were still active. They were engaged in "hanging around" together joining in gossip. Their business was not a business of productivity.

The Workaholic

The term *workaholic* is used in two quite different ways in our culture. In popular usage the word describes a hard-working person who hardly ever stops to rest and has little time in his busy schedule for recreation and social amenities.

But there is a second way in which the word is used. It is used in a technical sense by psychologists. Here the term *workaholic* describes a nonproductive busybody who accomplishes little or no real work. This type of workaholic looks very busy. He is busy at creating an illusion of work.

I remember a fellow in our college class who seemed to have a remarkable level of discipline in the matter of studying. It seemed that every hour we were out of class he was at his desk, hard at work studying. There were no idle visits to the student union building, no participation in dorm antics. There was no play.

Yet when exam time rolled around he always did very poorly. He sometimes flunked his tests. I was amazed that such a disciplined effort yielded such little fruit. Then one evening I was able to observe my friend while he was "studying." He sat at his desk, his head propped up by his hands, intently staring at the book in front of him. His eyes were glazed. I watched for several minutes as he gazed blankly at the page. He didn't turn a page. He was at the desk. His eyes were on the book, but his mind was obviously somewhere else. I thought I was observing a man sleeping with his eyes wide open.

The neurotic workaholic loves to give the appearance of hard work. Frequently he is the first to arrive at the office and the last to leave. His light stays on at night. He carries a heavy briefcase wherever he goes. Often he is a disruptive force in the office. He loves to criticize coworkers for their failures. He covers his own tracks efficiently by shifting blame to others. He always appears busy, but his most significant characteristic is that he never produces. He is busy doing either nothing or the trivial. His business is a substitute for productive labor.

We must be careful here. The nonproducing workaholic displays many characteristics of people who are diligent and productive. Simply because a person arrives early and works late does not identify him as a producer.

The counterfeit imitates the genuine except at the points of production and the assumption of responsibility. The bogus worker appears busy, but he is marked by the two fatal flaws of nonproduction and chronic buck-passing. His criticism of others is an attempt to mask his own failure. This type of workaholic is a slothful person in disguise. The workaholic often fools fellow workers—in fact, he may even fool himself. But he does not fool God, who surely takes no pleasure in seeing unproductive workers covering up their lack of productivity.

Many Christians have grown up with the idea that a person should always look busy. Sociologists and historians have debated for years about the source of the so-called Protestant work ethic, but there is a general agreement that Protestants in northern Europe and America have often had an exalted view of work. Far from seeing it as a curse, many of us have been taught to see it as the great goal of life. The problem is that, where such a view prevails, there are still people who are lazy and unproductive. They don't want to be perceived that way, so they cover their tracks. These people burden themselves (and others) not only with their unproductive habits but also with constant patterns of deception.

The Sweet Sleep of the Worker

That we must work is a divine command. *That* we work and not be slothful is a moral matter. *Where* we work is a matter of prudence. The virtuous person is a working person. The wise person is one who marries his motivated ability pattern to his job.

Obviously it is not always possible to find a perfect job fit for our abilities. But much guilt and frustration can be avoided if we seek to know ourselves and seek as much as it is possible to find a good match in our jobs. Even in situations where we do not feel matched to our jobs, however, we are still under a divine mandate to work well. God is pleased to see us in jobs that are perfectly matched to our talents and needs, but He is also pleased that we work with dedication in whatever situation we find ourselves.

The Bible says that the sleep of a working man is sweet (Eccles. 5:12). Productive work may be tiresome, but it is also highly satisfying. It makes for a sleep that is not disturbed by fits of anxiety and frustration.

Anxious sleep often results from the guilt we feel for shirking our responsibilities. The anxiety builds up in direct proportion to the work we leave undone. I knew a woman who suffered from severe bouts of depression. She was under the care of a psychiatrist. Her depression attacks were finally seen to have a direct correlation to the amount of unironed clothes in her laundry basket. She hated to iron, and her family did not wear wash-and-wear clothes. As the clothes piled up in the laundry basket, so did her anxiety until she reached a fever pitch of depression.

I can relate to that. Though I'm not yet under the care of a psychiatrist, I feel anxiety related to unanswered mail. I hate to answer my mail. The more my mail stacks up, the worse I feel. It is a point of sloth in my life that brings the consequence of depressing guilt.

I once had an economics professor who, once a semester, stood on top of his desk and shouted his favorite law of economics: "You gotta work!" He got our attention. His manner of preaching may have been unorthodox, but with one sentence he captured the spirit of the Law of God. Work is our duty. It is our divine vocation. Each of us has a task to perform.

I can think of no words sweeter to the ear than to hear the words of Jesus: "Well done, thou good and faithful servant." I long to hear those words some-day. I am sure we all want to hear them. But if we are to receive that benediction from Christ, we must be diligent now, faithful to do the work He has called us to perform. In this we please Him.

THIRTEEN

~~~

The Sin of Dishonesty

Ａll men are liars," says Psalm 116:11. This is echoed in conclusion of the apostolic indictment of the human race. Paul declares: "Indeed, let God be true but every man a liar" (Rom. 3:4).

Dishonesty is a severe problem with us. We violate the truth in our speech, our actions, and our relationships. We lie to each other, to God, and to ourselves. This problem is found early in human history. The first recorded lie is uttered by the serpent in Eden. When the devil said to Eve, "You will not die," he was lying. It is the nature of Satan to lie. Jesus described Satan in this manner:

> You are of your father the devil, and the desires of your
> father you want to do. He was a murderer from the
> beginning, and does not stand in the truth, because there is
> no truth in him. When he speaks a lie, he speaks from his
> own resources, for he is a liar and the father of it. (John 8:44)

The conflict between God and Satan is focused on the issue of truth. God is the fountainhead of all truth; Satan is the father of lies. The central issue between Christ and the Antichrist is the issue of truth. The prefix "anti" that describes the Antichrist can mean either "against" or "in place of." The Antichrist fights against Christ. His chief ploy is to seek to replace Christ. He asserts himself as a substitute for Christ. He is the counterfeit, the fraud who works to supplant the genuine article. The Antichrist is a false Christ. In a word, he is a liar. He pretends to be something that he is not.

The Antichrist is the ultimate hypocrite. He is involved in the great deception. He performs lying signs and wonders. Everything about him is counterfeit. His goal is to undermine the truth, to obscure the truth from view. As Satan disguises himself as an angel of light, so the Antichrist tries to pass himself off as the Christ.

The Antichrist depends upon our cavalier attitude toward truth for his own power. He builds his kingdom upon the kind of lies that appeal to people who enjoy lies. We remember that in vivid contrast Jesus declared: "For this cause I was born, and for this cause I have come into the world, that I should bear witness to the truth. Everyone who is of the truth hears My voice" (John 18:37).

To be of the truth is to hear the voice of Christ. Christ is the very incarnation of truth. The battle between light and darkness, between Christ and Antichrist, is the battle between truth and falsehood.

As we made a brief survey of biblical passages concerning slothfulness, let us do the same with lying. The following represents a brief sampling of biblical comments:

> These six things the LORD hates,
> Yes, seven are an abomination to Him:
> A proud look,
> A lying tongue. . . . (Prov. 6:16, 17)

> Lying lips are an abomination to the LORD,
> But those who deal truthfully are His delight. (Prov. 12:22)

> A righteous man hates lying,
> But a wicked man is loathsome and comes to shame.
> (Prov. 13:5)

> A poor man is better than a liar. (Prov. 19:22)

> All liars shall have their part in the lake which burns with fire
> and brimstone, which is the second death. (Rev. 21:8)

Lying to Others

When we lie we usually do it to other people. We are motivated to lie by several factors. We note that lying is closely related to the other sins of pride and slothfulness. We lie to others because we fear that truth will injure our esteem. When our pride cannot bear that the truth be known about us, we cover our tracks by lying. We lie to escape punishment; we lie to cover up our guilt.

We also lie to hide our slothfulness. One of the most widespread forms of lying is via cheating. We cheat to conceal our lack of preparation. If we have not diligently prepared for an examination, we resort to cheating as a substitute for proper preparation. The grade we receive if we are not caught is a dishonest grade. This is particularly grievous when we cheat in competitive tests. Our cheating then becomes a form of stealing, as others are penalized by our dishonesty.

The golfer who cheats in a tournament steals from the other players who are the victims of the dishonesty. Thus by cheating we do violence to the truth and violate other people.

I am ashamed to recount an incident in which I was involved in college. I had a friend who had great difficulty with the study of Greek. Before every test we met together and I tutored him rigorously to help him get ready. He was barely passing as we came down to the wire, the final exam. During the final exam the professor left the room, leaving us on our "honor." We did not act in an honorable way.

My friend was seated next to me. As he got farther into the exam, his anxiety increased. He began to crane his neck to look at my paper. I helped him. I pushed my paper to the side of my desk so that he could get a clear view of it. I was obviously a willing accomplice in the deed.

When the exam grades were posted on the professor's office door, two grades were conspicuously absent. There was an asterisk next to my name and my friend's, with a note to "see the professor." My heart was pounding as I knocked on the professor's door.

The professor ushered me into his office. To my sick astonishment he produced a chart of every answer of every student to every question. The chart revealed that on several questions two people and only two people had the same wrong answer. The evidence was incontrovertible. The professor looked at me sadly and said, "I have just one question for you." "Yes, sir?" I replied. "Are the answers on your paper your own?" I replied, "Yes, but—" I started to confess my complicity in the scandal. He cut me off in midsentence.

"I don't want to hear it," the professor said. "All I want to know is, are your answers your own?" Again I said, "Yes," and he promptly dismissed me.

For reasons I do not understand but for which I am still grateful, the professor gave me no penalties. I received his utter mercy. My friend did not fare so well. He received an *F* for the entire course. The results were an academic disaster for him.

We both cheated. My help was motivated simply by compassion for his panic. I know that I took pride in his achievement because I was coaching him. I was cheating as much for me as I was for him. Either way we were being dishonest. I resolved from that day never to cheat on an exam in any way.

I also became sensitive to the temptations of cheating. I was later in charge of a youth group in a church. I had about thirty young people in the class. On one occasion I said to them, "Okay, let's get real honest here. How many of you ever cheat on tests?"

I was shocked by the response. Every hand in the room went up. I don't know if I was more shocked by the fact that they all did it or by the fact that they were all willing to admit it.

We then proceeded to a lengthy discussion about *why* they cheated. The answers they gave included: "My parents put so much pressure on me to make good grades." "Everyone else is cheating and it is the only way I can compete." "I don't want to look stupid." "The tests aren't fair."

We talked it out. As a group we resolved to change our habits. For the entire semester I asked them each week: "Did you cheat this week?" Some of them stopped cheating immediately. Others struggled with it deeply. What emerged was a camaraderie among them whereby they were encouraging each other toward honesty.

Not all lies to others are connected with our pride and slothfulness. Some are related to our desire for unjust gain. Salesmen, for example, seem to forget that under normal circumstances they are expected to tell the truth. For example, on a business transaction the truth is due to the buyer. They cannot hide behind a convenient policy of *caveat emptor* ("Let the buyer beware"). If my car has a hidden mechanical problem, it is my duty to make full disclosure of that when I go to sell it. It is fraud to sell things by false representation. The truth is due the buyer.

Only recently has the law in the United States required truth in lending and truth in advertising. Lenders can no longer conceal hidden costs with impunity. Advertisers are now libel if they make false claims about their products. To lie in lending, advertising, or selling is to be involved in a not so subtle form of theft.

Lying about Others

It is one thing to lie *to* others. It is still another matter to lie *about* others. This involves slander. To tell lies about other people is to cause them grave injury. The devil himself is the master of slander. He encourages his disciples to engage in gossip, backbiting, and slander. To steal a person's good name may be more harmful to the person than to steal their property.

God is so concerned about slander and lying about others that He included a prohibition against it in His Ten Commandments: "You shall not bear false witness against your neighbor" (Exod. 20:16).

The prohibition includes more than falsely accusing someone in a law court. The responsibility in Israel to tell the truth, the whole truth and nothing but the truth in a law court was taken very seriously. If perjury was committed in the courts, the penalties ranged all the way to the death penalty.

Justice cannot be maintained in the land unless the courts can be certain of the honesty of witnesses. But on a more daily basis, injurious lies can take the form of slander. Let us consider briefly the meaning and force of the verb *to slander*. To slander someone is to tell lies about him, lies that injure him. Slander involves making an unjust accusation. We have all felt the sting of being slandered. It is one thing to suffer injury for sins of which we are guilty. It is another thing to be punished for something we did not do. No one enjoys the pain of false accusation.

Jesus was a victim of slander throughout His entire public ministry. Even in the agony of death He was subjected to verbal abuse. During His crucifixion He was the subject of debate between the two thieves that were executed with Him. "Then one of the criminals who were hanged blasphemed Him, saying, 'If You are the Christ, save Yourself and us'" (Luke 23:39).

Indeed Jesus was the Christ. There was no "if" about it. Here the accusation against Him, which was made in mockery, was ironically true. The mocking of the first thief was an attempt to slander Jesus. The response of the second thief was noteworthy: "But the other, answering, rebuked him, saying, 'Do you not even fear God, seeing you are under the same condemnation? And we indeed justly, for we receive the due reward of our deeds; but this Man has done nothing wrong'" (Luke 23:40, 41).

Here the second thief acknowledged that his own punishment was just. He was guilty of the crimes for which he was being crucified. The other thief was likewise guilty. They were receiving justice. They were receiving what was *due* them. But Jesus was innocent of the charges against Him. He was a victim of false accusation. The cross—the central moment of all redemptive history—was, from a divine vantage point, the critical moment of salvation. Yet, from a human standpoint, it was the most vicious act of injustice ever committed in this world. It was the supreme act of slander in human history. Roman justice had declared that the innocent Son of God was worthy of death. The Jews, God's chosen people, those who expected a Messiah, had handed an innocent man over to the Romans.

The second thief set the record straight. "This man has done nothing amiss." Here the thief echoed the judgment of the Roman procurator, Pontius Pilate: "I have found no fault in this Man" (Luke 23:14). But Pilate, despite vindicating Jesus with these words, caved in to the clamoring crowd and allowed the punishment for the slanderous charges to be carried out. Pilate, acting as the Roman guardian of justice, spit in the face of justice to appease an angry mob.

However corrupt the second thief was, he used his last breaths fighting for truth. He died with a testimony to justice and a plea for mercy on his lips: "Lord, remember me when You come into Your kingdom" (Luke 23:42).

Jesus was obviously touched that his integrity was being defended by such a man as this. He was quick to respond with a promise of grace: "Assuredly, I say to you, today you will be with Me in Paradise" (Luke 23:43).

I suspect that the thief is still with Jesus in paradise. The devil is not. There is no room for slander in the kingdom of Christ.

I labor the point of slander's being an injurious lie because it is one of the chief works of the devil against God's people. To slander a person is to injure that person's reputation. Our reputations, our "good names," are important to our lives. Life is difficult enough without trying to operate with an evil reputation.

Lies for a Good Purpose

Jacob was a supplanter. He lived up to his name by stealing his brother Esau's birthright. The theft took place by deception. When Isaac grew old and was blind, Jacob disguised himself by putting animal skins on his body and, posing as his hairy brother Esau, fooled Isaac into giving him the patriarchal blessing. All of this was done with the help and guidance of Isaac's wife Rebekah. She was the Mother of the lie:

> Now therefore, my son, obey my voice according to what I
> command you. Go now to the flock and bring me from there
> two choice kids of the goats, and I will make savory food
> from them for your father, such as he loves. Then you shall
> take it to your father, that he may eat it, and that he may
> bless you before his death. (Gen. 27:8–10)

It might be argued that Rebekah was merely carrying out the will of God. God had ordained that the elder would serve the younger. Jacob was the child of promise. Rebekah was simply making sure that God's sovereign will was done.

However, God does not require the sins of humans to accomplish His holy will. He stands sovereign over sin but is not the author of sin. He accomplished His will through the example of Judas, but that did not absolve Judas of his crime. As in the case of Joseph's brothers, they meant it for evil, but God meant it for good. So Rebekah is still responsible for her sin. Her sin provoked an endless bitterness, an ongoing hatred between Esau and Jacob that carried over to their descendants. We might even say that part of the bloody struggle in Palestine today has its roots in one woman's unscrupulous lie.

But what of the lie of Rahab the harlot? Rahab made it to the roll call of heroes in Hebrews 11: "By faith the harlot Rahab did not perish with those who did not believe, when she had received the spies with peace" (Heb. 11:31).

We read of Rahab's trickery in Joshua 2:

> Then the woman took the two men and hid them; and she
> said, "Yes, the men came to me, but I did not know where they
> were from. And it happened as the gate was being shut, when
> it was dark, that the men went out. Where the men went I do
> not know; pursue them quickly, for you may overtake them."
> (Josh. 2:4, 5)

This is the record of a bold-faced lie. The issue is, then, was Rahab blessed by God because of her lie, or in spite of her lie? Some put Rahab in the same category as Rebekah, arguing that she was blessed in spite of the lie. This position assumes that lying is *always* wrong.

On the other hand, we have the principle that we must tell the truth *when the truth is due.* This position assumes that the truth is not always due. That is, not everyone is entitled to the truth.

Let me illustrate. When I lived in Holland, I lived in a home of a woman who had endured five years of Nazi occupation during World War II. It was the policy of the Germans to arrest young Dutchmen and ship them off to camps or to work projects for the Nazi war effort. This woman hollowed out a hiding place beneath the floorboards to hide her son. In this small cubicle she installed a ventilation fan and stored food provisions in the hiding place.

One day as the Nazis were searching the village for young men, the woman hid her son beneath the floor. Without knocking, the soldiers burst into the house armed with submachine guns. They rushed to the bedroom and searched the closets for evidence of young men's clothing. They felt the beds to see if they were warm. Finally they returned to the living room and stood over the very spot where the son was hidden. A soldier said to the woman: "Are you hiding any boys here?"

What was her moral responsibility? Should she have said, "Yes there is one under the floor?" I think not. She had the moral right to lie. The Nazis had no right to the truth. She replied, "No, there are no boys here." Thereupon the soldiers began to shoot up the floor, all the while watching the Mother's reaction for any hint of panic. She displayed no outward emotion, while inside she was in stark terror.

Finally the soldiers left. Panic-stricken, the mother rushed to the hiding place. Her son emerged unscathed. Her deception had saved him.

We are not required to tell robbers where we have hidden our valuables. Soldiers are not required to tell the enemy where their comrades are positioned. Truth is to be told to those who are due it. We are not pleasing God when we tell the truth to people who do not deserve the truth.

Lying to Ourselves

One of the most difficult tasks we ever have is to tell the truth about ourselves to ourselves. On the surface it would seem incredible that this is difficult. Who knows more about ourselves than ourselves?

Yet the one person we must want to have a good opinion of ourself is ourself. It is painful in the extreme to face the darker side of our personalities with the stark truth. Usually it takes nothing less than the supernatural power of divine conviction for us to come to grips with personal reality. Indeed we are fortunate that the Holy Spirit does not reveal the full truth about ourselves to us all at once. Who could possibly bear such a full self-revelation? One glimpse of the holiness of God had Isaiah cursing himself. Job and Habakkuk almost perished when God gave them an unveiled view of themselves.

We lie to ourselves. We view our own actions in the best of all possible lights. Where we are quick to judge others harshly, we are equally quick to excuse ourselves. We are masters of the art of rationalization.

We remember David, a man after God's own heart. When he fell into sin with Bathsheba, he called upon all of his cunning to mask his fault from himself. He added murder by proxy to his crime by using his authority to send Bathsheba's husband, Uriah, to the front lines in combat.

After taking Bathsheba for his own, David was confronted by the prophet Nathan. Nathan approached the king with a seemingly harmless parable:

> Then the LORD sent Nathan to David. And he came to him,
> and said to him; "There were two men in one city, one rich
> and the other poor. The rich man had exceedingly many
> flocks and herds. But the poor man had nothing, except one
> little ewe lamb which he had bought and nourished; and
> it grew up together with him and with his children. It ate
> of his own food and drank from his own cup and lay in his
> bosom; and it was like a daughter to him.

> And a traveler came to the rich man, who refused to take
> from his own flock and from his own herd to prepare one for
> the wayfaring man who had come to him; but he took the
> poor man's lamb and prepared it for the man who had come
> to him." (2 Sam. 12:1–4)

When David heard this story from the prophet's lips he was furious. The narrative declares: "Then David's anger was greatly aroused against the man, and he said to Nathan, 'As the LORD lives, the man who has done this shall surely die! And he shall restore fourfold for the lamb, because he did this thing and because he had no pity' " (2 Sam. 12:5, 6).

Then Nathan, at the risk of his own life, put the sword deeply into David's soul. He cried out to the king: "You are the man!"

David was shattered. His repentance was as severe as his crime. He saturated his pillow with tears. Out of his stricken conscience he penned the immortal lines of the Fifty-first Psalm. But David could not see his own guilt directly. Only when Nathan held up a mirror in front of him by disguising the sin could David see it. He recognized it clearly when it was cloaked in the story of another man's crime. Yet even then he did not make the personal application until Nathan pointed his finger in David's face.

David was not alone. In this tendency toward self-deceit, David is Everyman.

Lying to God

We lie to others, we lie to ourselves. But our sin is compounded infinitely when we lie to God. Lying to God is as foolish as it is irreverent. It is foolish to think that we can deceive Him. Every secret thought in our heart is known to Him totally. No mountain is big enough to cover our guilt from His penetrating gaze.

We lie to God in a multitude of ways. Since Eden we have tried to conceal our shame by hiding from Him. We violate His truth. We break our covenants with Him. To swear an oath to God and to break it is to lie to Him.

The clearest example we have in Scripture of people lying to God is found in the story of Ananias and Sapphira:

> But a certain man named Ananias, with Sapphira his wife,
> sold a possession. And he kept back part of the proceeds, his
> wife also being aware of it, and brought a certain part and
> laid it at the apostles' feet. But Peter said, "Ananias, why has
> Satan filled your heart to lie to the Holy Spirit and keep back

> part of the price of the land for yourself? While it remained,
> was it not your own? And after it was sold, was it not in your
> own control? Why have you conceived this thing in your
> heart? You have not lied to men but to God." (Acts 5:1–4)

As soon as the indictment was uttered by Peter, Ananias breathed his last. Moments later he was joined in death by his wife. The judgment of God was swift and decisive. He refused to tolerate this dishonesty.

Acts tells us that as a result of the penalty imposed upon Ananias and Sapphira "great fear came upon all the church" (Acts 5:11).

The sin of Ananias and Sapphira was not that they refused to sell all of their possessions. That is not a universal requirement upon the church. Their sin was of lying. They made a pledge to God that they did not keep.

The healthy fear that gripped the church in the first century has long since evaporated. In the modern church we know that when pledges are made for giving, we cannot hope to receive more than 80 or 85 percent of the pledges made. The church still has the spirit of Ananias' lying to God.

Jesus came to bear witness to the truth. His people are called to be people of truth. As Christians we are to put away our fallen tendency to lie. We are to be done with lies. If we are to strive toward integrity, our striving must be toward truthfulness.

Truth is sacred because God is a God of truth. He has nothing to do with falsehood. His word can be trusted absolutely. We are to mirror that kind of fidelity to truth. We are to tell the truth, do the truth, and live the truth. In so doing we please the God of truth.

FOURTEEN

❦

Doctrine and Life

N ot doctrine, but *life*—that is what really matters. This is a sentiment often expressed in Christian circles. The idea is simple: God is less concerned about what we believe than He is about how we live. Creeds and dogma are unimportant. What matters is outward behavior. *Orthopraxy*, not *orthodoxy,* is what counts. We may more completely please God with right behavior than with right thinking.

This is a false dilemma with perilous consequences. Right thinking and right living go together. We may distinguish them, but to separate them is deadly. We can have right theories without right practice. We can also have right practice without right theory, but only by accident as a happy inconsistency.

The disparaging of doctrine usually follows a common pattern. We begin by recognizing that there are people who have all the correct theological answers but who live scandalous lives. The devil can make a high score on a theology test. It was the demons who first recognized Jesus as the Son of God before the disciples did, but the demons hated the truth they recognized so clearly. There are many people who know truth about God but who are living lives that could not possibly please God.

The Leaders' Treason

There is a deep suspicion in the Christian community about theology, especially academic theology, and for good reason. The church has experienced what one scholar called "the treason of the intellectual." Much of the skepticism leveled against biblical Christianity has come from within the church. It was the church's theologians who declared the death of God. It is the theological seminaries that attack the trustworthiness of Scripture.

I remember my own rude awakening as a first-year seminary student. I was shocked to hear one of my professors not only deny the deity of Christ but attack it with a tone of hostility. I might have been less shocked had the professor expressed a deep personal crisis of faith in which he no longer could embrace the biblical faith. Had he made this confession with tears and a broken heart, I could have understood it. But his denial was couched in a kind of militancy against the biblical view of Jesus.

When I raised questions about this to him, my professor glared at me and said, "Young man, you have come to seminary with too many preconceived ideas." The preconceived idea for which I was rebuked was the belief in the deity of Christ.

I was bewildered. I naïvely assumed that everybody who went to a Christian seminary to prepare for the Christian ministry was already convinced of the deity of Christ. I couldn't imagine any other reason to be there. When I called attention to the fact that the creeds of our church clearly affirm the deity of Christ, the man replied (in private), "The orthodox creeds are full of——." (He did not delete the expletive.)

Countless college students have had similar experiences with professors at church-related colleges. A natural reaction to the pain and shock of this kind of skepticism is to retreat into a nonintellectual haven of faith. The seductive temptation is to think, *If this is what academic theology produces, then who needs it? I'm going to keep my faith simple and avoid any involvement with theology.*

We must not assume that because someone is a theological scholar that he is a Christian. We may not assume that because someone is an ordained minister he is necessarily a Christian. Sadly, there are many people who enter the ministry for the wrong reasons. Some make theological skepticism a profession. There are those who are motivated to study Christian theology out of a burning desire to disprove, neutralize, or change Christianity. Natural man has enough enmity toward God to make a lifelong crusade against Him. There is an enemy within the church.

We have heard enough testimonies from clergy who declare they have been converted after their ordination to know that many are in fact ordained in unbelief. American colonial pastor Gilbert Tennent once wrote an essay entitled "The Dangers of an Unconverted Clergy." Tennent was not merely crying wolf. There are wolves out there in sheep's clothing. They masquerade as men and women of God while inwardly being at war with God. That is nothing new. We remember that the most hostile group toward Jesus in His earthly life was the clergy of His day, the scribes and the Pharisees.

People seek ordination for all sorts of reasons. One reason is to legitimatize their unbelief. Another reason, as we have seen, is to work against Christ from within. And there are many who are genuine humanitarians who see the church as a marvelous institution of social concern. Where else can a person find such a well-established platform for community influence?

When a businessman moves into a new community, he must work hard at establishing new relationships. If he is to rise to a position of community prominence and influence, he must face the reality that it takes time and effort to do it. When a new minister comes to town, he instantly steps into a position of community leadership. The influence of the local church may be waning, but it is still a reality. The minister has an instant platform from which to exert influence. He has a pulpit. He has a congregation. He has a church program. The wages may not be the best, but the opportunities for exerting influence and community leadership are great. A pulpit beats a soapbox for those motivated to persuade people to their own viewpoints.

There are other factors that play a role, and some are painful to relate. One ignoble motivation was felt sharply in the sixties. Seminary enrollment brought with it a deferment from the military draft. Some students were quite candid about it. A three-year tour of seminary seemed a better option than a tour of duty in Vietnam or exile to Canada.

But we dare not paint the whole house with the same brush. The vast majority of clergy are in the ministry out of a sincere desire to serve God. There are lots of sheep in sheep's clothing. Indeed, they are more than sheep; they are shepherds. These pastors love God and they love their people. With all their failings, they still try to please God and to lead other people to do so.

The Need for Doctrine

The church needs dedicated pastors. It also needs dedicated teachers of theology. The church has always benefited greatly from the work of sound theologians. I return again and again to the insights of Augustine, the cogency of Thomas Aquinas, the brilliance of Calvin, the passion of Luther. These men feed my mind and my soul.

We all need good teachers. I know that I cannot do without them. But how do we find them? What are the marks of a good teacher of theology?

Finding good teachers is like finding a good doctor. We want a doctor who knows what he is doing and who is a person we can trust with our bodies. If the doctor is warm and kind but doesn't know medicine, we are in deep trouble. It is small consolation to me if he holds my hand while he injects the wrong medicine into my bloodstream.

On the other hand, there are highly skilled professional physicians who have little personal regard for their patients. They know how to treat diseases but don't know how to treat people.

If possible, I want a doctor who is a master of medical knowledge and who will also value me as a person. Medically, that is the best of all possible worlds.

In theology we need teachers who display a high degree of skill and knowledge coupled with a deep love for God. Loving God is not a prejudicial barrier to a correct understanding of the things of God. On the contrary. A heart that is disposed toward God will only enhance the theologian's knowledge of God.

Professor G. C. Berkouwer of the Free University of Amsterdam once remarked in class, "Gentlemen, all great theologians begin and end their work with doxology!" Doxology—the writings of the great masters breathe a spirit of doxology. Their work goes beyond analysis and exposition to praise. Read the works of the apostle Paul, the premier theologian of the church. In the midst of his heaviest treatment of election, he interrupts the flow of his thought to exclaim, "O the depths and the riches of His mercy!" (Rom. 11:33).

We find that same spirit of doxology in the giants of church history. We can't miss it in Augustine, Athanasius, Anselm, Aquinas, Luther, Calvin, and Edwards, to mention the finest. None of these is infallible. We can find points of disagreement among them. Yet there is a remarkable and profound unity among them regarding the essential doctrines of the faith. Hear what C. S. Lewis once observed:

> In the days when I still hated Christianity, I learned to recognize, like some all too familiar smell, that almost unvarying something which met me, now in Puritan Bunyan, now in Anglican Hooker, now in Thomist Dante. It was there (honeyed and floral) in Francois de Sales; it was there (grave and homely) in Spenser and Walton; it was there (grim and manful) in Pascal and Johnson; there again, with a mild frightening, Paradisial flavor, in Vaughan and Boehme and Traherne. In the urban sobriety of the eighteenth century one was not safe—Law and Butler were two lions in the path. The supposed "Paganism" of the Elizabethans could not keep it out; it lay in wait where a man might have supposed himself safest, in the very centre of *The Faerie Queene* and the *Arcadia*. It was, of course, varied; and yet—after all—so unmistakably the same; recognizable, not to be evaded, the odour which is death to us until we allow it to become life.[1]

Now read the works of twentieth-century critical theologian Rudolf Bultmann. Bultmann displays an uncanny technical erudition. His critical skills are noteworthy. Yet it would require the lamp of Diogenes to find a single note of

1.   C. S. Lewis, *God in the Dock*, ed. Walter Hooper (Grand Rapids: Eerdmans, 1970), 203–204.

doxology in all his writings. That should tell us something. We do well to wonder if a man who cannot praise God is going to please God with his vast learning.

We still face the dilemma of a vast public fear of theology. At times I have been critical of Christian bookstores. So much of what sells as teaching is theologically weak. It is often not only simple (which is a virtue), but simplistic (which is a harmful vice). There is much doxology, but little theology. Some literature found in Christian bookstores manifests a serious ignorance of orthodox theology. It is simply bad teaching. It is well-intentioned bad teaching. But it is still bad teaching.

For me to criticize Christian bookstores and Christian publishers is to bite the hand that feeds me. But if that hand is feeding harmful food to Christ's sheep, then somebody needs to bite it.

I have pleaded with booksellers and publishers to promote the writings of the great masters. The usual response is that the great masters don't sell well to the general public. I still plead. I'm convinced that if the industry promoted the classics, the classics would sell.

I once ordered John Murray's *Principles of Conduct* for a seminary course. The publisher notified me that it was out of print. I pitched a fit. I begged the publisher to reprint it, even offering to raise the finances necessary to do it. The book was too important to allow it to slip into publishing purgatory. To my great joy the publisher relented and issued a new edition.

I would be delighted to see bookstores bury all my books in the basement or put them to the torch if they would replace them with the works of Luther, Augustine, Edwards, and the rest. What do I know that I haven't learned from them? The only difference between them and me is that their work is better thought out and much better written. I am sure that James Boice, J. I. Packer, Charles Colson, and a host of contemporary writers would say the same thing. We are at best dwarfs standing on the shoulders of the giants.

We need sound doctrine. The Spirit of holiness is also the Spirit of truth. Truth and righteousness go together. True living flows out of true thinking. Our lives can change externally without changing internally. All that achieves is to qualify us to be Pharisees. The Spirit goes to the root of the matter.

It is good trees that produce good fruit. It is the transformed mind that yields a transformed life. How we think about God is the most vital influence to how we respond to God. Repentance itself is a change of mind before it ever yields a change of behavior.

We must reject a false dichotomy between doctrine and life. We can have sound doctrine without a sanctified life. But it is extremely difficult to progress in sanctification without sound doctrine. Sound doctrine is not a sufficient condition to produce a sound life. It does not yield sanctification automatically. Sound doctrine is a *necessary* condition for sanctification. It is a vital prerequisite. It is like oxygen and fire. The mere presence of oxygen does not guarantee a fire, but you can't have a fire without it.

Consciousness, Conviction, Conscience

Why? Why is sound doctrine necessary for sanctification? For real sanctification to occur in the Christian life at least three absolute changes are necessary. There must be a change in our consciousness. There must be a change in our convictions. There must be a change in our conscience. Consciousness, conviction, and conscience—these three are all vital to our sanctification.

Consciousness involves knowledge. Before we can willfully do what God commands and what pleases Him, we must first understand what it is that God requires. From the Law comes a knowledge of sin. Also from the Law comes a knowledge of righteousness.

A person could "accidentally" obey the law without doing so consciously. But such an action would have no moral virtue to it. Suppose a man enjoys driving his car at fifty miles an hour. It pleases him to ride at that rate of speed. He drives his car at fifty miles an hour in fifty-five-mile-per-hour zones and in fifteen-mile-per-hour zones. When he drives in the fifty-five-mile-per-hour zone, he is within the speed limit. He is obeying the law. But when he goes fifty in a fifteen-mile-per-hour zone, he is a menace to those around him.

Suppose our mythical driver systematically refuses to look at speed limit signs. He averts his gaze from any sign that even appears to mark a speed limit. He keeps himself purposefully unconscious of speed limits. At times he "happens" to obey the law, but purely by coincidence. If the man wants to achieve moral virtue as a driver and always drive within the speed limit, he must first become aware, he must become *conscious* of the law.

But consciousness is not enough. We all have seen people who are quite conscious of the speed limits while they are violating them. We don't have to look beyond ourselves to discover the culprits. For our behavior to change we must move beyond consciousness to conviction.

Conviction is a matter of depth and intensity. It is one thing to be aware that a certain action is right. It is another to have a conviction about it. It is a lot easier for us to compromise our knowledge than to act against convictions. A conviction is knowledge that is settled. It has a firm hold on us. It goes beyond our brains and penetrates the conscience.

Our conscience acts as a kind of governor upon our behavior. It is the inner voice that either accuses us or excuses us. It monitors our behavior by way of approval or disapproval. The problem is that our conscience doesn't always tell us the truth. We are adept at training it in the direction of self-approval.

It is hard to live with a guilty conscience. Guilt feelings paralyze us. They can produce literal nausea. They can provoke psychosomatic illnesses. When we are assaulted by a guilty conscience, we can change our behavior or change our consciences. We can sear the conscience. We can dull its accusing tone by rationalization.

By repeating sins over and over again we can mute the inner voice of conscience. We fall into the decadence described by Paul in Romans 1 whereby we not only continue in sin but encourage others to join us in it. "Who, knowing the righteous judgment of God, that those who practice such things are worthy of death, not only do the same but also approve of those who practice them" (Rom. 1:32).

Recently, I watched a segment of the Phil Donahue show that featured an interview of actors and actresses who starred in pornographic movies. The film players insisted that (a) they felt no guilt and (b) they had high standards because they refused to participate in radical sexual violence or in the sexual exploitation of children. They had a conscience about violence and child exploitation which "excused" their lack of conscience in other areas.

The porn actors justified their behavior by appealing to the fact that they avoided more heinous sexual behavior than their own. Their remarks were a consummate display of self-deceit, whereby they casually called evil good. They played on a distinction between bad and worse. They considered their own evil good because it was not worse. Here wickedness was relativized so that their own conscience could excuse them.

This game is played on more stages than those that are X-rated. As long as I can point to some worse evil than my own, I can flatter myself with a distorted view of virtue and vice.

For the conscience to function in a godly way it must be influenced by godly convictions. To gain godly consciences, our consciousness of what is right and what is wrong must be sharpened. This involves the mind. It is a matter of doctrine.

Doctrine comes from the Word of God. The Word addresses our consciousness. It is given for our understanding. The Word engages the mind, not the elbow. The Word is the Spirit's book. The Holy Spirit inspires the Scriptures. He is the Revealer of truth.

But the Spirit's work does not stop in the inspiring of Scripture. The Spirit illumines the Word and applies the Word to us: "But God has revealed them to us through His Spirit. For the Spirit searches all things, yes, the deep things of God. For what man knows the things of a man except the spirit of the man which is in him? Even so no one know the things of God except the Spirit of God" (1 Cor. 2:10, 11).

I once heard Dr. David Hubbard, president of Fuller Theological Seminary, speak on this text. Dr. Hubbard explained the meaning of the Spirit's *searching* the things of God. Human beings search after things they do not have or do not know. The Holy Spirit is not an ignorant member of the Godhead who is desperately seeking to discover the truth of God. The Holy Spirit is God. All that the Father knows the Spirit already knows—He does not need to search after it.

Rather, the text refers to the Spirit's work of illumination for us. It is as though the Spirit puts a searchlight on the Word of God to help us see what is already there. He is assisting us in our search for understanding.

The Spirit is sent to instruct us and to convict us. He applies the intensity of knowledge that is conviction. Jesus promised the Holy Spirit for this purpose: "Nevertheless I tell you the truth. It is to your advantage that I go away; for if I do not go away, the Helper will not come to you; but if I depart, I will send Him to you. And when He has come, He will convict the world of sin, and of righteousness, and of judgment" (John 16:7, 8).

The progress from a changed consciousness to a changed conviction to a changed conscience is directed by the Holy Spirit. The Spirit works *with* the Word. He does not work against the Word or without the Word. The Word and Spirit go together. Doctrine and life go together. The will and the mind go together. To separate them is to frustrate the work of sanctification within us and to grieve the Holy Spirit. To separate them is to avoid the integrated, committed life that pleases God.

FIFTEEN

~⚬~

Never Give Up

S ir Winston Churchill returned to Eton, the scene of his childhood education. The students were assembled to hear a speech from Eton's most illustrious alumnus. Churchill was a word merchant, a master of the English language without peer, the king of repartee. Of course, he had been challenged in debate on the floor of Parliament by unarmed men. Fools took him on at dinner parties, always to rue the moment. Even the great playwright George Bernard Shaw had mustered his wit to foil the prime minister. Shaw, on the occasion of the opening of one of his plays, dispatched an acid-dripping invitation to Churchill: "Dear Mr. Prime Minister, here are two complimentary tickets to the opening night of my new play. One ticket is for you and the other for a friend . . . if you have one."

Churchill dispatched an immediate reply: "Dear Mr. Shaw. Thank you for your invitation and generous gift of tickets for your new play. Unfortunately, my schedule prohibits my attending opening night. However, I shall surely be in attendance on the second night . . . if there is one."

By the time Churchill returned to Eton, his fame as a speaker was already well-known to every British schoolboy. The moment was at hand to hear the great man display his oratory. The assembly was hushed as Churchill approached the podium. He grasped the lectern and thrust out his chin in bull-dog ferocity and said, "Never, never, never . . . give up." Then he sat down.

With one sentence he electrified his audience. One wonders how many times in how many young men's secret thoughts those words came back in a moment of crisis, a moment when the fearful totter between fight or flight.

Never give up. This is a message echoed again and again in Holy Writ. Consider Jesus the Author and the Finisher of our salvation. Jesus finishes what He starts. He did not spar with the devil for a season. He locked the enemy in combat to the end.

One of the most significant utterances ever to come from the mouth of Jesus was spoken on the cross. In the midst of this grand passion, as He suffered the paroxysms of the agony of death, Jesus managed to gasp, "It is finished." That is when Jesus quit life. When His task was finished. Not before. Not until. The work had to be finished.

Jesus said, "No one, having put his hand to the plow, and looking back, is fit for the kingdom of God" (Luke 9:62). Jesus' eyes were fixed forward. He set His face toward Jerusalem. Lot's wife looked back and became a pillar of salt. Jesus looked ahead and achieved the redemption of the world.

Paul stated it this way: "Forgetting those things which are behind and reaching forward to those things which are ahead, I press toward the goal for the prize of the upward call of God in Christ Jesus" (Phil. 3:13, 14).

We are called to *press* toward the mark of our high calling. To press is to use exertion. It is to apply pressure. The apostle is calling us to *effort*. The pursuit of righteousness is not a cavalier matter. There is no room for the easy-chair method of sanctification. Determination is important. Effort is important.

Both Passive and Active

One of the great distortions of the doctrine of sanctification may be found in the creed of quietism. Traditionally, quietism has referred to a kind of spiritual passivity that emphasizes divine activity and human inactivity. The popular slogan of quietism is, "Let go, and let God." The slogan has merit if it is intended to remind us that our spiritual progress cannot be achieved merely by our own efforts. Self-reformation is an exercise in futility if it proceeds without dependence upon the grace of God. But there is a better way to express this dependence. Rather than "Let go, and let God," we ought to say, "Hang on, and trust God."

To be sanctified involves work. The apostle exhorts Christians to a life of work: "Work out your own salvation with fear and trembling; for it is God who works in you both to will and to do for His good pleasure" (Phil. 2:12, 13).

Sanctification is cooperative. There are two partners involved in the work. I must work and God will work. If ever the extrabiblical maxim "God helps those who help themselves" had any truth, it is at this point. We are not called to sit back and let God do all the work. We are called to work, and to work hard. To work something out with fear and trembling is to work with devout and conscientious rigor. It is to work with care, with a profound concern with the end result.

I remember working in the yard as a boy. I worked on our family's yard as well as on the yards of our neighbors. I distinctly recall that I approached the tasks differently. When I worked at home my only concern was to finish the job in a hurry so I could go out and play. Trimming around trees and along sidewalks was either perfunctory or nonexistent.

Working in neighbors' yards was different. Here I was getting paid. My labor was being evaluated. I pressed harder. I paid more attention to detail. There was fear and trembling in my effort.

When I become a man I still had to do yard work. My care for detail went even deeper. Now I experienced *ownership*. It was *my* lawn I was working on. No one was paying me to trim around the trees. No one was looking over my shoulder to evaluate me. But it was *my* lawn. I wanted it to look nice. I cared about the results. (However, I was still in a hurry so I could go out and play!)

I was soon frustrated when I enlisted the help of my son. I noticed that he didn't care much about trimming around trees. He was fast with the mower. Zip, zip, the job was done. Not much fear. Not much trembling. He had a basketball game on the schedule. I thought to myself, *"Doesn't he have any pride in our lawn?"* Then I discovered the sins of the fathers being visited on the third generation. This wasn't a chip off the old block; this was the old block himself. I wonder if he will trim around trees when he has his own lawn. I suspect he will, for he, like everyone, will put forth effort when he sees the end result as important.

If we live to please God, we must constantly remind ourselves that our effort is extremely important. Our salvation doesn't end when we are reborn. True, the Spirit does the work of regeneration by Himself. Regeneration is monergistic, not synergistic. I am quiet, passive, when the Spirit does His work of quickening my soul. But then the work begins. I must work out my salvation. I must press toward the mark. Though the Spirit always helps us, we must *work* out our salvation.

The Violent People of the Kingdom

Jesus once made a remark that has puzzled Bible readers for centuries. He declared: "And from the days of John the Baptist until now the kingdom of heaven suffers violence, and the violent take it by force" (Matt. 11:12).

What did Jesus mean? How does the kingdom suffer violence? On the surface it seems to suggest that people can storm the gates of heaven and gain entrance by some sort of power play. It suggests that unworthy people can besiege the kingdom with military strength. But this interpretation does violence to everything the Bible teaches about the nature of God's kingdom. God is not powerless to prevent the unworthy from sneaking into His presence. No man by sheer effort can gain access to the Father. God's fortress is not vulnerable to thieves and robbers. The pagan can lay siege to the heavenly Jerusalem yet never provoke the surrender of Zion.

No, I think Jonathan Edwards was correct when he saw this verse as referring to the passion by which new believers pursue their quest for God's kingdom. It describes the zeal by which those who are awakened by the Spirit press into the kingdom. With the announcement of John the Baptist of the approaching kingdom, a great awakening occurred in Israel. People flocked to the Jordan to receive the preparatory baptism of John.

Jesus took the announcement one step further. Where John said, "The kingdom of heaven is at hand" (Matt. 3:2), Jesus declared the very presence of the kingdom (Luke 17:21). With the appearance of Jesus the king of the kingdom arrived. This sparked an unprecedented national repentance. Those who were awakened *rushed* to embrace Christ. The repentant sinner leaves no stone unturned to embrace his king. The zeal and the passion of the newly awakened is forceful. It is violent not in the sense of the use of physical arms but in its urgency and intensity. (The New International Version reads "forceful men lay hold of it" instead of "the violent take it by force," and this may be a more accurate translation.)

This urgency and intensity requires a pressing into the kingdom. It means a determined effort with one's eyes fixed upon the goal. Indeed, there is an analogy drawn from warfare. When the gates of a walled city are opened, the victorious do not hesitate to push through. No soldier surrenders to lethargy or weariness at the moment of triumph.

Those who press into the kingdom sign up for the duration. We are not permitted the luxury of quitting. We cannot retire from sanctification. There are no pensions in the kingdom of God. We are called to endure to the end. When we dedicate ourselves to God, we dedicate ourselves to lifelong service. The phrase "full-time Christian service" applies not only to pastors and missionaries, but to everyone.

The author of the Epistle to the Hebrews describes the Christian life as a battle—even unto death.

> Therefore we also, since we are surrounded by so great a
> cloud of witnesses, let us lay aside every weight, and the sin
> which so easily ensnares us, and let us run with endurance
> the race that is set before us, looking unto Jesus, the author
> and finisher of our faith. . . . You have not yet resisted to
> bloodshed, striving against sin. (Heb. 12:1, 2, 4)

When we seek to overcome besetting sins, we are easily frustrated, easily defeated. One straw breaks the back of the camel. We surrender before we resist unto blood.

Repeated failures do little to inspire confidence. This is why we are called to forget the things that are behind. We must forget the failures. We must not wallow in defeat. We must press on toward the mark. We must never, never, never give up.

Our goal is not trivial. It is worth fighting for. It is worth fear and trembling. It is the high calling of Christ. Indeed, it is the highest calling. It is worth more effort than it takes to win a golf tournament. It is infinitely more important than trimming around trees. It is the calling of Jesus. It is worth all the blood, all the sweat, all the tears.

Again, the exhortation of the author of Hebrews is vivid:

> Now no chastening seems to be joyful for the present, but grievous; nevertheless, afterward it yields the peaceable fruit of righteousness to those who have been trained by it. Therefore, strengthen the hands which hang down and the feeble knees, and make straight paths for your feet, so that what is lame may not be dislocated, but rather be healed. (Heb. 12:11–13)

The author of Hebrews was elaborating on an earlier point. "And you have forgotten the exhortation which speaks to you as sons: 'My son, do not despise the chastening of the LORD, nor be discouraged when you are rebuked by Him; for whom the Lord loves He chastens, and scourges every son whom He receives' " (Heb. 12:5, 6).

Hebrews makes it clear that we are not bastards; we are sons. Our Father disciplines us precisely because He loves us. At times His hand is heavy upon us. That does not mean that He treats us in a heavy-handed manner. But the weight of His divine touch of discipline can easily overcome us. His chastening seems grievous. We respond with drooping hands and weak knees. Who wouldn't be weak-kneed in the face of divine discipline?

But the discipline of God is not meant to destroy us but to heal us. The treatment is painful for a season. Knee braces are not comfortable. But the goal of the Father's discipline is training. It yields the fruit we are all seeking, the *peaceable fruit of righteousness*.

That fruit is worth the effort. It is worth the struggle. The discipline we endure is not worthy to be compared with the fruit that lies beyond it.

Here again are the words of Hebrews:

> For you have not come to the mountain that may be touched and that burned with fire, and to blackness and darkness and tempest, and the sound of a trumpet and the

voice of words, so that those who heard it begged that the
word should not be spoken to them anymore. (For they
could not endure what was commanded: "And if so much
as a beast touches the mountain, it shall be stoned or thrust
through with an arrow." And so terrifying was the sight
that Moses said, "I am exceedingly afraid and trembling.")
(Heb. 12:18–21)

This is not our experience. Burning hills. Fierce storms. Black smoke.
Sounds of trumpets and thundering words. This was the experience of the
children of Israel at Mount Sinai. It was a time of terror. It left the people beg-
ging for relief. Even Moses was frightened in the extreme. The author mentions
this ancient moment of terror for purposes of contrast:

But you have come to Mount Zion and to the city of the living
God, the heavenly Jerusalem, to an innumerable company of
angels, to the general assembly and church of the firstborn
who are registered in heaven, to God the Judge of all, to the
spirits of just men made perfect, to Jesus the Mediator of
the new covenant, and to the blood of sprinkling that speaks
better things than that of Abel. (Heb. 12:22–24)

We are the new Israel. Our Exodus is infinitely greater than the one out of
Egypt. Our Mediator dwarfs Moses by comparison. Our mountain is not Sinai
but the eternal mountain of Zion. We enter into heaven. We join the multitude
of angels. We enjoy the communion of all the saints. We are sprinkled by the
blood of Christ, whose blood is of more import than all the sacrifices ever
offered.

It is for this eternal home that we endure. Who can quit in such a venture?
Who will not rise after stumbling to pursue afresh such a destiny?

There is a conclusion to the matter: "Therefore, since we are receiving a
kingdom which cannot be shaken, let us have grace, by which we may serve
God acceptably with reverence and godly fear. For our God is a consuming fire"
(Heb. 12:28, 29).

It is for this consuming fire that we live. It is Him that we strive to please.
It is for Him that we rise up again after repeated failures. It is He who is our
destiny.